T0305649

'This is an important, topical and practical book that covers the profound consequences of the Covid-19 pandemic in the workplace. The authors, with their different expertise and backgrounds, offer a thoughtful and well-researched understanding of how the world has changed for people at work. It is comprehensive and critical, well-edited and thorough. I will, I believe, turn out to be a classic that analyses the new world order.'
— **Adrian Furnham,** *Professor at the Norwegian Business School, Norway*

'A winner for a no-win environment. Two academic stars organize diverse yet complementary chapters into a focused book, coming at an ideal time. Risks factors escalated during COVID while sources of renewal to mitigate burnout were stymied or compromised. Great burnout lessons from the pandemic!'
— **James Campbell Quick,** *FSAScot, FAPA,*
Distinguished University Professor & Professor Emeritus,
The University of Texas at Arlington, USA

Burnout While Working

This book offers an extensive look into the ways living through the COVID-19 pandemic has deepened our understanding of the crises people experience in their relationships with work. Leading experts explore burnout as an occupational phenomenon that arises through mismatches between workplace and individuals on the day-to-day patterns in work life.

By disrupting where, when, and how people worked, pandemic measures upset the delicate balances in place regarding core areas of work life. Chapters examine the profound implications of social distancing on the quality and frequency of social encounters among colleagues, with management, and with clientele. The book covers a variety of occupational groups such as those in the healthcare and education sectors, and demonstrates the advantages and strains that come with working from home. The authors also consider the broader social context of working through the pandemic regarding risks and rewards for essential workers. By focusing on changes in organisational structures, policies, and practices, this book looks at effective ways forward in both recovering from this pandemic and preparing for further workplace disruptions.

A wide audience of students and researchers in psychology, management, business, healthcare, and social sciences, as well as policy makers in government and professional organisations, will benefit from this detailed insight into the ways COVID-19 has affected contemporary work attitudes and practices.

Michael P. Leiter, PhD has researched burnout extensively as a Professor and Canada Research Chair at Acadia University in Canada and as Professor of Organisational Psychology at Deakin University in Australia. He currently provides research and consulting services on burnout and workplace civility to organisations around the world.

Cary L. Cooper, CBE is the 50th Anniversary Professor of Organisational Psychology & Health at the ALLIANCE Manchester Business School, University of Manchester, UK, and Chair of the National Forum for Health & Wellbeing at Work (comprised of 45 global employers). He was knighted by the Queen for services to the social sciences in 2014, and was made an Honorary Fellow of the Royal College of Physicians and the British Psychological Society.

Current Issues in Work and Organizational Psychology
Series Editor: Cary L. Cooper

Current Issues in Work and Organizational Psychology is a series of edited books that reflect the state-of-the-art areas of current and emerging interest in the psychological study of employees, workplaces, and organisations.

Each volume is tightly focused on a particular topic and consists of seven to ten chapters contributed by international experts. The editors of individual volumes are leading figures in their areas and provide an introductory overview.

Example topics include: digital media at work, work and the family, workaholism, modern job design, positive occupational health, and individualised deals.

For more information about this series, please visit: https://www.routledge.com/Current-Issues-in-Work-and-Organizational-Psychology/book-series/CURRENTISSUES

Burnout While Working
Lessons from Pandemic and Beyond

**Edited by Michael P. Leiter and
Cary L. Cooper**

LONDON AND NEW YORK

Cover image: © Getty Images

First published 2023
by Routledge
4 Park Square, Milton Park, Abingdon, Oxon OX14 4RN

and by Routledge
605 Third Avenue, New York, NY 10158

Routledge is an imprint of the Taylor & Francis Group, an informa business

British Library Cataloguing-in-Publication Data
A catalogue record for this book is available from the British Library

Library of Congress Cataloguing-in-Publication Data
Names: Leiter, Michael P., editor. | Cooper, Cary L., editor.
Title: Burnout while working: lessons from pandemic and beyond / edited by Michael P. Leiter and Cary L. Cooper.
Description: First Edition. | New York, NY : Routledge, 2023. | Series: Current issues in work and organizational psychology | Includes bibliographical references and index. | Summary: "This book offers an extensive look into the ways living through the COVID-19 pandemic has deepened our understanding of the crises people experience in their relationships with work. Leading experts explore burnout as an occupational phenomenon that arises through mismatches between workplace and individuals on the day-to-day patterns in work life. A wide audience of students and researchers in psychology, management, business, healthcare, and social sciences, as well as policy makers in government and professional organizations, will benefit from this detailed insight into the ways COVID-19 has affected contemporary work attitudes and practices"-- Provided by publisher.
Identifiers: LCCN 2022035316 (print) | LCCN 2022035317 (ebook) | ISBN 9781032168418 (hardback) | ISBN 9781032168418 (paperback) | ISBN 9781003250531 (ebook)
Subjects: LCSH: Burn out (Psychology) | Work environment. | Personnel management. | COVID-19 Pandemic, 2020---Influence.
Classification: LCC BF481 .B857 2023 (print) | LCC BF481 (ebook) | DDC 158.7/23--dc23/eng/20220725
LC record available at https://lccn.loc.gov/2022035316
LC ebook record available at https://lccn.loc.gov/2022035317

ISBN: 978-1-032-16841-8 (hbk)
ISBN: 978-1-032-15874-7 (pbk)
ISBN: 978-1-003-25053-1 (ebk)

DOI: 10.4324/9781003250531

Typeset in Bembo
by MPS Limited, Dehradun

Contents

Contributors

Ángela C. Asensio is a Professor of Social Psychology at the Faculty of Social and Labor Sciences at the University of Zaragoza, Spain. She is currently working towards her Masters in Occupational Health and Safety, with a speciality in ergonomics and applied psychosociology.

Jeff Babb is an Associate Professor with the Department of Mathematics & Statistics at the University of Winnipeg, Canada. He has extensive statistical consulting experience with industry, government, and academia in the planning, design, implementation, analysis, and reporting of scientific research projects and in the design and analysis of questionnaires and surveys.

Sean Becker is currently working at the Veteran Affairs National Center for Organizational Development and finishing his PhD in Industrial/ Organizational and Human Factors Psychology at Wright State University, USA. His research focuses on scale development, occupational stress, and selection.

Caroline Biron is a Full Professor and Director of the Center of Expertise in Occupational Health and Safety Management at Laval University, Canada. Her research includes the evaluation of programs and organisational interventions aimed at improving the well-being of people and organisational performance and the process for developing and implementing occupational health and safety interventions in organisations.

Cheyna Brower is a Personnel Psychologist at the National Center for Organization Development at the U.S. Department of Veteran Affairs, USA. She currently specialises in Data analysis and data product development for the VA research team.

Maria José Chambel is an Associate Professor with Aggregation at the Faculty of Psychology of the University of Lisbon, Portugal, teaching in the Work and Organizational Psychology field. She is a member of the Research Center for Psychological Science at the University of Lisbon and has participated in and coordinated several research projects.

Cary L. Cooper is the 50th Anniversary Professor of Organizational Psychology & Health at the ALLIANCE Manchester Business School, University of Manchester, UK, and Chair of the National Forum for Health & Wellbeing at Work (comprising 45 global employers). He was knighted by the Queen for services to the social sciences in 2014, and was made an Honorary Fellow of the Royal College of Physicians and the British Psychological Society.

Arla Day is a Full Professor of Industrial/Organizational Psychology and former Canada Research Chair at Saint Mary's University, Halifax, Canada. She is the Director of the CN Centre for Occupational Health and Safety.

Claude Fernet is a Full professor in the Department of Human Resources Management at the University of Quebec at Trois-Rivières, Canada. His teachings focus on leadership and the behavior of individuals and groups within organisations.

Aristides I. Ferreira is an Associate Professor at the University Institute of Lisbon, Portugal, where he is the Director of the Master programme in Human Resource Management and Organizational Consulting. He is also a member of the Scientific Board and a researcher at the Business Research Unit in the same institute.

Maura Galletta is an Associate Professor in the Department Medical Sciences and Public Health at the University of Cagliari, Italy. Her research includes work motivation, nursing turnover, organisational behaviours, and workplace wellbeing.

Santiago Gascón is a Professor at the Department of Psychology and Sociology at the University of Zaragoza, Spain. His research includes work stress and health as well as violence at work and in schools.

Jonathon R. B. Halbesleben is the Dean and Bodenstedt Chair and Professor of Management at the University of Texas at San Antonio, USA. His research involves employee well-being, work-family issues, and relationships in and out of the workplace.

Valérie Hervieux is currently completing her doctorate in management at the Faculty of Administrative Sciences at Laval University, Canada. She is working on her thesis project which aims to investigate the relationship between psychosocial risks, presenteeism, and physical activity.

Elaine L. Kinsella is a chartered psychologist with experience working in academia and business consultancy. Elaine is passionate about creatively using psychology to understand and tackle organisational, clinical, and social challenges. She currently works as a psychology lecturer and professional researcher at the University of Limerick, Ireland.

Michael P. Leiter has researched burnout extensively as a Professor and Canada Research Chair at Acadia University in Canada and as Professor of Organisational Psychology at Deakin University in Australia. He currently provides research and consulting services on burnout and workplace civility to organisations around the world.

Nuoxun Lin is completing their PhD in Philosophy at Lingnan University, Hong Kong. Their thesis aims to investigate the growth mindset and rational beliefs employees could use to enhance their job performance to face a competitive and everchanging workplace.

Chris Mahar is a psychology instructor and doctoral student at Saint Mary's University (SMU) in Halifax, Nova Scotia, Canada. During his Master of Science, Chris completed an internship with the Canadian Forces Leadership Institute at the Royal Military College in Kingston, Ontario, and he also completed independent contract work for the Institute. Upon graduating with a Master of Science, Chris was hired as an instructor for the Psychology Department at SMU and developed an independent consultancy with his partner. Chris returned to SMU to complete a PhD in Industrial/ Organisational Psychology, and is currently working on his dissertation.

Christina Maslach is a Professor of Psychology (Emerita) and a core researcher at the Healthy Workplaces Center at the University of California, Berkeley. She is the pioneer of research on the definition, predictors, and measurement of job burnout and created the Maslach Burnout Inventory (MBI), the most widely used instrument for measuring job burnout, and has written numerous articles and books, including The Truth About Burnout.

Katerine Osatuke is the Supervisory Health Scientist and Research Director at Department of Veterans Affairs, USA. Her research is focused on the models and processes of change, including individual, group, and organisational change. She also has background and interest in Abnormal Psychology, Health Psychology, and Clinical Psychology.

Igor Portoghese is a Research Fellow in the Department of Health Sciences and Public Health, University of Cagliari, Italy. His research focuses on investigating factors linked to the promotion of healthy workplaces in multi-professional teams, and includes work stress, burnout, team conflicts, team communication, and leadership.

Oi-ling Siu is Chair Professor of Psychology at Lingnan University, Hong Kong. Her research interests are in Occupational Health Psychology, specifically occupational stress, psychology of safety, and work–life balance.

Laura Sokal is a Professor of Education at the University of Winnipeg. She has published more than 60 peer-reviewed articles on topics such as psycho-social development, well-being, and inclusion in schools. An award-winning teacher, she enjoys learning with and from her students.

Rachel C. Sumner is a chartered psychologist specialising in psychobiology who brings with her a number of research interests and projects. One of these projects is CV19 Heroes, a long-running project tracking the welfare of frontline workers in the pandemic.

Lesley Eblie Trudel is the Associate Dean of the Faculty of Education at the University of Winnipeg, Canada. She has over 30 years of experience in K-12 public education, most recently as an Assistant Superintendent of Schools in Manitoba, Canada.

Colin P. West is a quantitative health sciences researcher whose work focuses primarily on physician well-being, evidence-based medicine and biostatistics, and medical education. Results of research conducted by Dr. West and his team have been published in multiple top-tier journals, including the *Lancet*, the *Journal of the American Medical Association*, *Annals of Internal Medicine*, and *JAMA Internal Medicine*.

Introduction

Michael P. Leiter[1] *and Cary L. Cooper*[2]

[1]*Acadia University, Canada*
[2]*University of Manchester, UK*

The COVID-19 pandemic profoundly affected every dimension of life around the world. Prior to the development of vaccines, the primary defence strategies were in the domain of human behaviour rather than medical science or pharmaceuticals. The SARS-COVID2 virus had the insidious quality of being contagious before carriers experienced symptoms. It was even communicable by people who never developed symptoms, when infected. This quality allowed the virus to spread extensively before people knew to take action.

The prime behavioural strategies had the common theme of creating physical distance between people, constructing physical barriers between people, or both. Many workplaces realised distancing through remote working in employees' homes. For jobs requiring people to be on site and to be interacting with others, physical barriers, personal protective equipment (PPE), and scheduling minimised contact with the potential for transmitting the virus. With "belonging" as a core quality of people, an abrupt drop in social contact at work had profound implications for the potential for fulfilment at work.

The response of workplaces to the crisis demonstrated that they could change rapidly when confronted with an immediate threat and pressured by government directives to take action. Clearly, these actions saved lives, and, with the help of financial support programs, allowed organisations to remain operating. However, the quick action, often based on little or no forward planning for such emergencies, created serious strain for employees. Ideally, organisations and their employees manage transitions to assure well-designed workplaces and work processes. Ideally, the core design elements of balance, rhythm, and unity shape the new situation (Maslach & Leiter, 2022). However, abrupt responses required during emergencies often create situations that are poorly matched with the needs, aspirations, and abilities of the people undergoing the change. The change process itself, as well as the mismatches they create across the core areas of worklife become drivers of exhaustion, cynicism, and inefficacy that define job burnout (Leiter & Maslach, 2004).

The editors felt that the field would benefit from an exploration of the burnout consequences of the Covid-19 epidemic, and its impact on people and organisations in the future. The book is comprised of 12 chapters, which highlight some interesting psychological outcomes of the pandemic, and how

DOI: 10.4324/9781003250531-1

this may have accelerated a major change in how people work post-pandemic and in the future. A great deal of research over the last couple of decades has suggested that there are two main overarching constructs related to stress and burnout, uncertainty and lack of control (Cooper, 2021). During Covid and Post-Covid, people were and are worried about their jobs, financial security, ongoing variants of the virus and what the future of the workplace will be like. They also feel that they have little control over many of these real or potential stressors, clearly a recipe for burnout and other stress-related outcomes. The contributors to this volume highlight some very important issues which have implications for the future of work, and the health and wellbeing of working people—with many lessons to learn for future crises. What follows is a brief summary of each of the chapters from our distinguished group of scholars in the field.

In Chapter 1 Rachel Sumner and Elaine Kinsella identify a potential candidate for a stressor that is distinct to the pandemic. The chapter explores a central aspect of professional identity. They propose that professionals' understanding of how the broader community values their profession can affect their self-evaluation. It may also inform their understanding of their workplace demands and the potential impact of their efforts. A specific mismatch explored here is the lack of unity in a vision for public health as source of expertise and services during a global initiative. The variety of experiences of public health personnel across locations and over the course of the pandemic. The process has some parallels with the impact of workplace incivility. The more symbolic exchanges with the community through media or political action have implications for the regard in which people are held.

In Chapter 2 Michael Leiter and Christina Maslach applied the six areas of worklife model to the pandemic's impact on the design and experience of work. Changes in worklife had diverse impacts on people that went beyond abrupt changes in the amount and type of their workload. For example, the lack of effective treatments or vaccines for the virus in the initial year of the pandemic had serious consequences for employees' sense of control as well as their possibilities for experiencing intrinsic rewards while doing their work. Regarding the moral dimensions of worklife, the differential impact of the pandemic created meaningful mismatches in employees' sense of fairness regarding work. Overall, abrupt changes in the nature of work required a deep reflection on the extent to which organisations could realise their core values.

In Chapter 3 Chris Mahar and Arla Day take a deep dive into shifts in the balance of demands and resources that occurred for people working during the pandemic. Of particular interest is the extent to which the pandemic introduced entirely new demands or required entirely new resources for people to thrive at work during this period. From another perspective, did coping with the demands of the pandemic call upon distinct resources from what pertained to workplaces beforehand. In some ways the experience had qualities of intensifying the rhythm of worklife; in other ways the pandemic upset the balance of resources available to people as they did their work. Overall, the chapter provides a framework for considering the diverse ways in which work changed during this time.

In Chapter 4 Valérie Hervieux, Claude Fernet, and Caroline Biron focus on the link of burnout with physical activity, exploring the connection of activity and mobility with burnout, especially the exhaustion dimension of the syndrome. The chapter convers the relevance of physical activity during the pandemic when many people found their usual settings for exercise and recreation unavailable due to restrictions. It also clarifies the apparent contradiction between the experience of exhaustion and the beneficial effects of exercise, despite the demands exercise make upon energy. The challenges of fitting physical activity into busy days managing work and family underscores the importance of maintaining a rhythm across life domains with a unity of purpose for maintaining wellbeing. The chapter reflects on recommendations for maintaining health and engagement both during the pandemic and in a post-pandemic phase.

In Chapter 5 Laura Sokal, Lesley Eblie Trudel, and Jeff Babb explore the experience of distancing as a reaction to the pandemic on schoolteachers. In light of the importance of social contact for people at work and elsewhere, the chapter focuses on research on teachers' response to distancing mandates in their schools during the pandemic. These initiatives, although necessary to reduce risk to teachers and students, created imbalances regarding teachers' motivation for belonging associated with their work. The chapter explores a multifaceted model regarding connectedness at work.

In Chapter 6 Santiago Gascón, María José Chambel, and Ángela Asensio present a deep exploration of exhaustion in their chapter. While acknowledging that many people found remote working to be to their liking, they reflect on the qualities of telework that make distinct demands on people. One important dimension concerns the rhythm of the workday that becomes difficult to maintain with no boundaries between work and home. Maintaining a balance in responding to demands can become strained when so many activities with different priorities occur in the same time and place. With coworkers and supervisors dispersed, maintaining unity of purpose becomes a much larger leadership task. The chapter reviews recommendations for managing transitions from one work modality to another.

In Chapter 7 Aristides Ferreira considers people who are reluctant to acknowledge the extent to which they are experiencing burnout. The chapter consider perspectives on this phenomenon, some of which emphasise the workplace context while others focus on personal characteristics. From the workplace perspective, employees have practical concerns about acknowledging their distress where the organisational culture conveys disrespect towards those considered weak or lacking sufficient dedication. From a personal perspective, individual employees' concerns about their self-image may deter them from acknowledging distress, regardless of their social context. These perspectives have implications for preventing and alleviating burnout.

Much of burnout research focused one healthcare. People working in healthcare experienced dramatic increases in work demands. They had the most intimate contact with people infected with the virus, putting themselves at risk.

In Chapter 8 Colin West applies the Areas of Worklife model to the work of physicians, noting that they experienced a lot of strain before the pandemic began. Worklife for physicians had its uplifting and rewarding qualities but, overall, was unsustainable. The design on day-to-day work for physicians has long been poorly designed, lacking the core elements of balance, rhythm, and unity (Maslach & Leiter, 2022). The skewed nature of work/home imbalance was one important dimension, but that balance of administrative to clinical tasks also created serious mismatches for them. The pre-existing strains across all six areas of worklife diminished physicians' capacity to sustain the extraordinary effort required in the initial phases of the pandemic. West's analysis covers the range of issues confronting physicians in the pandemic, noting the pertinence of specialties, work settings, and backgrounds to their vulnerability to experiencing aspects of burnout.

In Chapter 9 Cheyna Brower, Sean Becker, and Katerine Osatuke examine implications for burnout of the response of the United States Veterans Affairs organisation to the pandemic. As one of the largest healthcare organisations in the world, the Veterans Affairs provides lessons on the contribution of policy initiatives and support strategies during a major workplace transition as many of its roles shifted to telework. The chapter considers the ongoing pressures towards burnout inherent in the setting prior to the pandemic as well as the distinct contributions of the pandemic and steps taken to implement distancing in reaction to the pandemic. The chapter makes a case for focusing on changes in organisational structures, policies, and practices as the most productive way forward in both recovering from this pandemic and preparing for further workplace disruptions.

A definitive form of social distancing for office-based employment came from directives for people to work from their homes. Igor Portoghese and Maura Galleta explore the issues of preparation, training, and ergonomics involved in shifting work from the office to the home. In many situations, shifting work to home became a viable solution, but those solutions came at a cost to those who made that transition. One important feature explored in the chapter is the complete collapse of the already shaky boundary between work and family. Maintaining a workable balance was a challenge for people when people had a designated work setting. When locational boundaries disappeared, allocating time between the two domains became more difficult as well. In Chapter 10 Igor Portoghese and Maura Galleta note the additional challenges inherent in home-based work for people with small homes and small children. A contrasting perspective comes from people living alone for whom social distancing acquired an absolute quality.

In Chapter 11 Oi-ling Siu and Nuoxun Lin explore the application of work/home spillover models to the strains inherent in working from home during the pandemic. The complexity of roles competing for employees' limited energy within the same time and space require ongoing decisions and adjustments to keep things on course. The unplanned complexity of the situation 'often creates discordant rhythms in employees' lives as they contend with competing pressures. The chapter underscores the importance of employees' understanding of their situations. Although a rational mental framework for the experience of working from home is necessary for people to thrive, it is difficult to attain when people feel thrust into unwelcomed changes. Developing a sense of control can increase employees' chances of avoiding burnout or other stress reactions.

Although COVID seems to be an ongoing part of life, the response of workplaces and society in general to the disease changes over time. After an initial phase dominated by remote work, people began returning to work settings. Some people were delighted with the opportunity to return to the office; others had settled in nicely at home. In Chapter 12 Jonathon Halbesleben takes a close look at the process of people returning to work. This chapter explores contrasting models of employees' response to uncertain and changing situations during the transition back to work. From one perspective, ongoing stressors suggest that people will become accustomed to the situation they find themselves in. From another perspective, ongoing stressors suggest that employees' capacity to thrive will diminish their capacity over time. The Halbesleben reviews the issues requiring insight and research to guild decisions about providing support to employees when they are confronting challenging situations.

All of the contributions of our distinguished colleagues in this book will help to understand the impact of a once in a lifetime pandemic for most of us. It helps us to think differently about our lives and work, accelerating many trends in the workplace that are likely to be with us for many years to come (e. g., hybrid working, the empathic role of the line manager, work-life integration, the role of men in the family, long working hours the four-day working week, etc.). Major life events like the pandemic do change society. As President Franklin Delano Roosevelt said after the Great Depression of the 1930s:

> True individual freedom cannot exist with economic security and independence. People who are hungry and out of a job are the stuff of which dictatorships are made. The hopes of the Republic cannot forever tolerate either undeserved poverty or self-serving wealth.

Positives can come out of disasters and tragedies, opportunities to think differently about our lives, are working practices and our relationships, which can reduce the stresses and strains personally and communally.

We hope this book will help the reader to think differently and help to create a new future for work in our societies. Maybe we should take a lesson from the great social reformer John Ruskin who wrote at the beginning of the Industrial Revolution in 1851 about work: "In order that people may be happy in their work, these three things are needed: they must be fit for it, they must not do too much of it and they must have a sense of success in it."

6   *Michael P. Leiter and Cary L. Cooper*

References

Cooper, C. L. (Ed.) (2021). *Psychological insights for understanding Covide-19 and work.* New York & London: Routledge.

Leiter, M. P., & Maslach, C. (2004). Areas of worklife: A structured approach to organizational predictors of job burnout. In P. Perrewé & D. C. Ganster (Eds.). *Research in occupational stress and well being,* Vol. 3. Emotional and physiological processes and positive intervention strategies (pp. 91–134). Oxford, UK: JAI Press/Elsevier.

Maslach, C., & Leiter, M. P. (2022). *The burnout challenge: Managing relationships of people with their work.* Cambridge, MA: Harvard University Press.

1 High expectations and unreciprocated effort in societal exchange: Lessons from the pandemic about psychological forces that influence burnout

Rachel C. Sumner[1] *and Elaine L. Kinsella*[2]

[1]*Cardiff Metropolitan University, Cardiff, UK*
[2]*University of Limerick, Castletroy, Co. Limerick, Republic of Ireland*

The purpose of this chapter is to introduce and explore novel predictors of burnout that became apparent during the Covid-19 pandemic with a view to considering their application more broadly in other occupational and social contexts. Through our own work with frontline workers in the UK and Ireland[1], we developed the thesis that solidarity would be important to those whose work provides a fundamental and pivotal support to society. In testing that theory, we established that a sense of meaning appeared to function as a mechanism between solidarity and occupational welfare outcomes such as burnout.

In this chapter, we will explore these concepts more fully, by examining the likely precursors to the need for, and expectation of, solidarity. We take the perspective that meaning serves as a fulcrum to burnout, to either buffer (when plentiful) or to accelerate (when depleted). We posit that societal labelling of frontline workers early on in the pandemic established an enhanced sense of meaning to their work, and potentially their lives. This process of labelling may have also established a new relationship between the workers and society, consequently setting the terms for social exchange.

To make these complex ideas more tangible, it is helpful to consider how these processes may have operated during the Covid-19 pandemic at a general level. The positioning of these workers as *serving* society provided an augmented sense of meaning, potentially allowing them to endure the forthcoming hardships. Simultaneously, the media, governments, and public who used these labels set in motion a society-level social exchange protocol that was initially honoured, but appeared to degrade over time. Arguably, the lack of solidarity felt by those workers was the lack of enactment of the social exchange, undermining not just the agreement between society and these workers, but also their sense of meaning.

Our analysis provides a new lens with which to consider the precursors to burnout, situating meaning as being a critical contributor to the process of burnout that can and has been externally influenced by society placing labels

DOI: 10.4324/9781003250531-2

on these workers. These labels, in turn, established the terms of social ex-change, which was ultimately not perceived to be reciprocated, initiating a steep decline of workers' feelings of meaning, leading to a profound descent into burnout. With these novel constructions of burnout pathways, we con-sider a re-framing of the examination of social factors in burnout to incorporate—where relevant—factors that exist beyond the direct workplace environment.

The Covid-19 pandemic: New labels, new risks, and new meanings

During the early months of the Covid-19 pandemic, many societies came to a near standstill during periods of "lockdown." Citizens were required to stay at home with the exception of workers that provided an *essential* public service. Occupational sectors and roles that were deemed critical to the functioning of societies, but that had previously operated with limited public awareness or acknowledgement, were suddenly receiving widespread attention. In the context of the looming threat of a deadly virus rapidly circulating around the world, people who were leaving their home to play their role in the fight against the virus, were not only labelled "essential" but were also, hailed as heroes. The attribution of such labels was accompanied with an outpouring of political and public support, and gratitude for their sacrifices in an un-precedented global emergency. There was widespread support for these workers—they were providing not just their standard work or service, but also, an additional service to humanity in keeping society going through such a tumultuous and dangerous time. In a matter of weeks, it appeared that the status of frontline workers was elevated to honorary level, and citizens rallied behind their heroes by adhering to public health guidelines and distancing from others, apparently united against a common threat.

The term "essential" workers (sometimes "key" workers also) has been adopted internationally to apply to workers that offer an essential service, (often) dealing directly with the public, and who are unable to work remotely during crises. In prior public health emergencies, the concept of the "frontline" was usually considered to be those working in healthcare; however, those deemed essential during Covid-19 have also been, by default, frontline. They have been those workers who have had to face the dangers of being infected with Covid, have had to deal with the direct and indirect consequences of the pandemic (such as supporting those infected, but also dealing with societal fallout such as panic buying), and have been the only ones permitted to leave their house to work because of the essential service their roles serve to society. As such, the range of workers deemed to be on this frontline due to their "essential" status expanded to include those working across health and social care, civil defence, essential retail, education (in some countries), and those maintaining and serving the community infrastructures—with the majority of those having never re-ceived training for crisis or emergency response. The everyday undertakings of these essential workers contained new elements of danger, organisational pressure, and societal expectations. As a result, these workers as a collective became increasingly prominent in the public eye.

Arguably these early moves in the pandemic triggered a series of social and psychological consequences that are relevant to understanding burnout trajectories over the duration of what was to unfold. In the very early stages, labelling frontline workers as "essential," and subsequently as "heroes," offered an initial greater surge of meaning to frontline workers, allowing them to sustain tremendous hardships due to their now serving a new and critical "greater good" (Kinsella et al., 2021). By asserting that these workers were essential and were their heroes, the public conferred a sense of debt and gratitude to them, thereby setting the terms of social exchange. In ordaining these labels, the public also positioned themselves as being a part of the society the workers were tasked to protect. During those early weeks and months, gestures of solidarity offered support to frontline workers in coping with the physical and psychological threats presented by the onset of the pandemic and associated challenges (Kinsella et al., 2021), confirming and fulfilling this social exchange. This sentiment of solidarity ensured that society was not just rallying behind their essential worker heroes, but was enacting that support by adhering to pandemic safeguards, preventing an unmanageable and catastrophic burden of infection.

Unfortunately, the solidarity perceived and felt by many essential workers dissipated over time. Some frontline workers attributed this change in sentiment and behaviour to being initiated by widely publicised instances of rule breaking by leadership.

In the UK, there were several notable confirmed and alleged instances of rule infraction by figures in leadership. In May 2020, news media stories emerged following investigations by two UK national newspapers that the UK Prime Minister's senior advisor, Dominic Cummings, had travelled across the country with his family during some of the strictest movement regulations enforced in the nation during March 2020. To make matters worse, Cummings believed that he and family members had already contracted SARS-CoV-2 prior to travel. He declined to apologise after widespread news reporting, and continued with his role in leadership, despite calls for him to step down or to be dismissed. The Prime Minister of the UK and many other leading members of the UK parliament were also embroiled in allegations regarding the infraction of distancing and gathering regulations throughout the pandemic and received fixed-penalty notices. In Ireland, 80 people gathered in August 2020 at an Irish parliamentary (Oireachtas) Golf Society event just one day after gathering restrictions had been made tighter by the government, allowing meetings of no more than six people. Even prior to this move towards more stringent measures, this meeting would still have constituted an infraction (where no more than 50 people were allowed to meet). The leadership breaches were seen to spark a chain reaction in the behaviour of others (Kinsella et al., 2022), initiating in the public a reduced will (or perhaps energy) to adhere to guidance. Frontline workers perceived these changes as reduced solidarity, which was related to a range of negative psychological effects (see solidarity appraisal: Sumner & Kinsella, 2021b, 2022). Importantly, in these analyses meaning was shown to have decreased across the course of the pandemic, and appeared to serve as an important mechanism in the relationship between appraisals of solidarity and welfare in frontline workers (Sumner & Kinsella, 2022).

Meaningfulness as a counter to burnout

The literature surrounding meaningful work has been replete with theoretical frameworks and constructs to make sense of what constitutes meaningful work, or otherwise what factors are associated with deriving meaning from work. A review of this work conducted by Rosso and colleagues (2010) brought together a vast volume of literature to tease apart the various aspects that underlie meaningfulness derived through work. First, someone's work may be a fundamental expression of who they are, what their values are, and therefore, the meaning derived from their work aligns to the enactment of their values. Second, meaning may be derived through the setting and achievement of goals within a work setting. Third, meaning from work can be derived through the answering of a calling, that one's work serves a higher purpose that may be called for personally or from a society to fulfil a moral or social need. Regardless of how meaning is derived through work, the fact that it can and is derived through work also provides a potential protective factor against burnout.

When considering the three core facets of burnout as defined by Maslach and Jackson (1981), we can observe an almost direct antithesis in some of the conceptual facets of meaningful work. The concept of cynicism or depersonalisation can be countered by the concept of purpose; reduced efficacy is opposed by the self-efficacy that is kindled by meaningful work; and emotional exhaustion is contrasted by motivation. Meaningful work is described to provide a great deal many other positive boons to wellbeing and job satisfaction (see Rosso et al., 2010 for a full review), but these three aspects do offer a direct and (in some cases) almost perfect opposite to the characteristics of burnout. Since this review, further theoretical work has suggested that work provides several latent and manifest aspects of meaning to one's life, such as the ability to express one's identity through work, that work provides a means of self-determination through actualising autonomy, competence, and relatedness, and that work provides the ability to accomplish and enhance a sense of comprehension to one's experiences (Autin et al., 2022; Steger & Dik, 2010). What is not currently clear, however, is whether a loss of meaning is a precursor to burnout, or if burnout processes trigger a loss of meaning, or, indeed, if burnout can occur whilst meaning is still retained.

The idea that meaning may be central to the process of burnout is not new, and an existential theory to burnout has been posited that describes a loss of meaning as a necessary process within the trajectory of burning out (Pines, 1993). Longitudinal work that has since been carried out to examine the relationship between meaning and burnout has elucidated this to some extent, with the context of the pandemic providing an important opportunity to capture and explore these two concepts. An excellent example of this comes from a study that captured data on meaning and burnout pre-pandemic, and then subsequently reassessed these aspects mid- and post-surge in the first wave of Covid-19, finding no difference in burnout across these time points (Uong et al., 2021). A subsequent commentary on this work attempted to explain this null finding by drawing on related work on disaster theory that describes initial public states in disasters as being characterised by altruism and solidarity, factors that may be supportive of meaning and therefore sufficient to buffer against burnout during such a period of stress and distress (Zuniga & Mahan, 2021). Related work predating the pandemic has also shown that meaning appears to be protective of burnout longitudinally in this population (Bayer et al., 2021), and our own work from a broad range of frontline workers in the UK and Ireland showed that in the initial stages of the pandemic, meaning was negatively associated with burnout also (Sumner & Kinsella, 2021a).

There is much to deconstruct in the pandemic context with regard to influences on meaning and burnout. Our own research has employed a variety of methods and collected data at several points, and associated findings can help to elucidate some aspects of these processes. Through a mixture of longitudinal surveying, cross-sectional and prospective analyses, and qualitative investigations, we can offer a roadmap of frontline workers' experiences that was characterised by an initial enhancement to meaning (from labelling) followed by a profound depletion that surpasses the original setpoint (from a perceived failure of social exchange), resulting in a variety of negative sequalae including burnout.

Labelling: Setting the tone for meaning and the terms of exchange

Sociologists and psychologists have studied labels for many decades, particularly in relation to how aspects of the self and identity, as well as behaviour, may be determined or influenced by the terms used to describe or classify them (e.g., modified labelling theory: Link et al., 1989). Some of these ideas date back to Durkeim, where he considers how labels associated with criminal activity may influence subsequent criminal behaviour (Durkheim, 2005). Despite the fact that frontline workers have been labelled extensively, there has been very little consideration of how these labels were internalised by frontline workers, and how they may have influenced others' expectations of the frontline. While the extent that the label of "burnout" is perceived to be stigmatising has been considered previously (Bianchi et al., 2016), there appears to be no existing work that considers the role of labelling as a precursor to burnout.

The "essential" worker

The terms "essential" or "key" worker, adopted by many nations in conceptualising their frontline, served to underscore the criticality of their work and their position in society at a time of crisis. As a result of these labels, many workers were lauded and celebrated as "essential" in the fight against a virus, shining a much-needed light on the importance of hygiene services, public transport, logistics, essential retail, and auxiliary roles within health and care systems (Kinsella et al., 2021). Work can be a way to derive meaning from one's life (Baumeister, 1991), and in times of heightened public appreciation for one's role and efforts, this is all the more so, particularly for those in roles that were previously low status and may also be low paid (Kinsella et al., 2021; Smith et al., 2020).

In line with the existential theory of burnout (Pines, 1993), the labels "essential" or "key" worker may have provided motivation and meaning to workers. Indeed, the labels may have provided an *extrinsic* calling from society that increased the meaning derived from their work (Baumeister, 1991; De Camargo & Whiley, 2020; Rosso et al., 2010; Sharma et al., 2022; Zhou et al., 2021). This calling was reinforced by the rhetoric employed by many governments, where the societal call-to-arms for essential workers was evocative of those made during times of war. This language was used at the beginning of the pandemic by leadership in many nations, and constituted a deliberate and very clear means of rallying those whose role it was to "serve" to be brave and to step up (Benziman, 2020). The evocation of serving a higher purpose or greater good, or otherwise contributing to something that will benefit broader society, is a powerful means to imbue work (and perhaps too one's life) with meaning (Rosso et al., 2010; Steger & Dik, 2010). Being designated as belonging to a group that is the frontline—the barrier between society and disaster—carries with it a heavy weight of profound purpose and duty (Zuniga & Mahan, 2021). This relates to ideas of *transcendence*, where the connection of the self and one's goals to that of a greater entity, including of society (Pratt et al., 2006; Rosso et al., 2010). This calling will have been interpreted differently by many across the course of the pandemic, with some finding profound pride and positivity in being able to contribute in times of crisis (Billings et al., 2021; Kinsella et al., 2021; Sharma et al., 2022), but also potentially feeling a sense of dread and fear that they are obliged to be placed in danger and distress (Billings et al., 2021; Koontalay et al., 2021).

The "hero"

The extraordinary efforts and sacrifices have quite rightly earned those in these essential or "key" worker roles the label of hero, with the public all over the world applauding and displaying signs of gratitude for their heroes. Yet, the labelling of another as hero carries with it many connotations. In most cases, the feelings about the label are markedly different between the giver (the onlooker) and the recipient (the hero). The person who is called a hero frequently feels deeply uncomfortable with that classification, often insisting that anyone would have done similar in their position (Walker et al., 2010). Work from the pandemic has also highlighted this eschewal as a discomfort with the label both from the perspective of a lack of identification with it, but also from the sense that it places unrealistic expectations on those it is given to (Cox, 2020; Einboden, 2020; Kinsella & Sumner, 2021).

The label of hero carries with it relatively universal characteristics: heroes are considered to have attributes associated with selflessness, bravery, moral integrity, the protection of others, and a consistency of acting with determination (Kinsella et al., 2015b). For those called "hero," there is a reasonable expectation that those who give the label mean it: that they admire and respect the person or people to whom they give that label because they are thought of positively (Kinsella et al., 2015a). Because the understanding of what it means to be a hero is so universal (Allison & Goethals, 2011; Frisk, 2019; Kinsella et al., 2015b), those who receive the label are as aware as those giving it what it means. Receiving that label connotes regard and esteem from those that give it; a recognition that the hero is worthy of admiration, respect, and gratitude (see the hero contract: Sumner & Kinsella, 2021b). This *hero contract* constitutes a type of relational psychological contract (Millward & Hopkins, 1998; Rousseau & Parks, 1993) whereby the attribution of the label from those that the worker indirectly serves (i.e., the general public rather than their specific patients, customers, or clients) implies a sentiment or expected behaviour from them toward the recipients of the label.

So, alongside the labelling of being "essential," these workers were also elevated to the status of "hero," potentially setting the terms for social exchange between the workers and those giving the labels (society). The labelling imposed on these workers elevated their feelings of meaning and purpose in their role, potentially providing the means for burnout to be buffered during a time of undoubted extreme stress and worry. The capacity for the elevated meaning to be reinforced through social exchange was initially realised in the demonstrations of solidarity from leadership and from the public. These labels and the sense of calling or transcendence they may imbue are ultimately fragile and temporary if not supported by consistent behaviour from onlookers (De Camargo & Whiley, 2020). Unfortunately, what eventually transpired during the pandemic was widely publicised rule breaking and noncompliance, which served to not only undermine the transcendence the labelling gave, but also ultimately to a general trend towards loss of meaning and heightened risk of burnout.

Social exchange and burnout

The emphasis made on social factors within occupational settings and their potential impact on burnout is a central focus of research in the field (Buunk & Schaufeli, 1993). The idea of effort-reward imbalance in certain professional settings as being a key precursor to burnout, alongside a variety of other occupational health and wellbeing outcomes, has been well established (Siegrist, 2002). The social aspect of this is such that there must be a perception of equivocal reciprocated return from others (in the form of effort, or at least commitment to reaching shared goals) to match the input made by the worker (Buunk & Schaufeli, 1993; Schaufeli et al., 1996). This is likely to be of particular concern for those professions where the actions of the other in the equation (usually patient or service user) do not adequately meet the actions put in by the worker. A good example of this is where those in the medical professions work hard to support their patients, but their efforts are ultimately thwarted due to the patient not following their advice or guidance (Buunk & Schaufeli, 1993). The failure of social exchange has been shown to be related to emotional exhaustion in particular (Petrou et al., 2011; Rose et al., 2010), and would, therefore, constitute a pathway to burnout in itself in this context beyond the added layers that the labelling appears to have had.

Whilst social exchange has received some attention in the context of burnout, it has previously been examined (in a similar fashion to the existential theories of burnout) with the view of occurring specifically within the working context, typically in the workplace itself. As mentioned above, in this time of crisis, where vast swathes of working roles have been designated as "essential" and as heroes of the hour, society itself has positioned itself as being the client of those workers, essentially locating the social exchange much more broadly. Society has initiated and reinforced the rhetoric of their providing a service to humanity, and so the context of social factors relating to burnout becomes relocated to a macro-level interaction between the worker and society-as-client. The terms of the social exchange in this context are not as concrete as those having previously been established in burnout theory, but rather rely on reciprocity in generalised exchange principles (Molm, 2010; Molm et al., 2007). Here, the workers are not reliant on objective or tangible objects of exchange, rather they are reliant on a sentiment of support, a collective commitment to work toward the same goal, which we have conceptualised as *solidarity*, and is supported in the social exchange literature as being related to a more generalised exchange between one and many (Molm et al., 2007). In this context of having established the terms for social (or societal) exchange, whether or not society upholds their end of the bargain not only has the potential to induce burnout through unhonoured social exchange, but the failure to act in solidarity also directly undermines the workers' sense of meaning.

Social exchange has also been hinted at within the literature concerning meaningful work, particularly with relevance to transcendence. Here, key others (in this case leadership) need to ensure integrity to foster the meaningfulness of work, in that they need to ensure an alignment of their words and deeds that support the narrative of the meaning of the individual's work in order to sustain that concept of transcendence (Pratt et al., 2006; Rosso et al., 2010). Leadership acting with integrity to the concept of meaning in the individual's work is said to function through two mechanisms: providing a role model by which to live the ideology of the meaning of that work, and by building trust in the system in which that person is working (Pratt et al., 2006). It is likely that this is also a form of social exchange, or psychological contract akin to the *hero contract*, that as a label is given (and a meaning invoked) that an expectation of behaviour on the part of the person giving the label is set (Sumner & Kinsella, 2021b). What was witnessed, in the two nations where our study was set, was that after leadership had given the label of "hero" and "essential worker" to these individuals, they broke their own rules to minimise the infection rate to lower worker burden and distress. This fundamentally violated the ideology of thenewly augmented meaning for the roles of frontline workers, and dishonoured the societal exchange.

In sum, frontline workers reported an elevation in their sense of meaning as the "essential worker" and "hero" labels were internalised through the call-to-arms from leadership and broader society in the early months of the pandemic. This labelling also initiated a process of social exchange. By designating frontline workers as the first line of defence, leaders and members of the general public agreed tosupport the efforts of the workers. During the pandemic, this involved minimising the community infection rates either through legislation (in the case of leadership) or the adherence to that legislation (in the case of the leadership and the public). Unfortunately, what was observed in the UK and Ireland, was that the sentiment of support and solidarity for the heroes rapidly dissolved with the emergence of leadership contravening its own rules (Davies et al., 2021; Fancourt et al., 2020; Faulkner, 2020). These occurrences acted as a catalyst for the undermining of health protection safeguards from the public, resulting in a weakened sense of solidarity from these groups by frontline workers (Sumner & Kinsella, 2021b, 2022). The incongruence between the words and deeds of the leaders that inspired the augmented sense of meaning in these workers along with the consequent social exchange not being seen to be honoured devalued these labels, potentially devaluing the workers' sense of meaning in and of itself.

Labelling, meaning, and social exchange: an integration

Throughout this chapter we have posited several key points, bringing together disparate theories from occupational and social psychology, to highlight the very specific and unique context of frontline working during in the pandemic. The present work adds to existing theory on burnout by highlighting the need to consider broader social factors beyond the workplace when seeking to make sense of such a complex personal process that can be influenced by the action or inaction of broader society. The consideration of the precursors to the issues we have so far observed in our own work sets a scene of society as a whole placing demands and pressures on workers, playing a part in their burnout. How much of this process is avoidable, and how much is inevitable in a disaster scenario, is not yet known. The ability for the public, who face their own distress, torment, and exhaustion with the various elements of pandemic life, to maintain support and solidarity for their essential workers indefinitely is a question that is hard to answer. What we have seen in the UK and Ireland, however, has been a pre-ventable loss of solidarity, initiated by the incongruence of behaviour on the part of leadership. Whilst the factors highlighted herein will not be relevant to every occupational scenario, it does account for factors presented by a very specific scenario that may be translatable to other contexts and occupational sectors.

This consilience of concepts and theoretical perspectives has been the result of efforts to make sense of the unfolding story written by frontline workers in our own work following their experiences during the pandemic. This thesis was born from a combination of methods and data collected at key points during the pandemic that highlighted: 1) that frontline workers felt an enhanced sense of meaning and calling from their work, particularly during the first wave (Kinsella et al., 2021), 2) that meaning in life was protective of burnout during this same period (Sumner & Kinsella, 2021a), 3) that since this time, the emergence of widely publicised rule breaking on the part of governments and the public was uniquely and profoundly hurtful, degrading their sense of meaning (Sumner & Kinsella, 2021b), and 4) that the concept of solidarity was related to a variety of markers of worker welfare via its relationship to meaning (Sumner & Kinsella, 2022). Notably, throughout our work we have captured data on participants' meaning in life, not just the meaning derived from their work. The fact that meaning in their lives declined over this time is a stark warning not just to occupational outcomes such as burnout, but also to fundamental mental health outcomes that exist beyond the occupational context.

Points for future research

Whilst the theoretical constructions made within this chapter have been based on evidence that has emerged in the pandemic, it is at present still incomplete in its understanding of how burnout may or may not develop when related to both meaning and social exchange. Fundamentally, what is not known at this stage is whether the loss of meaning is a characteristic of burnout, or whether it is a precursor to burnout. From our own research, we have found that meaning has decreased over time (Sumner & Kinsella, 2022), however levels of burnout in this latest analysis were not vastly larger than that recorded at baseline (Sumner & Kinsella, 2021a). It is noted that the sample sizes in the more recent analyses were significantly smaller, and it is very likely that those lost to follow-up may be so due to high levels of burnout, and therefore the level of burnout observed at the 12-month timepoint may not be an accurate reflection of the situation for all in our sample. It is also not known how the facets of burnout may correspond to changes in meaning. Given that there are aspects to meaningful work that sit counter to the component aspects of burnout, it is unknown as yet whether the degradation of meaning runs parallel to the increase in these counter concepts in burnout. Practically, it is also important to investigate the existential aspects of burnout more closely with regard to certain occupations.

It has been argued that burnout may be more common in "human services" professions because these roles are selected by those who wish to use them as a vehicle to manifest meaning in their lives (Pines, 1993), yet others have argued that burnout resulting from existential mechanisms is a product of poor fit on the part of the worker and their values to the overt outcomes of that work (Längle, 2003). This somewhat collides with the prior point, in that it is important to understand the linear and temporal processes of the meaning–burnout dynamics, however it is also important when considering how some occupations may be more vulnerable to burnout via existential threat.

Finally, it will be important to consider whether social exchange that is honoured may prevent burnout even in high-stakes, high stress scenarios. There are potentially other aspects of one's working life beyond the honouring of social exchange that can harm meaning also, so it is possible that (as is the case with many concepts in the psychology of stress and wellbeing) that the honouring of social exchange may not confer protection, but may merely prevent from further harm. Of importance, the concept of considering social factors beyond the direct working context or environment to burnout is of importance. There are many roles and occupational activities that sit under broad public scrutiny (such as those in the military, those in politics, and indeed any role if it has the media spotlight shone sufficiently on it), and it is possible that public sentiment or tone, particularly if this involves labelling or the invocation of transcendence, may be important considerations in the pathways to burnout.

Implications for applications in work psychology

Whilst this work is deeply rooted within the cultural, occupational, and political contexts of the pandemic, being developed from work in the UK and Ireland during Covid-19, there are likely implications and applications for these concepts that endure beyond these specific bounds. Labelling of workers occurs very frequently in occupational contexts as a means for motivation, reward, and recognition of efforts. Labels that are often given may centre around key performance indicators, such as "top performer" or "highest seller," or even more global personal attributes such as "rising star" or "future leader," but regardless of whether they speak to the attributes of someone as an employee or as a person, they must be given with care. Invoking transcendence through a "greater good" by labelling someone a hero has clearly been problematic when this has not been coupled with consistent action on the part of the person—or persons—giving the label, and it is likely that this is needed in other scenarios of workplace labelling also. Whilst "highflyer" may not invoke transcendence, it does also potentially set the terms for some sort of exchange, where after being given a label of success, the recipient of that label will reasonably expect behaviour that is congruent with that appraisal. Above all, it is important to remember that the higher the pedestal that we put others, the further they have to fall, so all labels should be given with care and consciousness of action on the part of the person giving the label.

Note

1 See: www.cv19heroes.com

References

Allison, S. T., & Goethals, G. R. (2011). *Heroes: What they do and why we need them.* New York. Oxford University Press.

Autin, K. L., Herdt, M. E., Garcia, R. G., & Ezema, G. N. (2022). Basic psychological need satisfaction, autonomous motivation, and meaningful work: A self-determination theory perspective. *Journal of Career Assessment*, *30*(1), 78–93. 10.1177/10690727211018647

Baumeister, R. F. (1991). *Meanings of life.* New York. Guilford Press.

Bayer, N. D., Taylor, A., Fallon, A., Wang, H., Santolaya, J. L., Bamat, T. W., & Washington, N. (2021). Pediatric residents' sense of meaning in their work: Is this value related to higher specialty satisfaction and reduced burnout? *Academic Pediatrics*, *21*(3), 557–563. 10.1016/j.acap.2020.10.012

Benziman, Y. (2020). "Winning" the "battle" and "beating" the COVID-19 "enemy": Leaders' use of war frames to define the pandemic. *Peace and Conflict: Journal of Peace Psychology*, *26*(3), 247–256. 10.1037/pac0000494

Bianchi, R., Verkuilen, J., Brisson, R., Schonfeld, I. S., & Laurent, E. (2016). Burnout and depression: Label-related stigma, help-seeking, and syndrome overlap. *Psychiatry Research*, *245*, 91–98. 10.1016/j.psychres.2016.08.025

Billings, J., Abou Seif, N., Hegarty, S., Ondruskova, T., Soulios, E., Bloomfield, M., & Greene, T. (2021). What support do frontline workers want? A qualitative study of health and social care workers' experiences and views of psychosocial support during the COVID-19 pandemic. *PloS one*, *16*(9), e0256454. 10.1371/journal.pone.0256454

Billings, J., Ching, B. C. F., Gkofa, V., Greene, T., & Bloomfield, M. (2021). Experiences of frontline healthcare workers and their views about support during COVID-19 and previous pandemics: A systematic review and qualitative meta-synthesis. *BMC Health Services Research*, *21*(1), 923. 10.1186/s12913-021-06917-z

Buunk, B. P., & Schaufeli, W. B. (1993). Burnout: A perspective from social comparison theory. In W. B. Schaufeli, C. Maslach, & T. Marek (Eds.). *Professional burnout: Recent developments in theory and research* (pp. 53–69). Philadelphia. Taylor & Francis.

Cox, C. L. (2020). 'Healthcare Heroes': Problems with media focus on heroism from healthcare workers during the COVID-19 pandemic. *Journal of Medical Ethics*, *46*(8), 510–513. 10.1136/medethics-2020-106398

Davies, B., Lalot, F., Peitz, L., Heering, M. S., Ozkececi, H., Babaian, J., Davies Hayon, K., Broadwood, J., & Abrams, D. (2021). Changes in political trust in Britain during the COVID-19 pandemic in 2020: Integrated public opinion evidence and implications. *Humanities and Social Sciences Communications*, *8*(1), 166. 10.1057/s41599-021-00850-6

De Camargo, C. R., & Whiley, L. A. (2020). The mythologisation of key workers: Occupational prestige gained, sustained … And lost? *International Journal of Sociology and Social Policy*, *40*(9/10), 849–859. 10.1108/IJSSP-07-2020-0310

Durkheim, E. (2002). *Suicide: A study in sociology.* New York. Routledge.

Einboden, R. (2020). SuperNurse? Troubling the hero discourse in COVID times. *Health*, *24*(4), 343–347. 10.1177/1363459320934280

Fancourt, D., Steptoe, A., & Wright, L. (2020). The Cummings effect: politics, trust, and behaviours during the COVID-19 pandemic. *The Lancet*, *396*(10249), 464–465. 10.1016/S0140-6736(20)31690-1

Faulkner, P. (2020). Lockdown: A case study in how to lose trust and undermine compliance. *Global Discourse, 11,* 497–515. 10.1332/204378921X16106635782045

Frisk, K. (2019). What makes a hero? Theorising the social structuring of heroism. *Sociology, 53*(1), 87. 10.1177/0038038518764568

Kinsella, E. L., Hughes, S., Lemon, S., Stonebridge, N., & Sumner, R. C. (2021). "We shouldn't waste a good crisis": The lived experience of working on the frontline through the first surge (and beyond) of COVID-19 in the UK and Ireland. *Psychology & Health,* 1–27. 10.1080/08870446.2021.1928668

Kinsella, E. L., Muldoon, O. T., Lemon, S., Stonebridge, N., Hughes, S., & Sumner, R. C. (2022). In it together?: Exploring solidarity with frontline workers in the United Kingdom and Ireland during COVID-19. *British Journal of Social Psychology.* 2022 Sep 12. 10.1111/bjso.12579. Epub ahead of print. PMID: 36097335.

Kinsella, E. L., Ritchie, T. D., & Igou, E. R. (2015a). Lay perspectives on the social and psychological functions of heroes. *Frontiers in Psychology, 6,* 130. 10.3389/fpsyg.2015.00130

Kinsella, E. L., Ritchie, T. D., & Igou, E. R. (2015b). Zeroing in on heroes: A prototype analysis of hero features. *Journal of Personality and Social Psychology, 108*(1), 114-127. 10.1 037/a0038463

Kinsella, E. L., & Sumner, R. C. (2021). High ideals: The misappropriation and re-appropriation of the heroic label in the midst of a global pandemic. *Journal of Medical Ethics, 48*(3), 198-199. https://doi.org/10.1136/medethics-2021-107236

Koontalay, A., Suksatan, W., Prabsangob, K., & Sadang, J. M. (2021). Healthcare workers' burdens during the COVID-19 pandemic: A qualitative systematic review. *Journal of Multidisciplinary Healthcare, 14,* 3015–3025. 10.2147/JMDH.S330041

Längle, A. (2003). Burnout–Existential meaning and possibilities of prevention. *European Psychotherapy, 4,* 107–121.

Link, B. G., Cullen, F. T., Struening, E., Shrout, P. E., & Dohrenwend, B. P. (1989). A modified labeling theory approach to mental disorders: An empirical assessment. *American Sociological Review,* 400–423. 10.2307/2095613

Maslach, C., & Jackson, S. E. (1981). The measurement of experienced burnout. *Journal of Organizational Behavior, 2*(2), 99–113. 10.1002/job.4030020205

Millward, L. J., & Hopkins, L. J. (1998). Psychological contracts, organizational and job commitment. *Journal of Applied Social Psychology, 28*(16), 1530–1556.

Molm, L. D. (2010). The structure of reciprocity. *Social Psychology Quarterly, 73*(2), 119–131. 10.1177/0190272510369079

Molm, L. D., Collett, J. L., & Schaefer, D. R. (2007). Building solidarity through generalized exchange: A theory of reciprocity. *American Journal of Sociology, 113*(1), 205–242 10.1086/517900.

Petrou, P., Kouvonen, A., & Karanika-Murray, M. (2011). Social exchange at work and emotional exhaustion: The role of personality. *Journal of Applied Social Psychology, 41*(9), 2165–2199. 10.1111/j.1559-1816.2011.00812.x

Pines, A. M. (1993). Burnout: An existential perspective. In W. B. Schaufeli, C. Maslach, & T. Marek (Eds.). *Professional burnout: Recent developments in theory and research* (pp. 33–52). Philadelphia, PA. Taylor & Francis.

Pratt, M. G., Rockmann, K. W., & Kaufmann, J. B. (2006). Constructing professional identity: The role of work and identity learning cycles in the customization of identity among medical residents. *Academy of Management Journal, 49*(2), 235–262. 10.5465/amj.2006.20786060

Rose, J., Madurai, T., Thomas, K., Duffy, B., & Oyebode, J. (2010). Reciprocity and burnout in direct care staff. *Clinical Psychology & Psychotherapy, 17*(6), 455–462. 10.1002/cpp.688.

Rosso, B. D., Dekas, K. H., & Wrzesniewski, A. (2010). On the meaning of work: A theoretical integration and review. *Research in Organizational Behavior, 30,* 91–127. 10.1016/j.riob.2010.09.001

Rousseau, D. M., & Parks, J. M. (1993). The contracts of individuals and organizations. *Research in Organizational Behavior, 15*(1), 1–43.

Schaufeli, W. B., Dierendonck, D. V., & Gorp, K. V. (1996). Burnout and reciprocity: Towards a dual-level social exchange model. *Work & Stress, 10*(3), 225–237. 10.1080/02678379608256802

Sharma, D., Ghosh, K., Mishra, M., & Anand, S. (2022). You stay home, but we can't: Invisible 'dirty' work as calling amid COVID-19 pandemic. *Journal of Vocational Behavior, 132,* 103667. 10.1016/j.jvb.2021.103667

Siegrist, J. (2002). Effort-reward imbalance at work and health. In P. L. Perrewé & D. C. Ganster (Eds.). *Historical and current perspectives on stress and health,* Bingley, UK. Emerald Group Publishing Limited.

Smith, S., Woo Baidal, J., Wilner, P. J., & Ienuso, J. (2020). The heroes and heroines: Supporting the front line in New York City during Covid-19. *NEJM Catalyst Innovations in Care Delivery,* 15 Jul 2020. 10.1056/CAT.20.0285

Steger, M. F., & Dik, B. J. (2010). Work as meaning: Individual and organizational benefits of engaging in meaningful work. In P. A. Linley, S. Harrington, & N. Garcea (Eds.). *The Oxford handbook of positive psychology and work* (pp. 131–142). Oxford University Press. 10.1093/oxfordhb/9780195335446.001.0001

Sumner, R. C., & Kinsella, E. L. (2021a). Grace under pressure: Resilience, burnout, and wellbeing in frontline workers in the UK and Republic of Ireland during the SARS-CoV-2 pandemic. *Frontiers in Psychology, 11.* 576229. 10.3389/fpsyg.2020.576229

Sumner, R. C., & Kinsella, E. L. (2021b). "It's Like a Kick in the Teeth": The Emergence of Novel Predictors of Burnout in Frontline Workers During Covid-19. *Frontiers in Psychology, 12.* 645504. 10.3389/fpsyg.2021.645504

Sumner, R. C., & Kinsella, E. L. (2022). Solidarity appraisal, meaning, and markers of welfare in frontline workers in the UK and Ireland during the Covid-19 pandemic, *SSM Mental Health,* 2022 Dec, *2.* 100099. 10.1016/j.ssmmh.2022.100099. Epub 2022 Apr 19. PMID: 35463800; PMCID: PMC9017115.

Uong, A. M., Cabana, M. D., Serwint, J. R., Bernstein, C. A., & Schulte, E. E. (2021). Changes in pediatric faculty burnout during the COVID-19 pandemic. *Hospital Pediatrics, 11*(12), e364–e373. 10.1542/hpeds.2021-006045

Walker, L. J., Frimer, J. A., & Dunlop, W. L. (2010). Varieties of moral personality: Beyond the banality of heroism. *Journal of Personality, 78*(3), 907942. 10.1111/j.1467-6494.2010.00637.x.

Zhou, Y., Asante, E. A., Zhuang, Y., Wang, J., Zhu, Y., & Shen, L. (2021). Surviving an infectious disease outbreak: How does nurse calling influence performance during the COVID-19 fight? *Journal of Nursing Management, 29*(3), 421–431. 10.1111/jonm.13181

Zuniga, L. M., & Mahan, J. D. (2021). Averting burnout in pediatricians: Understanding the intersection of workload and meaning of work. *Hospital Pediatrics, 11*(12), e409–e411. 10.1542/hpeds.2021-006349

2 Pandemic implications for six areas of worklife

Michael P. Leiter[1] and Christina Maslach[2]

[1]*Psychology Department, Acadia University, Wolfville, Nova Scotia and Deakin University, Melbourne, Australia*
[2]*Psychology Department, University of California, Berkeley*

Relationships with work

Relationships of people with workplaces are fraught with expectations, obligations, and demands from both sides. Good matches reflect alignment, such that both workplaces and employees develop compatible accommodation with one another. That is, there is an ongoing alignment between what people seek from workplaces and what workplaces seek from people. A core construct of the Areas of Worklife model is that mismatches on any or all the key areas can contribute to job burnout (Leiter & Maslach 2004; Maslach & Leiter, 2022). This chapter considers the implications of the pandemic for the six areas of worklife. The impact includes the pandemic further aggravating existing mismatches as well as creating new mismatches. It is also important to acknowledge that, in some instances, pandemic-related changes in work contributed to improving matches between workers and their workplace.

Burnout has increased among many sectors during the pandemic, especially among healthcare providers (Bezek et al., 2022; Butler et al., 2021; Lasalvia et al., 2021). There is no evidence that the increase in burnout resulted from the pandemic causing an abrupt decrease in resilience. The evidence points towards the pandemic causing abrupt changes in the ways people interacted with their workplaces and with the people associated with their workplaces. It follows that the most effective response to increased exhaustion and cynicism would address changes in work design rather than in addressing individual shortcomings. Improving resilience misses an important point. Not that there is anything inherently wrong with improving resilience, but there is more to be gained from addressing the immediate source of the problem than in helping people endure the problem.

From the perspective of the Areas of Worklife model of burnout, the pandemic changed everything, or at least changed aspects of all six of the areas that the model identifies. This chapter begins with an overview of those changes with their implications for experiences of exhaustion, cynicism, and inefficacy. It then reflects on the lessons learned from the experience.

DOI: 10.4324/9781003250531-3

Areas of Worklife model

The Truth about Burnout (Maslach & Leiter, 1997) identified six areas of worklife for which research had established consistent links with the three dimensions of burnout: exhaustion, cynicism, and inefficacy. A core construct of the model contrasts matches versus mismatches in the interactions of people with worksettings. People differ on what they bring to their workplaces in terms of aspirations, motivations, needs, and preferences. There is no one size that fits all. Yet, a good match of workplaces with people remains important for people to experience engagement with their work. On the other side of the relationship, workplaces differ in their opportunities, cultures, practices, and restraints. There are a lot of sizes requiring someone to fit them. A good match is when what matters to people aligns well with what matters to workplaces. For example, some people may prefer continuous social encounters during their workdays while others may prefer long stretches of uninterrupted concentration on ideas with occasional encounters with others. Although there is no level of sociability at work that is perfect for everyone, the right level of sociability is a critical issue for everyone. To what extent can workplaces and people create a happy balance. Without resolution across the six areas of worklife, misalignments persist indefinitely.

To further complicate the challenge of sustaining a fulfilling, productive relationship of people with workplaces, the elements are in constant flux. People change over time. Their abilities, values, and hopes ebb and flow as people mature, learn, and gain experience. Workplaces evolve in line with developments in technologies, finance, and culture. Not only does one size not fit all, one size rarely fits anyone forever. Research on the model (Leiter & Maslach, 2004) led to developing the Areas of Worklife Scale (AWS; Leiter & Maslach, 2011), a 28-item questionnaire on which people indicate the extent to which the six areas of worklife are functioning well at their work, which has been used in research on the impact of COVID on worklife (Jarzynkowski et al., 2021).

The challenge to workplaces goes beyond providing an ideal setting. It requires developing the systems, leadership, and culture that encourages people to find what works best for their given situation in ways that meet their current responsibilities and goals. The point is not providing employees with the ideal workplace and then maintaining its pristine condition. Rather, the point is encouraging an ongoing dynamic in which people and workplaces accommodate one another in social context, a process that rests upon open and honest communication.

Workload

Workload captures the demands of work in the context of the resources available to address those demands. Subjective evaluations of workload respond to the number of tasks, the time requirements of those demands, their complexity, their emotional intensity, and the extent to which they are familiar or novel.

People evaluate workload in the context of relevant resources, including expertise, equipment, facilities, and support staff (Hill et al., 1992). People assess their work demands against the time and energy they have to apply to the job.

The pandemic was associated with increases in workload across many occupations and nationalities. For example, a survey of 439 pharmacists in the USA (Bakken & Winn, 2021) found that during the pandemic those with increased work hours and more intense work demands reported higher levels of exhaustion and depersonalisation. Spanish fashion retail employees (Rodríguez-López et al., 2021) reported greater exhaustion associated with increased work demands and uncertainty. A case study of two Chinese healthcare professionals (Kutlu et al., 2021; Zhou et al., 2022) reported that excessive workload appeared to be associated with them experiencing a second COVID-19 infection. Italian intensive care practitioners reported higher levels of burnout (Stocchetti, et al., 2021). A brief review of research on physicians' experiences of burnout while contending with the pandemic (Amanullah & Shankar, 2020) found that increased workload was a consistent theme of physicians' perspective on COVID's impact on their lives.

A survey of Australian teachers (Timms et al., 2007) found that abrupt increases in workload were associated with increased burnout among teachers. Disruptions to the established pattern of work make a noticeable impact on employees' subjective assessment of their workload. Although their formal workday maintains a designated amount of time, their assessment of demands upon them becomes more severe. The importance of change was evident in a longitudinal survey of employees of a Finnish forestry company (Leiter et al., 2013). Employees whose exhaustion and cynicism scores worsened over a three-year period were prescribed more anti-depressant and psychotropic medications over the subsequent decade. The worsening of exhaustion and cynicism made a contribution distinct from the absolute level of those scores.

The pandemic's impact was diverse across sectors. On one extreme, hospitality workload diminished abruptly as hotels, restaurants, and airlines shut down. Some people lost their jobs entirely, some were furloughed, and others worked reduced hours, all of which entailed a sharp reduction of workload. In contrast, healthcare experienced an immediate increase in work demands from patients experiencing serious symptoms of respiratory and other illnesses associated with the corona virus. Even within healthcare, the impact was complex in that elective surgeries and services unrelated to the virus were suspended. Working from home freed people from the demands of commuting and travelling for work, but it often added demands by increasing the length of the workday through a plethora of zoom meetings and the requirement that people integrate work within childcare demands.

The virus's impact on workload went far beyond the quantity of tasks to be addressed. First, the virus was, in itself, a new and serious workplace hazard with the potential for causing serious illness or death. Even mild infections could block a person's capacity to work or participate in community life through isolation or quarantine. These hazards contribute to anxiety that can be an energy-depleting experience with a potential to interfere with recovery by preventing sleep.

Second, continuing businesses managed their contacts with people through a variety of strategies to maintain distance. These processes required learning new skills to manage the technology and to present oneself as a competent professional on client calls and video meetings. Working from home often required upgrading equipment, furniture, and connections to attain a level of participation. These requirements not only entailed expense, but the time to set things up.

Third, change also makes demands on people. Responses to the pandemic disrupted established routines, shut down locations, and required new ways of maintaining contact with colleagues and customers. These changes increased the level of uncertainty that prompt anxiety and worry.

In changing the locations, processes, and linkages of work, reactions to the pandemic increased workload in ways that depleted personal resources of time, energy, and enthusiasm. To some extent, other aspects of the pandemic response—its novelty and community-building qualities—could offset the impact of increased workload. However, the long duration of the pandemic response tended to maintain its exhausting qualities. That is, people can return to their usual routine after a brief period of intense work demands, but an ongoing, chronic intensity profoundly changes peoples' relationships with work.

Control

Although workload often is seen as the driving force behind experiences of burnout, the Areas of Worklife model places control at the pivotal position among the six areas (Gascón et al., 2013; Leiter & Shaughnessy, 2006). To the extent that people can exert control in their jobs, they can improve their situation at work. Control over the amount, pace, or complexity of work demands has significant implications for how people experience workload. Choices over the people with whom one works can shape one's sense of community. Access to institutional decision-making allows people to create a better match concerning rewards or fair access to opportunities. Autonomy regarding the way people spend time at work opens possibilities for pursuing what truly matters, leading to a better match on values. The potential for control to shape other areas of worklife give control a foundational role in the Areas of Worklife model.

In its early stages, the pandemic engendered considerable uncertainty in being a novel corona virus. Predicting the disease's trajectory, transmission, and impact required research and clinical practice. The reliable foundation for contemporary healthcare comes from protocols established through clinical trials using randomised controls to identify effective treatments (Sackett & Rosenberg, 1995). During the first wave of the pandemic, doctors and nurses were functioning without sufficient information to exercise control in their interactions with patients. They scrambled to keep people breathing, prompting a search for mechanical ventilators that were eventually found to have mixed results (Tobin et al., 2020; Wunsch, 2020). Research supporting specific treatments was slow to emerge.

In addition to limited efficacy in clinical practice, the potential for contracting the disease while interacting with patients introduced further uncertainty. The virus posed the risk of serious disease that was at times fatal. In the initial phase of the pandemic, personal protective equipment (PPE) was in short supply. There was also uncertainty on what equipment provided the best protection, and inconsistencies in uses of the PPE. The effectiveness of PPE among healthcare workers varied according to workers' health conditions (obesity, smoking, diabetes), ventilation in work areas, length of work shifts, the quality of PPE manufacture, mask fit, and length of time wearing PPE (Galanis et al., 2021). Without access to high quality equipment, thorough training on its use, and well-designed work areas, it was difficult for workers to feel in control of their interactions with the virus.

Changes in worklife that exacerbated mismatches on other areas of worklife had implications as well for employees' sense of control in their work. For example, shifting from face-to-face meetings to video calls moved people into a different mode of interacting. Video calls not only depend on a high quality, reliable internet connection, they also have their own social norms for presentation and participation. It takes some concerted effort for people to become comfortably adept at managing a new social media with its cybersecurity implications (Okereafor & Manny, 2020; Taber et al., 2021).

The pandemic and the policy reactions to it disrupted broadly and deeply. The disruption itself cast doubt on employees' sense of control over many aspects of their lives. Remote working loosened managers' sense of control regarding their domains, as it left them with fewer options for monitoring employees' behaviour. Their diminished control did not directly contribute to greater control for employees, as control does not operate as a zero-sum game. Often less control for one person signals less control for everyone. People required considerable experience working in the new world created by the pandemic, in order to feel in control of their job.

Reward

A good alignment of people with their work also rests on meaningful rewards—both intrinsic and extrinsic. The pandemic had the potential to disrupt both dimensions of reward. The immediate impact of myriad strategies for social distancing was on the intrinsic quality of interactions between employees and their service recipients. Usually, these encounters would have provided moments in which employees exercised their expertise, by providing relevant technical or medical services, but the face-to-face encounters provided the medium for realising therapeutic relationships. In contrast, social distancing (whether through PPE, physical distance, or electronic mediation such as Zoom) diminished the range of subtle cues to which employees usually respond (Earle & Freddolino, 2022). Distancing also constrained the potential for service recipients to perceive the various supportive communications that employees were sending their way (Twenge et al., 2018). That is, some subtle gestures, facial expressions, or voice modulations may fail to transmit through social distancing.

Distancing changed more than social contact; it changed workflow as well. For those who had developed intrinsically satisfying rhythms to their work, new constraints were not welcomed (Sweeny et al., 2020). Whether conducting medical procedures, checking out groceries, delivering packages, or going to meetings, people had to accommodate to changes in procedures and processes. Specific tasks often required more time, different pacing, or different locations.

However, working during the pandemic also had its rewards as well as its challenges. For example, working at home presented challenges to many (especially to parents of young children), but was a boon to some (whose home environments were more comfortable and pleasant than the conditions of their job). The ability to do one's work without having to commute (which is often time-consuming, expensive, frustrating, and unpleasant) was a major improvement for many people. For some nurses, the pandemic has confirmed their sense of calling in their profession. Student nurses and newly graduated nurses moved more rapidly into practice with higher levels of responsibility that they found to be intrinsically rewarding. In addition to wider opportunities for action, the pandemic situation strengthened their sense of professional identity that was highly rewarding as well (Swift et al., 2020).

Rewards at work are pleasant in themselves but they also provide confirmation that the relationship with work is going well. Disruptions of the intrinsically motivating aspects of being on the job and functioning in familiar patterns can challenge employees' sense of wellbeing as well as their identity. People have the capacity to develop new patterns that work well but doing so requires concerted effort and some time. The most direct connection of rewards with job burnout is with employees' sense of efficacy. Both intrinsic and extrinsic rewards at work support feelings of confidence and accomplishment.

Community

Despite a strong case for social motivation being a universal human quality (Deci & Ryan, 2000), there is evidence that people differ greatly in that motive's power as well as in the routes through which people prefer to pursue fulfilling that motive (Dunbar, 1998; Hill, 1987; Wardhaugh & Fuller, 2021). Yet again, one size does not fit all. Some people thrive in jobs that entail nearly constant social interaction while others find such settings overwhelming. It need not be lacking any social motivation, but the types and quantities of social encounters that they find fulfilling have a different quality. Because of the range of preferences and inclinations that people have concerning social engagement, the important issue for a fulfilling worklife is alignment: do workplaces and the job roles match the social motivations and capabilities of their employees. Without a simple solution that fits all or even most people, people can find themselves in work situations that align poorly with the ways in which they want to engage socially at work. The extent to which people can shape their social participation at work has implications for their potential to find fulfillment at work.

Workplace cultures are stable over years and can remain resistant to efforts to change them deliberately (Braithwaite, et al., 2017). That stability implies that the quality of match regarding community is likely to remain as it is for a long time. A good match bodes well for the future, but a mismatch is likely to maintain without good fortune or focused efforts to bring about change in workgroup dynamics. For example, a survey of hospital employees found that 75% of those who described their social encounters with co-workers as uncivil at baseline also described their encounters as uncivil one year later. Consistently, 67% of those of those who described their social encounters with co-workers as respectful at baseline also described their encounters as re-spectful one year later (Leiter et al., 2011; Leiter et al., 2012). People and their relationships tend to maintain over time.

Countering stability over time is the diversity of social roles across the workgroups that a large organisation encompasses. This diversity offers solutions for people experiencing mismatches within the community domain. They may be able to shift to a role more compatible with their skills and inclinations, while remaining with the same employer (Broom et al., 2015).

In addition to disrupting contact with customers, patients, or students, social distancing upset relationships between employees and their manager, as well as among co-workers. The social environments of workplaces define a sense of community for people, addressing a widely held need for belonging or re-latedness (Deci & Ryan, 2000). Even for settings in which people continued working onsite, such as healthcare, workgroup interactions changed. Hospitals reconfigured teams, reassigning people from areas in which services were suspended to areas of high demand, such as respiratory therapies. Such changes were especially disruptive when employees had little or no choice regarding the reassignment (Gilles et al., 2021). These social encounters play an integral role in professional identities.

In their workplace communities, people develop distinct roles that become central to their identity at work. They define these roles partially through the social encounters that are integral to their jobs. For example, there are rules or established practices on the ways nurses interact with patients or supervisors lead workgroup meetings. Beyond these defined roles, people bring a personal style to those defined encounters. Nurses may vary in the amount of emotional support they bring to patient encounters. Supervisors vary in the openness to debate from workgroup members. People have discretion regarding their participation in informal workplace communities. Over time, they establish persistent patterns of encounters among members of workgroups.

Workplace changes in response to the pandemic disrupted both occupational and informal social networks with implications for employee wellbeing (Maunder et al., 2021). For example, in a survey of Canadian physicians in 2020, those whose MBI scores indicated a burnout profile (high exhaustion, cynicism, and inefficacy), reported lower levels of respect from colleagues combined with higher frequency of conflict at work (Bailey et al., 2021). Whereas much of contemporary work occurs through integrating contributions from people with distinct technical skills, disrupting among co-workers and the social make-up of workgroups has direct implications for the way people experience their work (Sargeant et al., 2008).

For some people, reassignment to a new team can be a change for the better. Workgroups vary in the extent to which their social culture conveys respect and civility (Cortina et al., 2001; Leiter et al., 2011). Those in less civil settings may find reassignment to be an opportunity for creating a better relationship with work.

However, whereas the primary theme of workplace responses to the pandemic was social distancing, the social environments of workplaces lost intimacy, intensity, and prevalence. Whatever its form, physical isolation prompted emotional isolation (Anderson & Kelliher, 2020) resulting in greater mismatches on the community are of worklife for most people. A survey of the law enforcement sector found that extraverts had a more difficult transition to working from home (Langvik et al., 2021). Distancing was a serious challenge for people for whom social interaction was a central part of their identity and the way in which they did their work.

The central quality of workplace responses to the pandemic increased distance between people. These efforts—especially working from home and wearing high quality masks when near people—were effective at reducing transmission. They made a big difference prior to readily available vaccines. They did, however, come at a cost. In the immediate term, workplaces had few options for supporting people distressed by social distancing. The crisis framework of the early pandemic narrowed focus to fundamental points of survival. However, as the pandemic persisted, the need for action to improve the quality of workplace cultures increased in urgency.

Fairness

Establishing fairness at work presents challenges that are inherent in hierarchical structures (Kwok, 2021), in that epistemic injustice—discrediting people of low status—is endemic to bureaucratic systems. Fricker (2007) distinguishes two forms within the domain of epistemic injustice. Testimonial injustice arises from hierarchical inclinations to distrust people of lower status who are often assumed to be less knowledgeable, intelligent, or emotionally stable. Hermeneutical injustice arises from lower status people lacking voice in the process of defining shared concepts. That is, formal and informal leaders have a larger voice in defining workplace values and the domain of valid ideas.

Lower status members of hierarchies may have difficulty in understanding distressing experiences at work and little success in explaining their distress to others because they do not work within the jargon and implicit assumptions shared among higher status people.

The abrupt changes responding to the pandemic arose from government mandates, such as stay-at-home orders or from corporate leadership, such as cancelling the National Basketball Association season in the United States. They reflected a view of the world that made sense to decision makers. The decisions often had foundations in existing public health practice or in research pertaining to containing contagion. These actions made sense to a lot of people who complied with confidence.

One place that failed to jibe with many people's understanding was the designation of "essential worker." Although the designation encompassed high-status people in healthcare, firefighting, and police, it also included many low-status people in sectors including maintenance or food processing, delivery, and sales. Although compelled to work by being designated as essential, low-status people had fewer protections based on access to distancing and PPE, and less discretion about when and where to work. They retained their right to mobility while that of others was restricted, but they at time relinquished their right to health (Rubenstein & Decamp, 2020).

Those who did have access to PPE had concerns about its availability and quality. These views were related to physician's level of cynicism and exhaustion (Bailey et al., 2021). For example, only 10% of participants rated PPE to be inadequate, but 84% of those showed either a Burnout or Disengaged (high cynicism only) profile while only 6% of those rating PPE as inadequate showed an Engaged profile. The adequacy of protective equipment pertains to healthcare regarding the wellbeing of both those providing services and patients. Institutional failures to prepare and to respond to major health crises undermine the confidence of their physicians, nurses, and other employees (Ansell et al., 2021).

Although working from home protected employees from contact with the virus, the approach raised fairness issues about workload and work/non-work boundaries. For some, the transition to working from home went smoothly. For others it entailed major disruptions to their worklife. People with an already established home office benefitted from the transition (Allen et al., 2021). Both the available space—separated from the domestic domain of the home—as well as appropriate furniture and information technology—eased the transition (Lapierre, et al., 2016). Those with long and expensive commutes also benefitted from the transition.

A major predictor of strain for those working from home pertained to childcare responsibilities (Bezak et al., 2022). With schools and childcare facilities closing, the boundary between work and personal life became more permeable. Building on differences in parental responsibilities across many cultures, gender wage and influence disparities increased during the pandemic (Adams-Prassl et al., 2020; Hipp & Bünning, 2021) with many women leaving the workforce at least temporarily at the cost of current and future earnings. The suspension of childcare and education services removed critical infrastructure for parents' capacity to participate in work. Preschool children clamor for constant attention; school-aged children often need parental help or monitoring to participate in online schooling (Cotofan et al., 2021). The disappearance of distinct times and places for work and childcare activities created distress for parents working from home.

In many ways changes in worklife created mismatches regarding fairness. Enacted policies had differential impacts on people, often placing greater burdens on those less able to manage them. Remote work gave greater autonomy for some but also constrained employees' access to procedures for addressing problems they were experiencing at work.

Values

Value congruence pertains to employees' assessment of the fit between their personal values and the lived values of their employer (Leiter & Maslach, 2004). It also pertains to value congruence among members of workgroups as well as congruence of employees' values with the lived values of their service recipients (Sumner & Kinsella, 2021). The capacity to pursue work that furthers core values opens possibilities for greater engagement with work, reducing pressures towards cynicism or other forms of disengagement from work.

The pandemic was an occasion for co-workers to pull together, sustaining a spirit of camaraderie during their efforts against a clear and powerful adversary while other groups fragmented over conflicts and mistrust (Butler et al., 2021). A critical issue among the physicians surveyed appeared to be the extent to which workgroups had articulated shared values on critical issues pertaining to their work. A pervasive value conflict concerned the relative priority of the physicians' personal safety relative to the obligation to patient care. When physicians felt isolated from their colleagues or even actively ostracised when spending time with COVID patients, they developed harshly negative evaluations of those colleagues.

In contrast, other settings found the pandemic to be an opportunity to reflect on the value of their activities, when they discovered that they could curtail some activities with little impact on their patients' wellbeing (Sumner & Kinsella, 2021). They identified activities that had continued primarily through inertia rather than through maintaining a discernable value addition to their productivity. For example, one setting found that patients meeting with a physical therapist online provided service as good as an in-person visit with an orthopaedist with fewer costs and greater patient safety. Another setting reduced the availability of some radiology treatments to terminally ill patients. The pandemic provided the impetus to reflect on their practice. However, it was the shared professional values combined with a reflective, shared decision-making process that permitting the groups to make consequential changes to their practice.

Healthcare providers who had confidence in their organisation's policies for managing the pandemic experienced less exhaustion and cynicism (Jarzynkowski et al., 2021; Matsuo et al., 2021). Both the organisations' demonstrated values regarding patient care and employee safety provided indicators of core values. A survey of nurses using the Areas of Worklife Scale that assesses the six areas of workload, control, reward, community, fairness, and values, found that value congruence of employees with their organisations was a primary predictor of low levels of exhaustion and cynicism (Apaydin et al., 2021).

Workplace changes in reactions to the pandemic had implications across the six areas of worklife. The response showed that workplaces had the capacity to make major changes quickly when facing a major threat to people and to organisational viability. In making quick, wide-sweeping changes, workplaces and governments did not anticipate all of the implications or downstream consequences. Some policies improved the quality of worklife for some people while creating mismatches for others. The disruption of workflow may at times have slowed the capacity of workplaces to respond effectively to employees' distress.

The Areas of Worklife model provides a framework to reflect on the broad implications of major workplace changes. In the first instance, changes occur in response to an identified need, such as the need to reduce vulnerability of people to an infectious agent. However, this necessary response—i.e., PPE—affects more than the identified problem. It also affects work patterns, intrinsic rewards, and social dynamics within workplaces. A compete plan includes reflections on these downstream consequences in order to develop effective responses to accommodate those effects.

Implications for actions

Maslach and Leiter (2022) propose the six areas of worklife as focus points for intervention in efforts to prevent or alleviate burnout. The critical issue for each area of worklife is the degree of match or mismatch of people with their worksetting. Good matches may reflect good fortune: the workplace selected the right person for the job. Neither had to change to accommodate to the other. Alternatively, good matches could reflect flexibility: although matches may not be perfect from the start, both people and workplaces have sufficient latitude to find a viable solution. With flexibility, a perfect match need not remain pristine forever: both the job and the person have enough breathing room to accommodate one other as both develop.

Despite consistent patterns in relationships of the areas of worklife with the dimensions of burnout, making meaningful change requires problem solving that fits a solution to the situation. People and workplaces vary greatly in important ways. Identifying, executing, and evaluating strategies for improving the quality of worklife requires thoughtful and well-informed action.

Maslach and Leiter (2022) note three guidelines for organisational interventions. First is having a *collaborative* process that integrates views from people in management, supervision, and front-line work. The experience of parti-cipating in a change process increases confidence from all involved (Portoghese et al., 2012). Second is *customisation*, by adapting the action to the setting and the people who put the plan into action. The process of custo-mising a program requires leaders to attend carefully to the distinct char-acteristics of their situation and to listen attentively to the people involved. It produces something that makes sense to those who put the plan into action. Third is the workplace making an enduring *commitment* to the initiative. People often resist change (Beer et al., 1990). People may also be sceptical about leadership's commitment to an initiative. It is important to persist. It is also important to respond to critiques of the plan, making adjustments that further the process of customising to the present situation.

The action process begins with identifying the areas of worklife in which people are experiencing mismatches. The project may gather this information informally through reflections on experiences or systematically through con-ducting surveys across the workplace. Projects using a quantitative measure, such as the Areas of Worklife Scale, often supplement these measures with conversations or formal interviews to capture the ways in which people ex-perience mismatches. The stories generated through these conversations give more substance to the quantitative data.

The project team then shifts to generating possibilities for creating better matches between people and their workplaces. They focus on how work can be different rather than how people can better tolerate work continuing to be the same. Having generated some possibilities for change, the project team chooses one as the starting point. A workplace can only handle so many in-itiatives, especially a workplace trending towards burnout. Doing one in-itiative well builds credibility that provides a useful first step towards change. The focus may not be the most severe mismatch identified in the process. Although it is important to address an issue closely connected to employees' experience of burnout, it is also important to address issues for which there are feasible options for change. For example, unmanageable workload is often the most obvious contributor to exhaustion (Barello et al., 2020), but during peak demand generated by a crisis, a workplace may have few options. Shifting the focus to strengthening value congruence may be a more feasible option to have meaningful impact (Teisberg et al., 2020).

By considering burnout as a relationship breakdown, this approach broadens possibilities for action. Approaches that consider only one side of the re-lationship limit their impact by doing so. Treating the individual through resilience training or workplace health programs may be successful in in-creasing what people can endure at work, but they work within the constraints of human endurance. The capacity of people to endure adverse conditions is partly a function of their physical health, but it also is a function of their attitudes towards work (Cham et al., 2021). So, while mindfulness training may reduce feelings of exhaustion and cynicism (Roeser, 2013), it does not explicitly address the conditions at work that contribute to those experiences.

In contrast, initiatives to develop workplaces without directly involving the relevant people often miss the point. They may solve one problem—e.g., introducing barriers that reduce the potential of a virus transmitting—but fail to appreciate the full ramifications of that change in practice. The Six Areas of Worklife model directs attention to the broad range of dimensions on which people connect or disconnect with their workplaces. Thorough reflection on those points reduces the chances of implementing changes with severe unforeseen consequences. Although serious threats to health and safety at work call for timely action, avoiding unintended harm increases those initiatives' positive contribution. It also increases employees' confidence in workplace leadership when contending with a major challenge.

The process elements of collaboration, customisation, and commitment encourage a process that focuses on the relationships of people with their workplaces. Employees judging management's response to the COVID pandemic report greater cynicism combined with intentions to quit their jobs (El-liethiey & Atalla, 2021). Some situations may benefit from concerted efforts to build trust among employees. Actively involving a diverse range of people in the planning, execution, and evaluation of workplace initiatives creates a means of building trust through an open process. When time and resources are tight and consequences serious, the advantages of such an approach can greatly outweigh its demands.

Conclusion

To avoid wasting the crisis created by a global pandemic the challenge is to apply lessons learned—both to recover from this event and to prepare for the next. The scope and speed in the reactions of workplaces to the pandemic established that major change can occur. The distress reported broadly established as well that abrupt change that addresses one problem can create serious distress with the potential to undermine constructive reactions to the crisis at hand.

Maslach and Leiter (2022) noted that a useful guideline for future action is to consider basic elements of design: balance, rhythm, and unity. For example, challenges arose from the abrupt shift to people leaving offices to work from home. One such challenge was maintaining contact with people who were continually out of sight for extended periods. The proliferation of video platforms for online meetings—for example Zoom—fulfilled that need in many ways but needed to be used with discretion. Reflecting on quality of balance can alert leaders to the tension between staying in touch and being intrusive. Yes, people may become lonely when working remotely, but they also may thrive on the opportunities for deep work when freed from interruptions.

The pandemic arising from SARS-COVID2 prompted major changes in worklife as governments, workplaces, and individuals changed major aspects of what they did. Early results from research indicate a range of impacts from these changes. Many actions taken in this period helped people manage their contact with the virus. Some brought unforeseen benefits; some entailed costs that were not anticipated or appreciated at the time. Improving and expanding frameworks for understanding job burnout and strategies for taking action to address this problem can contribute to more effective responses to future crises.

References

Adams-Prassl, A., Boneva, T., Golin, M., & Rauh, C. (2020). Inequality in the impact of the coronavirus shock: Evidence from real time surveys. *Journal of Public Economics, 189,* 104245.

Allen, T. D., Merlo, K., Lawrence, R. C., Slutsky, J., & Gray, C. E. (2021). Boundary management and work-nonwork balance while working from home. *Applied Psychology, 70*(1), 60–84.

Amanullah, S. & Ramesh Shankar, R. (2020). The impact of COVID-19 on physician burnout globally: A review. *Healthcare, 8,* 421–433.

Anderson, D. & Kelliher, C. (2020). Enforced remote working and the work-life interface during lockdown. *Gender in Management: An International Journal.*

Ansell, C., Sørensen, E., & Torfing, J. (2021). The COVID-19 pandemic as a game changer for public administration and leadership? The need for robust governance responses to turbulent problems. *Public Management Review, 23*(7), 949–960.

Apaydin, E. A., Rose, D. E., Yano, E. M., Shekelle, P. G., McGowan, M. G., Antonini, T. L., ... & Stockdale, S. E. (2021). Burnout among primary care healthcare workers during the COVID-19 pandemic. *Journal of Occupational and Environmental Medicine, 63*(8), 642.

Bailey, J., Wong, M., Bailey, K., Banfield, J. C., Barry, G., Kirkland, S., & Leiter, M. P. (2021). Pandemic-related factors predicting physician burnout beyond established organizational factors: cross-sectional results from the COPING survey. *Psychology, Health & Medicine, 26,* 1–10. 10.1080/13548506.2021.1990366. https://www.tandfonline.com/doi/abs/10.1080/13548506.2021.1990366

Bakken, B. K. & Winn, A. N. (2021). Clinician burnout during the COVID-19 pandemic before vaccine administration. *Journal of the American Pharmacists Association, 61*(5), e71–e77.

Barello, S., Palamenghi, L., & Graffigna, G. (2020). Stressors and resources for healthcare professionals during the Covid-19 pandemic: Lesson learned from Italy. *Frontiers in Psychology, 11,* 2179.

Beer, M., Eisenstat, R. A., & Spector, B. (1990). Why change programs don't produce change, *Harvard Business Review, 60*(6) 158–166.

Bezak, E., Carson-Chahhoud, K. V., Marcu, L. G., Stoeva, M., Lhotska, L., Barabino, G. A., ... & Frize, M. (2022). The biggest challenges resulting from the COVID-19 pandemic on gender-related work from home in biomedical fields—World-wide qualitative survey analysis. *International Journal of Environmental Research and Public Health, 19*(5), 3109.

Braithwaite, J., Herkes, J., Ludlow, K., Testa, L., & Lamprell, G. (2017). Association between organisational and workplace cultures, and patient outcomes: Systematic review. *BMJ Open, 7*(11), 1–11. e017708.

Broom, A., Kirby, E., Good, P., Wootton, J., Yates, P., & Hardy, J. (2015). Negotiating futility, managing emotions: Nursing the transition to palliative care. *Qualitative Health Research, 25*(3), 299–309.

Butler, C. R., Wong, S. P., Vig, E. K., Neely, C. S., & O'Hare, A. M. (2021). Professional roles and relationships during the COVID-19 pandemic: A qualitative study among US clinicians. *BMJ Open, 11*(3), e047782.

Cham, B. S., Boeing, A. A., Wilson, M. D., Griffin, M. A., & Jorritsma, K. (2021). Endurance in extreme work environments. *Organizational Psychology Review, 11*(4), 343–364.

Cortina, L. M., Magley, V. J., Williams, J. H., & Langhout, R. D. (2001). Incivility in the workplace: incidence and impact. *Journal of Occupational Health Psychology, 6*(1), 64–80.

Cotofan, M., De Neve, J. E., Golin, M., Kaats, M., & Ward, G. (2021). Work and well-being during COVID-19: Impact, inequalities, resilience, and the future of work. *World Happiness Report*, 153–190.

Deci, E. L. & Ryan, R. M. (2000). The "what" and "why" of goal pursuits: Human needs and the self-determination of behavior. *Psychological Inquiry, 11*(4), 227–268.

Dunbar, R. I. M. (1998). *Grooming, gossip, and the evolution of language*. Cambridge, Mass: Harvard University Press.

Earle, M. J. & Freddolino, P. P. (2022). Meeting the practice challenges of COVID-19: MSW students' perceptions of e-therapy and the therapeutic alliance. *Clinical Social Work Journal, 50*(1), 76–85.

El-liethiey, N. S. & Atalla, A. D. (2021). Relationship between organizational cynicism and nurses' intension for turnover as perceived by nurses. *Egyptian Journal of Health Care, 12*(2), 383–397.

Fricker, M. (2007). *Epistemic injustice: Power and the ethics of knowing*. Oxford, UK: Oxford University Press.

Galanis, P., Vraka, I., Fragkou, D., Bilali, A., & Kaitelidou, D. (2021). Impact of personal protective equipment use on health care workers' physical health during the COVID-19 pandemic: A systematic review and meta-analysis. *American Journal of Infection Control, 49*(10), 1305–1315.

Gascón, S., Leiter, M. P., Stright, N., Santed, M. A., Montero-Marín, J., Andrés, E., ... & García-Campayo, J. (2013). A factor confirmation and convergent validity of the "areas of worklife scale" (AWS) to Spanish translation. *Health and Quality of Life Outcomes, 11*(1), 1–11.

Gilles, I., Mabire, C., Perriraz, M., & Peytremann-Bridevaux, I. (2021). Workplace well-being and intent to stay by health care workers reassigned during the First COVID-19 wave: Results of a swiss survey. *International Journal of Environmental Research and Public Health, 18*(17), 1–13. 10.3390/ijerph18178976

Hill, C. A. (1987). Affiliation motivation: People who need people … but in different ways. *Journal of Personality and Social Psychology, 52*(5), 1008.

Hill, S. G., Iavecchia, H. P., Byers, J. C., Bittner Jr, A. C., Zaklade, A. L., & Christ, R. E. (1992). Comparison of four subjective workload rating scales. *Human Factors, 34*(4), 429–439.

Hipp, L. & Bünning, M. (2021). Parenthood as a driver of increased gender inequality during COVID-19? Exploratory evidence from Germany. *European Societies, 23*(sup1), S658–S673.

Jarzynkowski, P., Piotrkowska, R., Mędrzycka-Dąbrowska, W., & Książek, J. (2021). Areas of work life as predictors of occupational burnout of nurses and doctors in operating theaters in Poland—Multicenter Studies. In *Healthcare, 10*, 26–37.

Kutlu, Ö., Çetinkaya, P. Ö., Kandemir, M. H., Temel, M. T., & Aybal, T. (2021). The burnout and workload impact on recurrent COVID-19: Analysis of two healthcare professionals. *International Journal of Clinical Practice, 75*(7), 2–3. 10.1111/ijcp.14136.

Kwok, C. (2021). Epistemic injustice in workplace hierarchies: Power, knowledge and status. *Philosophy & Social Criticism*, *47*(9), 1104–1131.

Langvik, E., Karlsen, H. R., Saksvik-Lehouillier, I., & Sørengaard, T. A. (2021). Police employees working from home during COVID-19 lockdown: Those with higher score on extraversion miss their colleagues more and are more likely to socialize with colleagues outside work. *Personality and Individual Differences*, *179*, 110924.

Lapierre, L. M., Van Steenbergen, E. F., Peeters, M. C., & Kluwer, E. S. (2016). Juggling work and family responsibilities when involuntarily working more from home: A multi-wave study of financial sales professionals. *Journal of Organizational Behavior*, *37*(6), 804–822.

Lasalvia, A., Amaddeo, F., Porru, S., Carta, A., Tardivo, S., Bovo, C., ... & Bonetto, C. (2021). Levels of burn-out among healthcare workers during the COVID-19 pandemic and their associated factors: A cross-sectional study in a tertiary hospital of a highly burdened area of north-east Italy. *BMJ Open*, *11*(1), e045127.

Leiter, M. P., Day, A., Oore, D. G., & Spence Laschinger, H. K. (2012). Getting better and staying better: Assessing civility, incivility, distress, and job attitudes one year after a civility intervention. *Journal of Occupational Health Psychology*, *17*(4), 425–437.

Leiter, M. P., Hakanen, J., Toppinen-Tanner, S., Ahola, K., Koskinen, A., & Väänänen, A. (2013). Changes in burnout: A 12-year cohort study on organizational predictors and health outcomes. *Journal of Organizational Behavior*, *34*, 959–973. 10.1002/job.1830.

Leiter, M. P., Laschinger, H. K. S., Day, A., & Gilin Oore, D. (2011). The impact of civility interventions on employee social behavior, distress, and attitudes. *Journal of Applied Psychology*, *96*(6), 1258–1272.

Leiter, M. P. & Maslach, C. (2004). Areas of worklife: A structured approach to organizational predictors of job burnout. In P. Perrewé & D. C. Ganster (Eds.). *Research in occupational stress and well being: Vol. 3. Emotional and physiological processes and positive intervention strategies* (pp. 91–134). Oxford, UK: JAI Press/Elsevier.

Leiter, M. P., & Maslach, C. (2011). *Areas of worklife scale manual* (5th Edition). Menlo Park, CA: Mind Garden Publishing.

Leiter, M. P., & Shaughnessy, K. (2006). The areas of worklife model of burnout: tests of mediation relationships. *Ergonomia: An International Journal*, *28*(4), 327–341.

Maslach, C., & Leiter, M. P. (1997). *The truth about burnout*. San Francisco: Jossey-Bass.

Maslach, C., & Leiter, M. P. (2022). *The burnout challenge*. Cambridge: Harvard University Press.

Matsuo, T., Taki, F., Kobayashi, D., Jinta, T., Suzuki, C., Ayabe, A., ... & Fukui, T. (2021). Health care worker burnout after the first wave of the coronavirus disease 2019 (COVID-19) pandemic in Japan. *Journal of Occupational Health*, *63*(1), e12247.

Maunder, R. G., Heeney, N. D., & Strudwick, G. (2021). Burnout in hospital-based healthcare workers during COVID-19. *Science Briefs of the Ontario COVID-19 Science Advisory Table*, *2*, 46.

Okereafor, K., & Manny, P. (2020). Understanding cybersecurity challenges of telecommuting and video conferencing applications in the COVID-19 pandemic. *International Journal in IT and Engineering*, *8*, 13–23.

Portoghese, I., Galletta, M., Battistelli, A., Saiani, L., Penna, M. P., & Allegrini, E. (2012). Change-related expectations and commitment to change of nurses: The role of leadership and communication. *Journal of Nursing Management*, *20*(5), 582–591.

Rodríguez-López, A. M., Rubio-Valdehita, S., & Díaz-Ramiro, E. M. (2021). Influence of the COVID-19 pandemic on mental workload and burnout of fashion retailing workers in Spain. *International Journal of Environmental Research and Public Health*, *18*(3), 983.

Roeser, R. W., Schonert-Reichl, K. A., Jha, A., Cullen, M., Wallace, L., Wilensky, R., ... & Harrison, J. (2013). Mindfulness training and reductions in teacher stress and burnout: Results from two randomized, waitlist-control field trials. *Journal of Educational Psychology*, *105*(3), 787–804.

Rubenstein, L. & Decamp, M. (2020). Revisiting restrictions of rights after COVID-19. *Health and Human Rights*, *22*(2), 321.

Sackett, D. L., & Rosenberg, W. M. C. (1995). On the need for evidence-based medicine. *Journal of Public Health*, *17*(3), 330–334.

Sargeant, J., Loney, E., & Murphy, G. (2008). Effective interprofessional teams: "contact is not enough" to build a team. *Journal of Continuing Education in the Health Professions*, *28*(4), 228–234.

Sorenson, C., Japinga, M., Crook, H., & McClellan, M. (2020). Building a better health care system Post-Covid-19: Steps for reducing low-value and Wasteful care. *NEJM Catalyst Innovations in Care Delivery*, *1*(4), 1–12.

Stocchetti, N., Segre, G., Zanier, E. R., Zanetti, M., Campi, R., Scarpellini, F., ... & Bonati, M. (2021). Burnout in intensive care unit workers during the second wave of the covid-19 pandemic: A single center cross-sectional Italian study. *International Journal of Environmental Research and Public Health*, *18*(11), 6102.

Sumner, R. C. & Kinsella, E. L. (2021). "It's Like a Kick in the Teeth": The emergence of novel predictors of burnout in frontline workers during Covid-19. *Frontiers in Psychology*, *12*, 1875.

Sweeny, K., Rankin, K., Cheng, X., Hou, L., Long, F., Meng, Y., ... & Zhang, W. (2020). Flow in the time of COVID-19: Findings from China. *PloS One*, *15*(11), e0242043.

Swift, A., Banks, L., Baleswaran, A., Cooke, N., Little, C., McGrath, L., ... & Williams, G. (2020). COVID-19 and student nurses: A view from England. *Journal of Clinical Nursing*, *29*(17-18) 3111-3114 . 10.1111/jocn.15298

Taber, L., Dominguez, S., & Whittaker, S. (2021). Cats, Kids, and video calls: How working from home affects media self-presentation. *Human–Computer Interaction*, *5*, 1–26.

Teisberg, E., Wallace, S., & O'Hara, S. (2020). Defining and implementing value-based health care: A strategic framework. *Academic Medicine*, *95*(5), 682–685.

Timms, C., Graham, D., & Cottrell, D. (2007). "I just want to teach": Queensland independent schoolteachers and their workload. *Journal of Educational Administration*, *45*, 569–586

Tobin, M. J., Laghi, F., & Jubran, A. (2020). Caution about early intubation and mechanical ventilation in COVID-19. *Annals of Intensive Care*, *10*(1), 1–3.

Twenge, J. M., Martin, G. N., & Campbell, W. K. (2018). Decreases in psychological well-being among American adolescents after 2012 and links to screen time during the rise of smartphone technology. *Emotion*, *18*(6), 765.

Wardhaugh, R. & Fuller, J. M. (2021). *An introduction to sociolinguistics*. Hoboken, New Jersey: John Wiley & Sons.

Wunsch, H. (2020). Mechanical ventilation in COVID-19: Interpreting the current epidemiology. *American Journal of Respiratory and Critical Care Medicine*, *202*(1), 1–4.

Zhou, A. Y., Hann, M., Panagioti, M., Patel, M., Agius, R., Van Tongeren, M., ... & Bower, P. (2022). Cross-sectional study exploring the association between stressors and burnout in junior doctors during the COVID-19 pandemic in the United Kingdom. *Journal of Occupational Health*, *64*(1), e12311.

3 Job burnout: The epidemic within a pandemic

Chris Mahar and Arla Day

Department of Psychology Saint Mary's University Halifax, NS Canada

As others have discussed throughout this book, we have a good under-standing of the antecedents and outcomes of burnout. Burnout had been labelled a growing "epidemic" (Moukarzel et al., 2019; Sanfilippo et al., 2017), even before the pandemic began. The pandemic intensified workers' levels of stress and strain as well as their levels of burnout, especially for younger, less experienced, female, and frontline workers (Amanullah & Shankar, 2020; Azoulay et al., 2020; Denning et al., 2021; Dimitriu et al., 2020; Giusti et al., 2020; Kannampallil et al., 2020; Meyer et al., 2021; Morgantini et al., 2020; Wu et al., 2020). There is considerable evidence to suggest that adverse conditions, such as traumatic events, natural disasters, and pandemics lead to the development of, and increase in, burnout (Chemali et al., 2019; Mattei et al., 2017; Maunder et al., 2006), although less is known about the specific reasons that burnout tends to increase. Workers' experiences during the pandemic provided valuable insights into how people react to, and cope with, different job and life demands, and they provided a novel perspective on examining burnout in the future. Several key questions about burnout stem from our experiences with the pandemic: What work and non-work factors exacerbated or alleviated workers' levels of burnout? What information can these experiences provide for us to deal with job burnout post-pandemic?

Therefore, we review both the seminal burnout work and recent studies in the context of the pandemic, focusing on what we have a solid understanding of and the antecedents that have received less empirical attention. We argue that the lessons learned from working through a pandemic can help to shape our future workplaces to effectively address job burnout. This work is integrated with existing burnout models into a new framework of burnout, with a focus on the mechanisms by which work demands may create or exacerbate burnout, as well as on the resources that may help to reduce burnout and to mitigate the negative effects of demands.

Understanding burnout

Freudenberger (1974) considered burnout to be non-specific psychosocial and medical-biological symptoms that develop because of excessive demands for energy

DOI: 10.4324/9781003250531-4

at work. Burnout is classified as an occupational syndrome by the World Health Organisation, such that it is not a medical condition (ICD-11; WHO, 2022). The WHO defines burnout based on Maslach and Jackson's (1981) three-component model of the syndrome, involving emotional exhaustion (i.e., the depletion of emotional resources leading to exhaustion), depersonalisation or cynicism (i.e., the development of negative attitudes and feelings toward clients), and personal accomplishment or professional efficacy (i.e., the tendency to evaluate oneself negatively regarding their work with clients; Maslach et al., 2001; Maslach & Jackson, 1981). Although some researchers define job burnout only in terms of emotional exhaustion (McCormack et al., 2018), the inclusion of the other two components provides more breadth to the theory and a more accurate assessment of the entire syndrome of burnout. Moreover, there is some evidence to suggest that we need to look at all three components as a syndrome, because personal accomplishment develops independently from emotional exhaustion and depersonalisation (Lee & Ashforth, 1996). Workers who work in "people-oriented" occupations, such as nurses and teachers, tend to be the most vulnerable to burnout (Martínez-López et al., 2020; Maslach & Jackson, 1981; Shanafelt et al., 2012). However, it has been argued that burnout applies to any job in which fatigue and exhaustion may occur (Alarcon, 2011; Demerouti et al., 2001).

Antecedents of job burnout: What we know

Many studies, including several meta-analyses, have examined the antecedents of burnout (Alarcon, 2011; Alarcon et al., 2009; Aronsson et al., 2017; Lee & Ashforth, 1996; Lee et al., 2011; Shin et al., 2014; Shoji et al., 2016; Swider & Zimmerman, 2010). We can cluster these antecedents into three distinct categories: organisational (i.e., environment), job, and individual (Chen et al., 2012). Organisational antecedents involve the macro aspects of the work environment, in terms of culture, organisation size, structure/hierarchy, and type of business/industry. Job-based antecedents are the actual job demands, overload, and relationships with colleagues. Finally, individual-based antecedents refer to the personal experiences and characteristics of individual workers (Chen et al., 2012).

Job antecedents

The preponderance of studies in this area has focused on the impact of job/work factors on burnout. In general, typical job demands and stressors, such as role ambiguity and conflict, team cohesion, lack of superior/leader support, workload, lack of job control and autonomy (Alarcon, 2011; Alarcon et al., 2009; Aronsson et al., 2017; Lee & Ashforth, 1996; Lee et al., 2011; Schaufeli & Buunk, 2003; Shin et al., 2014; Shoji et al., 2016; Swider & Zimmerman, 2010) all affect burnout.

Several meta-analyses have provided support for these relationships. Role ambiguity, role conflict, and work overload are positively related to burnout, whereas autonomy and job control are negatively related to burnout (Alarcon, 2011). As well, for mental health professionals, over-involvement, job control, and professional identity are related to all three burnout components (Lee et al., 2011). Finally, there is moderate evidence for the relationship between low job control, high workload, and high workplace support with emotional exhaustion. There is somewhat limited evidence for the relationship between psychological demands, emotional demands, patient demands, and supervisor and co-worker support with emotional exhaustion and depersonalisation (Aronsson et al., 2017).

Organisational antecedents

The idea that the organisational environment influences burnout is not new. Organisational culture and structure are associated with burnout (Leiter & Maslach, 1999). In fact, Leiter and Maslach (2001) argued that burnout is more a function of organisations' dysfunctional structures, such as its size, culture, and ownership, rather than of individual characteristics. For example, compared to nurses at public hospitals, nurses at private (for-profit) hospitals have higher levels of burnout (Hansen et al., 2009). In their systematic review of early career stage of physicians, Hariharan and Griffin (2019) found that uncooperative colleagues, workplace culture, and supervisor support were moderately related to burnout.

Individual antecedents

In addition to job and organisational antecedents, personal characteristics and social factors, such as emotional stability, negative affect, optimism, self-esteem, efficacy, over-involvement, coping styles, and social factors (e.g., social supports) all tend to be related to burnout (Alarcon, 2011; Alarcon et al., 2009; Aronsson et al., 2017; Lee & Ashforth, 1996; Lee et al., 2011; Schaufeli & Buunk, 2003; Shin et al., 2014; Shoji et al., 2016; Swider & Zimmerman, 2010).

Swider and Zimmerman (2010) conducted a meta-analysis to further understand the relationship between personality variables and burnout. Across the 115 studies in their meta-analysis, all Big 5 personality components (i.e., neuroticism, extroversion, agreeableness, conscientiousness, openness to experience) were related to all three burnout components. However, the relationship between openness to experience and burnout was weak (Swider & Zimmerman, 2010). In terms of coping strategies, both problem- and emotion-focused coping are related to the three components of burnout (Shin et al., 2014). Depersonalisation and reduced personal accomplishment are negatively related to seeking social support, and cognitive reappraisal is negatively related to emotional exhaustion and personal accomplishment (Shin et al., 2014), such that those who were able to reappraise a stressful situation in a more positive light tended to report less emotional exhaustion and more personal accomplishment. Conversely, early career physicians who engaged in maladaptive coping tended to have higher burnout (Shin et al., 2014).

Despite some research suggesting an effect of these individual characteristics on personal health, wellbeing, and burnout, some researchers argue that we have focused too much on individual factors at the cost of ignoring the workplace (Chen et al., 2012), whereas other researchers have argued that research on these individual-based antecedents tend to be very limited in scope (Alarcon et al., 2009; Swider & Zimmerman, 2010). Therefore, we look at these variables not as the ultimate explanation of burnout (i.e., in a blame-the-victim mentality), but as a piece of the greater puzzle to understanding burnout.

Covid-19 & burnout

The Covid-19 pandemic is considered unique compared to past pandemics, such as Ebola and Severe Acute Respiratory Syndrome (SARS), because it spread more widely across the globe, it could be spread asymptomatically (i.e., increases spread), and it has had a high mortality rate (Vu et al., 2022). Pandemic restrictions created new demands and challenges for workers across occupations. There was an unprecedented, global, and simultaneous shift from working in offices to working remotely. The pandemic increased health concerns of workers, and it changed the way most workers, anyone from front-line grocery store employees to caregivers, completed their daily tasks (Azoulay et al., 2020). It also shut down many industries, putting many workers out of work, reducing work hours for others, and increasing health fears and worries about job loss (Bahadirli & Sagaltici, 2021).

As a result of these challenges, many workers reported higher levels of burnout, whereby the pandemic highlighted and intensified some of the typical burnout reactions (Denning et al., 2021; Ma et al., 2021; Sayılan et al., 2021). Giusti et al. (2020) found that 76% of their sample of healthcare professionals reported burnout. Several systematic reviews during the pandemic have been conducted. In their systematic review on the prevalence of burnout during the SARS, MERS, and Covid-19 outbreaks, Magnavita et al. (2021) found that the prevalence rates of burnout during the Covid-19 pandemic were similar to the levels reported during the SARS and MERS outbreaks, and higher than pre-pandemic levels. Similarly, nurses experienced greater burnout during Covid-19 compared to pre-pandemic levels (Galanis et al., 2021). These levels even exceed pre-pandemic levels of burnout experienced by palliative care nurses, who generally tend to experience the greatest level of burnout (Galanis et al., 2021). Furthermore, physician burnout during the first wave of the pandemic increased compared to pre-pandemic levels (Amanullah & Shankar, 2020), and general healthcare workers' levels of emotional exhaustion were significantly higher during Covid-19 compared to pre-pandemic levels (Barello et al., 2020).

Creating a burnout framework

Given this increase in levels of burnout, the question remains as to the specific reasons why burnout increased during the pandemic. That is, what were the specific demands—and their mechanisms—that increased levels of burnout. The answer may be as simple as that workers' "regular" demands increased during the Covid-19 pandemic, which led to increased burnout. However, there are several other hypotheses and rationales that may help to explain this relationship and help us to better understand the experience of burnout. We incorporated the work on burnout, and what we learned from the pandemic, with existing models of burnout (e.g., the Job Demands-Resources model (JD-R; Demerouti et al., 2001); the transactional model of stress (Lazarus & Folkman, 1984), and Hobfoll's (1989) Conservation of Resources Model (i.e., COR) to provide a more comprehensive explanation of the process of demand and resource appraisal, and identified four overriding hypotheses that may help us to understand the relationship better (see Figure 3.1):

A. **Increased/Intensified Demands Hypothesis:** Changes to the work environment (e.g., remote work) intensified existing work problems and increased levels of traditional (pre-Covid-19) work stressors, resulting in higher levels of burnout.
B. **Covid-Specific Demands Hypothesis:** Covid-19 created work demands/stressors that were unique, or at least less typical (e.g., health fears), which increased burnout. Certain industries and jobs may have been more susceptible to these specific demands.
C. **Reduced Resources Hypothesis:** There were fewer work, personal, and social resources available to workers during the pandemic leading to greater burnout.
D. **Increased Vulnerability Hypothesis:** Certain groups (e.g., women, younger workers) were more vulnerable, and experienced a disproportionate amount of negative pandemic outcomes, thus making them more susceptible to burnout.

A. Increased/intensified levels of "Typical" demands hypothesis

Perhaps the most parsimonious reason for increased burnout during the pandemic is that there was an increase in the same demands that workers faced before the pandemic. That is, the pandemic and resultant changes to the work environment (e.g., remote work) merely augmented the level/amount of pre-Covid-19 stressors (i.e., workload and role ambiguity), exacerbating already existing work problems, and thereby creating higher levels of burnout. For example, if workers were unclear about their job roles, working alone with little guidance increased feelings of ambiguity and a lack of support. There is some evidence to support the hypothesis that increased demands, in terms of workload/overload, strained workplace relationships, economic stressors, and role uncertainty/ambiguity were associated with increased levels of burnout.

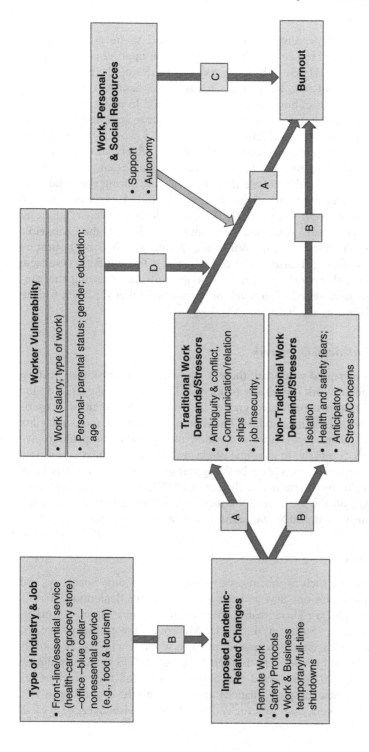

Figure 3.1 Burnout Framework and competing hypotheses to help examine the demands - burnout relationship.

Workload/Overload

High workload and perceived work overload tend to be associated with burnout (Alarcon, 2011; Lee & Ashforth, 1996; Sanfilippo et al., 2017), and one of the key increased demands that workers faced during the pandemic was an increased workload (i.e., Bradley & Chahar, 2020; Sant'Ana et al., 2020), leading to higher levels of burnout (Giusti et al., 2020). In many countries and workplaces, the pandemic lockdowns required a shift to remote work involving installation of home workstations, and created a work agenda that required learning new technology and work practices, which led to extra work for the individual (Sant'Ana et al., 2020). For example, many nurses were expected to work more than twice their normal shift during the pandemic, which led to significant increases in work overload and experienced stress (Manzano García & Ayala Calvo, 2021). Work overload has been a significant predictor of physician wellbeing and burnout during the pandemic (Amanullah & Shankar, 2020; de Wit et al., 2020), as well as on healthcare professionals' wellbeing (Bahadirli & Sagaltici, 2021). There is fairly consistent research showing that work overload and long work hours during the pandemic was associated with higher levels of burnout (Dosil et al., 2020; Galanis et al., 2021; Giusti et al., 2020).

Strained social relationships at work

In addition to increased workload, there is evidence of an erosion of positive social exchanges at work during the pandemic. El Ghaziri et al. (2022) found that 37.4% of nurses experienced greater incivility, 31.8% of nurses experienced more cyber-bullying, and 45.7% of nurses witnessed more incivility from registered nurses, supervisors, and middle management compared to pre-pandemic levels. Similarly, in a sample of general workers in Japan, compared to pre-pandemic levels, workplace bullying was greater than two times more likely to occur during the pandemic (Iida et al., 2021). This erosion of positive social exchanges on the job during the pandemic is related to increases in job burnout (Azoulay et al., 2020; Manzano García & Ayala Calvo, 2021).

Economic stressors

Economic stressors, such as job insecurity, perceived income adequacy, and underemployment, are not new and can lead to resource depletion (Hobfoll, 1989). For example, we know that economic hardship in temporary workers can lead to burnout (Striler et al., 2021). Moreover, the pandemic created substantially new concerns for a large number of workers who had previously enjoyed financial and job security. In their report of the US workforce during Covid-19, Cigna (2020) reported that about 20% of full-time workers reported experiencing a fair/poor financial situation, with this rate rising to 41% for furloughed workers, and 58% for laid-off workers. Moreover, 85% of all furloughed and laid-off workers reported experiencing stress due to current economic uncertainty.

These data support Sinclair et al.'s (2020) assertion that the pandemic exacerbated economic stressors, and that one's economic situation would have a significant impact on the ability to cope with the pandemic (i.e., higher financial resources improve ability to cope with massive disruptions related to the pandemic, such as homeschooling, access to Personal Protective Equipment (i.e., PPE), and withstanding food and household item shortages), which, in turn, would have a negative impact on health and well-being (i.e., stress symptoms, burnout, and mental health issues; Sinclair et al., 2020). During the pandemic, decreasing outpatient revenue, salary and benefit reduction, and increased use of telemedicine was a significant stressor leading to increased frontline healthcare worker burnout (Bradley & Chahar, 2020).

Increased uncertainty & ambiguity

In addition to the demands resulting from remote work, one of the key aspects of the pandemic was the uncertainty about what it was, how to address it, and how to stay safe. In general, job ambiguity and uncertainty, as well as fear of the unknown, tend to be associated with increased stress and burnout (Alarcon, 2011; Babamiri et al., 2022; Bahadirli & Sagaltici, 2021; Martínez-López et al., 2020). Employees tend to be much more likely to be able to tolerate stressful situations when they are viewed as temporary, and when the end of the event is predictable (DiStaso & Shoss, 2020). At the beginning of the pandemic, the lack of knowledge about the virus by official sources caused high anxiety and increased burnout in health professionals (Martínez-López et al., 2020). Frontline healthcare professionals experienced considerable perceptions of uncertainty during the pandemic due to the ambiguity around protocols and treatments required to manage Covid-19, and the immediate saturation of critical cases within hospitals (Di Monte et al., 2020). The main cause of stress and eventual burnout for frontline healthcare workers in Iran was uncertainty surrounding when the pandemic would end (Babamiri et al., 2022). Various psychological issues experienced by emergency physicians, such as burnout, anxiety, avoidance, and depression, have been associated with the uncertainty related to the Covid-19 virus (e.g., when will the pandemic end? What are the long-term effects of the virus?; Bahadirli & Sagaltici, 2021). During the pandemic, many healthcare professionals were required to adopt new roles, which dramatically increased feelings of uncertainty, and these professionals were twice as likely to experience burnout (Ferry et al., 2021).

Work–non-work interface & burnout

The interaction between work and non-work also was underscored during the pandemic. Several meta-analyses have found that the interface between work and non-work (e.g., work-family conflict; work–non-work balance, etc.)

tends to be related to burnout (Amstad et al., 2011; Lee et al., 2013; Reichl et al., 2014; Xu & Cao, 2019). During the Covid-19 pandemic, both work interference with family and family interference with work were positively related to burnout (Barriga-Medina et al., 2021), and daily work-family conflict was positively related to both emotional exhaustion and depersonalisation in physicians and nurses (Blanco-Donoso et al., 2021). Similarly, Cotel et al. (2021) found that work-family conflict was positively related to all three components of job burnout for healthcare workers. Clearly, work and non-work conflict is positively related to employee burnout pre and post Covid-19 pandemic.

B. "Non-traditional" Covid-specific demands hypothesis

According to estimates by the WHO (2022), there are 530,266, 292 confirmed cases of Covid-19 worldwide, with more than 6,299,364 confirmed deaths as of June 2022. In addition to the substantial impact on physical health, the pandemic created fear and worry. It also resulted in many substantial changes to workers work environment and job activities, including their hours of work and work location. Thus, many workers experienced high levels of work stressors that they personally had not experienced prior to the pandemic (Koch & Schermuly, 2021). Although these demands existed in workplaces, the majority of the workforce may not have experienced them. For example, job loss was a new concern for many workers who previously had experienced job security. Prior to the pandemic, remote work (i.e., teleworking, telecommuting, distributed work, flexible work arrangements, etc.) was not a prevalent practice, and in many organisations, it was considered a benefit only granted in special circumstances. Because of this inexperience with remote working, many employees and employers were ill prepared to deal with this dramatic change (Wang et al., 2021). Many workers also hadn't had to deal with specific, and substantial, health and safety concerns that were associated with Covid-19. Any work environment changes are a significant underlying cause of work stress (Jex & Yankelevich, 2008), and Covid-19-related changes and demands probably have a similar impact.

Health & safety concerns/fears

One of most salient aspects of the pandemic was fear of contracting the virus, and the impact of Covid-19 not only on one's own health, but also on the health of others, which increased feelings of fear and vulnerability. Most workers in the majority of first world countries have not recently experienced global war, famine, or pandemics. Although some occupations have faced substantial health concerns on a daily basis pre-pandemic (e.g., healthcare workers, police officers, workers dealing with toxic chemicals, etc.), prior to the pandemic, the threat of getting seriously sick and potentially dying, simply by being at work was very low. With the onset of the pandemic, these safety issues became front and centre for many workers who had not directly experienced these issues before; therefore, many workers reported feeling more vulnerable and worrying more about their own health and the health of their loved ones (Babamiri et al., 2022; Bahadirli et al., 2021; Ferry et al., 2021; Martínez-López et al., 2020). Furthermore, workplace safety issues, such as inadequate or lack of human resources, lack of specialised training, and decreased safety protocols, were all negatively related to burnout (Galanis et al., 2021).

Healthcare workers and frontline workers were most at risk. Healthcare workers were constantly exposed to the Covid-19 virus, which increased a real sense of danger and uncertainty in their daily activities (Xiang et al., 2020), especially considering the high rates of infection for workers in healthcare (Martínez-López et al., 2020). Issues related to PPE and the lack of, constantly changing, or contradictory information about the Covid-19 virus fuelled anxiety and fear, especially for healthcare workers (Bradley & Chahar, 2020; de Wit et al., 2020; Dimitriu et al., 2020; Martínez-López et al., 2020). Fear of infection (i.e., contracting the virus, and spreading the virus to friends and family) was the highest rated stressor for Spanish nurses during the first Covid-19 wave (Lorente et al., 2021). In fact, the main source of stress experienced by frontline physicians and nurses during the pandemic was fear of contracting Covid-19 and spreading the infection amongst family members (Wu et al., 2020). Specifically, over two-thirds of the sample experienced moderate to severe levels of emotional exhaustion and reduced professional efficacy, and over one-quarter reported moderate to severe levels of depersonalisation; therefore, fear of infection fuelled higher levels of burnout (Giusti et al., 2020). Emergency nurses' fear of Covid-19 (e.g., fear due to PPE issues, spreading the virus, no definitive treatment or cure) was positively related to their emotional exhaustion and depersonalisation, and negatively related to their sense of personal accomplishment (Ahorsu et al., 2022). Finally, Galanis et al. (2021) conducted a systematic review and found that nurses experienced elevated emotional exhaustion during the pandemic, which was related to being a high-risk group due to close contact with Covid-19 patients, and fear of the consequences of the disease.

A significant safety concern for many healthcare professionals during the pandemic involved safety measures related to PPE, such as shortages of appropriate PPE, as well as a lack of access to specialised training for correct use of PPE, which led to the experience of high levels of stress (Bradley & Chahar, 2020; de Wit et al., 2020; Dimitriu et al., 2020; Galanis et al., 2021; Martinez-Lopez et al., 2020). In Japan, PPE shortages and frequent reuse of single-use PPE were a significant work-related stressor for healthcare workers (Unoki et al., 2020). The lack of adequate PPE during the pandemic was related to an increase in burnout in several studies of physicians (Alrawashdeh et al., 2021; Tuna & Özdin, 2021) and for healthcare professionals across 60 countries (Morgantini et al., 2020).

Similarly, the actual use of PPE was a significant stressor to workers. For example, wearing multiple layers of PPE led to heat stress in nurses (Unoki et al., 2020), and the amount of time wearing a mask was related to higher stress levels in nurses (Hoedl et al., 2021), which may then lead to higher levels of burnout. Lack of familiarity and training in using PPE also was related to increased levels of anxiety and burnout in Japanese nurses, pharmacists, and specialty technologists (Matsuo et al., 2020; Matsuo et al., 2021). Proper specialised training to eliminate the incorrect use of PPE is essential for reducing healthcare worker anxiety, and it is considered a significant resource for reducing job burnout (Matsuo et al., 2021). For example, physician burnout was associated with a lack of Covid-19 training on how to correctly use PPE (Tuna & Özdin, 2021). PPE related concerns also were positively related to burnout for National Health Services (i.e., NHS) frontline and back office workers in the United States (Gemine et al., 2021).

Anticipatory work concerns

Related to the area of specific health concerns/worries about Covid-19 is the more general area involving worry and anticipatory stress about one's work. Human behaviour is motivated by predictions and expectations about the future (DiStaso & Shoss, 2020). Many workers experienced isolation, ambiguous expectations, and transitioning to new technology with little or no support from their organisation; therefore, the probability of experiencing anticipatory stress was high. However, there is little research that has focussed on how employees' stress reactions are shaped by what they anticipate to occur on-the-job in the future, such as changes to workload (Casper & Sonnentag, 2020; Casper et al., 2017; DiStaso & Shoss, 2020). Although several models of stress do include future-oriented anticipations that have an impact on stress and strain, such as COR's (Hobfoll, 1989) focus on the threat of resource loss, and Lazarus and Folkman's (1984) threat appraisal component, research on anticipatory stress and burnout, to date, is scant. Anticipated increases in workload (i.e., anticipated stress) exacerbate the positive relationship between workload and emotional strain; however, anticipated workload reduction also buffers the relationship between workload and emotional strain (DiStaso & Shoss, 2020). Work-related worry and high workload anticipation (i.e., anticipatory stress related to workload to occur on the following day) during the evening is positively related to emotional exhaustion the following morning (Casper & Sonnentag, 2020). Anticipatory traumatic reaction (i.e., ATR; future-focused distress due to exposure to media and social discussions about disasters or large-scale threats) is related to stress, anxiety, depression, and negative cognitions (Hopwood et al., 2019b). Therefore, anticipatory stress potentially leads to experienced emotional strain, lack of vigour, low task performance, physical and emotional exhaustion, stress, anxiety, depression, and negative cognitions (Casper & Sonnentag, 2020; Casper et al., 2017; DiStaso & Shoss, 2020; Hopwood et al., 2019b). For example, emergency air medical health professionals (i.e., those who care for and transport patients via helicopters from remote and sometimes dangerous areas) who reported higher concern about medical issues (e.g., patient care) tended to have higher levels of emotional exhaustion and depersonalisation, even when controlling for their degree of worry about catastrophic events (i.e., helicopter crashes; Day et al., 2009).

Hopwood et al. (2019a) found that anticipatory traumatic reaction (i.e., ATR) is related to high levels of job burnout (i.e., emotional exhaustion and cynicism) in youth workers. The preservative cognition hypothesis poses that people develop future-oriented cognitive appraisals of stressful situations and events. People view the future through the lens of the present and make predictions about how they will feel in the future based on how they currently feel. Therefore, people who are currently experiencing a great deal of stress will anticipate also experiencing a great deal of stress in the future (Puig-Perez et al., 2022).

The pandemic has involved many significant stressors, including health risks and death of self, friends, and family members, social isolation, job loss, work-hour reductions, forced remote working arrangements, risk of hospital over-capacity and cancellation of medical procedures, and food and medical supply shortages. Media coverage of Covid-19 is expected to intensify stress and fear related to the pandemic due to an increase in anticipatory stress (Hopwood et al., 2019a). Therefore, due to the extended duration of the pandemic, it is reasonable to assume that people will anticipate significant stress in the future, which is expected to lead to potential physical and psychological health risks (e.g., burnout), especially because the high levels of arousal are prolonged (Puig-Perez et al., 2022).

Remote work

Remote work is not new and typically has been seen as a perk that was granted to a small number of workers. The en-masse, pandemic enforced remote work, which occurred in a matter of days for many, was a gateway for new demands and stressors for workers, who had little time to prepare or attain the needed resources to do their work tasks remotely. Even though remote work may have provided opportunities for workers (e.g., increased job autonomy, Wang et al., 2021; reduced commuting; more time with family, Orr & Savage, 2021), it also offered several demands, including isolation (Wang et al., 2021), work "hassles" (interruptions; Wang et al., 2021; technology challenges; Sharma & Bumb, 2021; Shao et al., 2021), and communication challenges (Shao et al., 2021; Shockley et al., 2021), all of which affected worker well-being and functioning. As well, working from home also influenced workers non-work domains, such as family time (Wang et al., 2021).

Social isolation

Remote work involves significantly fewer face-to-face work-related and social interactions with co-workers, supervisors, and clients. According to Self-Determination Theory (i.e., SDT), human beings have a need for relatedness, or a desire to feel connected and interact with others (Deci & Ryan, 2000). In fact, social isolation and prolonged feelings of distress can lead to sustained arousal and fatigue, which is related to a variety of somatic issues (Cho et al., 2019; Shevlin et al., 2020). Social isolation is considered a primary public health concern for the elderly because it intensifies autoimmune, cardiovascular, mental, neurocognitive, depression, and anxiety issues (Lippi et al., 2020). Social isolation also exacerbates depression and anxiety in youths, and leads to significant deterioration for those with pre-existing illness/disease (Lippi et al., 2020).

Although Covid-19 restrictions varied from country to country, much of the global population experienced "lockdown" conditions during the pandemic. In some areas, people were only allowed to leave their homes for essential reasons, such as to work (i.e., essential work, which includes healthcare, policing, armed forces, firefighting, and critical services and manufacturing) and to purchase food and medicine. Furthermore, when exiting the home, people were required to engage in physical/social distancing to decrease the spread of the virus, which further reduced social interaction (Ingram et al., 2021; Lippi et al., 2020). Limiting social contact through pandemic lockdown procedures may have increased the need for relatedness leading to feelings of loneliness.

There was some evidence that feelings of loneliness increased during the pandemic due to social isolation (Lippi et al., 2020), and these feelings were related to a variety of negative outcomes, such as anxiety and depression, and job burnout (Lippi et al., 2020; Rudert et al., 2021). Similarly, extended periods of social isolation during the pandemic led to cognitive decline, which increased over the course of the pandemic (Ingram et al., 2021), and fewer social contacts during lockdown was associated with higher stress, fatigue, and Covid-19-related worries (Nitschke et al., 2021). The pandemic increased feelings of loneliness (Buecker & Horstmann, 2021; Wang et al., 2021), which tends to be associated with higher burnout (Ofei-Dodoo et al., 2021).

Similarly, remote workers who were isolated from their co-workers tended to experience higher burnout (Maneechaeye, 2021). Perceived work-related social isolation during the pandemic is positively related to job burnout, and negatively related to job engagement (Aarebrot & Oppedal, 2021). Loneliness also may have been exacerbated because of a need to isolate from one's social network. Loneliness due to reduced personal relationships was positively related to job burnout and depression in family medicine physicians (Ofei-Dodoo et al., 2021). Moreover, sometimes this isolation can interact with the fear of Covid-19. Boyraz et al. (2020) argued that a person's perceived vulnerability to Covid-19 increases Covid-19-related worries, which then leads to an increased sense of social isolation and traumatic stress.

Communication hassles

The quantity and quality of communications, and communication expectations, are all critical components necessary for enhanced productivity of remote workers (Shockley et al., 2021). Communicating remotely can restrict the richness of information and fails to relay social cues necessary for mutual understanding of the message compared to face-to-face communication (Shao et al., 2021). Unfortunately, ineffective communication is one of many challenges for remote workers during the pandemic (Shockley et al., 2021; Wang et al., 2021).

Given that remote work relies heavily on Information Communication Technology (i.e., ICT) for communication and collaboration, communication challenges of remote work may be exacerbated if workers face additional technology-related communication stressors or demands (Day et al., 2012). Due to the hasty adaptation of remote work, especially at the beginning of the pandemic, employees found it very difficult to get their home office ready for day-to-day operations. As well, often, specialised and necessary equipment and software were less accessible and worked less efficiently than they did at the permanent work site. Furthermore, remote workers were much less likely to receive timely IT technical support and feedback during the pandemic (Shao et al., 2021). Remote workers' work-related frustration was exacerbated due to frequent IT issues, especially at the beginning of the pandemic (Wang et al., 2021). Remote work led to more technological issues and decreased resources to deal with technical issues, which was a significant pandemic-related stressor for workers (Shao et al., 2021). Remote-based communication was considered to be inefficient, and frequent ICT issues exacerbated worker frustration (Wang et al., 2021). As such, poor communication quality was associated with burnout in remote workers (Shockley et al., 2021).

Work and non-work-based interruptions during working hours tended to increase dramatically during the pandemic, especially for remote workers (Leroy et al., 2021). Work-based multitasking and surprise interruptions increased as a result of the pandemic, as did non-work-based interruptions (e.g., intrusions, distractions, and multitasking; Leroy et al., 2021). These work-based intrusions were positively related to work-family conflict and negatively related to performance, whereas work-based multitasking, and non-work-based intrusions and distractions were positively related to emotional exhaustion (Leroy et al., 2021).

C. Reduced resources hypothesis

Another potential hypothesis focuses on the resources available to the worker rather than on the demands or stressors. That is, it is possible that burnout increased due to significant reductions in work, personal, and social resources during the pandemic. According to COR, people strive to obtain, maintain, and protect what they value. These resources may include support, money, tools, and personal characteristics. When resources are lost, threatened, or are unable to be obtained, strain is likely to occur (Hobfoll, 1989). When demands exceed resources for a significant period of time, emotional exhaustion is likely to occur, which can lead to cynicism and a lack of professional efficacy (Alarcon, 2011; Hobfoll, 1989).

Job resources, such as leader support, role clarity, and job autonomy can help to buffer/mitigate the negative impact that excessive demands have on an employee's physical and psychological well-being (Demerouti et al., 2001). Studies have shown that a multitude of resources were found to buffer the negative impact of virus outbreaks on well-being and burnout. In their meta-analysis of healthcare workers during virus outbreaks (e.g., SARS, COV, MERS, Ebola, various influenza A types), Kisely et al. (2020) found that a multitude of resources (e.g., adequate time-off from work, access to psychological interventions, developing and enforcing staff support protocols, and feeling adequately trained and educated to deal with the situation) were found to buffer the stressor-burnout relationship. Several studies have demonstrated that support was negatively related to burnout during the pandemic (Galanis et al., 2021; Kisely et al., 2020). However, support does not always buffer the effect of pandemic-related demands on burnout (Zhou et al., 2022).

Job resources, including resilience, were found to be associated with lower levels of emotional exhaustion during the pandemic (Barello et al., 2021). Similarly, job resources related to safety (e.g., safety systems, communication, decision-making, situational awareness, fatigue management, and participation in decision-making) were all significantly related to lower emotional exhaustion of general workers in Italy. Moreover, they buffered the relationship between perceived risk of being infected at work and emotional exhaustion (Falco et al., 2021). Overall, across all of these studies, we see the importance resources helping to reduce levels of worker burnout, and in some cases, potentially buffering the negative impacts of Covid-19 stressors on burnout (Barello et al., 2021; Falco et al., 2021; Galanis et al., 2021; Kisely et al., 2020; Zhou et al., 2022).

Another theory that has been bandied about in organisations and social media is that workers have become less resilient, and as such, they are experiencing greater levels of burnout. This debate originated not only with regard to Covid-19, but also as a more general dismissal of worker experiences. Typically, this hypothesis states that individuals become less resilient as they age, or a certain generation of workers is less resilient than a previous generation, or workers have become less resilient due to the pandemic. Based on a sample of 5000 full- and part-time workers in the US, Cigna (2020) reported that 63% of full-time workers have either low or moderate levels of resilience, which they argue puts the workers at risk of not being able to overcome adversity.

Research on the aforementioned assumptions is very limited, if not non-existent. Moreover, there is less evidence to suggest that an event such as a pandemic would reduce one's level of resilience. Indeed, many definitions of resilience highlight the role that adversity plays in developing or increasing resilience (McGee et al., 2018). However, Kuntz (2021) acknowledges that acute stressors, such as the Covid-19 pandemic, can be a double-edged sword: they can be debilitating and trauma inducing, or they can be a catalyst to growth. In examining data reported by Cigna (2020), it is notable that the laid-off workers have the lowest resilience (i.e., compared to full-time, part-time, and furloughed workers). Although their data is cross-sectional, it may be easier to suggest that being laid off resulted in lower resilience rather than the alternative suggestion (i.e., less resilience "caused" them to be laid off). Obviously, other third-variable explanations (e.g., lower resilient workers work in more vulnerable industries that are susceptible to lay-offs) are possible, but these findings are worth further examination using longitudinal data.

Although very few studies have been conducted that compare pre- and post-Covid-19 levels of resilience, some research shows that the resilience-burnout relationship remained the same. In general, higher levels of resilience are associated with lower job burnout, even during the pandemic (Baskin & Bartlett, 2021; Di Monte et al., 2020; Hu et al., 2020), especially in terms of protecting one's levels of personal accomplishment (Di Monte et al., 2020; Vagni et al., 2021). For example, Chinese healthcare worker's levels of resilience were negatively related to burnout during the pandemic, and post-traumatic growth was found to be negatively related to personal accomplishment (Lyu et al., 2021).

Baskin and Bartlett (2021) reviewed 32 Covid-19 resilience studies and found that nurses in the US (n=3 studies) experienced decreased resilience during the Covid-19 pandemic compared to non-pandemic levels. Conversely, nurses working in China (n=11 studies) experienced increased resilience. Moreover, studies conducted in all other countries included in the paper (i.e., Iran: n=2; Italy: n=1; France: n=1; Japan: n=1; Saudi Arabia: n=1; Singapore: n=1: India: n=2: Turkey: n=3; the Philippines: n=1; Canada: n=1; Spain: n=2; the United Kingdom: n=1; and Ethiopia: n=1) found no pre- versus post-pandemic changes in resilience. Interestingly, high levels of burnout may subsequently lead to decreased resilience. Employees experiencing high levels of burnout pre-pandemic tended to experience significant reductions in psychological capital during the pandemic (i.e., psychological capital involves a state of positive psychological development characterised by self-efficacy, optimism, hope, and resilience; Meseguer de Pedro et al., 2021).

D. Increased vulnerability

It is also interesting to note the differential impact that the pandemic had on different occupations and categories of workers. That is, the impact of the pandemic on workers depended somewhat on who they were, where they worked, and what they did, which sometimes created new vulnerable populations and/or increased the vulnerability of current at-risk groups. For example, several vulnerable groups, such as the elderly, minorities, and people with pre-existing conditions experienced higher rates of emotional exhaustion and fatigue during the pandemic (da Silva, 2021). As well, women experienced more burnout during the pandemic than did men (Peck, 2021). Workers in the accommodation and food service industry faced the largest changes in their employment status (e.g., job loss; reduced work hours). Work stoppages impacted women, younger workers, and lower educated workers to a greater degree than they affected men, older workers, and higher educated workers, respectively (Eurostat, 2021).

Most studies didn't directly address these vulnerable workers, or even look at multiple industries. Understandably, the majority of studies examined health-care workers who were at the frontline of the pandemic, and faced serious health risks, isolation from family (i.e., to avoid transmission), and high levels of burnout (e.g., Ma et al., 2021). However, there was limited research examining essential front-line workers that weren't in safety or health positions. For example, grocery store and gas station workers had to deal with the public throughout the pandemic, yet little is known about their health and wellbeing. Therefore, we need to speak of these industry and personal factors as potential moderators of the demands-burnout relationship. Moreover, people in lower-salaried positions were more extremely affected by the pandemic (e.g., reduced hours and job loss; Blundell et al., 2020), which can have a substantial impact on their wellbeing and burnout. These issues extend past the pandemic, and we need a better understanding of these types of under-studied workers and their experience of burnout.

Discussion

Lessons learned, future research, & practical implications

Not only has the pandemic directly affected individual physical and psychological health, it also has negatively impacted the work world, creating more work demands and negative health outcomes, including burnout. What have we learned from working through the pandemic that can help us to better understand burnout and to help improve the work experience, not only during pandemics and other crises, but also during times of non-crises? Although our categorisation of "traditional" versus "new" demands and stressors may seem a bit arbitrary, their distinction is primarily important to underscore the differential treatment they have received in the extant literature. Their importance (i.e., need for further study) continues even as the pandemic wanes. In our integration of the seminal burnout research with the current work on burnout during the pandemic, we have noted many similar findings/trends and we have identified areas that require more research. That is, what have we learned about burnout during the pandemic that will help us understand burnout in general? What resources from the pandemic can help us to buffer the demands-burnout relationship?

Future research

We can use the presented framework, in terms of traditional stressors, and "new" (or understudied Covid-related) stressors, resources, and vulnerability and contextual issues, as a useful structure to build an agenda for future research in burnout.

Extending traditional stressor research

Although the literature is well established regarding antecedents of burnout, the pandemic offered a perspective of the issues that we still need to examine, as well as identified some of our existing ideas about burnout that we need to challenge. For example, it is possible that Covid-19 may have changed workers, especially younger workers, expectations about work. Whereas recent generations of workers have been prioritising issues of balance and quality of life, Cotofan et al. (2020) suggested that "young people who come of age during this crisis may be more likely to prioritise financial security than job meaning or purpose as they enter the workforce." (p. 177). The veracity of this potential shift needs to be examined, as well as the potential impact on burnout and workplace functioning.

Health & safety future research

Health concerns and fear of Covid-19 were significant stressors related to job burnout. However, safety and health concerns often are ignored in studies of burnout antecedents. What are the key aspects that contribute to burnout? What can organisations do to help reduce risk as well as worker fear/concern that can lead to burnout? We also should examine whether such fears/concerns are only related to emotional exhaustion, or whether they also impact cynicism and professional efficacy, either directly or indirectly through exhaustion.

Social isolation future research

Social isolation also has received little attention prior to the pandemic. Because organisations are turning to remote workforces, what can organisations do to support worker health and functioning, and create a strong work culture across remote workplaces to increase a sense of belonging? Are current models of leadership effective in addressing behaviours that leaders need to exhibit to support a remote workforce? The data from social isolation is critical to our understanding of burnout and human functioning. We also must remember that remote work is not necessarily socially isolating. We need to understand both the work and non-work factors that contribute to feelings of inclusion, and their relationship to burnout.

Work–non-work issues, remote work, & burnout research

Not only did the pandemic highlight the key aspects associated with burnout, it also highlighted the intersection of work–family issues and remote work (Leroy et al., 2021) with burnout. Some people like to keep their work and non-work roles segmented, whereas others do better when roles blend together and are integrated throughout the day (i.e., boundary-management preferences; Ashforth et al., 2000). Working remotely makes segmentation of work and family roles difficult, because both are taking place in the same location. Forced remote work may create difficulties for those with strong segmentation preferences due to increased role blurring, perceptions of work–family conflict, and difficulty detaching from work (Kossek et al., 2006). If organisations force employees to work remotely post-Covid-19, will workers experience increased feelings of isolation, disengagement, and burnout?

Conversely, if workers prefer more integrated models of work and life, will being forced back to the workplace result in greater perceived demands and, ultimately, more burnout? Pre-pandemic, employees cited that one of the main barriers to working remotely is an unsupportive organisational culture (Batt & Valcour, 2003), which can exist when organisations have a high face-time versus results-oriented culture, and reward people for physical presence at work (Shockley & Allen, 2010). How will employees fair now that pandemic restrictions are being lifted in many countries, and some employees are now expected to go back to work? Some employees and organisations prefer remote work for a variety of reasons, such as childcare, financial costs associated with commuting to work, increased family time, and improved employee performance (Baudot & Kelly, 2020; Ozimek, 2020). Some organisations and companies are resisting employees' desire for continuing remote work arrangements, which may lead to deleterious outcomes, such as turnover and work stress (De Smet et al., 2021). Organisations, if possible, need to adopt a more flexible approach to developing work arrangements for their employees.

Future research on resources as buffers

Given the significant effects of key job and organisational resources (e.g., support, training, etc.) on burnout, as well as their potential buffering effects, more intervention research is needed to examine not only the beneficial aspects of these resources, but also to examine the validity of programs to increase these resources as a means of reducing burnout. Integrating our review with works on intervention levels (i.e., primary, secondary, and tertiary interventions; Sauter et al., 1990) and Nielsen et al.'s (2018) "IGLOO" focus on the individual, group, leader, and overall organisation, we can look at the lessons learned to change the environment/organisation, support individual workers, foster positive group dynamics, and develop effective leaders. In the case of burnout research, primary interventions target the organisation/job and are aimed at preventing or reducing damaging stressors and demands that may lead to burnout. Secondary interventions target the individual in helping them have the skills and abilities to face unexpected demands. Finally tertiary interventions for burnout address the issue of "healing the wounded" after burnout has occurred (Sauter et al., 1990).

As easy as it is to "blame" individuals for developing burnout symptoms, the reality is that job burnout is defined in terms of organisational and job demands. Therefore, the first place to address burnout is to look to organisational resources. The importance, and sometimes scarcity, of these resources have become very apparent during the pandemic. Because there is evidence that social support at work significantly decreased during the pandemic, which then led to greater experienced burnout (Manzano García & Ayala Calvo, 2021), organisations should devise ways of developing stronger supports for workers and supervisors providing this support.

The research on individual resources is less developed, and arguably less accepted, in the workplace. Despite the fact that it is not helpful to "blame" individuals for stressors created by the pandemic, and by life and work in general, it is beneficial to help workers to develop their resources and capacity to deal with these negative events/circumstances when they are not easily changed. In situations where the demands can't be totally eliminated, supporting workers to cope with these demands is beneficial to both the worker and the overall organisation. For example, several systemic reviews have established that mindfulness training reduced emotional exhaustion and depersonalisation (Salvado et al., 2021; Suleiman-Martos et al., 2020; West et al., 2016).

Future research should examine the extent to which supportive resources can mitigate the negative effects of some of the less-studied factors, such as isolation and health and safety concerns, on the components of burnout. It also would be beneficial to look at the additive effects of these individual supports alongside job and organisational supports designed to reduce demands and risk. Moreover, many models of burnout and stress fail to explain individual differences regarding the appraisal of job demands and resources (Crawford et al., 2010). A focus on individual differences in demand/resource appraisal may help to better understand these relationships. For example, job crafting is proactive work behaviour where the employee actively changes the perceived characteristics of their job so that they have greater alignment with preferences, motives, and passions (Wrzesniewski & Dutton, 2001). Several studies have demonstrated that job crafting is related to higher wellbeing (Ciuhan et al., 2022), reduced job strain (Rudolph et al., 2017), and burnout (Pijpker et al. (2022). However, we need more research to understand how it is appraised, and how it may help to buffer the impact of external threats/demands on employee well-being and burnout.

Practical implications

The heart of the burnout definition is that the environment is creating demands that lead to worker exhaustion, cynicism, and reduced efficacy. Therefore, reducing burnout should target the environment. Organisational change is notoriously difficulty, and we avoid it in favour of "easier" changes focusing on individuals. However, at the onset of the pandemic, many organisations rapidly introduced new policies, switched to remote working environments, changed work systems, and reorganised their workforce, which belies the common wisdom espoused by many that organisations' have an "inability" to quickly adapt and accommodate workers. It may be true that organisations are "resistant to change," but we should take a step back from assuming that change is impossible, and work toward ways to identify how to help organisations change to support their employees. We need to work toward using organisation's ability to change to support worker health and organisation functioning, by reducing burnout at work. Organisations should examine mechanisms through which they can create long-term, sustainable changes to support both worker and overall workplace functioning.

It is possible to examine individual differences in burnout without actually blaming the individual. Despite the importance of changing the environment and reducing demands on workers, it is equally important to support workers and to help them to define successful performance, which could be accomplished through a focus on the use of job crafting and employee thriving. Individual, relational, contextual, and agentic characteristics lead to thriving at work, which results in positive employee outcomes, such as well-being, development, and health (Spreitzer et al., 2005) and a reduction in burnout (Kleine et al., 2019; Spreitzer et al., 2005).

The pandemic highlighted the importance of social interactions for individual health. Although there has been some work on group functioning and individual wellbeing, more work needs to be conducted on the impact of good, bad, and non-existent social interactions at work. Moreover, it can be argued that leaders are the keystone of organisations. The pressure on them to be "perfect" and in charge to ensure that everyone is happy and well can be destructive, especially in the context of a global pandemic. We can both develop and support leaders to help them to handle their own demands, as well as help them to support their staff's level of wellness.

Summary

Burnout reflects the relationship between employees and their organisation, in terms of a person–organisation dynamic. However, this relationship can be heavily influenced by external events, such as a pandemic. This chapter has examined burnout in the context of the Covid-19 pandemic, providing an opportunity to better understand the work and non-work factors that contribute to burnout. The model identifies both traditional demands and some understudied demands, whose importance were underscored by the pandemic. It also highlights the importance of work and non-work resources in helping individuals function through challenging situations. Finally, we identified the potential for differential effects of pandemics, and other major world and organisational events, on workers, such that we need to better understand how to support vulnerable workers. Future research needs to extend past work to help identify factors to support worker health and reduce burnout.

References

Aarebrot, K., & Oppedal, S. (2021). *The involuntary use of home office and perceived work related social isolation during the COVID-19 pandemic: Implications for work engagement and burnout in the Norwegian banking sector*. Thesis Master of Science, Campus Bergen: Norwegian School of Business.

Ahorsu, D. K., Lin, C. Y., Marznaki, Z. H., & H Pakpour, A. (2022). The association between fear of COVID-19 and mental health: The mediating roles of burnout and job stress among emergency nursing staff. *Nursing, 9*(2), 1147–1154.

Alarcon, G., Eschleman, K. J., & Bowling, N. A. (2009). Relationships between personality variables and burnout: A meta-analysis. *Work & Stress, 23*(3), 244–263.

Alarcon, G. M. (2011). A meta-analysis of burnout with job demands, resources, and attitudes. *Journal of Vocational Behavior, 79*(2), 549–562.

Alcover, C. M., Chambel, M. J., Fernández, J. J., & Rodríguez, F. (2018). Perceived organizational support-burnout-satisfaction relationship in workers with disabilities: The moderation of family support. *Scandinavian Journal of Psychology, 59*(4), 451–461.

Alrawashdeh, H. M., Al-Tammemi, A. A. B., Alzawahreh, M. K., Al-Tamimi, A., Elkholy, M., Al Sarireh, F., Abusamak, M., Elehamer, N. M. K., Malkawi, A., Al-Dolat, W., Abu-Ismail, L., Al-Far, A., & Ghoul, I. (2021). Occupational burnout and job satisfaction among physicians in times of COVID-19 crisis: A convergent parallel mixed-method study. *BMC Public Health, 21*(1), 1–18.

Amanullah, S. & Shankar, R. R. (2020). The impact of Covid-19 on physician burnout globally: A review. *Healthcare, 8*(421), 1–12.

Amstad, F. T., Meier, L. L., Fasel, U., Elfering, A., & Semmer, N. K. (2011). A meta-analysis of work–family conflict and various outcomes with a special emphasis on cross-domain versus matching-domain relations. *Journal of Occupational Health Psychology, 16*(2), 151–169.

Aronsson, G., Theorell, T., Grape, T., Hammarström, A., Hogstedt, C., Marteinsdottir, I., Skoog, I., Traskman-Bendz, L., & Hall, C. (2017). A systematic review including meta-analysis of work environment and burnout symptoms. *BMC Public Health, 17*(1), 1–13.

Ashforth, B. E., Kreiner, G. E., & Fugate, M. (2000). All in a day's work: Boundaries and micro role transitions. *Academy of Management review, 25*(3), 472–491.

Azoulay, E., De Waele, J., Ferrer, R., Staudinger, T., Borkowska, M., Povoa, P., Iliopoulou, K., Artigas, A., Schaller, S., Hari, M., Pellegrini, M., Darmon, M., Kesecioglu, J., & Cecconi, M. (2020). Symptoms of burnout in intensive care unit specialists facing the Covid-19 outbreak. *Annals of Intensive Care, 10*(110), 1–8. 10.1186/s13613-020-00722-3

Babamiri, M., Bashirian, S., Sohrabi, M. S., Heidarimoghadam, R., Mortezapoor, A., & Zareian, S. (2022). Burnout and mental health of COVID-19 frontline healthcare workers: Results from an online survey. *Iranian Journal of Psychiatry, 17*(2), 136–143.

Bahadirli, S., & Sagaltici, E. (2021). Burnout, job satisfaction, and psychological symptoms among emergency physicians during COVID-19 outbreak: A cross-sectional study. *Practitioner, 83*(25.1), 8–20.

Barello, S., Caruso, R., Palamenghi, L., Nania, T., Dellafiore, F., Bonetti, L., Silenzi, A., Marotta, C., & Graffigna, G. (2021). Factors associated with emotional exhaustion in healthcare professionals involved in the COVID-19 pandemic: an application of the job demands-resources model. *International Archives of Occupational and Environmental Health, 94*(8), 1751–1761.

Barello, S., Palamenghi, L., & Graffigna, G. (2020). Burnout and somatic symptoms among frontline healthcare professionals at the peak of the Italian COVID-19 pandemic. *Psychiatry Research, 290*, 113129.

Barriga Medina, H. R., Campoverde Aguirre, R., Coello-Montecel, D., Ochoa Pacheco, P., & Paredes-Aguirre, M. I. (2021). The influence of work–family conflict on burnout during the COVID-19 pandemic: The effect of teleworking overload. *International Journal of Environmental Research and Public Health, 18*(19), 10302–10323.

Baskin, R. G., & Bartlett, R. (2021). Healthcare worker resilience during the COVID-19 pandemic: An integrative review. *Journal of Nursing Management, 29*(8), 2329–2342.

Batt, R., & Valcour, P. M. (2003). Human resources practices as predictors of work-family outcomes and employee turnover. *Industrial Relations: A Journal of Economy and Society, 42*(2), 189–220.

Baudot, L., & Kelly, K. (2020). A survey of perceptions of remote work and work productivity in the United States during the COVID-19 shutdown. Available at SSRN 3646406.

Blanco-Donoso, L. M., Moreno-Jiménez, J., Hernández-Hurtado, M., Cifri-Gavela, J. L., Jacobs, S., & Garrosa, E. (2021). Daily work-family conflict and burnout to explain the leaving intentions and vitality levels of healthcare workers: Interactive effects using an experience-sampling method. *International Journal of Environmental Research and Public Health, 18*(4), 1932–1948.

Blundell, R., Costa Dias, M., Joyce, R., & Xu, X. (2020). COVID-19 and Inequalities. *Fiscal Studies, 41*(2), 291–319.

Boyraz, G., Legros, D. N., & Tigershtrom, A. (2020). COVID-19 and traumatic stress: The role of perceived vulnerability, COVID-19-related worries, and social isolation. *Journal of Anxiety Disorders, 76*, 1–9.

Bradley, M., & Chahar, P. (2020). Burnout of healthcare providers during COVID-19. *Cleveland Clinic Journal of Medicine, 89*(9), 1–3.

Buecker, S., & Horstmann, K. T. (2021). Loneliness and social isolation during the COVID-19 pandemic: A systematic review enriched with empirical evidence from a large-scale diary study. *European Psychologist, 26*(4), 272–284.

Casper, A., & Sonnentag, S. (2020). Feeling exhausted or vigorous in anticipation of high workload? The role of worry and planning during the evening. *Journal of Occupational and Organizational Psychology, 93*(1), 215–242.

Casper, A., Sonnentag, S., & Tremmel, S. (2017). Mindset matters: The role of employees' stress mindset for day-specific reactions to workload anticipation. *European Journal of Work and Organizational Psychology, 26*(6), 798–810.

Chemali, Z., Ezzeddine, F. L., Gelaye, B., Dossett, M. L., Salameh, J., Bizri, M., Dubale, B., & Fricchione, G. (2019). Burnout among healthcare providers in the complex environment of the Middle East: A systematic review. *BMC Public Health, 19*(1), 1–21.

Chen, H., Wu, P., & Wei, W. (2012). New perspective on job burnout: Exploring the root cause beyond general antecedents analysis. *Psychological Reports, 110*(3), 801–819.

Cho, J. H. J., Olmstead, R., Choi, H., Carrillo, C., Seeman, T. E., & Irwin, M. R. (2019). Associations of objective versus subjective social isolation with sleep disturbance, depression, and fatigue in community-dwelling older adults. *Aging & Mental Health, 23*(9), 1130–1138.

CIGNA Resilience Index: 2020 US Report (2020). Aaccessed at: https://cignaresilience.com/wp-content/uploads/2020/10/Cigna_ResilienceReport_FINAL.pdf

Ciuhan, G. C., Nicolau, R. G., & Iliescu, D. (2022). Perceived stress and wellbeing in romanian teachers during the COVID-19 pandemic: The intervening effects of job crafting and problem-focused coping. *Psychology in the Schools, 59*(9), 1–12.

Cotel, A., Golu, F., Pantea Stoian, A., Dimitriu, M., Socea, B., Cirstoveanu, C., Davitoiu, A. M., Alexe, F. J., & Oprea, B. (2021). Predictors of burnout in healthcare workers during the COVID-19 pandemic. *Healthcare, 9*(3), 304–311.

Cotofan, M., Cassar, L., Dur, R., & Meier, S. (2020). Macroeconomic conditions when young shape job preferences for life. *The Review of Economics and AStatistics, 104*(5), 1–20.

Crawford, E. R., LePine, J. A., & Rich, B. L. (2010). Linking job demands and resources to employee engagement and burnout: A theoretical extension and meta-analytic test. *Journal of Applied Psychology, 95*(5), 834–848.

da Silva, J. A. T. (2021). Corona exhaustion (CORONEX): COVID-19-induced exhaustion grinding down humanity. *Current Research in Behavioral Sciences, 2*(100014), 1–4.

Day, A., Paquet, S., Scott, N., & Hambley, L. (2012). Perceived information and communication technology (ICT) demands on employee outcomes: The moderating effect of organizational ICT support. *Journal of Occupational Health Psychology, 17*(4), 473–491.

Day, A. L., Sibley, A., Scott, N., Tallon, J. M., & Ackroyd-Stolarz, S. (2009). Workplace risks and stressors as predictors of burnout: The moderating impact of job control and team efficacy. *Canadian Journal of Administrative Sciences/Revue Canadienne des Sciences de l'Administration, 26*(1), 7–22.

Deci, E. L., & Ryan, R. M. (2000). The "what" and "why" of goal pursuits: Human needs and the self-determination of behavior. *Psychological Inquiry, 11*(4), 227–268.

Demerouti, E., Bakker, A. B., Nachreiner, F., & Schaufeli, W. B. (2001). The job-demands resources model of burnout. *Journal of Applied Psychology, 86*(3), 499–512.

Denning, M., Goh, E. T., Tan, B., Kanneganti, A., Almonte, M., Scott, A., Martin, G., Clarke, J., Sounderajah, V., Markar, S., Przybylowicz, J., Huak Chan, Y., Sia, C., Chua, Y. X., Sim, K., Lim, L., Tan, L., Tan, M., Sharma, V., Ooi, S., Winter Beatty, J., Flott, K., Mason, S., Chidambaram, S., Yalamanchili, S., Zbikowska, G., Fedorowski, J., Dykowska, G., Wells, M., Purkayastha, S., & Kinross, J. (2021). Determinants of burnout and other aspects of psychological well-being in healthcare workers during the COVID-19 pandemic: A multinational cross-sectional study. *Plos One, 16*(4), e0238666.

De Smet, A., Dowling, B., Mugayar-Baldocchi, M., & Schaninger, B. (2021, September 8). 'Great attrition' or 'great attraction'? The choice is yours. *The McKinsey Quarterly, 63*(1), 1–6.

de Wit, K., Mercuri, M., Wallner, C., Clayton, N., Archambault, P., Ritchie, K., Gerin-Lajoie, C., Gray, S., Schwartz, L., & Chan, T. (2020). Canadian emergency physician psychological distress and burnout during the first 10 weeks of COVID-19: A mixed-methods study. *Journal of the American College of Emergency Physicians, 1*(5), 1030–1038.

Dimitriu, M. C., Pantea-Stoian, A., Smaranda, A. C., Nica, A. A., Carap, A. C., Constantin, V. D., Davitoiu, A. M., Cirstoveanu, C., Bacalbasa, N., Bratu, O. G., Jacota-Alexe, F., Badiu, C. D., Smarandache, C. G., & Socea, B. (2020). Burnout syndrome in Romanian medical residents in time of the COVID-19 pandemic. *Medical Hypotheses, 144*, 109972.

Di Monte, C., Monaco, S., Mariani, R., & Di Trani, M. (2020). From resilience to burnout: Psychological features of Italian general practitioners during COVID-19 emergency. *Frontiers in Psychology*, 2476–2484.

DiStaso, M. J., & Shoss, M. K. (2020). Looking forward: How anticipated workload change influences the present workload–emotional strain relationship. *Journal of Occupational Health Psychology, 25*(6), 401–409.

Dosil, M., Ozamiz-Etxebarria, N., Redondo, I., Picaza, M., & Jaureguizar, J. (2020). Psychological symptoms in health professionals in Spain after the first wave of the COVID-19 pandemic. *Frontiers in Psychology, 11*, 1–11.

El Ghaziri, M., Johnson, S., Purpora, C., Simons, S., & Taylor, R. (2022). Registered nurses' experiences with incivility during the early phase of COVID-19 pandemic: Results of a multi-state survey. *Workplace Health & Safety, 70*(3), 148–160.

Eurostat (2021). COVID-19 labour effects across the income distribution. https://ec. europa.eu/eurostat/statistics-explained/index.php?title=COVID-19_labour_effects_ across_the_income_distribution

Falco, A., Girardi, D., Dal Corso, L., Yıldırım, M., & Converso, D. (2021). The perceived risk of being infected at work: An application of the job demands–resources model to workplace safety during the COVID-19 outbreak. *PloS One*, *16*(9), e0257197.

Ferry, A. V., Wereski, R., Strachan, F. E., & Mills, N. L. (2021). Predictors of UK healthcare worker burnout during the COVID-19 pandemic. *QJM: An International Journal of Medicine*, *114*(6), 374–380.

Freudenberger, H. J. (1974). Staff burn-out. *Journal of Social Issues*, *30*(1), 159–165.

Galanis, P., Vraka, I., Fragkou, D., Bilali, A., & Kaitelidou, D. (2021). Nurses' burnout and associated risk factors during the COVID-19 pandemic: A systematic review and meta-analysis. *Journal of Advanced Nursing*, *77*(8), 3286–3302.

Gemine, R., Davies, G. R., Tarrant, S., Davies, R. M., James, M., & Lewis, K. (2021). Factors associated with work-related burnout in NHS staff during COVID-19: A cross-sectional mixed methods study. *BMJ Open*, *11*(1), e042591.

Giusti, E. M., Pedroli, E., D'Aniello, G. E., Stramba Badiale, C., Pietrabissa, G., Manna, C., Badiale, M. S., Riva, G., Castelnuovo, G., & Molinari, E. (2020). The psychological impact of the COVID-19 outbreak on health professionals: A cross-sectional study. *Frontiers in Psychology*, *11*, 1684.

Hansen, N., Sverke, M., & Näswall, K. (2009). Predicting nurse burnout from demands and resources in three acute care hospitals under different forms of ownership: A cross-sectional questionnaire survey. *International Journal of Nursing Studies*, *46*(1), 96–107.

Hariharan, T. S., & Griffin, B. (2019). A review of the factors related to burnout at the early-career stage of medicine. *Medical Teacher*, *41*(12), 1380–1391.

Hobfoll, S. E. (1989). Conservation of resources: A new attempt at conceptualizing stress. *American Psychologist*, *44*(3), 513–524.

Hoedl, M., Eglseer, D., & Bauer, S. (2021). Associations between personal protective equipment and nursing staff stress during the COVID-19 pandemic. *Journal of Nursing Management*, *29*, 2374–2382.

Hopwood, T. L., Schutte, N. S., & Loi, N. M. (2019a). Anticipatory traumatic reaction: Outcomes arising from secondary exposure to disasters and large-scale threats. *Assessment*, *26*(8), 1427–1443.

Hopwood, T. L., Schutte, N. S., & Loi, N. M. (2019b). Stress responses to secondary trauma: Compassion fatigue and anticipatory traumatic reaction among youth workers. *The Social Science Journal*, *56*(3), 337–348.

Hu, D., Kong, Y., Li, W., Han, Q., Zhang, X., Zhu, L. X., & Zhu, J. (2020). Frontline nurses' burnout, anxiety, depression, and fear statuses and their associated factors during the COVID-19 outbreak in Wuhan, China: A large-scale cross-sectional study. *EClinicalMedicine*, *24*, 100424–100434.

Iida, M., Sasaki, N., Kuroda, R., Tsuno, K., & Kawakami, N. (2021). Increased COVID-19-related workplace bullying during its outbreak: A 2-month prospective cohort study of full-time employees in Japan. *Environmental and Occupational Health Practice*, *3*(1), 1–11.

Ingram, J., Hand, C. J., & Maciejewski, G. (2021). Social isolation during COVID-19 lockdown impairs cognitive function. *Applied Cognitive Psychology*, *35*(4), 935–947.

Jang, S., Allen, T. D., & Regina, J. (2021). Office housework, burnout, and promotion: Does gender matter?. *Journal of Business and Psychology*, *36*(5), 793–805.

Jex, S. M. & Yankelevich, M. (2008), *"Work stress"*, *The SAGE handbook of organizational behaviour*, Vol. *1*, (pp. 498–518). London: Sage Publications.

Kannampallil, T. G., Goss, C. W., Evanoff, B. A., Strickland, J. R., McAlister, R. P., & Duncan, J. (2020). Exposure to COVID-19 patients increases physician trainee stress and burnout. *PloS One*, *15*(8), e0237301.

Kisely, S., Warren, N., McMahon, L., Dalais, C., Henry, I., & Siskind, D. (2020). Occurrence, prevention, and management of the psychological effects of emerging virus outbreaks on healthcare workers: Rapid review and meta-analysis. *BMJ*, *369*, 1642–1652.

Kleine, A. K., Rudolph, C. W., & Zacher, H. (2019). Thriving at work: A meta-analysis. *Journal of Organizational Behavior*, *40*(9–10), 973–999.

Koch, J., & Schermuly, C. C. (2021). Managing the crisis: How COVID-19 demands interact with agile project management in predicting employee exhaustion. *British Journal of Management*, *32*(4), 1265–1283.

Kossek, E. E., Lautsch, B. A., & Eaton, S. C. (2006). Telecommuting, control, and boundary management: Correlates of policy use and practice, job control, and work–family effectiveness. *Journal of Vocational Behavior*, *68*(2), 347–367.

Kuntz, J. C. (2021). Resilience in times of global pandemic: Steering recovery and thriving trajectories. *Applied Psychology: An International Review*, *70*(1), 188–215.

Lazarus, R. S., & Folkman, S. (1984). *Stress, appraisal, and coping*. New York: Springer Publishing Company.

Lee, J., Lim, N., Yang, E., & Lee, S. M. (2011). Antecedents and consequences of three dimensions of burnout in psychotherapists: A meta-analysis. *Professional Psychology: Research and Practice*, *42*(3), 252–258.

Lee, R. T., & Ashforth, B. E. (1996). A meta-analytic examination of the correlates of the three dimensions of job burnout. *Journal of Applied Psychology*, *81*(2), 123–133.

Lee, R. T., Seo, B., Hladkyj, S., Lovell, B. L., & Schwartzmann, L. (2013). Correlates of physician burnout across regions and specialties: A meta-analysis. *Human Resources for Health*, *11*(1), 1–16.

Leiter, M. P., & Maslach, C. (1999). Six areas of worklife: A model of the organizational context of burnout. *Journal of Health and Human Services Administration*, *21*(4), 472–489.

Leiter, M. P., & Maslach, C. (2001). Burnout and quality in a sped-up world. *The Journal for Quality and Participation*, *24*(2), 48–51.

Leroy, S., Schmidt, A. M., & Madjar, N. (2021). Working from home during COVID-19: A study of the interruption landscape. *Journal of Applied Psychology*, *106*(10), 1448–1465.

Lippi, G., Henry, B. M., Bovo, C., & Sanchis-Gomar, F. (2020). Health risks and potential remedies during prolonged lockdowns for coronavirus disease 2019 (COVID-19). *Diagnosis*, *7*(2), 85–90.

Lorente, L., Vera, M., & Peiró, T. (2021). Nurses stressors and psychological distress during the COVID-19 pandemic: The mediating role of coping and resilience. *Journal of Advanced Nursing*, *77*(3), 1335–1344.

Lyu, Y., Yu, Y., Chen, S., Lu, S., & Ni, S. (2021). Positive functioning at work during COVID-19: Posttraumatic growth, resilience, and emotional exhaustion in Chinese frontline healthcare workers. *Applied Psychology: Health and Well-Being*, *13*(4), 871–886.

Ma, Y., Faraz, N. A., Ahmed, F., Iqbal, M. K., Saeed, U., Mughal, M. F., & Raza, A. (2021). Curbing nurses' burnout during COVID-19: The roles of servant leadership and psychological safety. *Journal of Nursing Management*, *29*(8), 2383–2391.

Magnavita, N., Chirico, F., Garbarino, S., Bragazzi, N. L., Santacroce, E., & Zaffina, S. (2021). SARS/MERS/SARS-CoV-2 outbreaks and burnout syndrome among health-care workers. An umbrella systematic review. *International Journal of Environmental Research and Public Health, 18*(8), 4361–4374.

Maneechaeye, P. (2021). Structural equation model evaluating the impact of isolation and workfamily conflict on burnout among teleworking professionals. *Kasetsart Journal of Social Sciences, 42*(3), 630–636.

Manzano García, G., & Ayala Calvo, J. C. (2021). The threat of COVID-19 and its influence on nursing staff burnout. *Journal of Advanced Nursing, 77*(2), 832–844.

Martínez-López, J. Á., Lázaro-Pérez, C., Gómez-Galán, J., & Fernández-Martínez, M. D. M. (2020). Psychological impact of COVID-19 emergency on health professionals: Burnout incidence at the most critical period in Spain. *Journal of Clinical Medicine, 9*(9), 3029, 3047.

Maslach, C., & Jackson, S. E. (1981). The measurement of experienced burnout. *Journal of Occupational Behavior, 2*, 99–113.

Maslach, C., Schaufeli, W. B., & Leiter, M. P. (2001). Job burnout. *Annual review of psychology, 52*(1), 397–422.

Matsuo, T., Kobayashi, D., Taki, F., Sakamoto, F., Uehara, Y., Mori, N., & Fukui, T. (2020). Prevalence of health care worker burnout during the coronavirus disease 2019 (COVID-19) pandemic in Japan. *JAMA Network, 3*(8), e2017271–e2017271.

Matsuo, T., Taki, F., Kobayashi, D., Jinta, T., Suzuki, C., Ayabe, A., Sakamoto, F., Kitaoka, A., Uehara, Y., Mori, N., & Fukui, T. (2021). Health care worker burnout after the first wave of the coronavirus disease 2019 (COVID-19) pandemic in Japan. *Journal of Occupational Health, 63*(1), 1–11.

Mattei, A., Fiasca, F., Mazzei, M., Abbossida, V., & Bianchini, V. (2017). Burnout among healthcare workers at L'Aquila: its prevalence and associated factors. *Psychology, Health & Medicine, 22*(10), 1262–1270.

Maunder, R. G., Lancee, W. J., Balderson, K. E., Bennett, J. P., Borgundvaag, B., Evans, S., … & Wasylenki, D. A. (2006). Long-term psychological and occupational effects of providing hospital healthcare during SARS outbreak. *Emerging Infectious Diseases, 12*(12), 1924–1932.

McCormack, H. M., MacIntyre, T. E., O'Shea, D., Herring, M. P., & Campbell, M. J. (2018). The prevalence and cause (s) of burnout among applied psychologists: A systematic review. *Frontiers in Psychology, 9* (1897), 1–19.

McGee, S. L., Höltge, J., Maercker, A., & Thoma, M. V. (2018). Sense of coherence and stress-related resilience: Investigating the mediating and moderating mechanisms in the development of resilience following stress or adversity. *Frontiers in Psychiatry, 9*, 378.

Meseguer de Pedro, M., Fernández-Valera, M. M., García-Izquierdo, M., & Soler-Sánchez, M. I. (2021). Burnout, psychological capital and health during COVID-19 social isolation: A longitudinal analysis. *International Journal of Environmental Research and Public Health, 18*(3), 1064–1074.

Meyer, B., Zill, A., Dilba, D., Gerlach, R., & Schumann, S. (2021). Employee psychological well-beingduring the Covid-19 pandemic in Germany: A longitudinal study of demands, resources, and exhaustion. *International Journal of Psychology, 56*(4), 532–550. 10.1002/ijop.12743.

Morgantini, L. A., Naha, U., Wang, H., Francavilla, S., Acar, Ö., Flores, J. M., Crivallero, S., Moreira, D., Abern, M., Eklund, M., Vigneswaran, H. T., & Weine, S. M. (2020). Factors contributing to healthcare professional burnout during the COVID-19 pandemic: A rapid turnaround global survey. *PloS One, 15*(9), e0238217.

Moukarzel, A., Michelet, P., Durand, A., Sebbane, M., Bourgeois, S., Markarian, T., Bompard, C., & Gentile, S. (2019). Burnout syndrome among emergency department staff: Prevalence and associated factors. *Biomedical Research International, 2019*, 1–10, 10.1155/2019/6462472.

Neveu, J. P. (2007). Jailed resources: Conservation of resources theory as applied to burnout among prison guards. *Journal of Organizational Behavior: The International Journal of Industrial, Occupational and Organizational Psychology and Behavior, 28*(1), 21–42.

Nielsen, K., Yarker, J., Munir, F., & Bültmann, U. (2018). IGLOO: An integrated framework for sustainable return to work in workers with common mental disorders. *Work & Stress, 32*(4), 400–417.

Nitschke, J. P., Forbes, P. A., Ali, N., Cutler, J., Apps, M. A., Lockwood, P. L., & Lamm, C. (2021). Resilience during uncertainty? Greater social connectedness during COVID-19 lockdown is associated with reduced distress and fatigue. *British Journal of Health Psychology, 26*(2), 553–569.

Ofei-Dodoo, S., Mullen, R., Pasternak, A., Hester, C. M., Callen, E., Bujold, E. J., Carroll, J. K., & Kimminau, K. S. (2021). Loneliness, burnout, and other types of emotional distress among family medicine physicians: Results from a national survey. *The Journal of the American Board of Family Medicine, 34*(3), 531–541.

Orr, A. E., & Savage, T. (2021). Expanding access to and ensuring equity in the benefits of remote work following the COVID-19 pandemic. *Journal of Science Policy and Governance, 18*(4), 1–8.

Ozimek, A. (2020). The future of remote work. Available at SSRN 3638597.

Peck, J. A. (2021). The disproportionate impact of COVID-19 on women relative to men: A conservation of resources perspective. *Gender, Work & Organization, 28*, 484–497.

Pijpker, R., Kerksieck, P., Tušl, M., De Bloom, J., Brauchli, R., & Bauer, G. F. (2022). The role of off-job crafting in burnout prevention during COVID-19 crisis: A longitudinal study. *International Journal of Environmental Research and Public Health, 19*(4), 2146–2159.

Puig-Perez, S., Cano-López, I., Martínez, P., Kozusznik, M. W., Alacreu-Crespo, A., Pulopulos, M. M., Duque, A., Almela, M., Alino, M., Garcia-Rubio, M. J., Pollak, A., & Kożusznik, B. (2022). Optimism as a protective factor against the psychological impact of COVID-19 pandemic through its effects on perceived stress and infection stress anticipation. *Current Psychology*, 1–15.

Reichl, C., Leiter, M. P., & Spinath, F. M. (2014). Work–nonwork conflict and burnout: A meta-analysis. *Human Relations, 67*(8), 979–1005.

Rudert, S. C., Gleibs, I. H., Gollwitzer, M., Häfner, M., Hajek, K. V., Harth, N. S., Hausser, J. A., Imhoff, R., & Schneider, D. (2021). Us and the virus: Understanding the COVID-19 pandemic through a social psychological lens. *European Psychologist, 26*(4), 259–271.

Rudolph, C. W., Katz, I. M., Lavigne, K. N., & Zacher, H. (2017). Job crafting: A meta-analysis of relationships with individual differences, job characteristics, and work outcomes. *Journal of Vocational Behavior, 102*, 112–138.

Salvado, M., Marques, D. L., Pires, I. M., & Silva, N. M. (2021). Mindfulness-based interventions to reduce burnout in primary healthcare professionals: A systematic review and meta-analysis. *Healthcare, 9*(10), 1342–1356.

Sanfilippo, F., Noto, A., Foresta, G., Santonocito, C., Palumbo, G., Arcadipane, A., Maybauer, D., & Maybauer, M. (2017). Incidence and factors associated with burnout in anesthesiology: A systematic review. *Biomedical Research International, 2017*, 1–10. 10.1155/2017/8648925.

Sant'Ana, G., Imoto, A. M., Amorim, F. F., Taminato, M., Peccin, M. S., Santana, L. A., Gottems, L. B. D., & Camargo, E. B. (2020). Infection and death in healthcare workers due to COVID-19: A systematic review. *Acta Paulista de Enfermagem*, *33*, 1–9.

Sauter, S. L., Murphy, L. R., & Hurrell, J. J. (1990). Prevention of work-related psychological disorders: A national strategy proposed by the National Institute for Occupational Safety and Health (NIOSH). *American Psychologist*, *45*(10), 1146–1158.

Sayılan, A. A., Kulakac, N., & Uzun, S. (2021). Burnout levels and sleep quality of COVID-19 heroes. *Perspectives in Psychiatric Care*, *57*, 1231–1236.

Schaufeli, W. B., & Buunk, B. P. (2003). Burnout: An overview of 25 years of research and theorizing. *The Handbook of Work and Health Psychology*, *2*(1), 282–424.

Shanafelt, T. D., Boone, S., Tan, L., Dyrbye, L. N., Sotile, W., Satele, D., West, C. P., Sloan, J., & Oreskovich, M. R. (2012). Burnout and satisfaction with work-life balance among US physicians relative to the general US population. *Archives of internal medicine*, *172*(18), 1377–1385.

Shao, Y., Fang, Y., Wang, M., Chang, C. H. D., & Wang, L. (2021). Making daily decisions to work from home or to work in the office: The impacts of daily work-and COVID-related stressors on next-day work location. *Journal of Applied Psychology*, *106*(6), 825–838.

Sharma, S., & Bumb, A. (2021). The challenges faced in technology-driven classes during covid-19. *International Journal of Distance Education Technologies*, *19*(1), 66–88.

Shevlin, M., Nolan, E., Owczarek, M., McBride, O., Murphy, J., Gibson Miller, J., Hartman, T. K., Levita, L., Mason, L., Martinez, A. P., McKay, R., Stocks, T. V. A., Bennett, K. M., Hyland, P., & Bentall, R. P. (2020). COVID-19-related anxiety predicts somatic symptoms in the UK population. *British Journal of Health Psychology*, *25*(4), 875–882.

Shin, H., Park, Y. M., Ying, J. Y., Kim, B., Noh, H., & Lee, S. M. (2014). Relationships between coping strategies and burnout symptoms: A meta-analytic approach. *Professional Psychology: Research and Practice*, *45*(1), 44–56.

Shockley, K. M., & Allen, T. D. (2010). Investigating the missing link in flexible work arrangement utilization: An individual difference perspective. *Journal of Vocational Behavior*, *76*(1), 131–142.

Shockley, K. M., Allen, T. D., Dodd, H., & Waiwood, A. M. (2021). Remote worker communication during COVID-19: The role of quantity, quality, and supervisor expectation-setting. *Journal of Applied Psychology*, *106*(10), 1466–1482.

Shoji, K., Cieslak, R., Smoktunowicz, E., Rogala, A., Benight, C. C., & Luszczynska, A. (2016). Associations between job burnout and self-efficacy: A meta-analysis. *Anxiety, Stress, & Coping*, *29*(4), 367–386.

Sinclair, R. R., Allen, T., Barber, L., Bergman, M., Britt, T., Butler, A., ... & Yuan, Z. (2020). Occupational health science in the time of COVID-19: Now more than ever. *Occupational Health Science*, *4*(1), 1–22.

Spreitzer, G., Sutcliffe, K., Dutton, J., Sonenshein, S., & Grant, A. M. (2005). A socially embedded model of thriving at work. *Organization Science*, *16*(5), 537–549.

Striler, J., Shoss, M., & Jex, S. (2021). The relationship between stressors of temporary work and counterproductive work behaviour. *Stress and Health*, *37*(2), 329–340.

Suleiman-Martos, N., Gomez-Urquiza, J. L., Aguayo-Estremera, R., Cañadas-De La Fuente, G. A., De La Fuente-Solana, E. I., & Albendín-García, L. (2020). The effect of mindfulness training on burnout syndrome in nursing: A systematic review and meta-analysis. *Journal of Advanced Nursing*, *76*(5), 1124–1140.

Swider, B. W., & Zimmerman, R. D. (2010). Born to burnout: A meta-analytic path model of personality, job burnout, and work outcomes. *Journal of Vocational behavior*, *76*(3), 487–506.

Tuna, T., & Özdin, S. (2021). Levels and predictors of anxiety, depression, and burnout syndrome in physicians during the COVID-19 pandemic. *International Journal of Mental Health and Addiction*, *19*(6), 2470–2483.

Unoki, T., Tamoto, M., Ouchi, A., Sakuramoto, H., Nakayama, A., Katayama, Y., Miyazaki, S., Yamada, T., Fujitani, S., Nishida, O., & Tabah, A. (2020). Personal protective equipment use by health-care workers in intensive care units during the COVID-19 pandemic in Japan: Comparative analysis with the PPE-SAFE survey. *Acute Medicine & Surgery*, *7*(1), e584, 1–7.

Vagni, M., Maiorano, T., Giostra, V., & Pajardi, D. (2021). Protective factors against emergency stress and burnout in healthcare and emergency workers during second wave of COVID-19. *Social Sciences*, *10*(5), 178–193.

Vu, T. V., Vo-Thanh, T., Chi, H., Nguyen, N. P., Nguyen, D. V., & Zaman, M. (2022). The role of perceived workplace safety practices and mindfulness in maintaining calm in employees during times of crisis. *Human Resource Management*, *61*(3), 315–333.

Wang, B., Liu, Y., Qian, J., & Parker, S. K. (2021). Achieving effective remote working during the COVID-19 pandemic: A work design perspective. *Applied Psychology*, *70*(1), 16–59.

West, C. P., Dyrbye, L. N., Erwin, P. J., & Shanafelt, T. D. (2016). Interventions to prevent and reduce physician burnout: A systematic review and meta-analysis. *The Lancet*, *388*(10057), 2272–2281.

Williams, E. S., Rathert, C., & Buttigieg, S. C. (2020). The personal and professional consequences of physician burnout: A systematic review of the literature. *Medical Care Research and Review*, *77*(5), 371–386.

World Health Organization (2022). https://www.who.int/emergencies/diseases/novel-coronavirus

Wrzesniewski, A., & Dutton, J. E. (2001). Crafting a job: Revisioning employees as active crafters of their work. *Academy of Management Review*, *26*(2), 179–201.

Wu, Y., Wang, J., Luo, C., Hu, S., Lin, X., Anderson, A. E., Bruera, E., Yang, X., Wei, S., & Qian, Y. (2020). A comparison of burnout frequency among oncology physicians and nurses working on the frontline and usual wards during the COVID-19 epidemic in Wuhan, China. *Journal of Pain and Symptom Management*, *60*(1), e60–e65.

Xiang, Y. T., Zhao, Y. J., Liu, Z. H., Li, X. H., Zhao, N., Cheung, T., & Ng, C. H. (2020). The COVID-19 outbreak and psychiatric hospitals in China: Managing challenges through mental health service reform. *International Journal of Biological Sciences*, *16*(10), 1741.

Xu, S., & Cao, Z. C. (2019). Antecedents and outcomes of work–nonwork conflict in hospitality: A meta-analysis. *International Journal of Contemporary Hospitality Management*, *31*(10), 3919–3942.

Zhou, T., Xu, C., Wang, C., Sha, S., Wang, Z., Zhou, Y., Zhang, X., Hu, D., Liu, Y., Tian, T., Liang, S., & Wang, Q. (2022). Burnout and well-being of healthcare workers in the post-pandemic period of COVID-19: A perspective from the job demands-resources model. *BMC Health Services Research*, *22*(1), 1–15.

4 What do we really understand about the relationship between physical activity and burnout?

Valérie Hervieux[1], *Claude Fernet*[2], *and Caroline Biron*[1]

[1]*Université Laval, Québec, Canada*
[2]*Université du Québec à Trois-Rivières, Québec, Canada*

Introduction

Physical activity is well-recognised for its physical and mental health benefits (Piercy et al., 2018) and in some cases is even used as a treatment for certain health problems such as depression (Mead et al., 2010). In a systematic review of the association between physical activity and burnout, the evidence on the negative relationship between physical activity and the core component of burnout (i.e., exhaustion) was considered moderate, whereas it was classified as strong for the interventional studies (Naczenski et al., 2017). The authors of the review report results supporting the hypothesis of a reciprocal relationship between physical activity and exhaustion in one longitudinal study (de Vries et al., 2016). More precisely, an increase in physical activity was associated with a decrease in exhaustion at follow-up (i.e., half-year time lag), while an increase in exhaustion was also associated with a decrease in physical activity at follow-up.

Although physical activity is considered by many researchers and health professionals as a potential avenue for preventing health problems, there are still some paradoxes unexplained. The purpose of this chapter is therefore to shed light on certain contradictions regarding physical activity and its potential benefits to help prevent burnout through the recovery process. Specifically, we attempt to provide some answers to the following critically important questions emerging from our reading of conflicting studies on the relationship between physical activity and burnout: Is physical activity practiced during work time as beneficial for health as when done during non-work time? Do only sedentary office workers benefit from occupational physical activity?

Before describing these contradictions, we first define burnout as well as the reasons that lead us to focus on the relationship between burnout and physical activity in the context of the COVID-19 pandemic.

The most widely accepted definition of burnout comes from Maslach and colleagues (Maslach & Jackson, 1981; Maslach et al., 2001) describing it as a three-dimensional syndrome encompassing emotional exhaustion (i.e., depletion of physical energy and fatigue), depersonalisation or cynicism (i.e., excessively detached or negative responses to others), and a reduced sense of personal accomplishment or professional efficacy (i.e., feelings of lack of work

DOI: 10.4324/9781003250531-5

productivity and achievement). Unlike psychological fatigue or psychological distress, non-specific states of mental health, burnout characterised an affective strain reaction to chronic work-related stress (Maslach, 1982).

Although mental health has been extensively studied in relation to physical activity (Eime et al., 2013; Raglin & Wilson, 2012), there is still little known regarding the association between physical activity and burnout and its underlying mechanisms (Abós et al., 2021; Carson et al., 2010; Gillet et al., 2022; Jonsdottir et al., 2010). Some studies have shown that leisure-time physical activity reduces the risk for emotional exhaustion (see Naczenski et al., 2017 for a systematic review) but little information is available in the context of the COVID-19 pandemic. Yet, only a month after the World Health Organisation (WHO) declared COVID-19 a pandemic, an international cross-sectional survey reported higher than usual rates of burnout among health care workers, particularly due to increased workloads and work stress (Morgantini et al., 2020). Given the length of the health crisis we have experienced (and continue to suffer), there have been several calls to establish recommendations for interventions known to be effective in mitigating the effects of this chronic work stress (Greenberg et al., 2020; Walton et al., 2020).

At the individual level, physical activity is one of the interventions that has been recommended to prevent burnout during COVID-19. Indeed, physical activity was the most common behaviour adopted by health care workers to counteract pandemic-related stressors (Shechter et al., 2020) despite the fact that many opportunities to be physically active have been suspended over the past two years, including physical education classes, fitness centres, and public parks. The fact remains that several group physical activities and team sports have been banned for several weeks or even several months in some countries, which has certainly harmed commitment and full participation (Bauman et al., 2012), while limiting the social contacts that are essential to individuals' well-being. However, such a decrease in overall physical activity was to be expected (Wolf et al., 2020).

The need to investigate the longitudinal relationship of the effect of the pandemic on physical activity and psychological strain reaction such as burnout was raised as early as the first year of the pandemic. (Jacob et al., 2020, p. 5): « *Researchers should now focus on utilizing longitudinal data when available to infer the direction of the association [between mental health and physical activity]* ». We join our voice to those researchers who call for the need to consider physical activity as a resource to reduce and prevent burnout, especially in a context where a generalised decrease in the level of physical activity is observed (López-Bueno et al., 2020; Sánchez-Sánchez et al., 2020) and work organisation transformation is characterised by a worrying increase in workload (Biron et al., 2022).

Beyond the importance of studying the positive and protective effect of physical activity on burnout, it is necessary to discuss the importance of physical activity in our workplaces in the aftermath of the pandemic. The pandemic brought several drastic changes to workplaces and to our life habits, particularly in terms of the new work organisation methods (i.e., hybrid and remote working). The promotion of physical activity as an intervention that can be promoted in the workplace in various ways appears to be very useful to prevent burnout in a post-pandemic context. This is especially true in the context where the boundaries between the professional and personal sphere have been blurred for many workers, increasing the risk of work overload and the need for effective recovery strategies such as physical activity.

Given that burnout describes a psychological state resulting from an "unhealthy relationship" that individuals develop as they work, it is apparent that burnout is largely the result of the professional sphere, but perhaps this focus on the occupational area is also reductionist and casts a shadow on other spheres of life (family, personal, social, etc.). Thus, it becomes even more interesting to investigate risk and protective factors, such as physical activity, that can primarily be applied in the work environment, but also in other life environments (personal sphere and spillover between work and non-work activities) (Ten Brummelhuis & Bakker, 2012). Recent studies have indeed showed that non-work factors could be antecedents of burnout (Bianchi et al., 2021; de Vries & Bakker, 2022). Since most studies on the subject have focused on emotional exhaustion (i.e., the depletion of the employee's emotional and physical resources), the exploration of recovery and detachment processes appears to be relevant when trying to understand how occupational physical activity is beneficial to prevent burnout. We now address the two questions of interest in this chapter.

Is physical activity practiced during work time as beneficial for health as when practiced during non-work time?

One of the paradoxes in the burnout literature is the one on occupational activity which states that physical activity at work impairs health, whereas off-job (or leisure-time) physical activity promotes it (Coenen et al., 2020; Holtermann et al., 2018). While studies focusing on leisure-time physical activity (LTPA) report many health benefits for individuals, others on occupational physical activity report conflicting results. Indeed, occupational physical activity is not consistently associated with improved health (Clays et al., 2014; Harari et al., 2015). A systematic review (Coenen et al., 2018) regarding the association between occupational physical activity and all-cause mortality indicates that higher level of occupational physical activity in men was associated with more detrimental health consequences, including all-cause mortality, even when adjusting for relevant factors such as leisure-time physical activity.

Studies that have looked at this paradox observed a distinction between different domains of physical activity that is relevant for predicting health problems. For example, de Vries and Bakker (2022) found that off-job physical activity was negatively related to burnout symptoms among employees with low physical job demands whereas it was positively related to burnout symptoms among those with high physical job demands. However, these relationships were no longer significant in the longitudinal analyses.

The recent study by Holtermann et al. (Holtermann et al., 2021) also adds evidence to support the physical activity paradox. Their results show that higher amounts of leisure-time physical activity were associated with reduced risk of major cardiovascular events and all-cause mortality, whereas higher levels of work-related physical activity were associated with increased risk. The results of those studies emphasize the need to clarify the context in which occupational physical activity is harmful to health.

Before we go further, the following section reviews the recovery process related to physical activity. Regular physical activity reduces the risk of prolonged stress reactions such as burnout by fostering psychological detachment from work (Geurts & Sonnentag, 2006; Sonnentag, 2012). Psychological detachment from work is an important recovery experience and is essential to employee well-being. Indeed, feeling "away" from work promotes a reduction in mental demands and consequently recovery (Kaplan, 1995). Employees who feel more detached from work outside working hours are more satisfied with their experience and report less emotional exhaustion and lower levels of work-related stress (Moreno-Jiménez et al., 2009; Siltaloppi et al., 2009; Sonnentag et al., 2010). Psychological detachment is also related to various aspects of job performance, such as task performance and proactive work behaviours (Binnewies et al., 2010). It is important to note that detachment from work during non-work time does not imply a disengaged attitude toward work (Sonnentag, 2012). It might also help employees appraise their workday as less threatening and hindering (Casper & Wehrt, 2021).

Physical activity is considered a recovery enhancing activity, which refers to the process by which an employee recovers during non-work time after exerting effort at work (Demerouti et al., 2009). The effects of recovery are reflected in the employee's psychological and physiological state after recovery (Sonnentag et al., 2017). Thus, the activities and experiences employees have during their non-work time have a significant impact on how they feel and behave at work. Spending recovery time (e.g., evenings or weekends) doing physical activities has been linked to increased well-being during the workday (Sonnentag, 2001). Failure to optimally recover on a daily basis will result in the employee accumulating stress and fatigue overload (Geurts & Sonnentag, 2006), which can ultimately increase the risk of burnout and worsen health problems (Demerouti et al., 2009). An employee who has sufficiently recovered from his or her last shift will be more likely to engage in work in the next shift and perform better than an employee who has not sufficiently recovered (Demerouti et al., 2010).

Theoretically, recovery from job demands, whether physical or cognitive, mainly occurs when the resources that are needed during work are no longer called upon during leisure time (Hobfoll et al., 2018; Meijman & Mulder, 1998). This means that to have a positive effect on recovery, physical activity should be practiced outside of work time. While it is practicing during work time, is it as beneficial for their health as done during non-work time? Is physical activity undertaken at work can still help to facilitate the recovery process by replenish resources?

The fact of taking part in a physical activity does not guarantee recovery. Indeed, if the person does not derive pleasure or recognition from the activity, it will not contribute to recovery (Demerouti et al., 2009). In short, it is not a specific physical activity per se that helps employees recover, but rather it is the motivational and psychological attributes attached to the activities that appear to be more important in determining the recovery potential of the activities. Interestingly, physical activity may also function as a distraction mechanism by allowing individuals to shift their attention away from stressful situations (Bijttebier et al., 2001). It is therefore reasonable to ask whether physical activity, when performed while working (e.g., during active meetings) or at work (e.g., during lunchtime), still promotes the detachment and distraction that are beneficial to employee health.

A central idea of the present chapter is that occupational physical activity (OPA) might be as beneficial as leisure-time physical activity when it is desired and valued by the employee and is associated with positive work-related thoughts, regardless of the physical demands of the job. Physical activity is recognised as a preventive measure for both mental and physical health. However, as we mentioned earlier, recent evidence suggests that the benefits of physical activity mainly depend on the context in which it is undertaken (de Vries & Bakker, 2022; Holtermann et al., 2021).

As some types of physical activities are more mandatory than others (i.e., physically demanding job tasks), it could potentially influence their effect on health and more specifically on burnout symptoms. The mandatory nature of physical activity would be a determining factor. If occupational physical activity is voluntary (i.e., not required for the job tasks), desired, and enjoyable, it might have the same beneficial effects as LTPA. Moreover, one of the reasons why OPA is detrimental to workers' health is that it is often performed with low worker control (Holtermann et al., 2018). Holtermann et al., (2018) argued that

> Limited control over work tasks, speed, schedule, protective clothing, psychosocial stressors and the surrounding environment may contribute to the detrimental effects of OPA. […] In contrast, LTPA can be performed under safer self-regulated conditions. Lack of worker control over OPA can lead to over exhaustion, which may explain the particularly increased risk in such vulnerable groups. (p. 149)

The results of a recent longitudinal study (de Vries & Bakker, 2022) showed that both OPA (assessed by the physical demands of work) and transportation physical activity were positively related to burnout symptoms. Domestic physical activity (e.g., doing housework, gardening), on the other hand, was not associated with burnout. Again, if OPA is voluntary and self-initiated (e.g., workers who suggest a walking meeting to a colleague) it could provide the beneficial effects that are observed during LTPA. This is the first lead regarding the conditions in which the occupational physical activity must be carried out to be beneficial for the health of the employees.

What seem to be beneficial in LTPA are the following aspects: voluntary (Isoard-Gautheur et al., 2019), desired, and enjoyable (Pressman et al., 2009). Moreover, leisure-time physical activities may be most conducive to recovery, as they often include challenging activities performed with significant others and provide excellent opportunities for mastery experiences and social support (Deci & Ryan, 2000). Physical activities performed in leisure time can contribute to the development of social resources. Engaging in physical activity with others can provide social support and help build a more supportive social network. Social support, in turn, can facilitate coping with stressful (work) situations and thus prevent burnout (Ozbay et al., 2007). However, these aspects are not exclusively restricted to LTPA. The social aspect is present in active breaks as well as in active meetings. The study of Michishita and colleagues (Michishita et al., 2016) showed that active breaks in groups strengthen relationships between employees by reducing the stress associated with hierarchical relationships. The authors of this study conclude that active breaks characterised by a 10-minute workout also improve friendliness and perceived support from employers.

Based on these observations, it could be hypothesised that when OPA is chosen and desired by the employees, it would be as beneficial as LTPA. The concept of control seems to be crucial to understand the effect of physical activity on employees' psychological health. Regarding job control, it is also interesting to note the findings from a recent longitudinal study conducted during the first year of the Covid-19 pandemic in Canada. The results of that study (Hervieux et al., 2022) with a representative sample of the Quebec population in terms of age, gender, living environment, education and language, demonstrate that the combination of high demands and high control (job categorised as "active" according to Karasek's Job Demand-Control model; Karasek, 1979), significantly increases the probability of becoming physically active among participants who were physically inactive at the beginning of the study. Authors conclude that job control might be an important resource for organisations interested in promoting physical activity among their employees, particularly in a post-pandemic context where flexible workplaces and working hours seem to be becoming more and more normal.

Another lead to help us understand how and when OPA might be as beneficial for health as LTPA is to look into the process of how daily positive experiences in physical activity may spill over and enrich the work domain. De Vries, Bakker, and Breevaart (2021) collected diary data from 59 employees who engaged in sports activities during their lunch break to investigate this positive spillover process. More precisely, they explored a "sports-to-work enrichment process by examining a contextual resource in the sports domain (i.e., satisfaction with sports performance) in relation to a favourable work outcome (i.e., creativity) through the generation of personal resources (i.e., vigour)" (p. 13). They found that satisfaction with sports performance was positively related to vigour (i.e., momentary cognitive liveliness and emotional energy) immediately after the break, but only when employees reflected positively on their work during the sports lunch break. Results also showed that on days employees felt more cognitive liveliness immediately after the lunch break, they were more creative when back at work. The fact of having performed a physical activity at work during the lunch break did not seem to hinder the recovery process, especially since the work-related ideas were present (but positive) in the workers' minds. This raises the question of the need to be "away from work" to really benefit from the recovery process. Those results highlight the fact that to be beneficial for health, OPA should be enjoyable and associated with positive thoughts about work when practicing physical activities.

Based on those observations, we propose that: *Physical activity, performed during work time, appears to be beneficial when it is voluntary, desirable, and accompanied with positive work reflection. Such physical activities can generate resources useful such as creativity.*

Do only sedentary office workers benefit from occupational physical activity?

While this chapter addresses part of the question about the benefits of occupational physical activity, other questions emerge from these responses. If occupational physical activity is voluntary, desirable, and accompanied with positive work reflection, does it mean that all employees, even those with high physical demands, will benefit from physical activity at work? Does it only benefit sedentary office workers to increase occupational physical activity as their job is mainly characterised by low physical demands? In the next few lines, we delve further into conflicting evidence to provide a more comprehensive understanding of the effect of leisure-time physical activity irrespective of the level of employees' occupational physical activity.

Over the last two decades, we observed a shift from manual labour jobs to highly sedentary service industry and office-based professions (Choi et al., 2010). Many interventions have been introduced in the workplace to reduce the negative health impacts of the modern office environment (Bantoft et al., 2016). Those interventions involve modifying the workplace to increase incidental activity and exercise during the workday (e.g., sit-stand or active workstations). Physical activity during work is increasingly encouraged. Knowing what we know regarding the occupational physical activity paradox, do only sedentary office workers will fully benefit from occupational physical activity?

Some important precision must be made regarding the occupational physical activity paradox. Many of the studies that have observed the paradox have used an entirely male sample which limits external validity (Clays et al., 2014; Harari et al., 2015) or have found differences in the effects which limits generalisations among women (Coenen et al., 2018; Smith et al., 2018). In addition, to measure occupational physical activity, most studies use the proxy physical demands. This categorises jobs with high physical demands as jobs with more occupational physical activity. However, to our knowledge, no studies have looked at sedentary jobs (those with low physical demands) that incorporate physical activity into their work. For example, if one office worker is doing active meetings to reduce is sedentary time at work, does the worker faces the same risks as the worker who have a physically demanding job?

Results of a study (Hervieux et al., 2021) that tested the concept of active meetings among sedentary workers might help to answer that question. This study conducted in Canada tested the concept of active meetings among sedentary office workers. Workplace meetings, whether virtual or face-to-face, are becoming increasingly common (Geimer et al., 2015) and contribute greatly to a sedentary lifestyle that is associated with several health harms (Chau et al., 2013; Katzmarzyk et al., 2009). Researchers investigated whether replacing sitting with a low- to moderate-intensity physical activity (i.e., stationary cycling) was beneficial for psychological health (measured by well-being and stress) and cognitive performance (measure by attention, focus and fatigue) among seven work teams from a large French University (n = 30). During the active meetings, the majority of participants achieved low to moderate physical intensity. Results also showed that physical activity during the active meeting had a positive effect on participants' perception of stress. Participants felt significantly less stressed. Participants also reported an increase in well-being during active meetings, although these results were not statistically significant. In terms of cognitive performance, physical activity did not seem to affect levels of attention, focus, and fatigue, since the researchers did not detect any significant difference between the two conditions. Thus, depending on the intensity chosen, active meetings could become a way to increase one's level of physical activity, and this, without negatively affecting work performance.

Although the physical activity was performed during work time, it seemed to have a restorative effect on the employees, as they reported less stress. Thus, it might be argued that physical activity that replaces a sedentary activity at work (even if performed during work time), plays its role as a recovery activity by reducing perceived stress. However, to determine whether this type of occupational physical activity is beneficial to employee health, it will be essential to conduct longitudinal studies and replicate the intervention on more than one occasion with a larger sample. The results of this study nevertheless provide an interesting avenue supporting the idea that sedentary workers would benefit from regular occupational physical activity.

It is important to highlight that an assumption is made about stress as one of the determinants of burnout. Several studies conducted in various job sectors have shown that work-related stress is associated with an increase in burnout symptoms (Lan et al., 2020; Peasley et al., 2020). Burnout may occur in response to chronic stressors on the job (Maslach et al., 2001). When employees work under conditions of limited resources or time, work overtime, have inadequate rest, or are assigned to meet unrealistic expectations, they are at higher risk of experiencing job stress and a sense of fatigue which in turn contribute to burnout.

In order to promote occupational physical activity in a more effective and balance way while responding to the current main challenges of occupational health and working life, Holtermann et al. (2019) proposed the Goldilocks Principle. Inspired by the Goldilocks fairy tale, it promotes a "just right" approach that can be used, according to these authors, to design productive work to be "just right" with respect to physical activity. "In many jobs, physical activity is, however, either too much/high/frequent or too little/low/infrequent to give positive biomechanical and cardiometabolic stimuli" (Holtermann et al., 2019). In other words, the Goldilocks Principle aims to promote health and physical capacity by designing physical activity during productive work to be "just right." In order to redesign work to better fit the Goldilocks Principle, Holtermann et al. (2019) proposed three types of modification: 1) changing how to perform the tasks, 2) changing time pattern of work tasks, and 3) introducing new tasks.

This theoretical proposal is partly supported by a recent study conducted by de Vries and Bakker (2022) which suggests that "employees' off-job physical activity should be tailored based on employees' level of physical activity at work to lower the risk of job burnout" (p. 12). In the same manner as the Goldilocks Principle, this means adapting LTPA, as opposed to work tasks or work design in the Goldilocks Principle, to OPA. Indeed, employees with physically demanding jobs might benefit more from recovery activities such as social and relaxation activities (Sonnentag et al., 2017). Inversely, employees with low physical job demands would benefit more from leisure-time physical activities as a recovery experience. Although this statement makes sense, it suggests a narrow understanding of a job, where physical effort can vary considerably depending on the job, but also on the tasks performed, which can vary just as much within the same job category. It also suggests that a worker should continually review his or her physical activities based on the level of effort expended at work, which can vary considerably from day to day. So, is it just a matter of the physical demands of the job?

Interestingly, Holtermann et al. (2013) already provide an answer to the question about the benefit of leisure-time physical activity among sedentary workers versus workers with high occupational physical activity. They investigated the preventive effect and survival benefit of leisure-time physical activity on cardiovascular and all-cause mortality in a prospective cohort of 7,411 males and 8,916 females aged 25 to 66 years. The results showed that high leisure-time physical activity consistently reduced the risk for all-cause and cardiovascular mortality in all groups of occupational physical activity (i.e., low, moderate, high, and very high occupational physical activity). In order words, the effect of leisure-time physical activity on cardiovascular and all-cause mortality seems to be independent of the level of occupational physical activity.

Given the conflicting evidence to date and the well-known evidence of physical activity on health, *we suggest that both sedentary employees and employees with high level of physical demands may benefit from leisure-time physical activity.* Future studies should include non-work-specific determinants (e.g., self-efficacy, motivation, off-duty responsibilities, etc.) in addition to measuring physical activity by dimension (occupational, transportation, domestic, or leisure), intensity and duration with objective measures when possible.

Conclusion

In this chapter, we have highlighted paradoxes and contradictions in the literature on physical activity and burnout to better distinguish what we know (and do not know) about this relationship. One paradox in this field is that physical activity appears to be beneficial for health during leisure time, but not when it is carried out as part of one's work. Another contradiction concerns the inconsistent results of intervention research aimed at increasing physical activity during working hours for both office workers and for workers with high physical demands. Considering that work constitutes the main domain for physical activity for a large proportion of the adult population worldwide (Lear et al., 2017; Strain et al., 2020), and given the high prevalence of burnout (Naczenski et al., 2017) and its negative consequences, it is valuable to examine how and when physical activity may act as a resource to prevent burnout. This chapter offers a nuanced look at the literature with a view to improve interventions so that they are better adapted to the psychological and physical demands of workers. This seems particularly relevant following the organisational transformations resulting from the COVID-19 pandemic.

In line with the evidence and suggestions presented in this chapter, it appears that it is valuable for employees to be physically active, in leisure-time as well as during work time, regardless of the nature of their work. The COVID-19 pandemic also reminds the employers on the need to encourage physical activity by designing work to make it a health enhancement opportunity and by creating a work environment culture that promotes a healthy lifestyle (at work and outside work).

References

Abós, Á., Sevil-Serrano, J., Julián-Clemente, J. A., Generelo, E., & García-González, L. (2021). Improving teachers' work-related outcomes through a group-based physical activity intervention during leisure-time. *The Journal of Experimental Education, 89*(2), 306–325.

Bantoft, C., Summers, M. J., Tranent, P. J., Palmer, M. A., Cooley, P. D., & Pedersen, S. J. (2016). Effect of standing or walking at a workstation on cognitive function: A randomized counterbalanced trial. *Human Factors, 58*(1), 140–149.

Bauman, A. E., Reis, R. S., Sallis, J. F., Wells, J. C., Loos, R. J., Martin, B. W., & Group, L. P. A. S. W. (2012). Correlates of physical activity: Why are some people physically active and others not? *The Lancet, 380*(9838), 258–271.

Bianchi, R., Manzano-García, G., & Rolland, J.-P. (2021). Is burnout primarily linked to work-situated factors? A relative weight analytic study. *Frontiers in Psychology, 11*, 3975. Article 623912.

Bijttebier, P., Vertommen, H., & Vander Steene, G. (2001). Assessment of cognitive coping styles: A closer look at situation-response inventories. *Clinical Psychology Review, 21*(1), 85–104.

Binnewies, C., Sonnentag, S., & Mojza, E. J. (2010). Recovery during the weekend and fluctuations in weekly job performance: A week-level study examining intra-individual relationships. *Journal of Occupational and Organizational Psychology, 83*(2), 419–441.

Biron, C., Karanika-Murray, M., Fernet, C., & Ivers, H. (2022). *Job demands and psychological distress during the pandemic: A four-wave population study of Quebec onsite, hybrid, and teleworkers.* Paper presented at the European Academy of Occupational Health Psychology, Bordeaux, France.

Carson, R. L., Baumgartner, J. J., Matthews, R. A., & Tsouloupas, C. N. (2010). Emotional exhaustion, absenteeism, and turnover intentions in childcare teachers: Examining the impact of physical activity behaviors. *Journal of Health Psychology, 15*(6), 905–914.

Casper, A., & Wehrt, W. (2021). The role of recovery for morning cognitive appraisal of work demands: A diary study. *Journal of Occupational Health Psychology, 27*(2), 207.

Chau, J. Y., Grunseit, A. C., Chey, T., Stamatakis, E., Brown, W. J., Matthews, C. E., ... & van der Ploeg, H. P. (2013). Daily sitting time and all-cause mortality: a meta-analysis. *PloS One, 8*(11), e80000.

Choi, B., Schnall, P. L., Yang, H., Dobson, M., Landsbergis, P., Israel, L., ...Baker, D. (2010). Sedentary work, low physical job demand, and obesity in US workers. *American Journal of Industrial Medicine, 53*(11), 1088–1101.

Clays, E., Lidegaard, M., De Bacquer, D., Van Herck, K., De Backer, G., Kittel, F., ... & Holtermann, A. (2014). The combined relationship of occupational and leisure-time physical activity with all-cause mortality among men, accounting for physical fitness. *American Journal of Epidemiology, 179*(5), 559–566.

Coenen, P., Huysmans, M. A., Holtermann, A., Krause, N., Van Mechelen, W., Straker, L. M., & Van Der Beek, A. J. (2018). Do highly physically active workers die early? A systematic review with meta-analysis of data from 193 696 participants. *British Journal of Sports Medicine, 52*(20), 1320–1326.

Coenen, P., Huysmans, M. A., Holtermann, A., Krause, N., Van Mechelen, W., Straker, L. M., & Van Der Beek, A. J. (2020). Towards a better understanding of the 'physical activity paradox': The need for a research agenda. *British Journal of Sports Medicine, 54*(17), 1055–1057.

de Vries, J. D., & Bakker, A. B. (2022). The physical activity paradox: A longitudinal study of the implications for burnout. *International Archives of Occupational and Environmental Health, 95*(5), 965–979.

de Vries, J. D., Bakker, A. B., & Breevaart, K. (2021). Sports lunch breaks, vigor, and creativity at work: A test of the work-home resources model. *International Journal of Sport and Exercise Psychology*, 1–23. 10.1080/1612197X.2021.1993960.

de Vries, J. D., Claessens, B. J., van Hooff, M. L., Geurts, S. A., van den Bossche, S. N., & Kompier, M. A. (2016). Disentangling longitudinal relations between physical activity, work-related fatigue, and task demands. *International Archives of Occupational and Environmental Health, 89*(1), 89–101.

Deci, E. L., & Ryan, R. M. (2000). The "what" and "why" of goal pursuits: Human needs and the self-determination of behavior. *Psychological Inquiry, 11*(4), 227–268.

Demerouti, E., Bakker, A. B., Geurts, S. A., & Taris, T. W. (2009). Daily recovery from work-related effort during non-work time. In Sonnentag, S., Perrewé, P. L., & Ganster, D. C. (Eds.), *Current perspectives on job-stress recovery: Research in occupational stress and well-being* (Vol. 7, pp. 85–123). Bingley, UK: JAI Press.

Demerouti, E., Cropanzano, R., Bakker, A., & Leiter, M. (2010). From thought to action: Employee work engagement and job performance. *Work Engagement: A Handbook of Essential Theory and Research, 65*, 147–163.

Eime, R. M., Young, J. A., Harvey, J. T., Charity, M. J., & Payne, W. R. (2013). A systematic review of the psychological and social benefits of participation in sport for children and adolescents: Informing development of a conceptual model of health through sport. *International Journal of Behavioral Nutrition and Physical Activity, 10*(1), 1–21.

Geimer, J. L., Leach, D. J., DeSimone, J. A., Rogelberg, S. G., & Warr, P. B. (2015). Meetings at work: Perceived effectiveness and recommended improvements. *Journal of Business Research, 68*(9), 2015–2026.

Geurts, S. A., & Sonnentag, S. (2006). Recovery as an explanatory mechanism in the relation between acute stress reactions and chronic health impairment. *Scandinavian Journal of Work, Environment & Health, 32*(6), 482–492.

Gillet, N., Morin, A. J. S., Sandrin, É., & Fernet, C. (2022). Predictors and outcomes of teachers' burnout trajectories over a seven-year period. *Teaching and Teacher Education, 117*, 103781. 10.1016/j.tate.2022.103781

Greenberg, N., Docherty, M., Gnanapragasam, S., & Wessely, S. (2020). Managing mental health challenges faced by healthcare workers during covid-19 pandemic. *BMJ (Clinical research ed.), 368*, m1211. 10.1136/bmj.m1211.

Harari, G., Green, M. S., & Zelber-Sagi, S. (2015). Combined association of occupational and leisure-time physical activity with all-cause and coronary heart disease mortality among a cohort of men followed-up for 22 years. *Occupational and Environmental Medicine, 72*(9), 617–624.

Hervieux, V., Ivers, H., Fernet, C., & Biron, C. (2022). The role of job control and job demands in becoming physically active during the COVID-19 pandemic: A three-wave longitudinal study. *International Journal of Environmental Research and Public Health, 19*(4), 2168.

Hervieux, V., Tremblay, A., & Biron, C. (2021). Active meeting: An intervention to promote health at work without impairing performance. *Applied Ergonomics, 90*. 103269. https://doi.org/10.1016/j.apergo.2020.103269

Hobfoll, S. E., Halbesleben, J., Neveu, J.-P., & Westman, M. (2018). Conservation of resources in the organizational context: The reality of resources and their consequences. *Annual Review of Organizational Psychology and Organizational Behavior, 5*, 103–128.

Holtermann, A., Krause, N., Van Der Beek, A. J., & Straker, L. (2018). *The physical activity paradox: Six reasons why occupational physical activity (OPA) does not confer the cardiovascular health benefits that leisure time physical activity does.* In (Vol. 52, pp. 149–150). BMJ Publishing Group Ltd and British Association of Sport and Exercise Medicine.

Holtermann, A., Marott, J. L., Gyntelberg, F., Søgaard, K., Suadicani, P., Mortensen, O. S., ...Schnohr, P. (2013). Does the benefit on survival from leisure time physical activity depend on physical activity at work? A prospective cohort study. *Plos One, 8*(1), e54548.

Holtermann, A., Mathiassen, S. E., & Straker, L. (2019). Promoting health and physical capacity during productive work: The Goldilocks Principle. *Scandinavian Journal of Work, Environment & Health, 45*(1), 90–97.

Holtermann, A., Schnohr, P., Nordestgaard, B. G., & Marott, J. L. (2021). The physical activity paradox in cardiovascular disease and all-cause mortality: The contemporary Copenhagen General Population Study with 104 046 adults. *European Heart Journal, 42*(15), 1499–1511.

Isoard-Gautheur, S., Ginoux, C., Gerber, M., & Sarrazin, P. (2019). The stress–burnout relationship: Examining the moderating effect of physical activity and intrinsic motivation for off-job physical activity. *Workplace Health & Safety, 67*(7), 350–360.

Jacob, L., Tully, M. A., Barnett, Y., Lopez-Sanchez, G. F., Butler, L., Schuch, F., …Grabovac, I. (2020). The relationship between physical activity and mental health in a sample of the UK public: A cross-sectional study during the implementation of COVID-19 social distancing measures. *Mental Health and Physical Activity, 19*, 100345.

Jonsdottir, I. H., Rödjer, L., Hadzibajramovic, E., Börjesson, M., & Ahlborg Jr, G. (2010). A prospective study of leisure-time physical activity and mental health in Swedish health care workers and social insurance officers. *Preventive Medicine, 51*(5), 373–377.

Kaplan, S. (1995). The restorative benefits of nature: Toward an integrative framework. *Journal of Environmental Psychology, 15*(3), 169–182.

Karasek, R. (1979). Job Demands, Job Decision Latitude, and Mental Strain - Implications for Job Redesign. *Administrative Science Quarterly, 24*(2), 285–308. Retrieved from <Go to ISI>://WOS:A1979GX41100007. 10.2307/2392498

Katzmarzyk, P. T., Church, T. S., Craig, C. L., & Bouchard, C. (2009). Sitting time and mortality from all causes, cardiovascular disease, and cancer. *Medicine Science in Sports Exercise, 41*(5), 998–1005.

Lan, Y.-L., Huang, W.-T., Kao, C.-L., & Wang, H.-J. (2020). The relationship between organizational climate, job stress, workplace burnout, and retention of pharmacists. *Journal of Occupational Health, 62*(1), e12079.

Lear, S. A., Hu, W., Rangarajan, S., Gasevic, D., Leong, D., Iqbal, R., …Kumar, R. (2017). The effect of physical activity on mortality and cardiovascular disease in 130 000 people from 17 high-income, middle-income, and low-income countries: The PURE study. *The Lancet, 390*(10113), 2643–2654.

López-Bueno, R., Calatayud, J., Andersen, L. L., Balsalobre-Fernández, C., Casaña, J., Casajús, J. A., …López-Sánchez, G. F. (2020). Immediate impact of the COVID-19 confinement on physical activity levels in Spanish adults. *Sustainability, 12*(14), 5708.

Maslach, C. (1982). *Burnout: The cost of caring.* New-York: Prentice-Hall.

Maslach, C., & Jackson, S. E. (1981). The measurement of experienced burnout. *Journal of Organizational Behavior, 2*(2), 99–113.

Maslach, C., Schaufeli, W. B., & Leiter, M. P. (2001). Job burnout. *Annual Review of Psychology, 52*(1), 397–422.

Mead, G. E., Morley, W., Campbell, P., Greig, C. A., McMurdo, M., & Lawlor, D. A. (2010). Exercise for depression. *Cochrane Database of Systematic Reviews, 2010*(1), [CD004366]. https://doi.org/10.1002/14651858.CD004366.pub4

Meijman, T. F., & Mulder, G. (1998). Psychological aspects of workload. In P. J. D. Drenth, H. Thierry, & C. J. D. Wolff (Eds.). *Handbook of work and organizational: Work psychology* (2nd ed., Vol. 2, pp. 5–33). Hove: Taylor & Francis: Psychology Press/Erlbaum (UK).

Michishita, R., Jiang, Y., Ariyoshi, D., Yoshida, M., Moriyama, H., & Yamato, H. (2016). The practice of active rest by workplace units improves personal relationships, mental health, and physical activity among workers. *Journal of Occupational Health, 59*(2), 122–130.

Moreno-Jiménez, B., Mayo, M., Sanz-Vergel, A. I., Geurts, S., Rodríguez-Muñoz, A., & Garrosa, E. (2009). Effects of work–family conflict on employees' well-being: The moderating role of recovery strategies. *Journal of Occupational Health Psychology*, *14*(4), 427.

Morgantini, L. A., Naha, U., Wang, H., Francavilla, S., Acar, Ö., Flores, J. M., ... & Eklund, M. (2020). Factors contributing to healthcare professional burnout during the COVID-19 pandemic: A rapid turnaround global survey. *Plos One*, *15*(9), e0238217.

Naczenski, L. M., de Vries, J. D., van Hooff, M. L., & Kompier, M. A. (2017). Systematic review of the association between physical activity and burnout. *Journal of Occupational Health*, *59*(6), 477–494.

Ozbay, F., Johnson, D. C., Dimoulas, E., Morgan III, C., Charney, D., & Southwick, S. (2007). Social support and resilience to stress: From neurobiology to clinical practice. *Psychiatry (Edgmont)*, *4*(5), 35.

Peasley, M. C., Hochstein, B., Britton, B. P., Srivastava, R. V., & Stewart, G. T. (2020). Can't leave it at home? The effects of personal stress on burnout and salesperson performance. *Journal of Business Research*, *117*, 58–70.

Piercy, K. L., Troiano, R. P., Ballard, R. M., Carlson, S. A., Fulton, J. E., Galuska, D. A., ... & Olson, R. D. (2018). The physical activity guidelines for Americans. *Journal of the American Medical Association*, *320*(19), 2020–2028.

Pressman, S. D., Matthews, K. A., Cohen, S., Martire, L. M., Scheier, M., Baum, A., & Schulz, R. (2009). Association of enjoyable leisure activities with psychological and physical well-being. *Psychosomatic Medicine*, *71*(7), 725.

Raglin, J. S., & Wilson, G. S. (2012). Exercise and its Effects on Mental Heatlh. In C. Bouchard, S. N. Blair, & W. Haskell (Eds.). *Physical Activity and Health* (2nd ed.). Human Kinetics.

Sánchez-Sánchez, E., Ramírez-Vargas, G., Avellaneda-López, Y., Orellana-Pecino, J. I., García-Marín, E., & Díaz-Jimenez, J. (2020). Eating habits and physical activity of the Spanish population during the COVID-19 pandemic period. *Nutrients*, *12*(9), 2826.

Shechter, A., Diaz, F., Moise, N., Anstey, D. E., Ye, S., Agarwal, S., ... & Chang, B. (2020). Psychological distress, coping behaviors, and preferences for support among New York healthcare workers during the COVID-19 pandemic. *General Hospital Psychiatry*, *66*, 1–8.

Siltaloppi, M., Kinnunen, U., & Feldt, T. (2009). Recovery experiences as moderators between psychosocial work characteristics and occupational well-being. *Work & Stress*, *23*(4), 330–348.

Smith, P., Ma, H., Glazier, R. H., Gilbert-Ouimet, M., & Mustard, C. (2018). The relationship between occupational standing and sitting and incident heart disease over a 12-year period in Ontario, Canada. *American Journal of Epidemiology*, *187*(1), 27–33.

Sonnentag, S. (2001). Work, recovery activities, and individual well-being: A diary study. *Journal of Occupational Health Psychology*, *6*(3), 196–210.

Sonnentag, S. (2012). Psychological detachment from work during leisure time: The benefits of mentally disengaging from work. *Current Directions in Psychological Science*, *21*(2), 114–118.

Sonnentag, S., Kuttler, I., & Fritz, C. (2010). Job stressors, emotional exhaustion, and need for recovery: A multi-source study on the benefits of psychological detachment. *Journal of Vocational Behavior*, *76*(3), 355–365.

Sonnentag, S., Venz, L., & Casper, A. (2017). Advances in recovery research: What have we learned? What should be done next? *Journal of Occupational Health Psychology*, *22*(3), 365.

Strain, T., Wijndaele, K., Garcia, L., Cowan, M., Guthold, R., Brage, S., & Bull, F. C. (2020). Levels of domain-specific physical activity at work, in the household, for travel and for leisure among 327 789 adults from 104 countries. *British Journal of Sports Medicine*, *54*(24), 1488–1497.

Ten Brummelhuis, L. L., & Bakker, A. B. (2012). A resource perspective on the work–home interface: The work–home resources model. *American Psychologist*, *67*(7), 545.

Walton, M., Murray, E., & Christian, M. D. (2020). Mental health care for medical staff and affiliated healthcare workers during the COVID-19 pandemic. *European Heart Journal: Acute Cardiovascular Care*, *9*(3), 241–247.

Wolf, S., Zeibig, J., Seiffer, B., Welkerling, J., Brokmeier, L., Atrott, B., Ehring, T. , Schuch, F. B. (2020). Can physical activity protect against depression and anxiety during the COVID-19 pandemic? A rapid systematic review. Res. Sq. 2020. Preprint PPR218366.

5 Teacher (Dis)connectedness and burnout during COVID-19

Laura Sokal, Lesley Eblie Trudel, and Jeff Babb
University of Winnipeg in Canada

Introduction to the problem

Copious research about teacher burnout has substantiated that supportive re-lationships have the capacity to ameliorate the effects of demanding teaching contexts (Loeb et al., 2005). Building on this research, we used a mixed methods research design to generate a robust understanding of the relationships between teacher burnout and possible protective effects of collegial relationships during a pandemic. We were especially interested in the effects of the pandemic on workplace factors such as connectedness and organisational commitment, which have been shown to affect teacher attrition (Jarzabkowski, 2003). Teacher at-trition was a concern pre-COVID-19 (Bakker & Demerouti, 2014), and fear of a mass exodus of teachers from the profession has been raised as a possible outcome of the pandemic (Holmes et al., 2020).

Models of teacher burnout

We used two well-supported models of teacher burnout as the theoretical foundation of this study. First, the Job Demands-Resources (JD-R) model was introduced to capture the changing dynamics within the context of a workplace (Bakker & Demerouti, 2007). The model considers the demands of the work role, including physical, emotional, psychological, social, and organisational aspects of the work that require sustained effort and skill. To balance these demands, resources in the form of physical, emotional, psychological, social, and organisational aspects of the workplace are used by employees to support the achievement of work goals. Such resources can include both those provided by the employer (for example, mentoring, or equipment) as well as those brought to the employment situation by employees (e.g., skills and efficacy) (Taris et al., 2017). The relationship between resources and demands is not static, and when an employee makes a subjective appraisal that there are insufficient resources to meet job demands, that person experiences stress (Bakker & Demerouti, 2007). Stress, in turn, can lead to burnout over time (Harmsen et al., 2018).

Maslach and her colleagues (1981, 1996) have generated over 50 years of re-search supporting their three-component model of burnout across occupations,

DOI: 10.4324/9781003250531-6

cultures, and time; hence this model was chosen as the second foundational theory in the current study. The first component of burnout in this model is exhaustion. Exhaustion captures the employee's perceptions of emotional and physical fatigue that are not adequately addressed during the "reset" time between work shifts. This component is understood to be the first stage in the progression toward burnout (Alarcon, 2011). The second component is termed "depersonalization" (Maslach & Jackson, 1981) and represents a withdrawal away from emotional commitment to relationships at work. For teachers, this may take the form of distancing themselves from students or developing apathy toward them. The third component is a loss of accomplishment—that is, the subjective appraisal that the employee is no longer meeting their work goals and roles.

Importance of collegiality to educators

One of the potential resources available to teachers to balance out their job demands is the relationship with other adults in their schools. By definition, collegiality includes social/emotional and professional aspects of workplace interactions (Jarzabkowski, 2003). The terms "collegiality" and "collaboration" have been used interchangeably in the literature, however Kelchtermans (2006) provided a useful differentiation between them: Collaboration describes a set of co-operative actions, whereas collegiality refers to the "quality of the relationships among staff members in a school" (p. 221) exemplified by "meaningful interactions rather than mere behaviours" (p. 222). Turner and Morelli (2017) highlighted the importance of strong relationships between teachers and their colleagues and administrators.

Over the past decade, the term collective efficacy has gained momentum in the research community (Donohoo, 2017). This construct builds on teachers' beliefs that they can influence student learning by working together to achieve successful outcomes. Collective efficacy of a school staff allows them to undertake challenging tasks, be more accepting of change, and be more likely to attempt novel instructional approaches. Canadian teachers have identified collegiality as being demonstrated through encouragement for and by peers, support, sharing, trust, mutual respect, and caring (Retallick & Butt, 2004). Collegiality is a component of successful organisations and is based on teamwork that includes regular interactions that are supportive of organisational goals (Leonard & Leonard, 2003). Of particular interest in the current study are pre-pandemic findings that collegiality serves as a protective factor against stress and burnout (Numeroff, 2005), as well as against attrition (Jarzabkowski, 2003).

Seminal, pre-COVID-19 work by Hargreaves and Fullan (1992) revealed a tension between the need for school-based collaboration and teachers' pre-service socialisation into a culture of teaching framed as individualised and isolated. They agreed that the ability to collaborate effectively was one of the key requisites of learning organisations. However, Hargreaves and Fullan (1992) found that provision of time for teachers to plan and work together did not always lead to greater collegiality, but occasionally led to conflict. Löfgren and Karlsson (2016) suggested that educational researchers have uncritically accepted a false dichotomy between isolation as "bad" and collaboration as "good." Nias (1999) concurred and suggested that a balance of collaboration and autonomy can support a collegial organisational culture.

Inter-dependence with colleagues can result in positive understandings of the ethics of care for colleagues, but it can also lead to over-extended teachers feeling that caring for their colleagues is yet another job demand (Nias, 1999), contributing further to their stress (Farber, 1999). Moreover, the more in-depth the interactions and relationships between teachers, the more likely they will reveal differences of opinion and potentially conflict (Erickson et al., 2005). If these conflicts are navigated in healthy ways, then community bonds can be enhanced (Achinstein, 2002), whereas unhealthy, unaddressed, or unresolved conflict can diminish collegiality (Kelchtermans, 2006). This range of possibilities based on teacher interactions is reflected in recent research by Chen (2020) showing that interactions with colleagues resulted in a range of positive (e.g., warmth, caring, happiness and satisfaction) and intense negative emotions result from peer competition. Thus, at their best, positive collegial relationships among teachers are most frequently cited as the reasons for teachers staying within the profession (Loeb et al., 2005), whereas lack of collegial support has been associated with teacher depression and anxiety (Mahan et al., 2010) and lack of teacher accomplishment (Halbesleben, 2006).

Within the context of the school setting, the importance of administrators to the development of teacher collegiality has been highlighted by several researchers. The vital role of administrators in fostering collegiality within their schools cannot be over stated (Chance & Segura, 2009). A key factor is that teachers in schools have sufficient opportunities to collaborate in ways that result in their understanding the value of interacting with their colleagues (Shah, 2012). Brunderman (2006) found that three types of administrator actions had the capacity to foster collegiality: (1) fostering commitment to organisational goals; (2) providing support for individual teachers; and (3) having high expectations. These were accomplished by (1) setting and sharing a clear vision for the organisation; (2) modelling desirable behaviours; and (3) providing challenging and engaging stimulation to teachers. Moreover, teacher collaboration and school culture are related bi-directionally: Giddens (1984) showed that the while organisational culture determines the frequency and nature of interactions among staff, the quality of those interactions and resulting collegiality influences organisational culture.

Shah (2012) found that collegial relationships between teachers were an important factor to their commitment to their school organisations, resulting in reform and renewal in organisations (Geijsel et al., 2003). Organisational commitment is a multidimensional concept that explains an individual's relationship with an organisation and may influence the decision to remain or depart from their role (Meyer & Allen, 1991). Further, it refers to one's level of belonging and desire to work hard toward an organisation's goals (Ketchand & Strawser, 2001). Moreover, organisational commitment has been shown to serve as a protective factor against teacher attrition (Chughtai & Zafar, 2006).

Challenges of COVID-19

Although evidence of collegial in-school relationships as a protective factor against teacher stress and eventual burnout has generally been well-documented, conditions specific to safety protocols required due to COVID-19 have created challenges to these relationships. While safety regulations were enacted differently across geographic locations during the pandemic, the specific conditions in the Manitoba schools that participated in the current study were certainly not unique. These included the requirement for everyone in schools to keep a distance of two meters from others while wearing masks at all times. Some teachers in Manitoba were concurrently teaching students face-to-face and online during the pandemic. Teachers experienced significantly altered teaching assignments; some teachers who would typically teach indoors (e.g., physical education within a gymnasium) were directed to teach outside for the entire school year. Music teachers could no longer engage students in playing wind instruments or singing. Staff rooms were closed or limited in capacity, as teachers who were eating lunch or having a drink on a break needed to take off their masks, so they often chose to eat alone in their classrooms or cars. In some schools, staff rooms remained opened for restricted numbers of teachers in rotation. In terms of formal and informal interactions, whole-staff meetings were conducted online. Moreover, teachers were neither team teaching (due to decreased maximum occupancy in each room) nor chatting informally in the hallways, as entrance and exit schedules and flow of traffic in hallways were staggered and regimented.

Links between the COVID-19 context, disconnection, and burnout

Collectively, the conditions required for safety during the pandemic have challenged teachers' opportunities for in-person interactions with other adults in their schools. We were interested in the effects over time of such conditions on teachers' burnout and stress, as well as their perceptions of relational support, connectedness, and organisational commitment.

Research questions

From the second to third wave of the COVID-19 pandemic,

1 Did teachers demonstrate higher levels of burnout?
2 Did teachers perceive consistent support from their relationships with administrators and colleagues?
3 Were teachers' perceptions of connectedness within their schools consistent?
4 What were the relationships between teachers' burnout, perceptions of support from in-school relationships, and their general organisational commitment and connectedness in their schools?
5 What factors did teachers believe affected their levels of connectedness, organisational commitment, and perception of support by others?

Design

As part of a larger research project, the data for this portion of the study were generated in three ways. First, division-wide surveys were completed in November 2020 and in April 2021. Teachers within a school division were invited through email invitations from their divisional administration and from their teachers' association to click on a link to access the consent form and survey. Second, following the November 2020 survey, a subgroup of 21 teachers was recruited by invitation, and this panel was interviewed individually by phone every two weeks from November 2020 to June 2021. Third, focus groups of teachers were conducted in Fall 2020 and Spring 2021 during the same school year. The focus group teachers were recruited by email invitations through their divisional administration and their teachers' association's email lists asking them to contact the researchers if they wished to take part in one of four focus groups offered at each time point. Participants for the telephone interviews and focus groups were purposely selected from the teachers who volunteered, in order to garner input from teachers with a broad range of teaching roles in schools (e.g., years of experience, gender, grades taught, subject areas).

Participants

All participants were teachers from one school division in Winnipeg, Manitoba, Canada. See Table 5.1 for demographic information about the teachers who responded to the survey at each time point. Demographic information about the teachers who were interviewed bi-weekly and those in the focus groups is presented in Tables 5.2 and 5.3.

Context

The first survey was conducted in November 2020 during the second wave of COVID-19, at which time the study participants had been teaching within pandemic conditions since March 2020. Except for a short period of online learning in spring 2020, the teachers had been teaching from their school-based classrooms in face-to-face or blended formats since the current school year began in September 2020. The school division in our study had the highest COVID-19 transmission rate among the city's school divisions and was located in a province that had the highest positive COVID-19 testing rates in Canada during the second and third waves of the pandemic, which occurred during the data collection periods for the current study. There were a number of additional contextual challenges that may have affected teachers in this division, including an expired collective agreement; the teachers being accidently provided with expired masks in the fall of 2020; a provincial review of its education system released in March 2021, which outlined a plan for sweeping changes including dissolving the school divisions; and finally, teachers in the study province were not prioritised for vaccination.

Table 5.1 Demographic information about the survey participants

Variable		Fall 2020 n	Spring 2020 n
Gender	Male	32	31
	Female	113	93
	Other	0	1
	Did not answer	2	5
Age	25 or younger	3	4
	26–30	28	22
	31–40	59	49
	41–50	39	35
	Over 50	16	19
	Did not answer	2	1
Teaching	1 year or less	6	6
Experience	2–5 years	26	29
	6–10 years	43	25
	11–15 years	35	29
	Over 15 years	37	41
Education	Less than Bachelor's	2	1
	Bachelor's degree	88	81
	Some grad work	32	24
	Masters	24	24
	Ph.D.	1	0
Grade(s)	Kindergarten	14	20
Taught	Grades 1–3	47	36
	Grades 4–6	54	45
	Grades 7–9	60	52
	Grades 10–12	52	46
Position	Permanent	133	112
Type	Term	10	15
	Substitute	4	2

Instruments

Survey

The survey was constructed of valid and reliable scales that have been used in the past to study teachers.

RESILIENCE AND BURNOUT

Teacher stress was measured using the Maslach Burnout Inventory for Educators (Maslach & Jackson, 1981). This 22-item instrument measures the characteristics of burnout, including exhaustion, depersonalisation, and personal accomplishment (Maslach et al., 1996). It uses a 7-point Likert scale indicating the frequency with which educators agree with the statements: 0 (never); 1 (a few times since the pandemic began); 2 (once a month or less);

Table 5.2 Demographic Information about the Panel of Bi-weekly Individual Interview Participants

Codename	Pronoun	Teaching Experience	Education	Position
Purple	She	12 years	Bachelor	High school
Goldfish	She	20 years	Master	Middle school
Orange	She	4 years	Bachelor	Middle school
Green	She	7 years	Post Baccalaureate	High school
Red	She	5 years	Some grad school	Elementary
Tracy	She	10 years	Bachelor	Elementary
Black	She	10 years	Bachelor	Middle and high school
Doc	She	13 years	Bachelor	High school
Watermelon	She	15 years	Bachelor	Elementary
Tree	She	19 years	Post Baccalaureate	Elementary
Jeter	They	2 years	Bachelor	Elementary physical education
Peyton	She	18 years	Post Baccalaureate	Elementary
Sally	She	17 years	Master	High school
Pink	She	19 years	Post Baccalaureate	High school
Blue	She	9 years	Post Baccalaureate	Elementary
Twila	She	37 years	Master	Elementary
Alex	She	11 years	Bachelor	Elementary and middle school
Katherine	She	21 years	Post Baccalaureate	Middle school
Bond	He	12 years	Master	High school
Itch	He	12 years	Master	High school
Loki	She	12 years	Post Baccalaureate	High school

3 (a few times a month); 4 (once a week); 5 (a few times a week) 6 (every day). Three examples of statements are: "I feel emotionally drained from work" (exhaustion); "I don't really care what happens to some students" (depersonalisation); and "I have accomplished many worthwhile things in this job" (accomplishment). Cronbach alpha values were calculated using the current data set for the sub-scales of exhaustion ($\alpha = .90$), cynicism ($\alpha = .75$), and accomplishment ($\alpha = .76$), and indicated good to excellent reliability.

ORGANISATIONAL COMMITMENT

This construct was measured using a three-item scale by Collie et al. (2016). Each question was measured on a 6-point Likert scale indicating low commitment (1-2), medium commitment (3-4) or high commitment (5-6). The three questions were: (1) "If you could go back to your university days and start over again, would you become a teacher or not?" (2) "How long do you plan to remain in the position of a school teacher?" (3) "How long do you plan to remain teaching at your current school?" A Cronbach alpha value was calculated using the current data set for this measure ($\alpha = .62$) and indicated adequate reliability.

Table 5.3 Demographic Information about the Focus Group Participants

Codename	Level	Position
Michelle	Elementary school	Learning Support Teacher
Clint	High school	Classroom Teacher
Linda	Middle school	Classroom Teacher
Anna	High school	Learning Support Teacher
Cora	High school	Music Teacher
Katrina	Elementary school	French Immersion Classroom Teacher
Atticus	Elementary school	Music Teacher
Lucy	Middle school	French Immersion Classroom Teacher
Julia	High school	Alternative Education Teacher
Harper	Early years	Classroom Teacher
Derek	Middle school	Classroom Teacher
Chris	Early years	Learning Support Teacher
Delilah	Middle school	French Immersion Classroom Teacher
Troy	High school	Band Teacher
Tatiana	Middle school	French Immersion Classroom Teacher
Darren	Early years	Physical Education Teacher
Brittany	Early years	French Immersion Classroom Teacher
Kiera	Kindergarten	Classroom Teacher
Tannis	Elementary	Classroom Teacher
Pearl	Early years	Physical Education/Classroom Teacher

TEACHER CONNECTEDNESS

The connectedness subscale of the Teacher Subjective Well-being Questionnaire (Renshaw, 2020) was used. This scale includes 4 items, and teachers responded using a 4-point Likert scale, including 1 (almost never), 2 (sometimes), 3 (often), 4 (almost always) in terms of feeling this way in the last month. An example item is "I feel I belong in this school." A Cronbach alpha value was calculated using the current data set for connectedness ($\alpha = .91$), which indicated excellent reliability. We chose this scale following the definition of collegiality offered by Kelchtermans (2006) as it relates to relationship qualities. All of the items of this scale relate to feelings of collegiality within the school, including teachers' perceptions that they belong, are cared for, are respected, and can be their authentic selves.

SCHOOL LEADERSHIP AND DIVISIONAL LEADERSHIP

The School and Divisional Leadership scale (Crosby, 2015) was used to determine teachers' perceptions of educational leadership in their context. Two subscales addressed this construct: 13 items measured school leadership, and 10 items measured divisional leadership. All items were scored in a 6-point Likert scale from 1 (strongly disagree) to 6 (strongly agree). Example items from the school leadership sub-scale included "The principal in this school is fair and open to teachers" and "Teachers feel comfortable raising issues and concerns that are important to them with the school administration."

Likewise, items from the divisional leadership sub-scale included "District leaders consistently support teachers" and "District office staff understand the problems schools are facing." Cronbach alpha values were calculated using the current data set for school leadership ($\alpha = .96$) and divisional leadership ($\alpha = .96$), and indicated excellent reliability for both sub-scales.

PERCEIVED SUPPORTS

Teachers were given the opportunity to rate job resources that supported them during the pandemic. Perceived support was measured on a Likert scale ranging from 1 (not at all) to 6 (a great deal). Of particular interest in the current study was the support of administrators and colleagues. This variable was measured with the following questions: "How much does this factor contribute to the support of your teaching during the COVID-19 pandemic? (1) support from administrators; (2) support from colleagues."

Interviews

Each interview began with a research assistant (RA) asking the participant how things had been in the previous two weeks. The RA probed to determine both positive and negative aspects of the teachers' experiences. Each week concluded with an open-ended question asking if there was anything else the teacher wanted to share. Between these two questions, there was a focus question each week. These questions were adjusted as pandemic conditions changed (Cresswell & Cresswell, 2018), in order to capture teachers' thinking about specific aspects. Data were coded into ten previously selected themes by two members of the research team each week, with each member coding the data from the same groups of teachers from week to week. These ten themes had been generated from open-ended questions in a larger data set in previous survey research on teacher stress during the COVID-19 pandemic using grounded theory substantive coding (Glaser, 1998). The three categories relevant to the current research included Communication, Administration, and Community, and therefore we considered data coded into these three themes in the current analysis. Comments coded into these three categories were re-analysed for emergent themes using theoretical coding (Strauss & Corbin, 1994). Over the course of the study, the researchers met regularly to discuss emerging themes, and to support the RAs in gathering rich and robust data from the participants. All interview data are reported using pseudonyms selected by the participants.

Focus groups

The focus groups took place over ZOOM during fall 2020 and spring 2021. There were 20 participants in the fall focus groups, and 11 of those returned for the spring focus groups. Focus groups included between two and six teachers and were held over a one-hour period in each case. The data were coded by the researchers using the same initial coding themes as were used with the interview data. All focus group data are reported using pseudonyms selected by the researchers.

Results

Quantitative findings

To address our first three research questions, we conducted an ANOVA with time of survey as the independent variable. Please see Table 5.4.

This ANOVA provided data from which to answer the first three research questions: From wave two to wave 3 of the Covid-19 pandemic, (1) Did teachers demonstrate higher levels of burnout? No. There were neither significant increases in exhaustion or depersonalisation, nor significant decreases in accomplishment over the six months from the second to the third wave of COVID-19. (2) Did teachers perceive consistent support from their relationships with administrators and colleagues? Yes. The analysis did not detect changes in perceived levels of support from administrators and colleagues between November 2020 and April 2021. (3) Were teachers' sense of connectedness within their school communities consistent over time? No. Teachers perceived lower levels of connectedness despite perceptions of consistent support from administrators (both onsite and divisional), colleagues, and parents. It is noteworthy that although the observed means on many scales changed from November 2020 to April 2021, only one variable demonstrated significant change: teachers' sense of connectedness decreased significantly (p-value = 0.022) from November to April.

To answer the fourth research question, we conducted correlational analysis on the variables of interest, found in Table 5.5.

The analysis revealed that, as expected based on prior research, all three components of burnout were correlated with one another. Furthermore, support from peers was significantly correlated with teachers' levels of depersonalisation and accomplishment (but not exhaustion). Connectedness was correlated with all components of burnout, support from administrators and colleagues, and with teachers' perceptions of their school and divisional leadership as well as teachers' levels of organisational commitment.

Qualitative findings

Our final research question asked about the factors teachers believed to have affected their levels of connectedness and perceptions of support by others. To answer this question, we turned to the interview and focus groups data and considered the comments of teachers that had been coded under the themes of

Table 5.4 ANOVA Comparing the Two Survey Periods

Variable	Survey Period	N	Mean	Difference in Means	SD	F	Significance probability	η^2
Exhaustion	Fall 2020	147	3.55		1.34	0.643	0.423	
	Spring 2021	130	3.68	−0.1276	1.30			
	Total	277	3.61		1.32			
Depersonalisation	Fall 2020	147	1.24		1.18	2.61	0.107	
	Spring 2021	130	1.48	−0.2358	1.25			
	Total	277	1.35		1.22			
Accomplishment	Fall 2020	147	4.25		0.99	1.296	0.256	
	Spring 2021	130	4.12	0.1337	0.96			
	Total	277	4.19		0.98			
Connectedness	Fall 2020	147	3.28		0.82	5.303	0.022	0.022
	Spring 2021	129	3.06	0.2244	0.79			
	Total	276	3.18		0.81			
School Leadership Quality	Fall 2020	147	4.30		1.30	0.585	0.445	
	Spring 2021	130	4.42	−0.1194	1.29			
	Total	277	4.35		1.30			
Divisional Leadership Quality	Fall 2020	144	3.43		1.29	0.513	0.474	
	Spring 2021	129	3.53	−0.1068	1.16			
	Total	273	3.48		1.23			

(Continued)

Table 5.4 (Continued)

Variable	Survey Period	N	Mean	Difference in Means	SD	F	Significance probability	η^2
Organisational Commitment	Fall 2020	147	2.46	0.09848	0.50	2.152	0.144	
	Spring 2021	130	2.37		0.53			
	Total	277	2.42		0.51			
Support from Administrator	Fall 2020	146	4.40	−0.20659	1.62	1.152	0.284	
	Spring 2021	130	4.60		1.51			
	Total	276	4.49		1.57			
Support from Colleagues	Fall 2020	145	4.85	0.07004	1.12	0.236	0.627	
	Spring 2021	130	4.78		1.31			
	Total	275	4.81		1.21			

Table 5.5 Pearson Correlations

		2	3	4	5	6	7	8	9
1. Exhaustion	Correlation	.556**	-.302**	-.339**	-.313**	-.380**	-.341**	-.315**	-0.017
	Sig. (2-tailed)	0	0	0	0	0	0	0	0.776
	N	277	277	277	273	277	276	276	275
2. Depersonalisation	Correlation		-.336**	-.366**	-.318**	-.282**	-.378**	-.258**	-.172**
	Sig. (2-tailed)		0	0	0	0	0	0	0.004
	N		277	277	273	277	276	276	275
3. Accomplishment	Correlation			.256**	.237**	.233**	.361**	.172**	.145*
	Sig. (2-tailed)			0	0	0	0	0.004	0.016
	N			277	273	277	276	276	275
4. School Leadership Quality	Correlation				.552**	.307**	.593**	.766**	.282**
	Sig. (2-tailed)				0	0	0	0	0
	N				273	277	276	276	275
5. Divisional Leadership	Correlation					.240**	.346**	.387**	0.065
	Sig. (2-tailed)					0	0	0	0.283
	N					273	272	272	271
6. Organisational Commitment	Correlation						.327**	.302**	0.076
	Sig. (2-tailed)						0	0	0.212
	N						276	272	275
7. Connectedness	Correlation							.500**	.363**
	Sig. (2-tailed)							0	0
	N							275	274

(Continued)

Table 5.5 (Continued)

	2	3	4	5	6	7	8	9
8. Support from Administrators	Correlation							.275**
	Sig. (2-tailed)							0
	N							275
9. Support from Peers	Correlation							
	Sig. (2-tailed)							
	N							

Notes

** Correlation is significant at the 0.01 level (2-tailed).

* Correlation is significant at the 0.05 level (2-tailed).

"communication," "administration," "community," over the course of six months of bi-weekly interviews as well as eight teacher focus groups. We first used open coding, as it is flexible to various research contexts, then axial coding, resulting in three emergent themes (Cresswell & Cresswell, 2018; Merrium & Tisdell, 2016): the importance of authentic interactions with colleagues, division between teachers based on perceptions of safety and emotional responses to COVID-19, and demoralisation of teachers as a response to government.

The importance of authentic interactions

Many teachers mourned the loss of their collegial school community in terms of both formal and informal interactions with colleagues. For example, Jeter said, "That has been the biggest difference—not getting that communal connection with parents and teachers has been very, very challenging." Katrina concurred: "I prefer being with colleagues. That's one thing that I missed a lot, is that collaboration and that feeling that you're [not] alone in your space." Doe similarly observed, "This year has been way less personal connection than any other year."

Fear of COVID transmission and the additional workload it precipitated were reasons teachers gave for decreased interactions with colleagues.

> I find there are very few staff in the staff room. You have to really go out of your way to engage with the staff, because I find a lot of teachers are just on their own little islands right now.

Purple attributed the lack of peer connection to the busy-ness of teaching during the pandemic. "I'm kind of one of those teachers that I'm kind of so busy, I'm a little bit socially isolated. I find I'm so busy that I don't get a lot of time to socialize."

In addition to COVID-19 challenges with physically meeting with colleagues and the extra time needed for job demands, Blue noted the effects of colleagues' morale on her own emotions, specifically the absence of her close colleague: "And today had to be a day where she couldn't be at work. That scares me, as we have amazing, awesome teachers who are starting to feel the burn, and the burn is coming from the extra workload." Watermelon was able to reset and find new connections with colleagues when their closer colleagues were away: "I have found a different group of people to eat with, so that has been nice to have that collegial connection, because my good friend went on leave for the month, so it has been lonely." Others found that the crisis of the pandemic served to bring teachers closer together. Doe observed, "I still find we rely on each other and maybe even more so, because we are all in this craziness together."

Several participants commented on the need for administrative support to foster opportunities for both collaboration and collegiality. Delilah observed,

I think if I'd have to say the biggest supports we have are what we call Professional Learning Communities at our school. So, what we do, we come together, and we're a group of like 6 teachers plus an administrator. We collaborate together in terms of being able to bring solutions to the issues different teachers are having because of COVID. That's been extremely helpful for me in managing my own mental health, because it gives me a sounding board.

Harper observed the importance of leaders who participated as part of the school-based team.

The admin. at my school have demonstrated that they really are part of the team. They're leading the team, but they've stepped up tremendously to the support our team at my school. They are covering classes every single day. So, they're leading by example for sure.

Others found that collegial interactions with peers were either non-existent or superficial. For example, while Harper appreciated the support of her administrator, she also observed a lack of opportunities for colleagues to engage together in authentic ways.

We haven't had almost any full staff opportunities to learn to empathise with one-another. I think that would be really nice for us to kind of work together, ask some of the more challenging questions, celebrate some of the successes happening, and I think that would be really good for our staff.

Bond found staff meetings frustrating:

I would say our administration are very poor at communicating, so people get into this weird position where they ask passive aggressive questions, because it is almost the only way to address issues sometimes. But the culture is just not great. You know what I have noticed? I think [principals are challenged with] just maintaining any sense of place: This is a school—we are a unit—we are a staff, [but] I think people have really drifted apart, as to be expected.

Tannis shared Bond's frustrations with not feeling heard.

I find we have meetings where we talk with admin. [where] they ask for input, and then we share our thoughts and concerns with them and then it's like 'ok, we are doing it anyways.' That leads to feelings of not being heard or not having that voice and [not] feeling valued as a professional. If you are not going to listen to feedback, don't ask the question.

Lucy also desired more authentic communication with colleagues.

> I think our staff would benefit from a staff-wide conversation about the hard questions, like, 'What feels hard, what gives you energy, what takes it away, what feels like a waste of time?' Those kind of questions I think need to be discussed as a whole staff. It can be hard to form a goal long-term, but that's part of why I like this job, is to have a learning plan and to get better, and I think it would be helpful to have moments as a whole group to really confer and discuss what feels hard right now.

Division between teachers

Second, we notice that there was divisiveness within the teachers within various schools based on both safety practices and emotions related to COVID-19.

DIVISION IN SAFETY PRACTICES

Some teachers were very uncomfortable with their division and colleagues who they perceived as either under- or over-responding to the safety protocols.

Peyton said, "I just wish that we could all be on the same page in regards to our profession and rules. Everywhere you go, there's different rules." Bond concurred with Peyton's observations about the lack of consistency and the resulting tensions related to safety.

> Where I work there is still people who are teaching who are not wearing a mask. I think there is ambiguity. We had our boss tell us in our virtual staff meeting 'Ok, everyone has to be wearing a mask.' But, there is still a handful of people you walk past their rooms—and all the kids are wearing masks—and they're not! And it is like, 'What the hell are you doing?' And there has been have been multiple tensions and confrontations about it over the past month between staff members.

Other teachers told us that their experiences in their schools were more consistent. Alex said,

> I know the school division has been quite strict—especially our school in the division. We have been much stricter in comparison to other schools in both the size of our cohorts, and not having any kind of groups or mixing. I know we've been very, very strict on that, and again it's one of those things where it's a good thing, right, cause it's keeping us safe, but at the same time you miss it—you wish in a way that you could loosen a bit of those restrictions.

DIVISION OF EMOTIONAL RESPONSES TO TEACHING DURING A PANDEMIC

The second topic of divisiveness related to teachers and administrators who were perceived as spreading toxic positivity within the school. Many teachers in our study could identify incidents of toxic positivity within their schools. Tree observed,

> I think toxic positivity would be the characteristic of not acknowledging the obvious struggles, and moving forward with unreasonable optimism. I know teachers who do that, and they usually burn out. It is like the-end-of-the-rope, last ditch effort to bring things all together. Like it is all falling to Hell, so you just decide to be positive, but it usually isn't genuine, and it does not reflect the actual state of affairs.

Doe's response to toxic positivity was to restrict her actions with these peers.

> I think a lot of the teachers who are toxically positive are in denial or in a state of emotional numbness, because regarding COVID we are all just trying to get through it right now. You don't have to be happy about it all the time, because that is not realistic. I tend to congregate with teachers who are more like me. I am positive a lot, but I am also super cynical.

Other teachers perceived that this expectation was placed on all members of the school staff by administrators. Peyton observed,

> I wish that my admin. especially would be honest in expressing that everything is not okay at this moment and everyone is not doing okay, but we're doing the best we can, as opposed to saying that 'everything is fine, we're all doing great, everyone is okay.'

In contrast, other teachers agreed that being positive is a part of being professional and is a reasonable expectation from administrators. Purple adhered to this belief:

> I find, as a teacher, sometimes you have to kind of do that, pretend a lot of the time, because you know, how we feel or how we present ourselves kind of leads into the students. So, I guess in a way it's probably good to be that way—being positive even if you're not feeling it.

Tracy reframed these expectations from administrators as positive professionalism.

> I do work for admin. who believes that, [but] I wouldn't have thought it was toxic necessarily. I would look at it more as professional positivity. If you aren't able to be positive, hold together, then it just kind of spirals, and then everyone is affected. I think in our school we hold it together for the kids, and address real issues when needed and as appropriate, but try and give them a safe haven away from this craziness.

Still other teachers adopted a positive approach as a means of collegiality and peer support. Tree, for example, found this approach to by adaptive for her. "There is only 6 of us on break during the same time, and we are trying to not talk about what the [COVID-19] numbers are that day—we try to talk about asinine things like TV." Twila, too, appreciated colleagues who adopted this approach. "Do you know I have colleagues around me that we can just keep humour going, and I think that again is in keeping with whom I am, and what I need to get through these times."

Demoralisation and devaluing by government

The third theme that arose related to feelings of demoralisation (Santoro, 2011) based in the political climate related to teachers and provoked by the announcements by the government during the pandemic. The level of vitriol expressed by teachers was unexpected as well as was the repeated, unprompted return to this topic across interviews, focus groups, teachers, and time points.

Watermelon's comments are representative: "It has been challenging to come to work with a positive attitude knowing we are not really backed by the government and aren't supported in ways that other careers have been supported." Loki concurred,

> The best of the best are no longer performing at their very best. Hearing government officials talk about education from a perspective that doesn't include any of the teacher's perspectives makes us feel very devalued and not heard. Overall, I just think that teachers are feeling that they are not able to deliver their best selves, and that just isn't the natural problems of the pandemic but the man-made problems of the government.

In light of the government announcement regarding its review and reform, announced between the second and third waves, as well as the ongoing lack of vaccination for teachers as a group, teachers said that they felt "defeated, forgotten, devastated, hopeless, disheartened" (Red) "upset," (Katherine) "knocked back on the moral side of things, anxious," (Watermelon), "super stressed, unsettled" (Sally). It was significant that lack of vaccination priority, the education review, and its upcoming changes to education in the study province were so salient as to be discussed a length as an additional factor in teacher stress, connectedness, and commitment during the pandemic.

Discussion

The analyses revealed both expected and unexpected findings, each with their own implications for supporting teachers as we navigate and recover from the COVID-19 pandemic.

In terms of the expected findings, the three components of burnout were correlated with one another, all in the expected directions. Moreover, teachers' higher perceptions of connectedness were correlated with lower exhaustion and depersonalisation, greater levels of accomplishment, administrative support, peer support, organisational commitment, and perceptions of both school and divisional leadership quality (Jarzabkowski, 2003; Numeroff, 2005). Furthermore, administrative support was correlated with lower exhaustion, depersonalisation, as well as higher accomplishment. These trends have been supported by past research (Brunderman, 2006; Shah, 2012).

In terms of unexpected findings, we were quite surprised to see that burnout did not progress significantly between November 2020 and April 2021, given that our previous research on a national sample of teachers demonstrated increasing burnout from April 2020 to October 2020 (Sokal et al., 2020a). We were similarly surprised to see that connectedness decreased while perceptions of support from administrators and peers, perceptions of school and leadership quality, and organisational commitment demonstrated no significant decreases. Together, these findings suggest that a teacher's general sense of connectedness cannot be reduced to a collection of individual ingredients, but rather it is a dynamic and complicated phenomenon (Hargreaves & Fullan, 1992; Löfgren & Karlsson, 2016), where nuanced interpretation is necessary. Indeed, while both peer and administrative support are correlated with connectedness, neither on its own was sufficient to prevent overall loss of connectedness in teachers in our sample.

Relationships with peers

While we found that peer support was correlated with lower levels of depersonalisation and higher levels of accomplishment, there were no significant correlations between peer support and exhaustion. This finding is similar to the findings of Leiter et al. (2015), who showed that peer relationships correlated differentially with the three components of burnout. They revealed that employees who avoided their co-workers due to lower workplace civility and trust concurrently avoided greater exhaustion and cynicism, but avoidance also correlated negatively with accomplishment. They concluded that avoidance can be a healthy way to cope with a negative work environment, but it also forgoes the decrease in workload that can occur when colleagues work together. The avoidance of the staff room described by Tree and the increased busy-ness resulting from social isolation described by Purple provide further evidence of these social dynamics occurring as they relate to burnout in teachers during the pandemic. Other research (Leiter, 2021) has found positive correlations between exhaustion, cynicism, and incivility, and also between accomplishment and civility, further supporting our interpretations of our qualitative data. Leiter's (2021) research considered civility and incivility from both colleagues and supervisors and suggested that both lateral and hierarchical structures are at play in teacher burnout. Of note in the current study is the context of the pandemic and its incumbent elevation of stress in teachers. This might result in detachment (Browers & Tomic, 2000) or in undermining behaviours such as poor communication or conflicts with others (Bakker & Wang, 2020). These behaviours in turn lead to greater job stress that creates a cyclical relationship with conflict and/or detachment in the workplace, similar to those described by some of the teachers in our study.

Relationships with administrators

Given that past research about teachers during the pandemic has shown that exhaustion responds best to a decrease in demands rather than an increase in resources (Sokal et al., 2020b) and given that administrators have more control over demands than do colleagues, the role of administrators in early burnout prevention is key. An important finding was that the support of leaders was significantly correlated with all the other variables of interest in our study. This points to the special role of leaders not only in supporting teachers, but also facilitating collegial relationships between them. Importantly, leaders cannot dictate or mandate collegiality, so fostering it takes planning and thoughtfulness (Leonard & Leonard, 2003), even more so during a crisis such as a pandemic when divisiveness around perceptions of safety and appropriate emotional responses to COVID-19 have created additional tensions in schools.

A complex and dynamic system

Shah (2011) conducted a review of barriers to collegiality and found that time constraints, conflict avoidance, lack of administrative support, teacher preferences for autonomy, and weak leadership were relevant prior to the pandemic. Based on the comments from the teachers in the current study, the pandemic has created additional challenges to opportunities to foster collegiality related to both peer and leadership dynamics, and our data supports the relationships between these encounters, connectedness, and burnout. Both the qualitative and quantitative data further substantiate that, for some of the teachers in our study, peer and administrative barriers were evident in their schools. Collectively, our findings support Leiter's claim that, "The capacity to capture the complexity and diversity of the workplace social encounters [is] key to refining theory and evaluating interventions" related to burnout (2021, p. 11). This observation is especially salient during the COVID-19 pandemic.

Limitations

All research has limitations, and ours is no exception. First, we were unable to use paired analyses from the first and second survey data set to match the responses of the same teacher over time. Although teachers who participated in the surveys were asked to choose and use a consistent code name for matching time one and time two survey data, many were unable to remember their codenames at the second point of data collection. Therefore, we treated the data sets as independent samples even though we were aware that many of the same teachers participated in both surveys. Second, while some of the teachers in our survey, interview, and focus group samples took stress leaves during our study, none of the interview or focus group teachers left the study. However, given the high incidence of stress leaves among Manitoba teachers during the pandemic, it is likely that some of the teachers who did not complete the survey at time two were on stress leaves and/or were experiencing burnout. The inability to include these teachers in the time two data may have artificially enhanced the desirability of the time two scores in our entire sample. Finally, all the data sources involved self-reporting. Observational data collection was prohibited due to restricted entry to schools as well as occupancy limitation in classrooms during the study period. The addition of observational data would likely generate greater confirmation of our findings.

Despite these limitations, the current research has provided an interesting examination of the ways teachers have navigated the COVID-19 pandemic with special attention to their levels of burnout and (dis)connectedness. Our new awareness of the decline in teacher connectedness will serve as an important reminder of the role and responsibility of administrators to ensure that collegiality is fostered and restored as we recover from the pandemic.

Acknowledgements

This project was vetted for adherence with national ethics policies (HE#14993) and funded by a grant from the Social Sciences and Humanities Research Council of Canada (#1008-2020-0015).

References

Achinstein, B. (2002). Conflict amid community: The micropolitics of teacher collaboration. *Teachers College Record, 104*, 421–455.

Alarcon, G. M. (2011). A meta-analysis of burnout with job demands, resources, and attitudes. *Journal of Vocational Behavior, 79*(2), 549–562. 10.1016/j.jvb.2011.03.007

Bakker, A. B., & Demerouti, E. (2007). The job demands-resources model: State of the art. *Journal of Managerial Psychology, 22*, 309–328. 10.1108/01425450710826122

Bakker, A. B., & Demerouti, E. (2014). Job demands-resources theory. In C. Cooper & P. Chen (Eds.). *Wellbeing: A complete reference guide* (pp. 37–64). Chichester: Wiley-Blackwell.

Bakker, A. B., & Wang, Y. (2020). Self-undermining behavior at work: Evidence of construct and predictive validity. *International Journal of Stress Management, 27*(3), 241–251. 10.1037/str0000150

Browers, A. & Tomic, W. (2000). A longitudinal study of teacher burnout and perceived self-efficacy in classroom management. *Teaching and Teacher Education, 16*, 239–253.

Brunderman, L. (2006). *Leadership practices that support collegiality in schools.* Doctoral Dissertation. University of Arizona. Azy_etd_1886_sip1_m.pdf

Chance, P., & Segura, S. (2009). A rural high school's collaborative approach to school improvement. *Journal of Research in Rural Education, 24*(5), 1–12.

Chen, J. (2020). Teacher emotions in their professional lives: Implications for teacher development. *Asia-Pacific Journal of Teacher Education, 48*(5), 491–507.

Chughtai, A., & Zafar, S. (2006). Antecedents and consequences of organizational commitment among Pakistani university teachers. *Applied HRM Research, 11*(1), 39–64.

Collie, R. J., Shapka, J. D., Perry, N. E., & Martin, A. J. (2016). Teachers' psychological functioning in the workplace: Exploring the roles of contextual beliefs, need satisfaction, and personal characteristics. *Journal of Educational Psychology, 108*(6), 788–799.

Cresswell, J., & Cresswell, J. D. (2018). *Research design*. Los Angeles: Sage.

Crosby, K. S. (2015). The relationship between administrative support and burnout. In Turnaround Schools. *Online Theses and Dissertations*, 355. https://encompass.eku.edu/etd/355

Donohoo, J. (2017). Collective teacher efficacy research: Implications for professional learning. *Journal of Professional Capital & Community, 2*(2), 101–116.

Erickson, G., Minnes Brandes, G., Mitchell, I. & Mitchell, J. (2005) Collaborative teacher learning: Findings from two professional development projects. *Teaching and Teacher Education, 21*, 787–798.

Farber, B. (1999). Inconsequentiality – The key to understanding teacher burnout. In R. Vandenberghe & M. Huberman (Eds.). *Understanding and preventing teacher burnout. A sourcebook of international research and practice* (pp. 159–165). Cambridge: Cambridge University Press.

Geijsel, F., Sleegers, P., Leithwood, K. & Jantzi, D. (2003). Transformational leadership effects on teachers' commitment and effort toward school reform. *Journal of Educational Administration, 41*(3), 228–256. 10.1108/09578230310474403

Giddens, A. (1984). *The constitution of society*. Cambridge-Oxford: Polity Press.

Glaser, B. G. (1998). *Doing grounded theory – Issues and discussions*. Mill Valley, CA: Sociology Press.

Halbesleben, J. (2006). Sources of social support and burnout: A meta-analytic test of the conservation of resources model. *Journal of Applied Psychology, 91*, 1134–1145. 10.1037/0021-9010.91.5.1134

Hargreaves, A. (1995). Beyond collaboration: Critical teacher development in the postmodern age. In J. Smyth (ed.) *Critical Discourses on Teacher Development* (pp. 149–179). London, UK: Cassell.

Hargreaves, A. & Fullan, M. (Eds.) (1992). *Understanding teacher development*. New York: Teachers College Press.

Harmsen, R., Helms-Lorenz, M., Maulana, R., & van Veen, K. (2018). The relationship between beginning teachers' stress causes, stress responses, teaching behaviour and attrition. *Teachers and Teaching, 24*(6), 626–643. 10.1080/13540602.2018.1465404

Holmes, E., O'Connor, R., Perry, V., Tracey, I., Wessly, S., Arseneault, L., … Ballard, C. (2020). Multi-disciplinary research priorities for the COVID-19 pandemic: A call for action for mental health sciences. *Lancet Psychiatry, 7*, 547–560. 10.1016/S2215-0366(20)30168-1

Jarzabkowski, L. M. (2003). Teacher collegiality in a remote Australian school. *Journal of Research in Rural Education, 18*(3), 139–144.

Kelchtermans, G. (2006). Teacher collaboration and collegiality as workplace conditions: A review. *Zeitschrift für Pädagogik, 52*, 220–237.

Ketchand, A. A., & Strawser, J. R. (2001). Multiple dimensions of organizational commitment: Implications for future accounting research. *Behavioral Research in Accounting, 13*(1), 222–252. 10.2308/bria.2001.13.1.221

Leiter, M. P. (2021). Assessment of workplace social encounters: Social profiles, burnout, and engagement. *International Journal of Environmental Research in Public Health, 18*, 3533. https://doi.org/10.3390/

Leiter, M., Day, A., & Price, L. (2015). Attachment styles at work: Measurement, collegial relationships, and burnout. *Burnout Research, 2*, 25–35.

Leonard, L., & Leonard, P. (2003). The continuing trouble with collaboration: Teachers talk. *Current Issues in Education [On-line], 6*(15). tp://cie.ed.asu.edu/volume6/number15/.

Loeb, S., Darling-Hammond, L., & Luczak, J. (2005). How teaching conditions predict teacher turnover in California schools. *Peabody Journal of Education, 84,* 44–70.

Löfgren, H. & Karlsson, M. (2016). Emotional aspects of teacher collegiality: A narrative approach. *Teaching and Teacher Education, 60,* 270–280. 10.1016/j.tate.2016.08.022

Mahan, P., Mahan, M., Park, N., Shelton, C., Brown, K. & Weaver, M. (2010). Work environment stressors, social support, anxiety, and depression amog secondary school teachers. *AAOHN Journal, 58,* 197–205.

Maslach, C., & Jackson, S. E. (1981). The measurement of experienced burnout. *Journal of Occupational Behaviour, 2,* 99–113.

Maslach, C., Jackson, S. E., & Schwab, R. L. (1996). Maslach burnout inventory – Educators survey (mbi-es). In C. Maslach, S. E. Jackson, & M. P. Leiter. *MBI Study* (3rd ed). Palo Alto, CA: Consulting Psychologists Press.

Merrium, S. & Tisdell, E. (2016). *Qualitative research methods.* San Francisco: Jossey-Bass.

Meyer, J. P., & Allen, N. J. (1991). A three-component conceptualization of organizational commitment. *Human Resource Management Review, 1*(1), 61e89. 10.1016/1053-4822(91)90011-Z.

Nias, J. (1999). Teachers' moral purposes: Stress, vulnerability, and strength. In R. Vandenberghe, & A. M. Huberman (eds.), *Understanding and Preventing Teacher Burnout: A Sourcebook of International Research and Practice* (pp. 223–237). Cambridge: Cambridge University Press.

Numeroff, D. (2005). *Teacher collegiality and collaboration in exemplary high school math departments.* Doctoral dissertation, Florida Atlantic University, AAT 3162664.

Renshaw, T. L. (2020). *Teacher Subjective Wellbeing Questionnaire (TSWQ): Measure and user guide.* Open Science Framework. https://osf.io/6548v

Retallick, J. & Butt, R. (2004). Professional well-being and learning: A study of teacher-peer workplace relationships. *Journal of Educational Enquiry, 5*(1), 85–99.

Santoro, D. A. (2011). Good teaching in difficult times: Demoralization in the pursuit of good work. *American Journal of Education, 118*(1), 1–23. 10.1086/662010

Shah, M. (2011). The dimensionality of teacher collegiality and the development of teacher collegiality scale. *Journal of Studies in Education International Journal of Education, 3*(2), E10.

Shah, M. (2012). The importance and benefits of teacher collegiality on schools—A literature review. *Social and Behavioral Sciences, 46,* 1242–1246.

Sokal, L., Eblie Trudel, L., & Babb, J. (2020a). COVID-19's Second Wave: How are teachers faring with the return to physical schools? *EdCan Network.* https://edcan.atavist.com/teacher-covid-survey-2

Sokal, L., Eblie Trudel, L., & Babb, J. (2020b). Supporting teachers in times of change: The job demands-resources model and teacher burnout during the COVID-19 pandemic. *International Journal of Contemporary Education, 3*(2), 67–74. http://redfame.com/journal/index.php/ijce/issue/view/243

Strauss, A., & Corbin, J. (1994). Grounded theory methodology: An overview. In N. Denzin & Y. Lincoln. *Handbook of qualitative research* (1st ed., pp. 273–284).Newbury Park, California: Sage.

Taris, T., Leisink, P., & Schaufeli, W. (2017). Applying occupational health theories to educator stress: Contributions of the jobs-demands resources model (pp. 237–260). In T. McIntyre, S. McIntyre, and D. Francis (Eds.), *Educator stress: An Occupational health perspective.* Huston, TX: Springer. 10.1007/978-3-319-53053-6_11

Turner, S. L., & Morelli, C. A. (2017). Five essential relationships every new teacher needs to build. *Kappa Delta Pi Record, 53*(3), 134–137.

6 "To the last drop." The acceleration of the exhaustion process due to the new working ways imposed by COVID-19

Santiago Gascón[1], *María José Chambel*[2], *and Ángela C. Asensio*[3]

[1]*Departamento de Psicología y Sociología, Universidad de Zaragoza (Spain)*
[2]*Facultade de Psicología, Universidade de Lisboa (Portugal)*
[3]*Facultad de Ciencias Sociales y del Trabajo, Universidad de Zaragoza (Spain)*

Introduction

The COVID-19 healthcare crisis brought with it the generalisation of working methods that existed beforehand, namely working from home and on-line meetings. These professional modes, which came into being to reduce costs and time spent travelling to and from work (Costa et al., 2022) while also helping the reconciliation between professional and family life (Allen et al., 2022), entailed a hastened use of technology hitherto unknown for the majority of employees (Morrison et al., 2019).

From the onset of the global healthcare crisis, teleworking has been the most used solution as a means of continuing production or services, maintaining safety standards to contain the virus and offering major advantages, even for professionals for whom this mode had never been applied (Arrivillaga, 2022). Everything suggests that this manner of undertaking professional tasks outside the traditional working ethos, through information and communications technology, is here to stay and few could envisage a post-pandemic world without this form of working (Bailey, 2002).

However, owing to multiple reasons, namely its implementation without suitable planning beforehand on the part of the organisation and its employees, the ease with which the boundaries between time spent working and that devoted to our families can disappear, or the lack of training in technological usage, teleworking has shown itself prone to certain psychosocial risks, even being viewed as an "accelerator" of the burnout process (Van Steenbergen, 2018).

The concept of "burnout," under study for decades in diverse professions, is now under a different spotlight, owing to the insertion of these new organisational methods. Professionals for different sectors were forced to tackle a situation in which they had to make decisions swiftly to be able to carry out essential tasks. Teleworking was introduced into sectors in which it would have been unthinkable beforehand: healthcare, education, the media, etc.,

DOI: 10.4324/9781003250531-7

(Gascón et al., 2021, Montero-Marín et al., 2013), whose professionals tried their hardest against an unprecedented backdrop, and in which challenges were overcome through the help of technology.

The hit-and-miss results of teleworking.

It has been proven that teleworking fosters autonomy and flexibility (Van Steenbergen, 2018) and research suggests that it can lessen the negative impact caused by overload leading to burnout, allowing for enhanced control on the part of the employee regarding the time management of their workload (Tavares 2017).

There is evidence that teleworking performed at high-intensity may create conflict in the family (personal life)—workplace relationship, though when the tasks and pace of work are more evenly spread out, working from home bestows benefits insomuch as its effect on employees' health and wellbeing.

On the one hand, research unearths that this manner of working weakens necessary social support through encouraging isolation, disconnection from superiors and colleagues, the lack of feedback and intrinsic rewards (Sardeshmukh et al., 2012), although it has also been proven that the exhaustion produced by overburdening workers may be softened if there is sustained support from supervisors (Chambel et al., 2022), thereby increasing levels of engagement (Gajendran & Harrison, 2007).

The positive effects of teleworking have been widely described (Bailey & Kurland, 2002), yet owing to the fact that during the COVID-19 pandemic it was an unchosen option for many professionals, and one which took up their entire working timetable, there has been an outpouring of studies that show how it can hasten the burnout process (Carvalho et al., 2021).

The number of variables involved and the interaction between remote working and health create major confusion when determining the positive and negative aspects of this working method (O´Neill et al., 2009). Beckel and Fisher (2022) embarked upon an in-depth review differentiating between predictive, mediative, and moderative variables in the relationship between teleworking and wellbeing. In a general sense, the studies coincide in the idea that the inherent characteristics of work, along with the resources to which the worker has access to tackle them are the main variables to explain burnout (Bakker & Demerouti, 2017; Ten Brummelhuis & Bakker, 2012).

The possibility of choosing between working from home as an option relates to health-based variables and reduces absenteeism, although whether this is genuinely reduced or if employees simply do not report their illness due to the fact that they can manage their tasks from home is cast into doubt. Females more often choose the alternative of working from home and are similarly more negatively affected owing to having to juggle family management while performing their professional duties within eyeshot of their children.

The flexibilisation of the workload through this method, on the one hand, facilitates the balance between personal and professional life (Allen et al., 2022), although the limits between time and space are more easily blurred, thus increasing the probability of conflict in both spheres (Graham et al., 2021). Studies carried out during the COVID-19 pandemic confirmed that the traditional spread of gender roles was maintained. Females have worked remotely and have continued to be main caregivers to children (Lyttelton et al., 2020), for this reason, they displayed greater indices of stress and lower levels of satisfaction in terms of professional performance. However, fathers who worked from home during almost the entire pandemic spoke positively of an increase in the amount of time they devoted to their children (Pineault et al., 2022).

Remote working is inextricably linked to the use of information and communications technology (ICT). Over the past few decades, the risks resulting from the improper use of computers and desks as the catalysts for ergonomic issues have been assessed. The abuse of videoconference meetings, the absence of breaks to rest between one and another, the over-exposure to screen time, increase, not solely the risk of suffering from musculoskeletal issues, but also mental overload and physical tiredness (Ganster et al., 2018). With regard to these technological demands, teleworkers reported that they had to bear the costs to purchase computers, cameras, or ergonomic chairs (Arrivillaga et al., 2022). All of the foregoing, alongside the distress caused by lack of familiarity with programmes and applications, or the increase of demands of an administrative nature were noted (Tarafdar et al., 2011).

Several studies have unearthed more symptoms related to stress and burnout in employees working remotely during COVID-19 (Graham et al., 2021; Song & Gao, 2020). However, the fact that in the research heterogeneous measurements have been used to assess items such as wellbeing, stress, burnout or engagement, contributes to the findings' ambiguity.

The ease with which the boundaries between work and family can be blurred, the dependency on ITC to try to tackle professional assignments, alongside a reduction of face-to-face communication, may have adverse effects on teleworkers (Henke et al., 2016).

Teleworking and burnout

In diverse research papers, the intense workload, reduced feedback and scant or zero social support perceived in remote working were predictors, not solely of emotional weariness, but moreover of other dimensions of burnout: cynicism and lack of personal realisation (Wang et al., 2021). In interviews performed on healthcare professionals, (Larranaga & Gascón, 2022) these stated that it was commonplace to hear their patients complaining about matters such as: "*I feel completely drained,*" "*My head feels empty,*" or "*I cannot focus on an idea.*" Cognitive symptoms such as the inability to process, to maintain attention, memory problems, especially working memory, are increasingly more common in healthcare surgeries (Schmitt et al., 2021). Likewise, the employees describe emotional symptoms, namely anxiety, stress, impotence due to wanting to work more but being unable to, self-critical thoughts, the sensation that work is meaningless, and the outlook is bleak, along with general malaise or insomnia (Mann & Holdsworth, 2003).

Indeed, in Spanish speaking countries, the references to "dwindling energy" or "running out of battery," have had a tell-tale effect on understanding wholly the process of burnout. The term "burnout," which originally came from colloquial usage in the USA (Schaufeli et al., 2009), has never been easily translated into Spanish, often turning to the expression "professional exhaustion syndrome" or simply using the English term (literally meaning wholly consumed by fire). Additionally, in Spanish the word to define "exhaustion" is *"agotamiento,"* which is used regardless of whichever type of tiredness it intends to refer to, without specifying its intensity or duration. This term has been used for situations relative to stress, without considering the different symptomatology that burnout syndrome entails. If the term *"agotamiento"* is analysed etymologically, derived from the Latin (a + gutta) which literally means "having consumed the last drop" (Galicia & Zermeño, 2009). Therefore, it illustrates the state of mental and emotional collapse described by some workers.

The construct of burnout, under study since 1974, was acknowledged as a occupational phenomenon by the WHO in its International Classification of Diseases (WHO, 2018). Despite this, it more often than not confused with illnesses such as stress or depression (Schaufeli et al., 2009). The hasty and massive insertion of teleworking during the COVID-19 healthcare crisis, as well as its implementation without suitable planning, might have contributed to an acceleration of the burnout process, which normally takes years to manifest.

Shared experiences described by those who have worked remotely throughout the pandemic were: the ease with which time limits are overlooked, working beyond the scheduled timetable and exceeding one's skills set, tackling too many requests at an accelerated pace, different data entry points (telephone, videoconference, WhatsApp, email), occasionally dealing with several screens and without time to process such requirements. To the foregoing, it must be added that employees, in a general sense, have faced this situation without suitable professional training and without a clear set of agreements with their companies (Carvalho et al., 2021).

To this hastened burnout process, we must add the psychosocial effect derived from the disproportionate use of ICT, which Brod (1984) termed "technostress" and defined it as "an adaptation disorder caused by the lack of ability to cope with these technological demands in a healthy manner," and that it is the result of the combination of information overload, anxiety, conflicts between roles and organisational aspects. Certain writers consider that "technostress" is the product of the mental exertion entailed in tackling different factors related to the use of technology: data collection fatigue, multitasking or IT issues (Brillhart, 2004). Tarafdar et al. (2011) highlights as consequences of technostress the overburdening of roles, with the subsequent increase in the perception of tasks' complexity, the downturn in professional satisfaction, reduced motivation, and innovation in the workplace, drops in productivity, dissatisfaction with the use of technology and the poor levels of organisational commitment. The evolution of ICTs has taken place at a greater pace that than the time required for workers to adapt to them when dealing with someone with standard computer proficiency, meaning the repercussions of this psychosocial risk are similar to those caused by stress: psychosomatic problems, anxiety, irritability, eye strain (Minaya Lozano, 2008).

However, become clear that employees around the globe has been deemed telework as positive experience and would like that this modality of work to be part of their reality in the post-Covid period. For example, in Europe, three quarters of employees have reported wishing to maintain telework, at least to some extent, in the post-crisis period (Eurofound, 2020); in the USA, three out of five employees who adopted telework during the Covid-19 pandemic would like to maintain this employment arrangement (Gaffney et al. 2021); in Australia, two-thirds of employees would like to have this opportunity after Covid-19 has been controlled (Nguyen & Armoogum, 2021). With the learning provided by the experience of telework in the context of this pandemic, in the future, organisations will be able to implement this employment arrangement as a new way of working, which may lead not only to improved work-family balance, but also to the achievement of work goals and better performance. Will be important that organisations provide all resources that employees need to perform that work, which includes competences, time, support, rewards, and any negative implications related to promotions or other organisational opportunities.

Future research lines

Thorough studies are needed on the health consequences of teleworking, which clearly define their aims: anxiety, depression, burnout, or other mental health indicators (O'Neill et al., 2009) and take into account the complexity of mediating and modulating variables. Future research should seek to identify what behaviours and resources of teleworking can be beneficial in meeting demands and what aspects contribute to exhaustion.

It has been found that the number of days and hours per week devoted to teleworking plays a crucial role in predicting job satisfaction and the health of teleworkers (Chambel et al., 2022). Full-time teleworkers report increased satisfaction when they have high levels of autonomy and family support supervision (Turetken et al., 2010). Golden (2006) reported that teleworkers' satisfaction increased to a point of hours, yet that this positive association between variables stabilised and began to decrease once high levels of teleworking hours are reached. Therefore, it seems necessary to ration the number of days and hours, as well as providing the option of combining working on site and remotely.

Another positive aspect that research allows for us to affirm regarding the teleworking and burnout relationship is that an important mediating variable is the perceived autonomy or control over the task (Van Steenbergen, 2018). While it has also been shown that work from home tends to blur the boundaries between the working world and the family and personal world (Kossek et al., 2006). Therefore, the research works' findings coincide in recommending to organisations and teleworkers the establishment of delimitation strategies such as: having a separate space or establishing a strict schedule, or combining breaks, moments for domestic tasks and/or childcare, or choosing to work in a shared room to increase the time devoted to the family (Matthews et al., 2010).

Leiter and colleagues proposed a "Double burnout process theory" (2008) that points out that work overload has a direct effect on emotional fatigue, the main dimension of burnout. Still other variables noted in the person-work relationship, such as the possibility of control over the task, the spirit of community, the possible intrinsic rewards generated by the work, or a feeling of justice and congruence between the values of the employee and those of its company, can act as moderators or buffers of the burnout experience. If for some reason the conditions of that organisation are modified (change of owners, policies, emergency situations, etc.), those variables that moderated the negative effects of the overload, can disappear, and quickly generate an increase, not only in emotional fatigue, but moreover in the other aspects of burnout, such as cynicism or the lack of personal achievement in the professional sphere.

Alongside exhaustion, these authors envisage a model of burnout in which the dimensions of depersonalisation and lack of personal accomplishment in the workplace come to the fore. Depersonalisation is engendered over time due to the inability to respond to the service receptors being provided or owing to the impossibility of remaining involved in workplace activities. The experience of chronic exhaustion or lack of involvement or cynicism erodes employees' beliefs on their powers to influence matters in their professional environment. These three independent experiences bring about the burnout syndrome in a widespread manner.

In previous studies, the six key areas forming one's professional life, mentioned beforehand, have displayed a contribution, whether positive or negative, to the development of the scale of burnout (Maslach & Leiter, 2008). With a view to optimising the results of teleworking and improving employees' wellbeing, it would be timely to analyse these areas bearing in mind new challenges faced.

Workload

The concepts of workload and control were already present in the *"Demand-Control model"* (Bakker et al., 2010). The most commonly found and evident aspect in any working environment and professional category is overload, since, working demands typically exceed people's operational capacities. Workload has a direct bearing with burnout, particularly with regard to emotional tiredness.

Throughout this chapter, we have seen how the relationship between wellbeing and the number of days devoted to working remotely trace out a curve in which, once a certain point has been passed, there is a drop off both in terms of employee effectiveness and their wellbeing. It has been proven that the ideal scenario is to schedule two days per week, in other words around 40% of the working timetable to working under this regime (Bailey et al, 2002). It is similarly important to mark out the limits regarding working schedules, days off and holidays, as well as not encroaching on time devoted to family and personal matters. Workers undergo listlessness if they must overcome too many challenges, if these must be tackled through diverse channels and if there are not sufficient remedies in place for recovery. Each employee must have suitable resources on hand: personal computer, programmes, ergonomic furniture, etc.

Control

The main advantage that has been ascertained with regard to teleworking is the increase in the flexibility and control the worker exerts over their tasks. This is true up to a certain point, as this variable similarly unearths ambiguous relationships regarding burnout. Working from home may nurture confusion regarding spaces and the invasion of one area encroaching on the time devoted to another, leading to a loss of control vis-à-vis the tasks that one wishes to perform and/or a conflict of roles, which may result in an increase in the hours devoted to work in order to accomplish targets set (Kossek et al., 2006).

The teleworking mode can allow for a person to organise their working days in such a way that the latter can be more smoothly arranged, though certain tasks entail the implication of other colleagues, supervisors, or clients who are not physically present, and this may bring with it tiresome waits, feelings of impotence and stress as a task cannot be continued.

Rewards

The rewards, whether these are financial, social, or intrinsic, may not be consistent with a worker's expectations. The situation of teleworking, the risk that it can entail is that the agreements between the company and the employee are not clearly stated: reduced salaries for working from home, increased expenses if the person has to purchase the necessary technology (Carvalho et al., 2021), reduced professional satisfaction due to the absence of acknowledgment on the part of management, co-workers, etc., all of the foregoing leading to negative consequences on the aspect of ineffectiveness.

Community

A fundamental aspect of these six areas of professional life, proposed by Leiter and community Maslach, is the one concerning community: a wide-ranging concept of social interaction in the workplace that ranges from negative issues, namely conflicts, to positive matters such as mutual support, the level of proximity between the members, or the capacity to work as a team (Novianti & Roz, 2020). Research confirms that teleworking, on the one hand reduces conflicts, however, it interrupts trusting relationships and social exchanges, being able thus to exert a negative influence on productivity (Eniola, 2022).

It is widely known that much more is produced and this is of a higher standard when the working environment is convivial, comfortable and when humour is a staple of professional life. Social support, on the part of the supervisors, co-workers, friends and family, is the variable that has appeared most, displaying a role as moderator in research works into stress and health (Lincoln, 2000). Similarly, in sociological and psychological studies, one of the many contributions that work has on the person is that it confirms their desire to belong to a group. There is a strong likelihood that working outside the office would entail an end to this perceived support or sense of belonging (Bailey & Kurland, 2002; Golden et al., 2008). Conversely, it has been shown that severe conflicts left unresolved may have a harmful effect on employees' health and wellbeing. This is a further aspect that is hard to overcome in remote working scenarios.

If autonomy has been considered as a strong point of teleworking, isolation is the most deleterious condition. At the onset of the COVID-19 pandemic, the major challenge was achieving the continuance of production, and this occurred largely due to the use of ICTs. As has been seen, not all workers had been provided with professional training in this sphere and the fact that they must tackle new and hitherto unknown technology has been as source of unease and tension. Implanting teleworking as an effective mode in the future entails the need for ICTs to be humanised, in such a way that they can become a useful tool to offer support and make the worker feel part of a team and thus a community. The quality of leadership diminishes through virtual work. Studies confirm that the positive impact perceived by the employees is lessened, with these stating that they receive less motivation, inspiration or challenging proposals from their bosses (Eniola, 2022). It is of the utmost importance for senior management and heads of human resources to harness this methodology to offer feedback, remain in close contact with the employees, and handle the needs that arise on a day-to-day basis. In this way, virtual leadership would reach a balance between control and support, thus fostering autonomy and self-regulation (Gan et al., 2022).

Fairness

A further area of importance is the sense of fairness, or the perception that the decisions made in the company are fair and that the worker feels they are treated with respect. This is essential to encourage a proper sense of community, appreciating clearly how conflicts are resolved, if each party involved is given a voice and the chance to participate in decision-making processes. In different studies, the employees who sense that their leaders are fair and supporting show less likelihood to feel burnt out and take on board organisational changes better, especially at more testing times (Ronen, & Mikulincer, 2009).

Values

To conclude, in the burnout process, the area of congruity between one's own values and those of the organisation takes on major relevance. In the congruity of values, both individual values, either consciously or subconsciously, as well as the corporate values of the organisation are involved (Gascón et al., 2021). People who work in a company with congruent values are more motivated to pursue shared aims and feel capacitated to accomplish their goals. A conflict of values may lead to a downturn in one's professional career, making them consider that they have wasted their talents and energy in trifling matters, even having behaved in contrary to their beliefs. Research work has found relationships between the incongruence in terms of values and burnout in different professions, with implications in three dimensions of the syndrome: erosion of energy, downturn in implication levels, leading them to feel demotivated and lacking a sense of realisation Leiter & Harvie, 1996).

In short, the fact that the organisation offers teleworking as an option, as well as the degree of formality of the agreements and the support perceived by colleagues and bosses have been shown as modulating variables of burnout (Collins et al., 2016; Graham et al., 2021). On the other hand, the social support variable seems to play a significant mediating role in employees' wellbeing (Graham, 2021). When the perceived support from the organisation is insufficient, the negative impact of isolation, along with the use of telework, increases stress and reduces job satisfaction.

Another significant variable is the "interdependence of tasks," or the extent to which a person depends on others to complete their work tasks (Golden, 2006). If the type of teleworking is overly interdependent, there is a risk of experiencing more frustration and burnout from the necessary continuous back-and-forth communication to complete tasks (Kaduk et al., 2019).

Discussion

The teleworking method offers major advantages for both organisations and employees, yet also, it is fraught with risks to health that hinge on a series of characteristics related to the workplace, to the context or to technology.

There is still much to be researched, certain teleworking variables might accelerate the burnout process. It is known that professional overburdening (taking on too many tasks in too short a timeframe) plays a crucial role in this process. We know that the symptoms come to light when the person, upon applying all of their armoury, slumps in defeat due to not having sufficient skills to tackle the situation. We also know that this entails a process in which different variables act as mediators or as moderators (Tarafdar et al., 2011).

The main findings on the relationship between remote working and burnout are related to the work setting and its characteristics, particularly the number of hours and days devoted to teleworking, autonomy, and support.

In the coming years, it is highly likely that we will witness the growth of teleworking to full-time employment (Tavares, 2017). This represents a reassuring challenge, as it will be more likely that parents can respond to their duties vis-à-vis their children better, and couples will enjoy more time together. Teleworking is the ideal method to foster the balance between professional and family life (Kossek et al., 2006), though it entails a greater risk of personal matters invading the working arena and vice versa. For this reason, both senior management as well as employees must set and stick to a series of clear agreements on timetables and expectations to respond to communications relating to work. Likewise, employees must notify their families of these agreements to lessen the risk of non-work-based interruptions.

Remote working can be feasible even in professions in which it had been hitherto considered unthinkable, yet it is vitally important that organisations have in place beforehand a clearly defined, properly disseminated, and inclusive teleworking policy, seeking out balancing flexibility and formality (Matthews et al., 2010). The heads of human resources departments must ensure clear principles to set out who is eligible for teleworking, where they will be located, when and how often an employee may telework. Research undertaken suggests that the optimum amount is 40% of the overall time, between two and eight hours per day.

The social backdrop within which teleworking is performed helps to define the relationship between teleworking and the worker's health. Workers' relationships with their superiors, colleagues and relatives, the feelings of isolation, may affect their wellbeing (Chambel et al., 2022). Senior management must identify resources, such as social support or flexibility to assuage the potential of reduced perceptions of autonomy.

It is vital that the organisation provides face-to-face interaction with these employees, especially those of the most recent intake, relying upon web conference platforms, informal channels, etc.

Conversely, it is well known that the prolonged use of personal computers, over-exposure to screen time and unsuitable working spaces can lead to musculoskeletal symptoms and cognitive type disorders (Ganster et al., 2018). The foregoing means that professional training must be provided, not only in new technologies, but also in their proper usage, along with strategies for rest and energy renewal, and undertaking physical activity (Díaz-Silveira et al., 2020). It is therefore essential to tackle remote working with the necessary ergonomic and ethnological resources, alongside ongoing training in the use of ICTs.

The COVID-19 healthcare crisis drove many organisations to adopt teleworking, and this situation must be viewed as an opportunity for change and learning, fostering reflection on experiences (Chambel et al., 2022). Teleworking may be particularly beneficial so that employees find a balance between the management of their personal and professional lives, and, consequently, obtain greater wellbeing.

References

Allen, T. D., Golden, T. D., & Shockley, K. M. (2022). How effective is telecommuting? Assessing the status of our scientific findings. *Psychological Science in the Public Interest, 15*, 40–68.

Arrivillaga, A., Garcia, W., & Gramajo, G. (2022). Impact on occupational health by teleworking during the Coronavirus disease (Covid 19) pandemic. *Safety and Health at Work, 13*, S173–S173.

Bailey, D. E., & Kurland, N. B. (2002). A review of telework research: Findings, new directions, and lessons for the study of modern work. *Journal of Organizational Behavior, 23*, 383–400.

Bakker, A. B., & Demerouti, E. (2017). Job demands-resources theory: Taking stock and looking forward. *Journal of Occupational Health Psychology, 23*, 272–285.

Bakker, A. B., Van Veldhoven, M., & Xanthopoulou, D. (2010). Beyond the demand-control model. *Journal of Personnel Psychology, 9*(1), 3–16.

Beauregard, T. A., & Basile, K. A. (2016). Strategies for successful telework: How effective employees manage work/home boundaries. *Strategic HR Review, 15*, 106–111.

Beckel J. L. O., & Fisher G. G. (2022). Telework and worker health and well-being: A review and recommendations for research and practice. *International Journal of Environmental Research and Public Health, 19*(7), 3879.

Brillhart, P. E. (2004). Technostress in the workplace managing stress in the electronic workplace. *Journal of American Academy of Business, 5*, 302–307.

Brod, C. (1982). Managing technostress: optimizing the use of computer technology. *Personnel Journal, 61*(10), 753–757.

Carvalho, V. S., Santos, A., Ribeiro, M. T., & Chambel, M. J. (2021). Please, do not interrupt me: Work–family balance and segmentation behavior as mediators of boundary violations and teleworkers' burnout and flourishing. *Sustainability, 13*(13), 7339.

Chambel, M. J., Castanheira, F., & Santos, A. (2022). Teleworking in times of COVID-19: the role of Family-Supportive supervisor behaviors in workers' work-family management, exhaustion, and work engagement. *The International Journal of Human Resource Management*, 1–36. 10.1080/09585192.2022.2063064.

Collins, A. M., Hislop, D., & Cartwright, S. (2016). Social support in the workplace between teleworkers, office-based colleagues, and supervisors. *New Technology, Work and Employment, 31*, 161–175.

Costa, C. S., Pitombo, C. S., & Souza, F. L. U. D. (2022). Travel behavior before and during the COVID-19 pandemic in Brazil: Mobility changes and transport policies for a sustainable transportation system in the post-pandemic period. *Sustainability, 14*(8), 4573.

Díaz-Silveira, C., Alcover, C. M., Burgos, F., Marcos, A., & Santed, M. A. (2020). Mindfulness versus physical exercise: effects of two recovery strategies on mental health, stress and immunoglobulin A during lunch breaks. A randomized controlled trial. *International Journal of Environmental Research and Public Health, 17*(8), 2839.

Eniola, O. (2022). Work-from-home engagement during COVID-19: implications for human resource management. *International Journal of Business and Management, 17*(3), 134.

Eurofound. (2020). *Living, working and COVID-19, COVID-19 series*. Dublin: Publications Office of the European Union. http://eurofound.link/covid19data

Gaffney, A. W., Himmelstein, D. U., & Woolhandler, S. (2021). Trends and Disparities in Teleworking during the COVID-19 Pandemic in the USA: May 2020–February 2021. *Journal of general internal medicine, 36*(11), 3647–3649.

Gajendran, R. S., & Harrison, D. A. (2007). The good, the bad, and the unknown about telecommuting: Meta-analysis of psychological mediators and individual consequences. *Journal of Applied Psychology, 92*, 1524–1541.

Galicia, F. A., & Zermeño, M. E. G. (2009). Estrés, agotamiento profesional (burnout) y salud en profesores de acuerdo a su tipo de contrato. *Ciencia & Trabajo, 12*(33), 172–176.

Gan, J., Zhou, Z. E., Tang, H., Ma, H., & Gan, Z. (2022). What it takes to be an effective "remote leader" during COVID-19 crisis: The combined effects of supervisor control and support behaviors. *International Journal of Human Resource Management*, 1–23. 10.1080/09585192.2022.2079953.

Ganster, D. C., Rosen, C. C., & Fisher, G. G. (2018). Long working hours and well-being what we know, what we do not know, and what we need to know. *Journal of Business and Psychology, 33*, 25–39.

Gascón, S., Fueyo-Díaz, R., Borao, L., Leiter, M. P., Fanlo-Zarazaga, Á., Oliván-Blázquez, B., & Aguilar-Latorre, A. (2021). Value conflict, lack of rewards, and sense of community as psychosocial risk factors of burnout in communication professionals (press, radio, and television). *International Journal of Environmental Research and Public Health, 18*(2), 365.

Golden, T. D. (2006). The role of relationships in understanding telecommuter satisfaction. *Journal of Organizational Behavior, 27*, 319–340.

Golden, T. D., & Veiga, J. F. (2005). The impact of extent of telecommuting on job satisfaction: Resolving inconsistent findings. *Journal of Management, 31*, 301–318.

Golden, T. D., Veiga, J. F., & Dino, R. N. (2008). The impact of professional isolation on teleworker job performance and turnover intentions: Does time spent teleworking, interacting face-to-face, or having access to communication-enhancing technology matter? *Journal of Applied Psychology, 93*(6), 1412.

Graham, M., Weale, V., Lambert, K. A., Kinsman, N., Stuckey, R., & Oakman, J. (2021). Working at home: The impact of COVID-19 on health, family-work-life conflict, gender, and parental responsibilities. *Journal of Occupational and Environmental Medicine, 63*, 938–948.

Henke, R. M., Benevent, R., Schulte, P., Rinehart, C., Crighton, K. A., & Corcoran, M. (2016). The effects of telecommuting intensity on employee health. *American Journal of Health Promotion, 30*, 604–612.

Kaduk, A., Genadek, K., Kelly, E. L., & Moen, P. (2019). Involuntary vs. voluntary flexible work: Insights for scholars and stakeholders. *Community, Work & Family, 22*, 412–442.

Kossek, E. E., Lautsch, B. A., & Eaton, S. C. (2006). Telecommuting, control, and boundary management: Correlates of policy use and practice, job control, and work-family effectiveness. *Journal of Vocational Behavior, 68*, 347–367.

Larranaga, J. & Gascón, S. (2022). *Las quejas de los pacientes en Atención Primaria durante la Pandemia COVID-19. Documento del Trabajo Fin de Grado de Psicología.* Zaragoza: Universidad de Zaragoza.

Leiter, M. P., & Harvie, P. L. (1996). Burnout among mental health workers: A review and a research agenda. *International Journal of Social Psychiatry, 42*(2), 90–101.

Leiter, M. P., Gascón, S., & Jarreta, M. B. M. (2008). A two process model of burnout: their relevance to Spanish and Canadian nurses. *Psychology in Spain,* (12), 37–45.

Lincoln, K. D. (2000). Social support, negative social interactions, and psychological well-being. *Social Service Review, 74*(2), 231–252.

Lyttelton, T., Zang, E., & Musick, K. (2020). Gender differences in telecommuting and implications for inequality at home and work. (July 8, 2020). Available at SSRN: https://ssrn.com/abstract=3645561 or 10.2139/ssrn.3645561

Mann, S., & Holdsworth, L. (2003). The psychological impact of teleworking: stress, emotions and health. *New Technology, Work and Employment, 18*(3), 196–211.

Maslach, C., & Leiter, M. P. (2008). *The truth about burnout: How organizations cause personal stress and what to do about it.* New York: John Wiley & Son.

Matthews, R. A., Barnes-Farrell, J. L., & Bulger, C. A. (2010). Advancing measurement of work and family domain characteristics. *Journal of Vocational Behavior, 77*, 447–460.

Minaya Lozano, G. (2008). Tecnoestrés: Identificación, valoración y control (II). *Gestión Práctica de Riesgos Laborales, 48*, 20–27.

Montero-Marin, J., Prado-Abril, J., Carrasco, J. M., Asensio-Martinez, A., Gascon, S., & Garcia-Campayo, J. (2013). Causes of discomfort in the academic workplace and their associations with the different burnout types: A mixed-methodology study. *BMC Public Health, 13*, 1240. 10.1186/1471-2458-13-1240

Morrison, J., Chigona, W., & Malanga, D. F. (2019). Factors that influence information technology workers' intention to telework: A South African perspective. In *Proceedings of the South African Institute of Computer Scientists and Information Technologists 2019* (pp. 1–10).

Novianti, K. R., & Roz, K. (2020). Teleworking and workload balance on job satisfaction: Indonesian public sector workers during Covid-19 pandemic. *APMBA (Asia Pacific Management and Business Application), 9*(1), 1–10.

Nguyen, M. H. , & Armoogum, J. (2021). Perception and preference for home-based telework in the covid-19 era: A gender-based analysis in Hanoi, Vietnam, *Sustainability, 13*(6), 3179.

O'Neill, T. A., Hambley, L. A., Greidanus, N. S., MacDonnel, R., & Kline, T. B. (2009). Predicting telework success: An exploration of personality, motivational, situational, and job characteristics. *New Technology, Work and Employment, 24*, 144–162.

Pineault, L. A., Brumley, K., & Baltes, B. B. (28 April 2022). You work from home, I work from home, we all work from home: Differences in work-family experiences by dyad-level work location configurations. In Proceedings of the *Society for Industrial and Organizational Psychology Annual Conference*, Seattle, WA, USA.

Ronen, S., & Mikulincer, M. (2009). Attachment orientations and job burnout: The mediating roles of team cohesion and organizational fairness. *Journal of Social and Personal Relationships, 26*(4), 549–567.

Sardeshmukh, S. R., Sharma, D., & Golden, T. D. (2012). Impact of telework on exhaustion and job engagement: A job demands and job resources model. *New Technology, Work and Employment, 27*(3), 193–207.

Schaufeli, W. B., Leiter, M. P., & Maslach, C. (2009). Burnout: 35 years of research and practice. *Career Development International, 14*(3), 204–220. 10.1108/13620430910966406.

Schmitt, J. B., Breuer, J., & Wulf, T. (2021). From cognitive overload to digital detox: Psychological implications of telework during the COVID-19 pandemic. *Computers in Human Behavior, 124*, 106899.

Song, Y., & Gao, J. (2020). Does telework stress employees out? A study on working at home and subjective well-being for wage/salary workers. *Journal of Happiness Studies, 21*, 1137–1155.

Tarafdar, M., Tu, Q., Ragu-Nathan, T. S., & Ragu-Nathan, B. S. (2011). Crossing to the dark side. *Communications of the ACM, 54*(9), 113–120.

Tavares, A. I. (2017). Telework and health effects review. *International Journal of Healthcare, 3*, 30–36.

Ten Brummelhuis, L. L., & Bakker, A. B. (2012). A resource perspective on the work-home interface: The work-home resources model. *American Psychologist, 67*, 545–556.

Turetken, O., Jain, A., Quesenberry, B., & Ngwenyama, O. (2010). An empirical investigation of the impact of individual and work characteristics on telecommuting success. *IEEE Transactions on Professional Communication, 54*, 56–67.

Van Steenbergen, E. F., van der Ven, C., Peeters, M. C., & Taris, T. W. (2018). Transitioning towards new ways of working: Do job demands, job resources, burnout, and engagement change? *Psychological Reports, 121*, 736–766.

Wang, B., Liu, Y., Qian, J., & Parker, S. K. (2021). Achieving effective remote working during the COVID-19 pandemic; A work design perspective. *Applied Psychology, 70*, 16–59.

World Health Organization. (2018). International classification of diseases for mortality and morbidity statistics (11th Revision). Available at https://icd.who.int/browse11/l-m/en

7 Hiding behind a mask: A multilevel perspective of burnout shame

Aristides I. Ferreira

Associate Professor, Researcher at BRU (Business Research Unit), Iscte – Instituto Universitário de Lisboa, Av. das Forças Armadas, Lisboa (Portugal)

Introduction

The Covid-19 pandemic context has added new individual, group, and organisational job-related factors that have increased the risk of burnout with a direct and indirect impact on the quality of life and other health-related outcomes (Leo et al., 2021). Accordingly, burnout is a syndrome that comprises three dimensions: emotional exhaustion, cynicism, and the lack of accomplishment (Maslach & Jackson, 1981). Mental fatigue or emotional exhaustion exists when employees feel tired and fatigued at work. Cynicism or depersonalisation includes negative feelings and perceptions about the people one works with. Finally, a lack of accomplishment represents diminished professional efficacy.

During the Covid-19 pandemic, the media showed examples of courageous workers risking their lives and devoting their time to save other people's lives. Front-line healthcare workers (e.g., nurses, doctors) and other essential works such as bus drivers, food producers, and suppliers appeared on television as heroes. However, there is always a price to pay. According to the literature, employees in general may experience periods of heroism or honeymoon characterised by periods of high resilience, and an increased sense of meaning about the desired behaviour (Brooks et al., 2019). When employees have to deal with prolonged stressful experiences, they tend to decrease resilience associated with a reduced perception of resources. Accordingly, several changes have appeared in employees' daily activities associated with the Covid-19 pandemic phenomena. In the current chapter, we explore how individuals restored their regular emotional and psychological functioning following a very demanding job task such as to deal with infectious people or restricted rules and regulations. Additionally, due to the confinement, employees were responsible for several multiple and demanding roles (e.g., work, taking care of children, home schooling). Employers faced new managerial challenges with remote work. Distant work brought important implications on social dynamics with social distancing affecting the relationships between coworkers, as well as between supervisors and subordinates. Some employees also face the social pressure of

DOI: 10.4324/9781003250531-8

being an "essential worker" while others (e.g., musicians, actors) perceived high job insecurity and fear of long-term unemployment.

Framed within the Job Demands-Resources theory (JD-R; Bakker & Demerouti, 2007) a model was conceptualised where the antecedents (i.e., demands) derived from the Covid-19 pandemic stressors increased the levels of burnout at work. Accordingly, the JD-R model, which is a well-established model, is an appropriate theory to explain how employees leverage job resources to deal with the Covid-19 job demands (Xie & Gruber, 2022). Essentially, burnout appears as a consequence of reduced resources (e.g., supervisor support) and the high demands imposed by the pandemic situation (e.g., multiple roles, remote work, work/home spillover, layoffs). As a consequence of their burnout, and under certain circumstance people tend to hide their burnout symptoms. Burnout shame appears in contexts of high presenteeism cultures and stigma associated with psychological and physical diseases. The Conservation of Resources theory (Hobfoll, 1989) explains that burned out employees hide their burnout because they develop emotional experiences of shame (i.e., being judged, rejected, and discriminated against) due to the need to retain and maintain their resources during times of uncertainty and insecurity. Therefore, a negative spiral of burnout and consequent negative outcomes (e.g., distress, poor well-being, low quality of life, and sub-optimal performance) appear associated to contexts where employees feel discomfort in reporting their health problems at work.

Covid-19 antecedents of burnout symptoms

Due to the pressure imposed by the Covid-19 pandemic, employees perceived increased task demands and complexity, high workloads, and lack of support from managers who were struggling with new challenges. Employees perceived that their time to restore physical and psychological disruptions of stress was suddenly shortened (Kuntz, 2021). In the healthcare sector the growing and competing demands was also associated with a lack of feedback, role ambiguity, and an absence of recognition from peers and supervisors. Additionally, some of them reported the absence of adequate personal protective equipment (e.g., masks, gloves, etc. …), difficulty to deal with the technological requirements of remote work (e.g., appropriate software and computers, strong WI-FI signal), and the perception that the use of remote technology was not compatible with job requirements.

Additionally, employees who were not "labeled" as front-line employees feared job insecurity and developed concerns about job loss which appeared in some situations as a primary source of stress. Also, employees from the services sector found several tensions often associated to poor team performance, absence of coordination and inadequate leadership roles. The literature suggested that the support received at home played a key role to help employees maintaining their levels of resilience when facing traumatic experiences such as an earthquake-related stress event (Malinen et al., 2019) and that this resilience is important to help individuals in different contexts, such as family, life in general and work domains.

During the initial period of the pandemic situation, remote work was not voluntary and implied a huge availability with greater intensity of tasks and responsibilities for employees (International Labour Organization, 2020). As a consequence, the Covid-19 pandemic brought challenges in terms of both work-family and family-work conflicts (Kumar et al., 2021). These tensions appeared due to the large amounts of time and energy working remotely at home to assure financial stability and employment. Employees developed cynicism and detachment from their sources of social support. Essentially the support from family and friends were significantly reduced (Kuntz, 2021). Empirical studies suggest that work-family conflicts were positively associated with physical fatigue and emotional exhaustion. There was a positive relationship between the two dimensions of the work–family boundaries (i.e., work interference on family and family interference on work) explained a significant proportion of the variance on physical and cognitive fatigue, and emotional exhaustion (Barriga Medina et al., 2021). In sum, the psychological detachment from work positively influences mental health, whereas conflicts with both work and family have a negative impact on mental health (Trógolo et al., 2022).

The use of personal protective equipment and other organisational and governmental regulations and protocols developed to reduce risk of contagion between individuals increased task demands and consequent emotional exhaustion (Kuntz, 2021). Employees received very precise and concrete guidelines to introduce physical and relational distance at the workplace in order to avoid possible contamination from work to home. Additionally, at the daily (and sometimes hourly) basis, individuals developed frustration and feelings of impotence associated with misinformation from the media, governments, and other people. The cumulative flow of information, and misinformation about conspiracy theories increased the feelings of cynicism and detachment from the daily tasks (Rapp et al., 2021).

With the pandemic context and the shift to remote work and home schooling the work-home boundary collapsed affecting individuals' well-being and quality of life. Interminable Zoom meetings mixed with taking care of children and performing other activities interfered with individuals' tasks to accomplish their work and it became more difficult for everyone to have an adequate healthier and relaxed life. Due to these occurrences, the literature showed some gender interactions with burnout, where IT professional women were more prone to suffer from work-family boundary stressors than male (Kumaresan et al., 2022). Women accumulated more roles at home and thus, had to deal with more difficulties to manage their emotional regulation skills. Due to the multiple roles, employees experienced more emotional exhaustion, became more cynical in their interaction with others and reduced their self-confidence and the capacity to accomplish the required tasks successfully (Maslach & Leiter, 2022).

The label "essential worker" during the Covid-19 pandemic was associated to a burden. Essentially, the health care professionals who were dealing everyday with life and death, included the risk of losing their own lives or even the risk to affect other close relatives with virus contagion, brought with them from the work where they had to contact with infected people at the daily basis. These traumatic experiences consumed numerous psychological resources as people were struggling to self-regulate their negative emotions (Baumeister, 2014). In fact, health care professionals were particularly vulnerable as they had to deal with the indirect trauma experienced by their patients and families and at the same time the direct trauma of personal harm from the virus. Research shows that the intensity of their involvement was positively and significantly associated with high emotional exhaustion at work (Caldas et al., 2021). This study also showed that those health care workers who prioritised the importance of protecting and stimulating the well-being of others, exacerbated the positive relationship between the intensity of involvement and their emotional exhaustion at work.

During the Covid-19 pandemic several governments imposed the obligation to stay safe at home, which had an impact on people's lives. In some sectors (e.g., artists, musicians, athletes, restaurants, hotels, bars and small shops) owners were obligated to close their doors. These severe restrictions in some countries took many months of lockdown, and affected the economy and the quality of life in general. As a consequence, some employees lost their jobs, while others feared to lose their own source of financial support. The changes introduced downsized some salaries and as a consequence many employees and families suffered income losses. Some employees have been asked to work shorter hours or even to work remotely under rather precarious conditions. The uncertainty and financial instability associated with the pandemic ended up directly affecting employees' mental health (Trógolo et al., 2022) and consequently, potentiating higher levels of burnout.

Additionally, the social dynamics of remote meetings, social distancing, the use of personal protective equipment brought dramatic consequence for employees' mental health. The daily exposure to images of death, threat of death due to contagion, or eventually the long-term Covid-19 effect associated with physical and psychological injuries increased the levels of anxiety (Greenberg et al., 2020). Also, the constant uncertainty or the fear of infecting other, more fragile family members, helped explain a very relevant amount of negative emotions associated with the pandemic experience. In line with previous studies on the Covid-19 pandemic-related job stressors (Zhou et al., 2022), the current conceptual model adopted the rationale of the Job Demands-Resources model to explain how increased job demands and reduced resources impacted the levels of burnout at work during the pandemic.

The moderating effect of social support

In the previous section, the demands or stressors imposed by the Covid-19 pandemic were introduced. Here, the resources of social support were integrated with the JD-R model, whose main proposition is that job demands, and job resources impact employee engagement, burnout, and job-related outcomes (Bakker & Demerouti, 2007). The moderating effects of social support on job-related stressors have been studied in other contexts and populations (Fong et al., 2018), although not extensively explored under the pandemic situation such as the Covid-19 outbreak. However, a recent study conducted with a sample of 3,477 healthcare workers from 22 hospitals in Beijing, China, revealed that social support was negatively associated with burnout (Zhou et al., 2022). Moreover, the same study that was conducted under pandemic prevention and control measures, showed that the perceived social support mitigated the adverse effects of pandemic-related job stressors. In this sense, it is expected that for low levels of social support the job stressors associated with the pandemic Covid-19 would be more associated with burnout.

Covid-19 and the advent of burnout shame at work

In the current chapter, shame was characterised as a "painful emotion that arises when an employee evaluates a threat to the self when he or she has fallen short of an important standard tied to a work-related identity" (Daniels & Robinson, 2019, p. 2450). Shame can be grouped into four categories (Van Vliet, 2008): i) as a perceived transgression to the moral, social and individual standards (e.g., becoming drunk in a social event; lying to a close person about sexual orientation; being caught stealing in a shopping); ii) personal failure (e.g., losing money in a casino or sporting bet; repeating the driving license test); iii) ostracism or social rejection (e.g., being ostracised after showing photos of a homosexual relationship; being rejected in a job interview due to a tattoo in the neck); and (d) trauma (e.g., being assaulted or being a victim of bullying at school).

In the current study, I want to identify the Covid-19 related factors that may cause burned out shame among employees. According to a model developed by Daniels and Robinson (2019) there are intrapsychic components of organisational shame. In organisational contexts, shame appears as a result of the discrepancies between employees' behaviour and the standards that were socially constructed. In other words, shame appears as a consequence of discrepancies between the self-evaluation that the person has deviated from the standard—as seen through the eyes of others. The authors also introduced the experience of vicarious shame which determines the degree to which the focal social entity (i.e., peer, supervisor) is relevant for the employee. Employees tend to evaluate themselves taking into account the evaluations of relevant individuals and groups. Therefore, they care about the evaluation of the groups to where they belong and also if the group evaluates their behaviour favourably or not. Accordingly, employees tend to develop behaviour that is not discrepant from the work-related identity (Daniels & Robinson, 2019). If employees fail to display a good image and behaviour congruent with the group or sector where they belong, their shame undermines the individual's positive self-concept, damages the individual's social relationships with other colleagues and supervisors, which in turn, may result in reduced sense of power and control. Due to shame, individuals may experience negative judgments (from oneself or from others), experience a painful sense of social isolation, and in some contexts, employees may try to rationalise or minimising the significance of the cause of shame through a process of denial or suppression (Van Vliet, 2008).

Similarly to what happened in previous pandemics (e.g., HIV, Ebola), the responses and consequences to Covid-19 brought the same or even exacerbated shameful experiences (Logie & Turan, 2020). Shame appeared as negative self-conscious emotions that could be caused by the Covid-19 pandemic (Cavalera, 2020). Employees who experienced shame due to the burnout associated to the stressors mentioned that they tended to hide from others at all costs. This involved feelings of rumination, confusion and even inability to communicate (Orth et al., 2006). Accordingly, it is understandable why shame is associated with several mental health problems, such as depression (Andrews et al., 2002), anxiety (O'Connor et al., 1999), and post-traumatic stress disorder (Leskela et al., 2002).

The literature revealed that the negative emotion of shame was associated with the construct of burnout (Livne-Ofer et al., 2019). However, there is a call for future studies mentioning that anger and hostility have been more frequently reported in the scientific literature and that there is a need to understand the underlying causes of shame as an important emotional reaction in the workplace (Livne-Ofer et al., 2019). According to the authors, the lack of studies approaching shame is related to the cognitive complexity associated with self-awareness and self-consciousness processes that are difficult to evaluate (Livne-Ofer et al., 2019). In a very demanding context attributed to the Covid-19 pandemic outbreak, recursive experiences of shame attributed to burnout symptoms serves the adaptive function of alerting employees to threats to their image and status in the company. In accordance, shame in employees with burnout occurs in response to possible rejections or separation from relevant individuals such as co-workers, supervisors or even family (Van Vliet, 2008). Emotions of shame in contexts where heroes appear everywhere and frequently, namely in the media and on social networks, can increase a global negative self-attribution associated with increased adverse effects on burnout. This negative spiral of burnout and shame of burnout that lead individuals to hide from others has received little attention from scholars and, therefore, deserves to be further explored (Cavalera, 2020). The imposed social dynamics of the Covid-19 pandemic (remote working, use of protective gear, multiple roles) and, in some sectors linked to health care and frontline workers, the increased demands and the pressure from managers and colleagues, pushed many workers to work, even when they were in burnout. This pressure resulted in increased burnout and in some cases the hiding of the disease, simply because it was not tolerable, or because there was a larger mission to fight the pandemic and help people. In some cases, the decision between showing that one was struggling with burnout and backing off, or going ahead and hiding the illness, led many people to choose the second option. Employees feared that their burnout attributes and the request to recover or slow down task demands being imposed by managers and colleagues was misinterpreted or evaluated negatively (Cavalera, 2020). What conditions led people to choose the second option is something that will be discussed in the next sections of the chapter.

The social support moderator and burnout shame

The Conservation of Resources (COR) theory (Hobfoll, 1989) aims to explain the motivation that drives individuals to maintain their existing resources and to achieve new resources. According to this theory, it is more difficult to lose resources then to gain resources. Hence, individuals tend to invest resources (i.e., go to work despite being ill / hide their burnout symptoms) to protect against resource loss (e.g., lack of social support), to recover from losses, and to gain resources (e.g., job stability, career visibility and public recognition). Employees who perceive a lack of supervisor support tend to develop more emotions of shame associated with high levels of self-criticism (Fatima et al., 2020). Shame at work can explain the relationship between negative feedback from a supervisor and performance on subsequent days (Xing et al., 2021). There is a link between social exchanges and shame and apparently shame appears as a mechanism to compensate resources lost due to burnout and the lack of social support. When burned out workers receive little social support (from supervisors and colleagues), they fear the loss of possible resources already gained (i.e., job stability, recognition), therefore they compensate for this loss by going to work hiding their burnout. The absence of perceived social support accentuates the perceived loss of resources and motivates people to develop active behaviour that drives them to go to work to mitigate possible losses. During the pandemic many workers perceived in the media, in social networks, recognised the importance of their work, often linked to saving lives. This perception led many people to feel ashamed of being in burnout, as if they were not allowed to be in burnout. The absence of a policy and support from colleagues and supervisors may have motivated burnout shaming behaviour.

The moderator role of stigmatisation

The World Health Organisation (WHO) identified stigma as one of the greatest obstacles for the treatment of mental and physical health. Stigma can be considered as an attribute, personality trait, psychological or physical disorder that marks individuals as being considered socially unaccepted because they are different from the standards of "normal" people with whom those individuals interact (Clough et al., 2019). Accordingly, there are four different types of stigma: i) personal—namely when an individual has stigmatising attitude towards others; ii) perceived—an individual's beliefs regarding others' stigmatising attitudes; iii) self-stigma—individual's stigmatising attitudes regarding themselves; and iv) structural stigma—intentional or unintentional practices and policies which impede stigmatised individuals' opportunities or well-being (Clough et al., 2019).

Over the decades, there have been several examples of social stigmatisation in previous pandemics, just to name a few examples: SARS, EBOLA, HVI/AIDS or H1N1 pandemics (Shultz et al., 2016). During all these pandemics, the world witnessed social phenomena of discrimination toward affected individuals or even specific communities. For example, the established link between homosexuals and the HIV/AIDS pandemic. The individual perception of negative stigma can lead to social isolation and shame for being ill. The increased perception of stigma and discrimination conducted to higher levels of depression and stress (Katafuchi et al., 2021; Pyle et al., 2015). In particular, stigma increased in patients with psychological disorders, essentially due to feelings of insecurity, loneliness, weakness which encouraged behaviour of avoidance and rejection (May et al., 2020) and inhibits individuals from accomplishing tasks (Bianchi et al., 2016). Therefore, individuals with psychological problems often face the burden of the social consequences that increase the already existing psychological problem. Specifically, during the Covid-19 pandemic, the literature revealed that stigmatisation was highly prevalent among individuals with Covid-19 and that this stigma increased in those with previously diagnosed psychiatric condition (Warren et al., 2022). Several individuals diagnosed with Covid-19 felt stigmatised with negative attitudes from co-workers and supervisors in their workplace.

The relationship between stigmatisation and health conditions linked to depression or burnout symptoms is not surprising (Pyle et al., 2015). In fact, employees with burnout tend to be stigmatised because they seem to be perceived as less competent and fragile than those who are not burned out (May et al., 2020). Therefore, in the current chapter burnout stigma will be distinguished from shame of burnout. Burnout stigma reflects the belief that employees with burnout are less competent than others (May et al., 2020). Shame of burnout is a complex cognitive process associated with self-awareness and self-consciousness processes (Livne-Ofer et al., 2019) associated with the perception that the individual failed and therefore, cannot follow the standards, rules and goals imposed by the company. These employees hide their burnout because they self-monitor their desire to cause a positive impression on others (Lim & Yang, 2015). The body and health condition associated to burnout says no, but the mind says yes and stimulates the person to go to work when they need to recover and maintain their lost resources. In the current chapter, a model is conceptualised in which a work context has a strong stigmatisation about burnout, as well as a greater tendency for people with burnout to hide their health condition and not report problems to their supervisors or colleagues.

The moderator role of presenteeism climate

Presenteeism refers to the act of being at work when you "should be at home either because you are ill or because you are working such long hours that you are no longer effective" (Cooper, 1996, p.15). Despite the absence of recent studies evaluating the role of presenteeism climates during the Covid-19 pandemic (Ferreira et al., 2022), it is important to note that companies that in the past promoted sickness presence at any cost, continue to encourage employees with burnout to go to work when they should effectively stay at home recovering from the illness. The financial crisis imposed by the Covid-19 has led many companies to adopt old strategies that are normally used to deal with difficulties, namely: downsizing or even closing which increases contexts of job insecurity (Lu et al., 2013), obsession with cost efficiency (Simpson, 1998) and increased internal competition (Ferreira et al., 2019). These measures are usually associated with cultures and climates of presenteeism, where: i) there is pressure form co-workers for competitiveness and to stay at work at any cost; ii) the belief that those who stay longer hours at work are more productive; iii) there are perceptions of difficulty replacement, where people go to work because they are aware that they cannot be easily replaced; iv) employees are aware of their health problem on their productivity; and finally v) supervisor distrust that characterises the perception that supervisors see absenteeism due to health problems as illegitimate (Ferreira et al., 2015).

In climates and cultures of presenteeism, employees seek to maintain the resources they have obtained so far (i.e., security, prestige, prospects for career advancement). Therefore, they sustain their behaviour in two important premises of the COR theory (Hobfoll, 1989), namely that: i) initial resource loss due to absence associated to burnout will lead to resource loss and opportunities in the future; ii) initial resource gains such as going to work with burnout and hiding their symptoms will lead to resource gains in the future. The shame resilience theory (Brown, 2006) explains that the feeling of shame appears associated with irrational beliefs when individuals cannot correspond to the expectations from colleagues, supervisors, and society. According to the theory, shame appears because people feel powerless and are convinced that they cannot find help to make the right decision. At the same time, the person develops feelings of isolation that are associated with the perception that they cannot receive support.

In sum, companies with climates and cultures of presenteeism provide the appropriate context for the development of shameful burnout since the competitiveness associated with such companies, challenges workers to maintain existing resources and obtain more resources (Hobfoll, 1989). It does not facilitate recovery but promotes behaviour where people must reveal to others that everything is okay with them and that illness is not an obstacle to individual performance and to the contribution of a common good, either for the company or society. During a Covid-19 pandemic, because of the antecedents described above, these effects become even more salient.

A conceptual model

Based on the JD-R model (Bakker & Demerouti, 2007), the present study conceptualises a model (Figure 7.1) to examine the effects of the Covid-19 pandemic-related job stressors (job demands) and perceived social support (job resources) on burnout as conceptualised by Maslach and Jackson (1981). According to the conceptual model and results supported by previous empirical studies (Kumar et al., 2021; Kuntz, 2021; Rapp et al., 2021; Trógolo et al., 2022; Zhou et al., 2022) Covid-19 emergent pandemic-related job stressors (e.g., social dynamics of remote meetings, the use of personal protective equipment, work-family conflicts, and the label of front-line employee) would positively predict burnout. Moreover, drawn on the JD-R model, perceived social support and organisational support would reduce the adverse effects of Covid-19 pandemic-related job stressors on burnout.

According to the COR theory (Hobfoll, 1989) employees are motivated to seek out and retain valuable resources. However, the pandemic increased levels of burnout occurring as a result of perceived or actual loss of different resources from employees. Being aware of this reality, many employees went to work sick with the burnout symptoms exacerbated by the pandemic. In the workplace, the demands associated with the pandemic did not promote a healthy work climate where health problems could be discussed and solved. Being aware of this new ab(normal) environment, many employees were hiding their burnout symptoms, developing what will be called in this chapter as burnout shame.

The process of burnout shame is in part induced by social comparisons and the perception that employees cannot follow the high standards, and the rules (Lewis, 1992) imposed by the demands associated with the specificities of the covid-19 pandemic context. Due to the pandemic-related job stressors, employees increased the perception of self-responsibility related to fear of failure to meet the desired social standards (Lim & Yang, 2015), which in certain circumstances implies to go to work even with burnout. Burnout shame appears when employees self-monitor their desire to cause a positive impression on colleagues, supervisors, and society in general.

Under certain conditions, burnout shame can be exacerbated. In the current conceptual model, the moderators social support, stigmatisation, and presenteeism climate were introduced. In contexts where employees found a lack of social support from peers and supervisors, there seems to be a higher tendency to increase self-criticism (Fatima et al., 2020) and to develop shame (Xing et al., 2021). As a consequence, the phenomenon of burnout shame appeared because employees protect themselves against resource lost and hide their burnout symptoms. Similarly to what happened in the past with previous pandemics such as SARS, EBOLA or HIV/AIDS (Shultz et al., 2016), in companies where employees perceived high levels of stigmatisation and discrimination, they tended to develop high levels of stress (Katafuchi et al., 2021; Pyle et al., 2015) encouraging behaviour of avoidance (May et al., 2020).

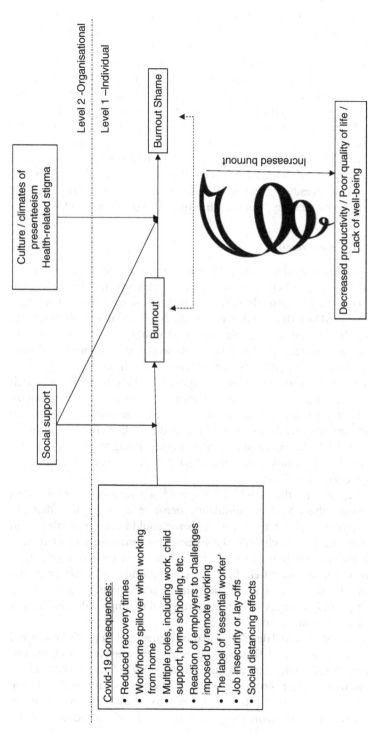

Figure 7.1 Conceptual model explaining how the demands imposed by Covid-19 explain burnout and burnout shame.

In contexts of high stigmatisation people tended to hide their problems and avoid communicating and discussing possible solutions for their health problem. Finally, the current model emphasised the role of presenteeism climate (or cultures) where the pandemic allowed the emergence of cultures of attendance (Ferreira et al., 2022). Organisations with high presenteeism climate/culture are characterised by pressure from colleagues to stay at work overtime, to increase perception of difficulty replacement, or even to have supervisors that see health problems as something that is not a legitimate cause for absenteeism. Being aware of these cultures of attendance, employees with burnout do not feel comfortable to recover easily from burnout. This model explains the dynamic relationship between burnout and burnout shame that tends to accentuate already existing levels of burnout. It is a negative spiral that affects decreased productivity, poor quality of life, and lack of well-being.

Implications and future research

The model presented in this chapter provides an interesting contribution to understand the burnout phenomenon associated with various stressor-related variables. Its conceptualisation allows to enrich the most established theoretical models such as the JD-R (Bakker & Demerouti, 2007) and the COR (Hobfoll, 1989) theories. Its development enables us to understand the emergence of very specific phenomena of burnout shame in which people with burnout syndrome go to work and in certain contexts develop shame and hide the problems associated with burnout from colleagues and supervisors. This multilevel approach also allows us to distinguish the concepts of stigmatisation with health problems and with burnout in particular from the phenomenon of shame that we can feel when we have burnout syndrome. Additionally, the studied conceptual model allows us to extend the literature of presenteeism (i.e., going to work when you are sick) by establishing a link between a negative emotion (shame) and a very specific health condition—burnout.

Furthermore, due to the Covid-19 imposed job-stressors, a multi-level model to capture the potential cumulative negative consequences that the interaction between burnout and burnout shame could have for employees in general is presented in this chapter. This study constitutes an important step where academicians and practitioners can be motivated to investigate these contributions in the burnout field further by considering the different angles and the different levels of analyses of the burnout phenomenon, as well as by introducing repeated measures designs with the goal to empirically understand the dynamics of burnout shame.

From the conceptual model developed in this chapter, new lines of research and contributions to burnout and shame, such as discrete negative emotion, can be better drawn. Based on the different causes of shame (Van Vliet, 2008)) and the three dimensions of burnout as conceptualised by Maslach and Jackson (1981), we may see the emergence of a new construct. In order to validate this new construct, Table 7.1 presents a set of items that, based on the good procedures for the

Table 7.1 Example of possible shame burnout items

	Emotional Exhaustion	Cynicism	Depersonalisation
Transgression to the standards	I feel that for my colleagues when I show signs of tiredness and exhaustion it is a sign of weakness.	I don't want others to see that due to exhaustion I cannot maintain the same levels of productivity.	I feel ashamed that I can no longer treat other people with respect and dignity.
Personal failure	I feel that I am failing when I am feeling burned out from all the work.	I try to hide my incapacity to accomplish my duties.	I feel shame for treating other people as if they were objects.
Social rejection	I feel discrimination when I show signals of being emotionally drained.	I make an extra effort to maintain my performance, for fear of being discriminated.	I am afraid that my indifference to people is starting to isolate me more and more.
Trauma	I feel frustrated by my job due to what I experienced during the Covid-19 pandemic.	The demands of the pandemic were so relevant that even today I try to disguise the difficulties that prevent me from achieving high performance.	I am afraid that people around me will blame me for the problems associated with the pandemic.

construction of psychological assessment instruments (c.f., Hinkin, 1995), may serve as a basis for the construction of a burnout shame scale. Hence, future studies may seek to understand how coping efforts to repair self-image could come with self-regulation, are associated with the emotion shame and how they may affect burnout; in particular, the emotional exhaustion dimension (Xing et al., 2021). However, future studies should take into account that previous studies found cultural differences in in the demonstration of certain emotions such as shame (Mosquera et al., 2000), therefore, future studies should consider the integration of cross-cultural perspectives.

According to the current theoretical assumptions, managers, work and organisational psychologists, and occupational health professionals should introduce regulatory processes to help employees cope with burnout in the post-pandemic context (Ramkissoon, 2021). Specifically, the literature (Di Benedetto & Swadling, 2014) suggests the adoption of mindfulness as a good practice to help people deal with burnout problems. For example, empirical evidence was found suggesting that some mindfulness practices (e.g., acting with awareness, non-reactivity to inner experience, the capacity to describe and non-judging of inner experience) were negatively and significantly correlated with burnout (Di Benedetto & Swadling, 2014).

There is also evidence that an eight-week mindfulness-based yoga group intervention decreased depression, anxiety, stress, increased health and wellbeing among health care professionals (Ofei-Dodoo et al., 2020). These activities are in line with the principles of psychological recovery where nature-based interventions (i.e., walking in direct contact with elements of nature such as animals, forests, rivers ...) play a very relevant role in burnout recovery (Bloomfield, 2017). There is evidence to suggest that the practices that involve contact with nature (e.g., deep breaths in nature, and positive environmental stimuli such as the contact with animals) and muscle relaxation intervention enhance vigor and energetic resources (Steidle et al., 2017) and improve workplace well-being (Sonnentag, 2012). In particular, group sharing experiences between members of organisations, who have symptoms of burnout in common resulting from Covid-19 and beyond, may be important in normalising the perception of being ill in the workplace. The possibility of relativising a health condition like burnout may help people to better understand their problems, reduce shame, and thus make better decisions that may lead to seeking help from specialised professionals.

Conclusions

During the Covid-19 pandemic, we have all been hearing and seeing its impact for the life of the entire human species on television and on social media in general. People were mobilised in a way that was unprecedented in recent human history. Many people were called to work on the front lines, to face the risk of death. Many had to deal with the life and death of millions of people around the world. Others had to improvise and reorganise to make their home a new workplace. This brought implications for the lives of countless families and resulted in burnout levels that in some cases became increasingly unsustainable. However, the media applauded and appealed to the "new heroes" who saved lives, who went to work when others were at home, or even who stayed home and performed multiple roles. What to do when this becomes the new normal? When society and our supervisors "force" us to always do a little more? Now that bosses are without the skills to focus on remote work and more focused on the survival of the business, social support no longer exists and with this, more burnout has appeared. Society and the whole environment created a kind of stigma about the disease. Being sick was not allowed. Companies have also developed cultures and climates of presenteeism. People walked among heroes, and this prevented many from showing their weaknesses, from showing that they were suffering and from asking for help. With this, this chapter shows us that we can easily understand the emergence of burnout shame. On the whole, people who were physically and psychologically exhausted, who had no energy, who dealt with their colleagues as if they were numbers, and who could no longer meet the new demands imposed by the job, hid their health conditions, were afraid to ask for help, and went to work in automatic mode as if they were zombies in the midst of heroes. They forgot that the heroes also needed help, needed to take off their cape and recover. This is one of the stories that the Covid-19 pandemic has brought us. It alerts us of the need for support, acceptance, knowledge that we are not all heroes at the same time, and that even in the midst of so many heroes, it is normal to ask for help.

References

Andrews, B., Qian, M., & Valentine, J. D. (2002). Predicting depressive symptoms with a new measure of shame: The experience of shame scale. *British Journal of Clinical Psychology, 41*, 29–42.

Bakker, A. B., & Demerouti, E. (2007). The job demands-resources model: State of the art. *Journal of Managerial Psychology, 22*(3), 309–328. 10.1108/02683940710733115

Barriga Medina, H. R., Campoverde Aguirre, R., Coello-Montecel, D., Ochoa Pacheco, P., & Paredes-Aguirre, M. I. (2021). The influence of work-family conflict on burnout during the COVID-19 pandemic: The effect of teleworking overload. *International Journal of Environmental Research and Public Health, 18*(19). 10302. https://doi.org/10.33 90/ ijerph181910302

Baumeister, R. F. (2014). Self-regulation, ego depletion, and inhibition. *Neuropsychologia, 65*, 313–319. 10.1016/j.neuropsycho-logia.2014.08.012

Bianchi, R., Verkuilen, J., Brisson, R., Schonfeld, I. S., & Laurent, E. (2016). Burnout and depression: Label-related stigma, help-seeking, and syndrome overlap. *Psychiatry Research, 245*, 91–98. 10.1016/j.psychres.2016.08.025

Bloomfield, D. (2017). What makes nature-based interventions for mental health successful? *BJPsych International, 14*, 82–85. 10.1192/S2056474000002063

Brooks, S., Dunn, R., Amlôt, R., Rubin, G., & Greenberg, N. (2019). Protecting the psychological wellbeing of staff exposed to disaster or emergency at work: A qual-itative study. *BMC Psychology, 7*(1), 78. https://doi.org/10.1186/s40359-019-0360-6

Brown, B. (2006). Shame resilience theory: A grounded theory study on women and shame. *Families in Society, 87*(1), 43e52.

Caldas, M. P., Ostermeier, K., & Cooper, D. (2021). When helping hurts: COVID-19 critical incident involvement and resource depletion in health care workers. *Journal of Applied Psychology, 106*(1), 29–47. 10.1037/apl0000850

Cavalera, C. (2020). COVID-19 psychological implications: The role of shame and guilt. *Frontiers in Psychology, 11*. 10.3389/fpsyg.2020.571828

Clough, B. A., Ireland, M. J., & March, S. (2019). Development of the SOSS-D: A scale to measure stigma of occupational stress and burnout in medical doctors. *Journal of Mental Health, 28*(1), 26–33. 10.1080/09638237.2017.1370642

Cooper, C. (1996). Hot under the colar. *The Times Higher Education Supplement*, June 21st.

Cortina, L. M., Sandy Hershcovis, M., & Clancy, K. B. H. (2022). The embodiment of insult: A theory of biobehavioral response to workplace incivility. *Journal of Management, 48*(3), 738–763. 10.1177/0149206321989798

Daniels, M. A., & Robinson, S. L. (2019). The shame of it all: A review of shame in organizational life. *Journal of Management, 45*(6), 2448–2473. 10.1177/014920631881 7604

Di Benedetto, M., & Swadling, M. (2014). Burnout in Australian psychologists: Correlations with work-setting, mindfulness and self-care behaviours. *Psychology, Health & Medicine, 19*, 705–715. 10.1080/13548506.2013.861602

Fatima, T., Majeed, M., & Jahanzeb, S. (2020). Supervisor undermining and submissive behavior: Shame resilience theory perspective. *European Management Journal, 38*(1), 191–203. 10.1016/j.emj.2019.07.003

Ferreira, A. I., Mach, M., Martinez, L. F., Brewster, C., Dagher, G., Perez-Nebra, A., & Lisovskaya, A. (2019). Working sick and out of sorts: A cross-cultural approach on presenteeism climate, organizational justice and work–family conflict. *The International Journal of Human Resource Management, 30*(19), 2754–2776. 10.1080/09585192.2017.1332673

Ferreira, A. I., Mach, M., Martinez, L. F., & Miraglia, M. (2022). Sickness presenteeism in the aftermath of COVID-19: Is presenteeism remote-work behavior the new (Ab) normal? *Frontiers in Psychology, 12,* 748053. 10.3389/fpsyg.2021.748053

Ferreira, A. I., Martinez, L. F., Cooper, C., & Gui, D. M. (2015). LMX as a negative predictor of presenteeism climate: A cross-cultural study in the financial and health sectors. *Journal of Organizational Effectiveness: People and Performance, 2*(3), 282–302.

Fong, L. H. N., Chui, P. M. W., Cheong, I. S. C., et al. (2018). Moderating effects of social support on job stress and turnover intentions. *Journal of Hospitality Mark Management, 27*(7), 795–810.

Greenberg, N., Docherty, M., Gnanapragasam, S., & Wessely, S. (2020). Managing mental health challenges faced by healthcare workers during covid-19 pandemic. *BMJ (Clinical research ed.),* 368, m1211. https://doi.org/10.1136/bmj.m1211

Hinkin, T. R. (1995). A review of scale development practices in the study of organizations. *Journal of Management, 21*(5), 967–988. 10.1177/014920639502100509

Hobfoll, S. E. (1989). Conservation of resources: A new attempt at conceptualizing stress. *American Psychologist, 44*(3), 513–524, 10.1037/0003-066X.44.3.513

International Labour Organization (2020). *Teleworking during the COVID-19 Pandemic and beyond: A Practical Guide.* Available online: https://www.ilo.org/moscow/news/WCMS_751232/lang--en/index.htm (accessed on 28 August 2021).

Katafuchi, Y., Kurita, K., & Managi, S. (2021). COVID-19 with stigma: Theory and evidence from mobility data. *Economics of Disasters and Climate Change, 5*(1), 1–25. 10.1007/s41885-020-00077-w

Kumaresan, A., Suganthirababu, P., Srinivasan, V., Vijay Chandhini, Y., Divyalaxmi, P., Alagesan, J., Vishnuram, S., Ramana, K., Prathap, L., Davis, K., & Kotowski, S. (2022). Prevalence of burnout syndrome among work-from-home IT professionals during the COVID-19 pandemic. *Work, 71*(2), 379–384. 10.3233/WOR-211040

Kumar, P., Singh, S. S., Pandey, A. K., Singh, R. K., Srivastava, P. K., Kumar, M., Dubey, S. K., Sah, U., Nandan, R., Singh, S. K., Agrawal, P., Kushwaha, A., Rani, M., Biswas, J. K., & Drews, M. (2021). Multi-level impacts of the COVID-19 lockdown on agricultural systems in India: The case of Uttar Pradesh. *Agricultural Systems, 187*(1).

Kuntz, J. C. (2021). Resilience in times of global pandemic: steering recovery and thriving trajectories. *Applied Psychology: An International Review, 70*(1), 188–215. 10.1111/apps.12296

Leo, C. G., Sabina, S., Tumolo, M. R., Bodini, A., Ponzini, G., Sabato, E., & Mincarone, P. (2021). Burnout among healthcare workers in the COVID 19 Era: A review of the existing literature. *Frontiers in Public Health, 9,* 750529. 10.3389/fpubh.2021.750529

Leskela, J., Dieperink, M., & Thuras, P. (2002). Shame and posttraumatic stress disorder. *Journal of Traumatic Stress, 15,* 223–226.

Lewis, M. (1992). *Shame: The exposed self.* New York, NY: Simon and Schuster.

Lim, M., & Yang, Y. (2015). Effects of users' envy and shame on social comparison that occurs on social network services. *Computers in Human Behavior, 51*(1), 300–311.

Livne-Ofer, E., Coyle-Shapiro, J. A.-M., & Pearce, J. L. (2019). Eyes wide open: Perceived exploitation and its consequences. *Academy of Management Journal, 62*(6), 1989–2018. 10.5465/amj.2017.1421

Logie, C. H., & Turan, J. M. (2020). How do we balance tensions between COVID-19 public health responses and stigma mitigation? Learning from HIV research. *AIDS and Behavior, 24*, 2003–2006. 10.1007/s10461-020-02856-8

Lu, L., Cooper, C. L., & Lin, H. Y. (2013). A cross-cultural examination of presenteeism and supervisory support. *Career Development International, 18*, 440–456.

Malinen, S., Hatton, T., Näswall, K., & Kuntz, J. C. (2019). Strategies to enhance employee well-being and organisational performance in a postcrisis environment: A case study. *Journal of Contingencies and Crisis Management, 27*(1), 79–86.

Maslach, C., & Jackson, S. E. (1981). The measurement of experienced burnout. *Journal of Organisational Behaviour, 2*, 99–113. 10.1002/job.4030020205

Maslach, C., & Leiter, M. P. (2022). Work changed forever. *Scientific American, 326*(3), 64–65.

May, R. W., Terman, J. M., Foster, G., Seibert, G. S., & Fincham, F. D. (2020). Burnout stigma inventory: Initial development and validation in industry and academia. *Frontiers in Psychology, 11*. 10.3389/fpsyg.2020.00391

Mosquera, P. M., Manstead, A. S. R., & Fischer, A. H. (2000). The role of honor-related values in the elicitation, experience, and communication of pride, shame, and anger: Spain and the Netherlands compared. *Personality and Social Psychology Bulletin, 26*, 833–844.

O'Connor, L. E., Berry, J. W., & Weiss, J. (1999). Interpersonal guilt, shame, and psychological problems. *Journal of Social and Clinical Psychology, 18*(2), 181–203.

Ofei-Dodoo, S., Cleland-Leighton, A., Nilsen, K., Cloward, J. L., & Casey, E. (2020). Impact of a mindfulness-based, workplace group yoga intervention on burnout, self-care, and compassion in health care professionals: A pilot study. *Journal of Occupational & Environmental Medicine, 62*(8), 581–587. 10.1097/JOM.0000000000001892

Orth, U., Berking, M., & Burkhardt, S. (2006). Self-conscious emotions and depression: Ruminating explains why shame but not guilt is maladaptive. *Personality and Social Psychology Bulletin, 32*, 1608–1619.

Pyle, M., Stewart, S. K., French, P., Byrne, R., Patterson, P., Gumley, A., et al. (2015). Internalized stigma, emotional dysfunction and unusual experiences in young people at risk of psychosis. *Early Intervention in Psychiatry 9*, 133–140. 10.1111/eip.12098

Ramkissoon, H. (2021). Place Affect Interventions During and After the COVID-19 Pandemic. *Frontiers in Psychology, 12*, 726685. 10.3389/fpsyg.2021.726685

Rapp, D. J., Hughey, J. M., & Kreiner, G. E. (2021). Boundary work as a buffer against burnout: Evidence from healthcare workers during the COVID-19 pandemic. *Journal of Applied Psychology, 106*(8), 1169–1187. 10.1037/apl0000951

Shultz, J. M., Cooper, J. L., Baingana, F., Oquendo, M. A., Espinel, Z., Althouse, B. M., & Rechkemmer, A. (2016). The role of fear-related behaviors in the 2013-2016 West Africa Ebola virus disease outbreak. *Current Psychiatry Reports, 18*(11), 104 10.1007/s11 920-016-0741-y

Simpson, R. (1998). Presenteeism, power and organizational change: Long hours as a career barrier and the impact on the working lives of women managers. *British Journal of Management, 9*, S37–S50.

Sonnentag, S. (2012). Psychological detachment from work during leisure time: the benefits of mentally disengaging from work. *Current Directions in Psychological Science, 21*, 114–118. 10.1177/0963721411434979

Steidle, A., Gonzalez-Morales, M. G., Hoppe, A., Michel, A., and O'shea, D. (2017). Energizing respites from work: a randomized controlled study on respite interventions. *European Journal of Work and Organizational Psychology*, *26*, 650–662. 10.1080/1359432 X.2017.134834

Trógolo, M. A., Moretti, L. S., & Medrano, L. A. (2022). A nationwide cross-sectional study of workers' mental health during the COVID-19 pandemic: Impact of changes in working conditions, financial hardships, psychological detachment from work and work-family interface. *BMC Psychology*, *10*(1). https://doi.org/10.1186/s40359-022-00783-y

Van Vliet, K. J. (2008). Shame and resilience in adulthood: A grounded theory study. *Journal of Counseling Psychology*, *55*(2), 233–245.

Warren, A. M., Khetan, R., Bennett, M., Pogue, J., Waddimba, A. C., Powers, M. B., & Sanchez, K. (2022). The relationship between stigma and mental health in a population of individuals with COVID-19. *Rehabilitation Psychology*, *67*(2), 226–230. 10.1037/ rep0000436

Xie, J., Ifie, K., & Gruber, T. (2022). The dual threat of COVID-19 to health and job security – Exploring the role of mindfulness in sustaining frontline employee-related outcomes. *Journal of Business Research*, *146*, 216–227. 10.1016/j.jbusres.2022.03.030

Xing, L., Jian-min (James), S., & Jepsen, D. (2021). Feeling shame in the workplace: Examining negative feedback as an antecedent and performance and well-being as consequences. *Journal of Organizational Behavior*, *42*(9), 1244–1260. 10.1002/job.2553

Zhou, T., Xu, C., Wang, C., Sha, S., Wang, Z., Zhou, Y., Zhang, X., Hu, D., Liu, Y., Tian, T., Liang, S., Zhou, L., & Wang, Q. (2022). Burnout and well-being of healthcare workers in the post-pandemic period of COVID-19: A perspective from the job demands-resources model. *BMC Health Services Research*, *22*(1). 284. https://doi.org/10.1186/s12913-022-07608-z

8 COVID-19 impact on health care worker burnout: Insights from the areas of worklife model for job burnout

Colin P. West

Professor of Medicine, Medical Education, and Biostatistics Division of General Internal Medicine, Department of Medicine, Division of Clinical Trials and Biostatistics, Department of Quantitative Health Sciences Mayo Clinic, Rochester, MN USA

COVID-19 and health care worker burnout

It is well established that health care worker well-being was severely challenged prior to the onset of the COVID-19 pandemic (National Academies of Sciences, Engineering, and Medicine, 2019). The high prevalence of burnout symptoms across health care professions is a major part of this crisis of distress (Dyrbye et al., 2019a; Dyrbye et al., 2020a; Dyrbye et al., 2021; Rotenstein et al., 2018; Shanafelt et al., 2022). The pandemic has exposed and exacerbated these problems, although the patterns of well-being and distress have proven to tell a more complex story than first appearances might suggest.

Differences over time and stages of the pandemic

Burnout has consistently differed across stages of the pandemic. For example, in the United States a national study demonstrated high burnout experiences during the first three to nine months of the pandemic (Prasad et al., 2021). A subsequent national study in the United States examining the subsequent six months, when many were hopeful that the worst had passed and before the Delta and Omicron variants became widespread, actually revealed lower degrees of burnout symptoms than documented over the previous decade (Shanafelt et al., 2022). As the pandemic continued, however, distress rebounded and burnout concerns have continued to rise (Office of the Surgeon General, 2022). Regional and international studies of health care workers have similarly documented substantial posttraumatic stress among other mental health consequences (Feingold et al., 2021; Johns et al., 2022; Yu et al., 2021).

One way to understand burnout experiences across the stages of the pandemic is to consider the emotional phases of disaster response (DeWolfe, 2000). Phase 1 (the pre-disaster phase) is characterised by uncertainty, relating to safety, adequacy of disaster preparations, and the future. Phase 2 is the disaster–impact phase, with varying effects ranging from disbelief to dismay to

DOI: 10.4324/9781003250531-9

panic, with rapid conversion to a focus on safety for ourselves and others. Phase 3 is the immediate response to the emergency, the heroic phase. Health care workers' core professional values, including altruism, drive behaviours to run towards the crisis we advise others to avoid. A surge of positive emotion marks the transition from Phase 3 into Phase 4, the honeymoon period. During this phase, a sense of community and shared purpose predominates. Aligned with these positive feelings, distress and burnout may be less experienced or perhaps suppressed early on in a disaster situation such as the COVID-19 pandemic.

Unfortunately, these positive emotions erode in the face of prolonged strain, and the disillusionment characterising Phase 5 sets in. This phase involves tension as health care workers' inherent optimism and hopefulness struggle against chronic stress, exhaustion, and discouragement. It is important to emphasise that health care workers are notably resilient at baseline, with a remarkable ability to bounce back from distress, at least in the short term (West et al., 2020). However, repeated disappointments and experiences with the disillusionment phase of the pandemic have eroded this resilience and promoted cynicism and emotional exhaustion, hallmarks of burnout. As support scales back, the gap between needs and resources drives further negativity (Demerouti et al., 2001). This phase of disaster response presents particular risks for mental health issues and the longer the disaster remains unresolved, the deeper and more entrenched the effects of disillusionment become.

The final emotional phase of disaster response is reconstruction, where recovery begins. Phase 6 can involve setbacks and acknowledgment of shared grief, but the overall trend is positive. Importantly, the goal of reconstruction and recovery is not just to restore the pre-disaster state but to achieve post-traumatic growth in response to the disaster experience. This can provide meaning to the disaster experience and hope that we are better prepared for future disasters. This model offers hope that current pandemic-associated distress and burnout can be overcome and possibly even open the door to larger solutions to promote well-being that were increasingly necessary even before the pandemic.

Differences across other factors

Burnout during the COVID-19 pandemic has also differed across medical specialties, job roles, geography, and other factors. For example, the initial surge of burnout symptoms during the pandemic particularly affected inpatient health care workers, social workers, employees working in lower-paid and assistant roles, women, and underrepresented groups such as Black health care workers (Prasad et al., 2021; Shanafelt et al., 2022). These disparities have continued as the pandemic has continued (Office of the Surgeon General, 2022). However, COVID-19 surges affected different parts of the world and different regions within countries at different times, so these impacts have been felt heterogeneously over time across these groups.

Regardless of the factors affecting COVID-19's impact on particular groups, common experiences have contributed to burnout resulting from or exacerbated by the pandemic. For example, inadequate access to personal protective equipment and experiencing substantial economic consequences has been associated with burnout risk (Shanafelt et al., 2022). Providing direct care for patients seriously affected by COVID-19, especially those who died from their infection, has also been linked to increased burnout risk along with risk of other mental health problems (Yu et al., 2021). Unfortunately, mistreatment from patients and families has become increasingly common over the course of the pandemic and is strongly associated with health care worker distress (Larkin, 2021; Dyrbye et al., 2022). On the other hand, perceived support from clinical leadership may mitigate burnout risks (Feingold et al., 2021; Shanafelt et al., 2022), and listening, protecting, preparing, supporting, and caring for health care workers can protect and promote well-being (Shanafelt et al., 2020).

The areas of worklife model and burnout during the COVID-19 pandemic

The Areas of Worklife model for job burnout identifies six dimensions of work experience that predict burnout if suboptimally manifested in the workplace: workload, control, reward, community, fairness, and values (Leiter & Maslach, 1999). Differing contributions from each area of worklife category may explain observed differences in COVID-19 impact and inform approaches to anticipate, mitigate, and even prevent burnout in different pandemic-impacted settings as illustrated in the Table.

Workload

Workload is a consistent driver of burnout across professions and studies. Health care workers need time to recover from the demands of work. Human performance follows standard principles set forth by the Yerkes-Dodson Law, namely that beyond a certain point performance suffers if demands persist unabated (Yerkes & Dodson, 1908). Though not unique to medicine, health care workers often view themselves as impervious to the effects of overwork and have poor insight into their own degree of distress (Shanafelt et al., 2014). In addition, core principles of medical professionalism can be misused and misconstrued to maintain or even glorify excessive workloads that cause individual distress (Ofri, 2019; West & Shanafelt, 2007).

Within the COVID-19 pandemic, the effect of workload on burnout has been obvious. During the initial phases of the pandemic many health care workers worked superhuman hours to staff hospitals and clinics. This workload worsened as colleagues fell ill or declined to participate in vaccination programs and were removed from their job roles. Physical and emotional exhaustion was inevitable under these circumstances, and when coupled with inadequate administrative support and insufficient measures to mitigate risks to self and family as previously described, mental health distress and burnout have predictably resulted.

Control

A sense of control, autonomy, and agency at work is aligned with well-being and incongruent with burnout. Control at work also supports other drivers of well-being by allowing individuals to structure work to manage workload, support community, and align organisational and personal values. It is important to note that autonomy at work does not mean individual prioritisation without consideration of team needs, but rather avoiding a sense of "being a cog in the machine" with no say in how work occurs to optimise well-being and hence performance.

One area where control has been adversely impacted by COVID-19 overlaps with the workload effects described above. When health care areas are short-staffed and professional values prompt individuals to fill gaps in patient care needs as a priority even when they are exhausted, job control can feel like an after-thought. Job roles have also become blurred as staffing shortages necessitate individuals taking on responsibilities outside their typical functions, leading to role conflict, ambiguity, and confusion. Again, burnout is an expected result in such circumstances.

Reward

Intrinsic and extrinsic rewards are essential elements of well-being at work. Intrinsic reward may derive from the "MVPs" of well-being (meaning, values, and purpose). Meaning-filled, value-aligned, purpose-driven work serves as an antidote to burnout. Particularly in a profession such as health care where responsibility for others is so central, ensuring that this work is meaningful is critical. Feeling too worn down emotionally to tap into meaning and purpose, or becoming increasingly depersonalised so that patients become objects and health care workers become callous to their experiences and needs, will exacerbate burnout risk.

Extrinsic reward involves feeling valued and recognised, with close relationship to fairness at work. In many regions, adequate personal protective equipment was not available during early waves of the COVID-19 pandemic. The assumption of undue risks that were forced upon health care workers, especially those on the front lines of care, sent a message that health care workers were not sufficiently valued, threatening their sense of extrinsic reward and promoting burnout. Another area affecting the reward drivers of burnout during the COVID-19 pandemic is the documented increase in mistreatment by patients and families experienced by health care workers (Dyrbye et al., 2022). Early in the pandemic public perception and appreciation was very high, manifesting in nightly bell-ringing and applause sessions in many parts of the world. Unfortunately this has given way to displays of frustration and anger, diminished trust and susceptibility to misinformation about public health measures for infection control and vaccination, and even acts of violence against health care workers. Each of these unfortunate changes contributes to health care workers feeling unappreciated despite the extremes to which many have gone to protect patients at risk to themselves and their families. It is not surprising that this would then foster burnout.

Community

Social support, connectedness, and a sense of community are major contributors to well-being, especially in team-oriented professions such as medicine. Unfortunately, the COVID-19 pandemic forced interpersonal isolation while at work, further aggravated by remote work requirements for many. Though not undesirable for all health care workers, many have found these experiences increasingly distressing over time. The fact that isolation during the pandemic is not just a work phenomenon but also affects relationships and connectedness at home has added to the negative impact of loss of community on overall well-being.

Belonging is a related construct that can affect burnout and extends beyond isolation and loneliness (Salles et al., 2019). Also, imposter syndrome affects many learners, practicing clinicians, and other health care workers across medical job roles. Associated feelings of self-doubt and inadequacy may not match actual skills, yet can contribute to withdrawal and isolation. As previously discussed, mistreatment, discrimination, and bias are additional common barriers to belonging disproportionately affecting marginalised and underrepresented groups of health care workers. These experiences have been demonstrated to affect many groups in medicine with attendant connections to burnout (Dyrbye et al., 2019b; Dyrbye et al., 2022; Larkin, 2021). These issues may not be specifically related to COVID-19, but the disconnection during the pandemic has served to sustain these negative influences on health care worker well-being. When these and other issues contribute to mental health concerns, help-seeking should be encouraged and normalised. Stigma around mental health care is a societal problem, but is especially prevalent in medicine with high rates of hesitancy to seek help when faced with substantial distress (Dyrbye et al., 2015; Dyrbye et al., 2017; Dyrbye et al., 2020b; Kelsey et al., 2021; Shanafelt et al., 2021). Mental health has become an increasingly serious concern given the strain of the pandemic, and support remains inadequate.

Fairness

Feeling treated equitably promotes a sense of community and aligns with well-being mediated by reward. Burnout develops when employees do not have a sense of mutual trust among colleagues and supervisors, cannot rely on consistent and balanced work expectations and resources, and do not feel respected at work.

The unequal burdens of pandemic-related workload and risk across specialties and job roles have threatened fairness. For example, hospital workers in emergency departments and intensive care units faced extreme stress during pandemic surges while elective surgeries were cancelled so some surgical staff had little or no work. Access to personal protective equipment and vaccines was not uniform early in the pandemic either. In addition, health care workers with less robust financial resources to withstand pandemic impacts such as furloughs and increased costs of living have been disproportionately affected. A less discussed source of inequities is the role of temporary or contract health care workers to fill needs during pandemic surges and staffing shortfalls. On the one hand, these care roles are necessary and workload distribution offers benefits to overtaxed employees. On the other hand, these workers have often been paid high premiums well above the compensation provided to regular employees, commonly leading to feelings of unfairness and lack of respect.

Values

Alignment of personal values with what employees see demonstrated in the operations of their organisations is another important contributor to well-being, especially in purpose-driven professions such as medicine. Value congruence supports maximal work effort in meaningful activities that reward both the health care worker and the organisation. In health care, this is often best expressed by mutual prioritisation of what is best for patients, recognising that patients are best cared for by employees who are themselves cared for (Thomas et al., 2018). When personal and organisational values diverge, or stated and experienced organisational priorities differ from one another, these conflicts cause emotional distress and even moral injury for health care workers.

During the COVID-19 pandemic, value congruence has been highly variable. At times, patient-centred care has been a unifying rallying point for health care workers and their organisations. At other times, some practices have been seen as slow to make necessary investments in staffing and personal protective equipment needs, quick to furlough employees and expose them to financial hardships, and unwilling to consistently enforce public health protocols to protect health care workers and their families from infection. These concerns have extended to confusion and misalignment of messaging from local and national governments as well, with the well documented policy inconsistencies and resulting infection statistics in the United States representing a prime example of the disruptive effects of such issues. These tensions have worsened distress, including burnout, for health care workers who have many other hardships to deal with in their daily work roles and no additional emotional bandwidth to absorb these external stressors.

Applications to burnout solutions

The alignment of the areas of worklife dimensions with burnout experiences of health care workers during the COVID-19 pandemic reinforces their importance as drivers requiring attention if burnout anticipation, mitigation, and prevention are to be successful. The relevance of areas of worklife domains within the COVID-19 pandemic offers insight into approaches to burnout both during the pandemic and after the global crisis has eased (Table).

To address workload, for example, medicine desperately needs a revised staffing model that incorporates a buffer for back-up roles when health care workers fall ill or become overextended. Unfortunately, resources have not kept pace to meet the increasingly high demands of health care outside of emergency situations like the pandemic, and the surge in workload during the pandemic laid bare how fragile and at time non-existent staffing back-up systems are. Building redundancy into health care structures is a necessity that requires different thinking from recent emphasis on "lean" business models. Placing the well-being of health care workers as a priority alongside that of patients themselves will demand transformed practice models and result in a more effective health care system.

These models will naturally lend themselves to increased control and autonomy at work, reduced role conflicts and ambiguity, and feelings of being treated fairly at work as demands shift from the impossible to the achievable. Feeling less stretched will allow greater connection with patients and patient-related meaning and purpose in work, supporting a sense of intrinsic reward and visible alignment of organisational values with individual health care worker values in service of patients. These models will also demonstrate how valued health care workers are, as opposed to the common sense during COVID-19 of health care workers as undersupported yet essential workers who have been taken for granted. Careful attention to communication and relationships with patients will be needed to clarify that these measures are ultimately aimed at improving patient care, especially if continuity in the short term may diminish. Health care workers will need to embrace hand-off and transition mechanisms to protect patients from errors at potential discontinuity points in staffing across health care worker job roles.

The pandemic has also reinforced the need to protect health care workers from the subset of patients and colleagues who expose them to mistreatment. Enhanced health care worker well-being would be expected to improve health care workers' ability to meaningfully engage with patients and promote satisfaction even during stressful times, but beyond this health care organisations must develop and enforce expected behaviours for all stakeholders in health care. This focus must include attention beyond individual human interactions to building trust between medicine as a profession and society as a whole and exposing misinformation that can be harmful to both health care workers and patients.

A third insight brought into clearer focus by the COVID-19 pandemic is that health care organisations should promote community by extending opportunities for health care workers to connect and share experiences for mutual support. An example is the COMPASS (COlleagues Meeting to Promote And Sustain Satisfaction) group approach developed and implemented at Mayo Clinic for physicians (West et al., 2014; West et al., 2021). This and other small-group

Table 8.1 Relationship of areas of worklife with COVID-19 and Associated Potential Solutions

Area of Worklife	Relationship with COVID-19	Associated Potential Solutions
Workload	Increased hours and work intensity during pandemic due to work volume and staff shortages	Implement staffing models with built-in redundancy to accommodate absences and distribute workload
Control	Work coverage mandates and extended roles beyond typical functions	Prioritise consistent job roles with adequate team support to allow health care workers to apply their unique skills
Reward	Inadequate displays of value evidenced by lack of personal protective equipment availability Increased mistreatment of health care workers by patients and families	Develop and enforce policies to protect health care workers from illness and mistreatment, promote trust between medicine and society, and connect health care workers with meaning and purpose in their work
Community	Isolation necessitated by infection protocols	Extend opportunities for health care workers to connect, share experiences, and build communities that function as safe spaces for well-being
Fairness	Inequitable exposure risks and work demands across job roles Disparities in compensation between employed health care workers and temporary or contract workers	Ensure appropriate workplace protections for higher-risk roles and equitable total work compensation (including salary and benefits) for similar job functions
Values	Insufficient investment in staffing and financial protections for health care workers Inconsistent enforcement of public health protocols to protect health care workers	Demonstrate how much health care workers are valued by placing highest priority on fully supporting them and aligning organisational values to optimise their ability to care for patients

approaches such as Schwartz Rounds and Balint groups could include other health care worker job roles and interdisciplinary teams, deliberately reach out to off-site employees and teleworkers, and more fully promote community across health care teams, a key areas of worklife domain. In addition to these active community-building mechanisms, destigmatised and confidential processes for mental health care must be made much more available to help health care workers. Medical licensure language has improved in recent years (American College of Physicians, 2022; Dyrbye et al., 2017; Saddawi-Konefka et al., 2021), but much more is needed to extend protections more broadly across all health care worker job roles.

Summary

Distress among HCWs was common before the COVID-19 pandemic, and has become an even more pressing issue as the pandemic has increased demands and strained resources across all of society. COVID-19's impact on health care worker well-being has differed across time, medical specialty, job roles, geography, and other factors in patterns well-predicted by the areas of worklife model for job burnout. This model's six dimensions of work experience that predict burnout if sub-optimally manifested in the workplace (workload, control, reward, community, fairness, and values) offers insight into solutions to reduce burnout and promote well-being as the pandemic continues and as medicine experiences post-traumatic growth in the future (Table 8.1).

References

American College of Physicians. (2022). *Advocacy Toolkit: Revising License and Credentialing Application to Not Ask About Mental Health.* https://www.acponline.org/practice-resources/physician-well-being-and-professional-fulfillment/advocacy-toolkit-revising-license-and-credentialing-applications-to-not-ask-about-mental-health

Demerouti, E., Bakker, A. B., Nachreiner, F., & Schaufeli, W. B. (2001). The job demands-resourcs model of burnout. *Journal of Applied Psychology, 86*(3), 499–512. 10.1037/0021-9010.86.3.499

DeWolfe, D. J. (2000). Training manual for mental health and human service workers in major disasters (2nd ed.). HHS publication no. ADM 90–538. U.S. Department of Health and Human Services, Substance Abuse and Mental Health Services Administration, Center for Mental Health Services. https://eric.ed.gov/?id=ED459383

Dyrbye, L. N., Eacker, A., Durning, S. J., Brazeau, C., Moutier, C., Massie, F. S., Satele, D., Sloan, J. A., & Shanafelt, T. D. (2015). The impact of stigma and personal experiences on the help-seeking behaviors of medical students with burnout. *Academic Medicine, 90*(7), 961–969. 10.1097/ACM.0000000000000655

Dyrbye, L. N., Herrin, J., West, C. P., Wittlin, N. M., Dovidio, J. F., Hardeman, R., Burke, S. E., Phelan, S., Onyeador, I. N., Cunningham, B., & Van Ryn, M. (2019b). Association of racial bias with burnout among resident physicians. *JAMA Network Open, 2*(7), e197457. 10.1001/jamanetwork.open.2019.7457

Dyrbye, L. N., Leep Hunderfund, A. N., Winters, R. C., Moeschler, S. M., Vaa Stelling, B. E., Dozois, E. J., Satele, D. V., & West, C. P. (2020b). *Academic Medicine, 96*(5), 701–708. 10.1097/ACM.0000000000003790

Dyrbye, L. N., West, C. P., Halasy, M., O'Laughlin, D. J., Satele, D., & Shanafelt, T. (2020a). Burnout and satisfaction with work-life integration among PAs relative to other workers. *JAAPA, 33*(5), 35–44. 10.1097/01.JAA.0000660156.17502.e6

Dyrbye, L. N., West, C. P., Johnson, P. O., Cipriano, P. F., Beatty, D. E., Peterson, C., Major-Elechi B., & Shanafelt, T. (2019a). Burnout and satisfaction with work-life integration among nurses. *Journal of Occupational and Environmental Medicine, 61*(8), 689–698. 10.1097/JOM.0000000000001637

Dyrbye, L. N., West, C. P., Kelsey, E. A., Gossard, A. A., Satele, D., & Shanafelt, T. (2021). A national study of personal accomplishment, burnout, and satisfaction with work-life integration among advance practice nurses relative to other workers. *Journal of the American Association of Nurse Practitioners, 33*(11), 896–906. 10.1097/JXX.0000000000000517

Dyrbye, L. N., West, C. P., Sinsky, C. A., Goeders, L. E., Satele, D. V., & Shanafelt, T. D. (2017). Medical licensure questions and physician reluctance to seek care for mental health conditions. *Mayo Clinic Proceedings*, *92*(10), 1486–1493. 10.1016/j.mayocp.2017. 06.020

Dyrbye, L. N., West, C. P., Sinsky, C. A., Trockel, M., Tutty, M., Satele, D., Carlasare, L., & Shanafelt, T. (2022). Physicians' experiences with mistreatment and discrimination by patients, families, and visitors and association with burnout. *JAMA Network Open*, *5*(5), e2213080. 10.1001/jamanetworkopen.2022.13080

Feingold, J. H., Peccoralo, L., Chan, C. C., Kaplan, C. A., Kaye-Kauderer, H., Charney, D., Verity, J., Hurtado, A., Burka, L., Syed, S. A., Murrough, J. W., Feder, A., Pietrzak, R. H., & Ripp, J. (2021). Psychological impact of the COVID-19 pandemic on frontline health care workers during the pandemic surge in New York City. *Chronic Stress*, *5*. 10.1177/2470547020977891. https://pubmed.ncbi.nlm.nih.gov/33598592/.

Johns, G., Waddington, L., & Samuel, V. (2022). Prevalence and predictors of mental health outcomes in UK doctors and final year medical students during the COVID-19 pandemic. *Journal of Affective Disorders*, *311*, 267–275. 10.1016/j.jad.2022.05.024

Kelsey, E. A., West, C. P., Cipriano, P. F., Peterson, C., Satele, D., Shanafelt, T., & Dyrbye, L. N. (2021). Suicidal ideation and attitudes toward help seeking in U.S. nurses relative to the general working population. *American Journal of Nursing*, *121*(11), 24–36. 10.1097/01.NAJ.0000798056.73563.fa

Larkin, H. (2021). Navigating attacks against health care workers in the COVID-19 era. *JAMA*, *325*(18), 1822–1824. 10.1001/jama.2021.2701

Leiter, M. P. & Maslach, C. (1999). Six areas of worklife: a model of the organizational context of burnout. *Journal of Health and Human Services Administration*, *21*(4), 472–498.

National Academies of Sciences, Engineering, and Medicine. (2019). *Taking Action Against Clinician Burnout: A Systems Approach to Professional Well-Being*. Washington, DC: The National Academies Press. 10.17226/25521.

Office of the Surgeon General. (2022). *Addressing Health Worker Burnout: The U.S. Surgeon General's Advisory on Building a Thriving Health Workforce*. https://www.hhs.gov/sites/default/files/health-worker-wellbeing-advisory.pdf

Ofri, D. (2019, June 8). The business of health care depends on exploiting doctors and nurses. *The New York Times*. https://www.nytimes.com/2019/06/08/opinion/sunday/hospitals-doctors-nurses-burnout.html

Prasad, K., McLoughlin, C., Stillman, M., Poplau, S., Goelz, E., Taylor, S., Nankivil, N., Brown, R., Linzer, M., Cappelucci, K., Barbouche, M., & Sinsky, C. A. (2021). Prevalence and correlates of stress and burnout among U.S. healthcare workers during the COVID-19 pandemic: A national cross-sectional survey study. *EClinicalMedicine*, *35*, 100879. 10.1016/j.eclinm.2021.100879

Rotenstein, L. S., Torre, M., Ramos, M. A., Rosales, R. C., Guille, C., Sen, S., & Mata, D. A. (2018). Prevalence of burnout among physicians: A systematic review. *JAMA*, *320*(11), 1131–1150. 10.1001/jama.2018.12777

Saddawi-Konefka, D., Brown, A., Eisenhart, I., Hicks, K., Barrett, E., & Gold, J. A. (2021). Consistency between state medical license applications and recommendations regarding physician mental health. *JAMA*, *325*(19), 2017–2018. 10.1001/jama.2021.2275

Salles, A., Wright, R. C., Milam, L., Panni, R. Z., Liebert, C. A., Lau, J. N., Lin, D. T., & Mueller, C. M. (2019). Social belonging as a predictor of surgical resident well-being and attrition. *Journal of Surgical Education*, *76*(2), 370–377. 10.1016/j.jsurg.2018.08.022

Shanafelt, T., Ripp, J., & Trockel, M. (2020). Understanding and addressing sources of anxiety among health care professionals during the COVID-19 pandemic. *JAMA*, *323*(21), 2133–2134. 10.1001/jama.2020.5893

Shanafelt, T. D., Dyrbye, L. N., West, C. P., Sinsky, C. A., Tutty, M., Carlasare, L. E., Wang, H., & Trockel, M. (2021). Suicidal ideation and attitudes regarding help seeking in US physicians relative to the US working population. *Mayo Clinic Proceedings*, *96*(8), 2067–2080. 10.1016/j.mayocp.2021.01.033

Shanafelt, T. D., Kaups, K. L., Nelson, H., Satele, D. V., Sloan, J. A., Oreskovich, M. R., & Dyrbye, L. N. (2014). An interactive individualized intervention to promote behavioral change to increase personal well-being in US surgeons. *Annals of Surgery*, *259*(1), 82–88. 10.1097/SLA.0b013e3182a58fa4

Shanafelt, T. D., West, C. P., Sinsky, C., Trockel, M., Tutty, M., Wang, H., Carlasare, L. E., & Dyrbye, L. N. (2022). Changes in burnout and satisfaction with work-life integration in physicians and the general US working population between 2011 and 2020. *Mayo Clinic Proceedings*, *97*(3), 491–506. 10.1016/j.mayocp.2021.11.021

Thomas, L. R., Ripp, J. A., & West, C. P. (2018). Charter on physician well-being. *JAMA*, *319*(15), 1541–1542. 10.1001/jama.2018.1331

West, C. P., Dyrbye, L. N., Rabatin, J. T., Call, T. G., Davidson, J. H., Multari, A., Romanski, S. A., Henriksen Hellyer, J. M., Sloan, J. A., & Shanafelt, T. D. (2014). *JAMA Internal Medicine*, *174*(4), 527–533. 10.1001/jamainternmed.2013.14387

West, C. P., Dyrbye, L. N., Satele, D. V., & Shanafelt, T. D. (2021). Colleagues Meeting to Promote and Sustain Satisfaction (COMPASS) groups for physician well-being: a randomized clinical trial. *Mayo Clinic Proceedings*, *96*(10), 2606–2614. 10.1016/j.mayocp.2021.02.028

West, C. P., Dyrbye, L. N., Sinsky, C., Trockel, M., Tutty, M., Nedelec, L., Carlasare, L. E., & Shanafelt, T. D. (2020). Resilience and burnout among physicians and the general US working population. *JAMA Network Open*, *3*(7), e209385. 10.1001/jamanetworkopen.2020.9385

West, C. P. & Shanafelt, T. D. (2007). The influence of personal and environmental factors on professionalism in medical education. *BMC Medical Education*, *7*, 29. 10.1186/1472-6920-7-29

Yerkes, R. M. & Dodson, J. D. (1908). The relation of strength of stimulus to rapidity of habit-formation. *Journal of Comparative Neurology and Psychology*, *18*(5), 459–482. 10.1002/cne.920180503

Yu, B., Barnett, D., Menon, V., Rabiee, L., De Castro, Y. S., Kasubhai, M., & Watkins, E. (2021). Healthcare worker trauma and related mental health outcomes during the COVID-19 outbreak in New York City. *PLOS ONE*, *17*(4), e0267315. 10.1371/journal.pone.0267315

9 Stress test: The impact of COVID on employee burnout in the Department of Veterans Affairs

Cheyna Brower, Sean Becker, and Katerine Osatuke
United States Department of Veterans Affairs

Introduction

It has been a long time since you have run this hard. You can feel the sweat bead on your forehead and run down your back. The pounding in your chest is something you could have expected but never fails to induce a little panic—should it be working this hard? You are not sure you could handle the embarrassment of breathing this hard *and* visibly panicking. I guess *this* is why it is called a stress test.

Stress tests are a cardiological test that measures the heart's ability to respond to external stress (e.g., exercise) in a controlled clinical environment. The goal is to identify underlying concerns like issues with your heart muscle or valves, inadequate blood supply, and electric stability of your heart at rest and during stress. The idea is to push the heart to uncomfortable feats in a controlled environment to monitor heart function and diagnose issues so that they can be treated before those issues can cause harm in an uncontrolled environment.

In many ways, this pandemic has put organisations around the world under a stress test. The Department of Veterans Affairs (VA) is no exception. While the environment is certainly not controlled, VA has been routinely monitoring organisational functioning and addressing underlying issues in real time while under the stress of ever-changing and uncertain circumstances. In this chapter, we take detailed a look at how the VA performed on burnout during this global crisis. Did VA pass? What did VA learned about its ability to respond to stress in an uncontrolled real-world crisis? What was learned about burnout?

About VA

The Department of Veterans Affairs (VA) is a United States federal organisation; it is the second-largest federal agency in the U.S.A. VA provides medical care, benefits, and burial services to US war veterans. These three lines of work fulfil three of VA's missions. VA is also charged with the "Fourth Mission" to improve the nation's preparedness for war, terrorism, natural disasters, and national emergencies such as the COVID-19 pandemic. Over

DOI: 10.4324/9781003250531-10

400,000 employees make up the VA across three administrations: Veterans Health Administration (VHA), Veterans Benefits Administration (VBA), and National Cemetery Administration (NCA). Most of these employees (88%) work within VHA to provide lifelong medical care to veterans.

The VA is a diverse workforce in almost every way measurable. Employees work across the entire US and several territories in both urban and rural settings. The VA encompasses many types of work environments including offices, hospitals, cemeteries, labs, and more. There are over 350 occupations employed by the VA across numerous settings (e.g., inpatient, research, loan guarantee service, grounds keeper, administrative, etc.). Employees are demographically diverse as well (see Table 9.1).

How COVID-19 changed VA

The COVID-19 Pandemic has changed the way many organisations and the VA function. The largest change that occurred in day-to-day operations was the shift

Table 9.1 2021 VA AES Demographics

Demographic	Percentage
Age	
Did Not Disclose	5%
25 and under	2%
26–29	4%
30–39	22%
40–49	26%
50–59	28%
60 or older	14%
Ethnicity	
Did Not Disclose	6%
Hispanic	10%
Not Hispanic	84%
Sex	
Did Not Disclose	5%
Female	59%
Male	36%
Race	
Did Not Disclose	8%
American Indian	1%
Asian	7%
Black	20%
Multi-Race	3%
Native Hawaiian	1%
White	58%

Note. Demographics shown as a percentage of all responses to the 2021 AES, N = 287,224.

to maximum telework and virtual work when possible, to ensure employee and Veteran safety. Leading up to the COVID-19 pandemic, VA was largely an in-person organisation with a minority (~20%) of employees who teleworked any amount and less than 5% who teleworked full time. Like much of the world, with almost no warning up to 60% of employees were suddenly working from home temporarily and many continued in some capacity long term (40% in 2021). In fact, almost 18% teleworked full-time in 2021, where almost 38% of the workforce reported that they cannot telework due to job duties (e.g., patient care, cemetery grounds keeping, cleaning staff, etc.). This change required a simultaneous cultural shift and technological shift. The technological shift was rapid and effective. Data speak to the cultural shift in a later section.

The onset of the pandemic and the VA's Fourth Mission to support the nation in times of crises demanded a rapid evaluation of the VA's readiness to support the United States in the event of the worst-case projections of the pandemic. This necessity was another challenge to day-to-day operations that subsided for many VA employees after a month or so. For example, most program offices that support medical facilities were tasked with evaluating how critical their services were and if or how they could shift to direct pandemic support if necessary. Medical providers were tasked with more long-term role changes. For example, when a surge in cases occurred, staff from other floors, services, or locations would step in to help care for the increase in COVID-19 patients.

Civil servants are notoriously mission driven; VA employees are no exception. Many employees hold highly lucrative skills in high demand (e.g., physicians, nurses, leaders, lawyers, researchers, etc.) but choose to work at VA for the mission and derive great meaning from caring for our nation's veterans. Although the onset of the pandemic did not change this, like many Americans, it forced each individual to confront their values and priorities. Some reflections centred around the purpose and meaning derived (or not) from work, whether to continue to work when the demands of parenthood are greater due to lack of support, and whether people felt valued and cared for by their workplaces. Within the private sector, this led to a "Great Resignation" (Person & Mutikani, 2021; U.S. Bureau of Labor Statistics, 2022; Ian Cook, 2021) and increase in burnout (Chor et al., 2021; Jalili et al., 2021; Torres et al., 2022). In this chapter, we examine whether VA suffered the same fate. In the next section, we discuss how burnout is measured and the experience of burnout in the VA pre-pandemic.

Burnout baseline in VA

Each year VA surveys the entire workforce about their workplace attitudes and perceptions. This All Employee Survey (AES) gives VA data which are then used to inform improvements, policy changes, better workforce support, and so forth. The VA AES had a response rate from 66–71% from 2019 to 2021, which is very high for an anonymous, voluntary organisational survey (Baruch & Holtom, 2008). There are 67 core questions that are stable over time.

Topics include attitudes and employee perceptions about their workgroups, supervisors, leadership, resources, diversity, equity, and inclusion, engagement, and more. During the pandemic, additional questions asked about the impact of COVID–19 and telework.

Burnout is among the topics surveyed consistently. VA follows the Maslach burnout model (Maslach et al., 1997) where burnout reflects three dimensions: emotional exhaustion, depersonalisation, and lack of personal accomplishment. Emotional exhaustion is the drained feeling people feel from enduring stress—feeling like their physical and emotional stores are depleted from being overworked. Depersonalisation is the interpersonal component of burnout that encompasses a feeling of callousness or emotional detachment (e.g., customers are seen as tasks, not as people). And a lack of personal accomplishment is characterised by feeling unproductive or ineffective at work, for example, feeling that one's work makes no meaningful difference. In the AES, burnout is measured by three items below. They have been sourced, with permission, from the Maslach Burnout Inventory (MBI; Maslach, & Jackson, 1981) in consultation with the authors of the MBI and previous research (see Yanchus et al., 2015) and validated as short-form burnout assessment for VA (Hernandez et al., 2014). The items for emotional exhaustion and depersonalisation were the items with the highest loading on their respective MBI factors whereas reduced personal accomplishment was the second highest loading item (see Yanchus et al., 2015). The three items are below:

Emotional Exhaustion: I feel burned out from my work.
Depersonalisation: I worry that this job is hardening me emotionally.
Reduced Personal Accomplishment (reverse-scored): I have accomplished many worthwhile things in this job.
Burnout Scale
1 = Never
2 = A few times a year or less
3 = Once a month or less
4 = A few times a month
5 = Once a week
6 = A few times a week
7 = Every day

To direct attention where it is most needed within VA, AES reports burnout results in a simplified manner. Burnout is dichotomised into high (experienced once a week or more often) vs low (experienced less frequently than once a week). AES data reports summarise what percentage of employees in VA workplaces report "high" burnout on all three dimensions above, on two, on one, or on none of the dimensions above. Burnout is largely characterised in this way within this chapter; however, we do reference individual symptoms of burnout where relevant.

Prior to the pandemic (2019), just under 5% of VA's workforce experienced high burnout (i.e., all three symptoms of burnout on a weekly basis), 23% experienced one symptom of burnout, 17% experienced 2 symptoms of burnout, and about half of the workforce (52%) did not experience any symptoms of burnout on a weekly basis. In 2019, on average emotional exhaustion, reduced personal accomplishment, and depersonalisation were experienced about a few times a year or less (2.39, 2.04, and 1.18, respectively). Additionally, burnout was mentioned within 2.3% of free text comments (an open-ended question on the AES, where employees have 400 characters to suggest what they see as the most needed improvements to their workplaces). This relatively low experience of burnout that was typical of the years leading up to the pandemic.

The experience of burnout varied within VA. Across administrations (i.e., VHA, VBA, and NCA), Veteran Benefits Administration (VBA) showed both the highest rates of burnout (i.e., highest % of employees with all three symptoms of burnout on a weekly basis) (8.67%). Veteran Health Administration felt slightly less burned out (4.7%), followed by National Cemetery Administration (3.03%). Based on feedback from VBA through free text comments on the AES, burnout seemed to be driven largely by sheer workload and production standards required to meet the demand from Veterans receiving their benefits. For example, VBA employees shared sentiments such as "The workload is not sustainable which is causing many employees to burnout," and "A lot of us are experiencing burnout due to high production standards and mandatory overtime. Other than that, this really is my dream job."

Office-setting occupations tended to be the most burned out. The experience of burnout varied by occupation families with office-setting occupations having some of the highest rates of burnout compared to occupations that require less office-oriented work. For example, some of the occupation families with the highest rates of burnout (i.e., highest % of employees with all three symptoms of burnout on a weekly basis) were VBA Benefits (employees charged with the bureaucracy of dispersing benefits to Veterans; 9.41%), VA Central Office (employees who write, evaluate, and enforce policy for the rest of VA; 7.07%), and NCA District (employees who deal with the bureaucracy of cemetery operations across regions; 5.56%), all office-based work. Occupations with some of the lowest levels of burnout were cemetery care employees (2.50%), Information Technology (3.70%), and physicians (3.88%), all occupations that go beyond the office. Similar occupation families reported symptoms of burnout most frequently (i.e., highest average score on emotional exhaustion, depersonalisation, and/or reduced personal achievement).

One notable exception is that physicians typically felt emotional exhaustion and depersonalisation more frequently than other occupations (i.e., 2.43 or between once a month and a few times a month and 1.90 or almost once a month) whereas reduced personal achievement was among the least frequently experienced compared to other occupation families (i.e., 1.79 or almost once a month). This experience of frequently feeling emotionally drained and detached while still feeling like your work is making a meaningful difference is typical among physicians (West et al., 2018), and reflects nature of care work which relies on the emotional labour of employees (Jeung et al., 2018).

Employees with more leadership responsibility felt less burned out and lower levels of leadership felt most emotionally exhausted and hardened. For example, 5.19% of individual contributors, 4.35% of supervisors, 3.11% of managers, and 1.97% of Senior Executives experienced high burnout. This seemed to be driven by whether or not employees felt like their work was making a meaningful difference because this pattern holds when looking at how frequently employees felt reduced personal accomplishment across leadership levels. However, when looking how often specific symptoms of burnout occur, supervisors felt emotional exhaustion and depersonalisation most frequently followed by team leads, managers, individual contributors, then finally executives. That is, lower-level leadership felt more emotionally exhausted and hardened than upper leadership or individual contributors, but still feel like they were meaningfully contributing at their job. This suggests that the rates of high burnout across leadership levels are driven by whether or not employees felt like they were accomplishing anything worthwhile.

Overall, workplace drivers of burnout were an unreasonable workload, deriving less meaning from work, less involvement with in decisions that affect their work, not feeling like their talents are being used, having low expectations that their feedback on the AES will be used to improve the workplace, less satisfaction with personal recognition for their hard work, supervisors inadequately setting challenging yet attainable goals, and not having the appropriate resources to be effective at their jobs (see Table 9.2). On the whole, this experience can be summed up as being asked too much with too few resources or support.

In the next sections, we look at the impact of the COVID-19 pandemic in 2020 on VA as a whole. Then we take a more detailed look at those who experienced the most burnout, the providers who most directly tackled the pandemic, and new drivers of burnout due to the pandemic. After that, we look at how the impact of the pandemic changed in 2021. Finally, we review lessons learned about burnout through the pandemic and outline the way VA is moving forward into the new normal.

Impact of COVID

The impact of COVID on burnout in the VA is a tale of two years. The experience of burnout throughout VA was different at the start of the pandemic in 2020 than it was as the pandemic wore on in 2021. Generally, burnout decreased in 2020 then increased beyond pre-pandemic levels in 2021 as the pandemic continued. In the following sections, we discuss the impact of the pandemic in each year and speak to the drivers and lessons learned through time, starting with 2020.

Table 9.2 2019 Scaled Regression Results Using Burnout as the Criterion

Predictor	b	b 95% CI [LL, UL]	beta	beta 95% CI [LL, UL]	r	Fit
(Intercept)	6.17**	[6.11, 6.24]				
Workload	−1.08**	[−1.16, −0.99]	−0.25	[−0.27, −0.23]	−0.52**	
More Than Paycheck	−0.79**	[−0.87, −0.71]	−0.18	[−0.20, −0.16]	−0.37**	
Talents Used	−0.44**	[−0.54, −0.34]	−0.10	[−0.12, −0.08]	−0.50**	
Decisional Involvement	−0.43**	[−0.55, −0.31]	−0.10	[−0.13, −0.07]	−0.52**	
AES Use Expectations	−0.43**	[−0.52, −0.33]	−0.10	[−0.12, −0.08]	−0.48**	
Personal Recognition	−0.32**	[−0.43, −0.21]	−0.07	[−0.10, −0.05]	−0.50**	
Supervisor Goal Setting	−0.20**	[−0.30, −0.09]	−0.05	[−0.07, −0.02]	−0.50**	
Resources	−0.16**	[−0.24, −0.07]	−0.04	[−0.06, −0.02]	−0.41**	
Extra Effort	0.16**	[0.08, 0.25]	0.04	[0.02, 0.06]	−0.25**	
						$R^2 = .412^{**}$
						95% CI [.40, .42]

Note. A significant *b*-weight indicates the beta-weight is also significant. *b* represents unstandardised regression weights. *beta* indicates the standardised regression weights. *r* represents the zero-order correlation. *LL* and *UL* indicate the lower and upper limits of a confidence interval, respectively.

* indicates $p < .05$.

Note
** indicates $p < .01$.

2020: Burnout during acute stress

In March of 2020, the collective stress test begins. The treadmill is on and the speed ramps up from a brisk walk (i.e., signals of a potential pandemic) to a sprint (i.e., all hands on deck preparing and caring for those affected). Given the demands of a pandemic, theory and previous evidence would suggest that burnout would increase (Marjanovic et al., 2007). Additionally, the majority of VA contributes to the medical care of veterans and, through the Fourth Mission, must be prepared to care for others during the pandemic. These factors plus uncertainty, change in employees personal and professional lives, and potential for substantial increase in workload only support the idea the burnout should increase.

However, overall burnout in VA decreased in 2020. That is, the rate of high burnout decreased slightly (i.e., 4.89% down from 4.99% in 2019; a difference of about 500 employees) and the frequency of burnout symptoms slightly decreased from 2019 (i.e., on average 2.37, 1.77, and 1.95 for emotional exhaustion, depersonalisation, and reduced personal achievement). Further, more employees felt no burnout symptoms (53.94% up from 51.67% or ~ 23,000 more employees who were not experiencing any symptoms of burnout). Additionally, burnout was mentioned within only 1.7% of free text comments (compared to 2.3% in 2019) where employees have 400 characters to suggest improvements to their workplace. Together this demonstrates that the rate and frequency experience of burnout decreased across the VA from 2019 to 2020 (see Table 9.3).

This surprising occurrence could be the result of several factors. First, burnout was measured during the annual AES administration in September 2020. This was unusual timing for the AES, which is typically administered in June of each year. The AES was delayed based on the request of Medical Center Directors and other input from the system that a delayed survey administration would help reduce the load on their frontline employees as they adjusted to the demands of the pandemic. Thus, it is possible that burnout was higher before the AES was administered and burnout could have been higher if administered on schedule in June. This is possible, but not likely given the response scale and frame of reference for the burnout scale. That is, the survey asks employees to think of their experience over the last 6 months and the scale asks about how frequently symptoms of burnout of experienced in terms of time that include year and months so respondents are likely to think over time rather than how they felt just in that moment.

Second, as mentioned previously VA is quite diverse thus the decrease could be driven by one or a few populations within the VA having improved experiences that influence the average. To examine this, we take a closer look at burnout throughout VA in the following paragraphs.

Each administration felt the impact of the pandemic differently. Veteran Benefit Administration enjoyed the most reduction in the frequency of burnout compared to Veteran Health Administration and National Cemetery

Table 9.3 Burnout in VA by Year

Year	N	Burnout 0 Symptoms	Burnout 1 Symptom	Burnout 2 Symptoms	Burnout All Symptoms	Exhaus-tion	Depersonal-isation	Reduced Personal Achievement
2019	256807	51.67%	22.91%	16.56%	4.99%	2.386	1.815	2.036
2020	288369	53.94%	22.87%	16.22%	4.82%	2.370	1.767	1.952
2021	287224	51.45%	23.03%	18.56%	5.02%	2.717	1.941	1.904

Note. Individuals were sorted into categories based on underlying burnout scores. If an individual had no scores 4 or above on any burnout dimension, they would be placed in Burnout 0 symptoms. If they had all scores 4 or above, they were placed in Burnout All Symptoms. The burnout dimensions were measured by one question from the Maslach Burnout Index, the response choices are as follows: 0 = Never, 1 = A few times a year or less, 2 = Once a month or less, 3 = A few times a month, 4 = Once a week, 5 = A few times a week, 6 = Every day.

Administration. For example, percentage of workers with high burnout remained steady within Veteran Health Administration and National Cemetery Administration from 2019 to 2020, however Veteran Benefit Administration saw a notable decrease in high burnout (i.e., -2.11% to 6.56%). The driver for this decrease was likely a change in workload. VBA is subject to high productivity standards in order to meet the needs of Veterans who are entitled to benefits. In 2020, there were a few changes that improved the experience of workload in VBA: 1) some reduced demand of services due to COVID-19 disruptions (i.e., workload reliant on exams provided outside of VA that were not conducted), 2) a dashboard for managing workload, and 3) more staff were hired than usual with the intent to reduce workload. In 2020, VBA was able to substantially reduce the backlog of veteran request that had been building up over time.

The shift to telework also disproportionately affected Veteran Benefit Administration compared to the other administrations because nearly the entire workforce was able to perform work duties from home. Pre-pandemic, 89% of Veteran Benefit Administration worked from home less than 5 days a week compared to 8% in 2020. Working from home made employees feel more productive and at least as connected to their co-workers as when everyone was in the office. When asked, 63% of Veteran Benefit Administration employees said that teleworking had a positive impact on their productivity, 27% reported a neutral impact, and 7% reported a negative impact on productivity. When asked how telework impacted how connected Veteran Benefit Administration employees felt with each other, 26% reported a positive impact, 55% reported neutral impact, and 17% reported negative impact. Because reducing workload and more human connection reduce burnout (Seppala & King, 2017), the positive impact on productivity and connectivity felt from maximum telework likely played a role in reducing burnout.

Despite the benefits of telework and resulting reduction of burnout, office workers were still more burned out than those who worked outside of office settings in 2020. Some of the occupation families with the highest rates of burnout in 2020 (i.e., highest percentage of employees with all three symptoms of burnout on a weekly basis) were VBA Benefits again (7.12%, -2.29% from 2019), Admin (5.35%), and NCA Central Office (5.03%). Although these occupation families were the most burned out in 2020, none experienced rates as high as 2019. Occupations with the lowest levels of burnout were NCA District employees (2.94%; had one of the highest burnout rates in 2019), Information Technology again (3.29%, -0.41% from 2019), and physicians again (3.32%, -0.62% from 2019). The occupation families that saw the greatest decrease in high burnout from 2019 were NCA District (-2.61%), VA Central Office (-2.41%), and VBA Benefits (-2.29%)—all groups that were disproportionately affected by maximum telework.

Similar occupation families felt symptoms of burnout most frequently (i.e., highest average score on emotional exhaustion, depersonalisation, and/or reduced personal achievement). One notable exception is that clinical providers, other than physicians and nurses, were among the those feeling emotionally exhausted most frequently (i.e., 2.44 or almost once a month). Another notable exception is the experience of physicians. Although they have low rates of high burnout, the average frequency of emotional exhaustion and depersonalisation are relatively high (2.36 and 1.85 respectively) and reduced personal accomplishment is among the lowest (1.70). Just as before the pandemic, physicians and clinical staff tend to have experiences of burnout symptoms that differ from other types of work. Their experience is characterised by high emotional exhaustion, depersonalisation less frequently, and reduced personal accomplishment the least frequently. Again, this experience is likely shaped by the unique role medical providers, in that the job requires extensive emotional labour which can drive emotional exhaustion and depersonalisation (Jeung et al., 2018). Further, since emotional labour is in part what makes a medical provider successful, the burnout symptom of reduced personal accomplishment is less influenced.

Burnout patterns across leadership levels stayed consistent in 2020. That is, more senior leaders continued to have lower rates of high burnout than those with less leadership responsibility. Although the pattern across leadership levels was the same, some levels of leadership felt slightly more burnout than pre-pandemic levels (i.e., Senior Executives + 0.64% to 2.64% and managers + 0.36% to 3.46% respectively) and others had lower than previous rates of burnout (i.e., individual contributors −0.21% to 4.98%). Overall, leadership appeared to absorb some of the stress in the system that made burnout more relevant for them and less relevant for individual contributors. This is likely due to the rapidly changing landscape the COVID-19 pandemic created. Leadership now had to make high-stakes decisions despite uncertainty based on often changing and inconsistent information. For example, the only constants about making decisions regarding COVID-19 was that safety was prioritised and that the information regarding what was safe would always change.

Beyond maximum telework, the VA employed just about every lever it could as a federal agency in the short term to reduce the burden on employees, which could have contributed to the decrease in burnout. For example, while most private healthcare organisations were reducing services provided and staff, there were special provisions made within VA to allow for rapid hiring of new staff to respond to and prepare for COVID-19 waves. This likely helped alleviate stress due to the pandemic but also answered a consistent call for more staff. For administrative or office work, flexible scheduling was prioritised wherever possible with parents in mind due to school and childcare closures. For example, in many cases the acceptable hours for working were extended or eliminated all together so that parents could work less during school hours while children were schooling from home.

In 2020, some the drivers of burnout shifted and changed with the beginning of the pandemic (see Table 4). Many of the same drivers from before the pandemic influenced burnout such as having an unreasonable workload, not deriving meaning from work, not being satisfied with recognition, not being involved enough in the decisions that affect work, not feeling like talents are used well, and supervisors not setting challenging yet attainable goals. In addition to these drivers, some pandemic specific influences became important to the experience of burnout. These influences include additional stress added to day-to-day work due to the pandemic, not knowing how to access help with stress, not feeling like their supervisor is looking out for their personal safety, and not knowing how to respond to signs of emotional or psychological distress in colleagues. Notably, the added stress due to COVID-19 had the largest effect on burnout, after workload (see Table 9.4). That is, pandemic-related stress was the second largest driver of burnout in 2020.

Burnout as experienced by those confronting the pandemic directly: medical care providers

Healthcare workers were celebrated as heroes in US culture in 2020. There were parades in town and city centres, additional pay, profusely expressed gratitude, and generally a sense that the work being done by healthcare workers was of the utmost value and meaningful work happening at the time. Social media posts circulated throughout the year sharing stories from healthcare workers of triumph and some of dismay that were met with overwhelming support and gratitude. In general, healthcare workers, especially those directly dealing with COVID-19 patients had seemingly unending support from the public. COVID-19 waves hit different parts of the country at different times. In the next paragraph, we take a look at burnout among those who bared the brunt of the pandemic: healthcare workers.

In 2020, the rate of high burnout slightly increased for nurses (+0.20%, about 147 nurses) and slightly decreased for physicians (−0.56%, about 111 physicians). Historically within VA, there has been a relatively small but persistent gap between burnout among physicians and nurses. That is, more nurses are burned out more frequently on average than physicians. The beginning of the pandemic changed this relationship in a couple keyways. First, the gap between the rate of nurses and physicians who are experiencing high burnout widened (i.e., 0.58 difference in 2019 to 1.35 percentage point difference in 2020; see Figure 9.1).

Second, the gap in average frequency of emotional exhaustion and depersonalisation nearly closed in 2020 (see Figure 9.2 and Figure 9.3). Physicians felt emotionally exhausted and hardened more frequently than before and nurses felt that less frequently, meeting at almost the same frequency on average. That is, nurses and physicians felt almost equally emotionally drained and callous within VA for the first time. The widening of the high burnout gap but closing of the gap in experience of emotional exhaustion and depersonalisation suggests that the high burnout gap is due to the difference in personal accomplishment (see Figure 9.4). That is nurses did not feel like they were being effective or that their work was making a difference.

Table 9.4 2020 Regression Results Using Burnout as the Criterion

Predictor	b	b 95% CI [LL, UL]	beta	beta 95% CI [LL, UL]	r	Fit
(Intercept)	6.05**	[5.99, 6.11]				
Workload	−0.96**	[−1.04, −0.88]	−0.23	[−0.24, −0.21]	−.51**	
COVID Additional Work Stress	0.79**	[0.73, 0.86]	0.19	[0.17, 0.20]	.33**	
More Than Paycheck	−0.67**	[−0.74, −0.60]	−0.16	[−0.17, −0.14]	−.35**	
Decisional Involvement	−0.45**	[−0.56, −0.34]	−0.11	[−0.13, −0.08]	−.52**	
Talents Used	−0.41**	[−0.51, −0.32]	−0.10	[−0.12, −0.07]	−.49**	
AES Use Expectations	−0.30**	[−0.39, −0.21]	−0.07	[−0.09, −0.05]	−.47**	
COVID Access Help	−0.30**	[−0.39, −0.21]	−0.07	[−0.09, −0.05]	−.41**	
Personal Recognition	−0.20**	[−0.30, −0.10]	−0.05	[−0.07, −0.02]	−.47**	
Supervisor Goal Setting	−0.19**	[−0.29, −0.09]	−0.04	[−0.07, −0.02]	−.49**	
COVID Supervisor Personal Safety	0.14**	[0.06, 0.22]	0.03	[0.01, 0.05]	−.36**	
COVID Help Colleagues	−0.13**	[−0.21, −0.04]	−0.03	[−0.05, −0.01]	−.33**	
						$R^2 = .440$**
						95% CI[.43, .45]

Note. A significant *b*-weight indicates the beta–weight and semi-partial correlation are also significant. *b* represents unstandardised regression weighs. *beta* indicates the standardised regression weights. *r* represents the zero-order correlation. *LL* and *UL* indicate the lower and upper limits of a confidence interval, respectively.
* indicates p < .05.

Note
** indicates p < .01.

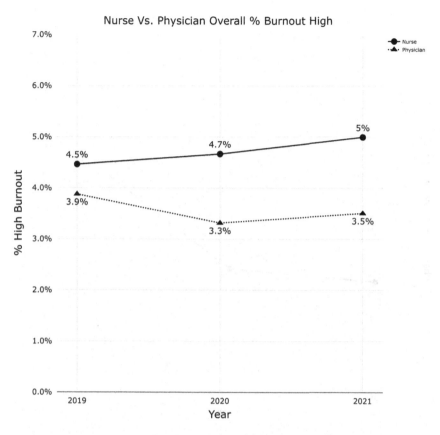

Figure 9.1 Nurse versus Physician High Burnout. The gap in rates of high burnout between nurses and physicians widened during the pandemic. Not that the Y-axis only shows 1–8% instead of the full range to illustrate the gap that would be too small to see if the full range of 1–100% were shown.

According to nurses and nurse supervisors, this lack of personal accomplishment could have been due to additional stress due to COVID-19 and workload. In particular, the added stress from having to work in a different clinic to make sure it was adequately staffed. Many clinics were short staffed due to illness or required quarantines. When that happened, nurses from other clinics would step in but did not always feel they had adequate support in the unfamiliar clinic. Thus, nurses that were filling in for other clinics might not have felt as effective or productive.

COVID-19 stress was an added driver of burnout in 2020. However, this seems to play out at the individual level and are influenced by personal experiences rather than external drivers (i.e., number of COVID-19 cases) (see Table 4). For example, the amount of added stress to an employee's day-to-day job, knowing how to access help in dealing with that stress, knowing how

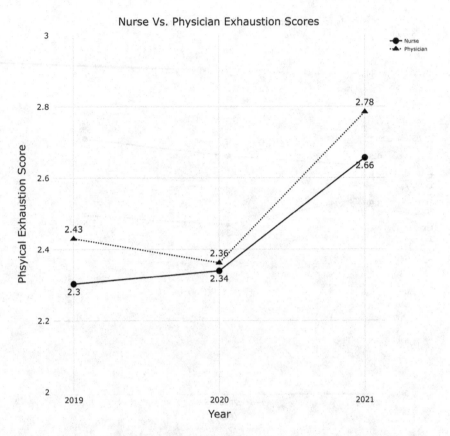

Figure 9.2 Nurse versus Physician Emotional Exhaustion Scores. In 2020, emotional exhaustion slightly increased for nurses and slightly decreased for physicians,
making their average scores more similar to each other. In 2021, both nurses and
physicians felt more emotionally exhausted, but nurses scores increased more.
Note that the Y-axis does not show the full range of possible scores (1–7) to
illustrate the difference between nurses and physicians, which is fairly small.

to respond to colleagues in distress, and knowing that your supervisor is
prioritising your safety predicted burnout. However, when comparing medical
centres that were experiencing high COVID-19 caseloads compared to those
were experiencing low COVID-19 cases, burnout was nearly identical (see
Table 9.5). The number of COVID-19 cases at the medical facility did not
seem to influence burnout.

Overall, the VA seemed to perform well under the acute stress of rapid
change, uncertainty, and high stakes. That is, the start of the pandemic added
stress to the day-to-day experience of nearly all VA employees (84%) however,
the individual and organisational efforts made to counter burnout worked to
not only prevent a rise in burnout but reduced it.

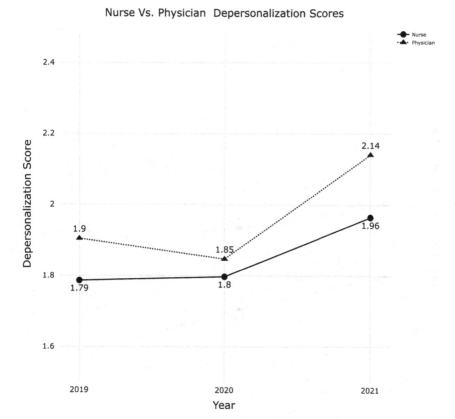

Figure 9.3 Nurses versus Physician Depersonalisation Scores. In 2020, depersonalisation slightly increased for nurses and slightly decreased for physicians, making their average scores more similar to each other. In 2021, both nurses and physicians felt more emotionally calloused, but nurses scores increased more. Note that the Y-axis does not show the full range of possible scores (1–7) to illustrate the difference between nurses and physicians, which is fairly small.

Impact of COVID in 2021: a feat of endurance, a new normal

The mileage on the treadmill is getting close to double digits. Even though you were told this was a relatively quick test to check-up on the ole ticker (i.e., "two weeks to flatten the [COVID-19 infection] curve"), the treadmill just will not stop (the COVID-19 infection curve did not flatten in two weeks). Your quick energy stores are depleted and you are digging deep—this is starting to feel more like a marathon (i.e., full-blown pandemic with endemic potential).

As the pandemic continued and evolved in nature, burnout in VA also changed. From the AES administration in September 2020 to the AES

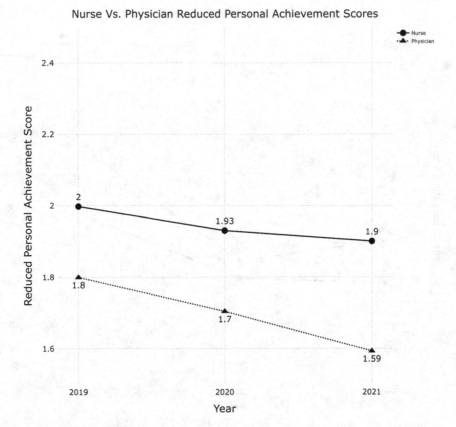

Figure 9.4 Nurses versus Physician Reduced Personal Accomplishment Scores. Both nurses and physicians felt more personally accomplished (therefore scores of reduced personal accomplishment decreased) throughout the pandemic. Note that the Y-axis does not show the full range of possible scores (1–7) to illustrate the difference between nurses and physicians, which is fairly small.

administration in June 2021 (the AES schedule resumed as it had in prior years), the experience of the pandemic had changed. Gone were the days of collectively celebrating healthcare workers through acts of kindness and grand gestures (e.g., parades, public signs showing gratitude, free services, and meals, etc.) or hazard pay. In its place arose the politicisation of COVID-19 and conspiracies or outright denial of the existence and severity of the illness. With the new year also came the COVID-19 vaccine effort. VA employees were responsible for administering millions of vaccinations to veterans, employees, and others. These changes and the enduring stress due to the COVID-19 pandemic took a toll on VA employees and their experience of burnout. In the following sections, we discuss burnout in VA and how it changed and stayed the same in the second year of the pandemic.

Table 9.5 Burnout Across VA by Covid Case Load

Year	Facility Classification	Total N	Burnout 0 Symptoms	Burnout 1 Symptoms	Burnout 2 Symptoms	Burnout High Symptoms
2020	Low	209176	53.9%	22.9%	16.3%	4.7%
2020	High	20162	53.6%	22.9%	16.5%	4.9%
2020	No Data	59031	54.2%	22.8%	15.8%	5.4%
2021	Low	200250	51.7%	22.9%	19.1%	5.0%
2021	High	26229	50.6%	23.2%	18.5%	4.8%
2021	No Data	60745	50.8%	23.3%	18.5%	5.6%

Note. Facilities that were classified as High were 2 standard deviations above the mean of covid cases at all VA facilities.

Overall, burnout levels rose from 2020 levels slightly past 2019 levels. As a whole, 5.02% of employees experienced high burnout and the average frequency of emotional exhaustion (2.71) and depersonalisation (1.94) were higher than both 2019 and 2020. However, reduced personal achievement fell slightly to an average of 1.90. Also, only 51.45% of employees were not experiencing any symptoms of burnout, slightly lower than both 2019 and 2020. That is, more employees felt slightly more emotionally drained and hardened, but felt like they were more effective at work.

While these changes overall are meaningful because they reflect the experiences of people working during and directly fighting a pandemic, the changes in burnout at the VA level are quite small. The rise in high burnout from 2020 to 2021 represents fewer than 600 more employees out of over 400,000. This number is surprisingly low given the challenges faced. In the next section, we take a look at who was experiencing burnout the most and what changes were faced in the second year of the pandemic.

Although office-setting workers still experienced the most burnout (VBA Benefits, 7.52%; VA Central Office, 5.24%), wage workers had the second highest rate of burnout and experienced the largest increase in burnout since 2020 (+1.32% to 5.66%, an additional 304 people). These employees do a wide range of work from food workers, cleaning staff, laundry, etc. Most of these employees work in a medical setting such as a hospital (89%) and did not telework (76%) because their work is not possible from home. Wage employees were also most likely to not be vaccinated (26.7% by June 2021) and were less trustful of the information provided by VA about the COVID-19 pandemic. Because wage workers were less likely to take the vaccine voluntarily and they were more likely to not trust COVID-19 information from the hospital they work at, it is likely that these employees were at minimum sceptical about COVID-19's existence and/or severity or the safety of the vaccine. This might suggest that wage workers did not feel like their safety was being prioritised by their leadership, which would contribute to burnout.

The pattern of burnout by leadership level stayed consistent. That is, the higher the leadership level, the lower the burnout. However, the slight shift observed in 2020 of increased burnout in higher leadership levels and reduced burnout for those without a leadership role trended back towards the status quo of pre-pandemic. That is, leadership (e.g., executives, managers, and supervisors) had slightly lower rates of burnout and individual contributors had slightly higher burnout rates (+0.28% to 5.26% or an addition 573 employees). Consistent with experiences both before and during the pandemic, the emotional exhaustion and depersonalisation are felt most frequently on average by lower-level leadership (e.g., supervisors, managers, and team leads) than upper leadership (e.g., executives) or individual contributors).

When looking at medical care providers, the gap in burnout between nurses and physicians that widened in 2020 persisted and increased in 2021. Both nurses (+0.33%, about 238 more nurses) and physicians (+0.19%, about 38 physicians) slightly increased in high burnout. Unlike physicians, nurses experienced a steady increase in burnout both years of the pandemic. This is likely due, in part, to the nature of nursing and how involved each nurse is with the hands-on care of their patient compared to physicians. Further, nurses consistently reported feeling short staffed due to illness, having to care for family, and some turnover due to high competition in the private sector (e.g., nurses were offered premium pay to travel where COVID-19 was worst at that moment in the private sector). In many facilities, nurses had to cross-train or uptrain to fill in for clinics they had little-to-no experience with (e.g., outpatient nurses uptraining to fill in for in-patient staff) and felt very short staffed.

The drivers of burnout were the same from 2020 to 2021. That is in addition to the pre-pandemic drivers of burnout (i.e., workload, meaning form work, recognition, decisional involvement, talents used, and goals), the pandemic-specific drivers of burnout (i.e., day-to-day stress due to COVID-19, safety not prioritised, not knowing how to respond to colleagues in distress) are still important. For some drivers, the size of the effect changed from 2020 (see Table 9.6). For example, employee's satisfaction with their involvement in decisions had a larger effect size than in either 2020 or 2019 suggesting that involvement in decisions had a bigger influence on burnout has the pandemic wore on than in the past. Similarly, satisfaction with recognition also had a larger effect on burnout than in past years.

Just like in 2020, facilities that had high COVID-19 cases at the time of the AES had nearly identical burnout and COVID-19 stress scores. This suggests that even for those who directly confronted the COVID-19 pandemic, the additional stress due to COVID-19 was not directly dependent on the caseload of COVID-19 but likely the environment and requirements or restrictions in place to prioritise safety. This could have been facilitated by some policies and flexibilities afforded during the pandemic. For example, VA employed traveling nurses who were available to go wherever COVID-19 was surging to help relieve some workload. While the restrictions in place by various authorities (e.g., VA leadership, local guidance, national guidance) did seem to contribute to burnout, it is likely that the lack of restrictions would have led to devastating burnout due to greater shortages of staff due to illness, greater death of co-workers, and greater death of patients.

Table 9.6 2020 Regression Results Using Burnout as the Criterion

Predictor	b	b 95% CI [LL, UL]	beta	beta 95% CI [LL, UL]	r	Fit
(Intercept)	6.05**	[5.99, 6.11]				
Workload	−0.96**	[−1.04, −0.88]	−0.23	[−0.24, −0.21]	−.51**	
COVID Additional Work Stress	0.79**	[0.73, 0.86]	0.19	[0.17, 0.20]	.33**	
More Than Paycheck	−0.67**	[−0.74, −0.60]	−0.16	[−0.17, −0.14]	−.35**	
Decisional Involvement	−0.45**	[−0.56, −0.34]	−0.11	[−0.13, −0.08]	−.52**	
Talents Used	−0.41**	[−0.51, −0.32]	−0.10	[−0.12, −0.07]	−.49**	
AES Use Expectations	−0.30**	[−0.39, −0.21]	−0.07	[−0.09, −0.05]	−.47**	
COVID Access Help	−0.30**	[−0.39, −0.21]	−0.07	[−0.09, −0.05]	−.41**	
Personal Recognition	−0.20**	[−0.30, −0.10]	−0.05	[−0.07, −0.02]	−.47**	
Supervisor Goal Setting	−0.19**	[−0.29, −0.09]	−0.04	[−0.07, −0.02]	−.49**	
COVID Supervisor Personal Safety	0.14**	[0.06, 0.22]	0.03	[0.01, 0.05]	−.36**	
COVID Help Colleagues	−0.13**	[−0.21, −0.04]	−0.03	[−0.05, −0.01]	−.33**	
						$R^2 = .44^{**}$
						95% CI [.43, .45]

Note. A significant *b*-weight indicates the beta-weight and semi-partial correlation are also significant. *b* represents unstandardised regression weights. *beta* indicates the standardised regression weights. *r* represents the zero-order correlation. *LL* and *UL* indicate the lower and upper limits of a confidence interval, respectively. * indicates $p < .05$.

Note
** indicates $p < .01$.

Overall, the increase in burnout in 2021 might represent a regression to the mean rather than a shift in the work environment. However, it could be a result of the ongoing stress due to the pandemic and operating at "full throttle" (a description by a medical centre director) for two years without a substantial break. Notably the burnout gap between nurses and physicians stayed wider than before the pandemic, suggesting that COVID-19 has impacted nurses and physicians differently. Much like 2020, the number of COVID-19 cases at a particular facility did not have a noticeable effect on the burnout experienced by that facility, demonstrating resilience among medical care providers during this ongoing crisis.

Lessons learned

The COVID-19 pandemic offered a few lessons on burnout. In this section we discuss what the pandemic has taught us about burnout. First, and perhaps most importantly, substantial burnout or substantial growth in burnout does not have to be an outcome of working during a global crisis such as a pandemic, even in workplaces that directly confront the pandemic—it is not inevitable. Going into the pandemic, literature suggested that burnout among employees (particularly healthcare workers) would likely grow (Dimitriu et al., 2020; Giusti et al., 2020; Kannampallil et al., 2020; Morgantini et al., 2020). Contrary to this expectation, within VA, burnout did not substantially grow overall and in many cases declined during the first year of the pandemic. This is in contrast with the private industry, particularly within healthcare where burnout soared (Sharifi et al., 2021).

The absence of a surge in burnout during the pandemic suggests that there are personal and organisational protective factors in place. Within VA there were several efforts that were made both pre-pandemic and during the pandemic that supported employees both personally and through organisational change. Although we do not have specific evaluation data to support the direct impact of each of these efforts to present, the efforts that leaders and employees cite as most helpful when asked were things like emergency staffing to keep workload more reasonable during surges of COVID-19, Employee Assistance Programs (EAP) to support employees when in distress, strong and supportive co-worker relationships, multiple employee recognition opportunities with prizes ranging from positive attention from leadership and colleagues to monetary awards, leaning into scheduling flexibility and maximum telework as much as possible, among other local efforts that were not system-wide.

Given the drivers of burnout within the VA specifically and across the literature (Kaltiainen & Hakanen, 2020; Mehta et al., 2021; Norful et al., 2021) these programs likely contributed to the relatively low prevalence of burnout during the pandemic. Some of these efforts, such as maximum telework, flexible scheduling, and additional staffing likely contributed to the surprising finding that non-medical and more office work-oriented jobs (e.g., VBA) experienced a notable reduction in burnout, especially in 2020 when these programs were first instituted.

This pandemic provided more evidence that medical providers are among the most resilient in the workforce. During the pandemic, the rate of medical care providers who experienced high burnout stayed steady, all things considered, with slight variations. Although some symptoms of burnout were felt more often than pre-pandemic (emotional exhaustion and depersonalisation), overall the increase was small, especially when considering the circumstances.

Another lesson learned during the pandemic was the ability of leadership to absorb some of the burnout or stress that could otherwise be felt by the front-line employee. This is aligned with the benefits of servant leadership (Kaltiainen & Hakanen, 2020), where leaders position themselves as supporting and facilitating the work down by individual contributors. This model of leadership is encouraged, trained, and supported throughout the VA and has been for several years. Having this leadership model in place likely allowed for as much of the uncertainty, decisional fatigue, and stress that might exacerbate supervisors and front-line employees to be handled at the leadership level, removing that burden from those working under their care. That is, leaders worked tirelessly to enact every policy that could reduce burden for those in their care while still carrying out the mission to serve Veterans.

The way forward

Although the rate and frequency of burnout experience within VA did not drastically increase, burnout is still an ongoing concern. With a workforce as a large as VA, even 5% is a substantial number of employees who deserve to not feel burned out at work and it would benefit VA to reduce that percentage as much as possible. Further, even though the pandemic did not substantially change burnout, it did substantially change many aspects of work and the workplace. At the highest leadership levels, VA has committed to continuing efforts that have helped manage burnout during the pandemic and beyond as the new normal is developed. For example, leaders at all levels are encouraging and making remote and telework available to jobs that can be done from home and expanding the definition of work that can be done from home without sacrificing care to Veterans.

Within VHA, a taskforce was formed, including employees from all levels of the organisation and multiple disciplines, to address burnout within Veteran Health Administration. Unlike many efforts to address burnout found within the literature (Goroll, 2020) and across the private industry, this task force is more focused on the organisational and work-related changes that can be made to change burnout than what individuals can do to take responsibility for their burnout. For example, there are taskforce workgroups focused on topics such as leadership and supervisor culture, organisational design, systems and solutions, recruitment and retention, employee well-being, and mental health. All these groups look for mechanisms within their scope that can be used to reduce and prevent burnout for employees.

This effort included searching the literature and speaking directly with employees to understand what would make the biggest difference in burnout. At the time of writing this chapter, employees had given feedback that centred largely around staffing and retention, workload management, reducing burdensome administrative tasks, and scheduling flexibility. Examples of employee-informed actions to reduce burnout include raising pay ceilings to allow for more competitive rates, allowing remote and/or alternative work schedules for positions not traditionally eligible, protecting time for professional development and well-being activities, developing integrated mental health crisis response to support employees, and shifting to shorter meetings (e.g., 25 minutes instead of 30 or 50 minutes instead of 60) as a standard to allow for time to reset before the next task. Some occupations are getting special attention, such as nursing. Because of the rising burnout rates within nursing and pervasive feeling of being short staffed, VA committed to hiring 70,000 nurses across facilities over the next 5 years. VA is committed to using any and all organisational mechanisms to reduce burnout, taking responsibility for the role the organisation plays in burnout rather than placing responsibility on individual employees. This commitment is likely responsible for the lack of rampant burnout rates within VA and will continue to improve burnout in the future.

Summary

In sum, burnout slightly decreased the first year of the pandemic then increased back to pre-pandemic levels in 2021. Within VA there were varied experiences of burnout. For example, Veteran Benefits Administration experienced the largest change, which was an overall reduction in burnout likely due in large to staffing, reduced workload, and maximum telework. Medical providers felt an increase in burnout, but it was relatively small with only 250 more employees (out of more than 90,000 employees) experiencing high burnout. This was in contrast to predictions from experts about how the pandemic would affect burnout in healthcare. This suggests that burnout is not inevitable and that organisations like the VA can implement policies to mitigate the effects of the pandemic. Additionally, it is important to note that the drivers of burnout did not change dramatically due to the pandemic, additional drivers due to the pandemic were additional day-to-day stress due to the pandemic and not knowing how to access help with stress, which does not represent a stark change from non-pandemic concerns and can be addressed with traditional individual or organisational burnout prevention techniques.

Conclusion

As the stress test winds down, VA demonstrated its resilience while fulfilling its mission in a time of crisis. Burnout was not inevitable and did not surge during the pandemic like predicted. However, chronic burnout remains and so does the possibility of COVID-19 becoming endemic. The VA demonstrated its ability to succeed during acute and enduring stress and learned how to manage burnout in uncertain and unprecedented crises. 2020 brought out the best in the organisation, plans were made despite the uncertainty, individuals found new enhanced meaning in work and the VA did everything within its power to support its employees. While 2021 brought no relief added new fervent opposition to safety measures and reduced public support for health care employees the VA employees proved resilient with minimal increases to burnout. Going forward, VA is working to internalise what has been learned from the success it achieved in this pandemic through policy and practice changes and continue to tackle chronic burnout. A key lesson that is being carried forward is the positive impact organisational and policy changes can have on burnout.

References

Baruch, Y., & Holtom, B. C. (2008). Survey response rate levels and trends in organizational research. *Human Relations*, *61*(8), 1139–1160. 10.1177/0018726708094863

Chor, W., Ng, W. M., Cheng, L., Situ, W., Chong, J. W., Ng, L., Mok, P. L., Yau, Y. W., & Lin, Z. (2021). Burnout amongst emergency healthcare workers during the COVID-19 pandemic: A multi-center study. *The American Journal of Emergency Medicine*, *46*, 700–702. 10.1016/j.ajem.2020.10.040

Cook, I. (2021, November 10). *Who is driving the great resignation?* Harvard Business Review. Retrieved September 6, 2021, from https://hbr.org/2021/09/who-is-driving-the-great-resignation

Dimitriu, M., Pantea-Stoian, A., Smaranda, A., Nica, A., Carap, A., Constantin, V., Davitoiu, A., Cirstoveanu, C., Bacalbasa, N., Bratu, O., et al. (2020). Burnout syndrome in Romanian medical residents in time of the COVID-19 pandemic. *Medical Hypotheses*, *144*, 109972.

Giusti, E., Pedroli, E., D'Aniello, G., Stramba Badiale, C., Pietrabissa, G., Manna, C., Stramba Badiale, M., Riva, G., Castelnuovo, G., Molinari, E. (2020). The psychological impact of the COVID-19 outbreak on health professionals: A cross-sectional study. *Frontiers in Psychology*, *11*, 1684.

Goroll, A. H. (2020). Addressing burnout—focus on systems, not resilience. *JAMA Network Open*, *3*(7), e209514–e209514. 10.1001/jamanetworkopen.2020.9514

Grow, H. M., McPhillips, H. A., & Batra, M. (2019). Understanding physician burnout. *Current Problems in Pediatric and Adolescent Health Care*, *49*(11), 100656. 10.1016/j.cppeds.2019.100656

Hernandez, W., Osatuke, K., & Ramsel, D. (2014). Factorial validity and measurement invariance of the MBI-HSS across occupations. Poster presented at the 122nd American Psychological Association Annual Convention, Washington, D.C., August, 20.

Jalili, M., Niroomand, M., Hadavand, F., Zeinali, K., & Fotouhi, A. (2021). Burnout among healthcare professionals during COVID-19 pandemic: a cross-sectional study. *International archives of occupational and environmental health*, *94*(6), 1345–1352.

Jeung, D. Y., Kim, C., & Chang, S. J. (2018). Emotional labor and burnout: A review of the literature. *Yonsei medical journal*, *59*(2), 187–193.

Kaltiainen, J., & Hakanen, J. (2020). Fostering task and adaptive performance through employee well-being: The role of servant leadership. *BRQ Business Research Quarterly*, *25*(1), 28–43. 10.1177/2340944420981599

Kannampallil, T., Goss, C., Evanoff, B., Strickland, J., McAlister, R., & Duncan, J. (2020). Exposure To COVID-19 Patients Increases Physician Trainee Stress and Burnout. *PLoS ONE*, *15*, e0237301.

Marjanovic, Z., Greenglass, E. R., & Coffey, S. (2007). The relevance of psychosocial variables and working conditions in predicting nurses' coping strategies during the SARS crisis: an online questionnaire survey. *International Journal of Nursing Studies, 44*(6), 991–998.

Maslach, C., Jackson, S. E., & Leiter, M. P. (1997). Maslach burnout inventory. Scarecrow Education.

Maslach, C., Jackson, S. E., & Leiter, M. P. (1996). *Maslach burnout inventory manual.* 3rd ed. Palo Alto, CA: Consulting Psychologists Press.

Maslach, C., & Jackson, S. E. (1981). *MBI: Maslach burnout inventory*, Palo Alto, CA, *1*(2), 49–78.

Maslach, C. & Leiter, M. P. (2017). New insights into burnout and health care: Strategies for improving civility and alleviating burnout. *Medical Teacher, 39*(2), 160–163, 10.1080/0142159X.2016.1248918

Mehta, A. B., Lockhart, S., Reed, K., Griesmer, C., Glasgow, R. E., Moss, M., Douglas, I. S., & Morris, M. A. (2021). Drivers of burnout among Critical Care Providers. *Chest, 161*(5), 1263–1274. 10.1016/j.chest.2021.11.034

Morgantini, L., Naha, U., Wang, H., Francavilla, S., Acar, Ö., Flores, J., Crivellaro, S., Moreira, D., Abern, M., Eklund, M., et al. (2020). Factors contributing to healthcare professional Burnout During The COVID-19 Pandemic: A Rapid Turnaround Global Survey. *PloS one, 15*(9), e0238217.

Norful, A. A., Rosenfeld, A., Schroeder, K., Travers, J. L., & Aliyu, S. (2021). Primary drivers and psychological manifestations of stress in frontline healthcare workforce during the initial COVID-19 outbreak in the United States. *General Hospital Psychiatry, 69*, 20–26. 10.1016/j.genhosppsych.2021.01.001

Person, & Mutikani, L. (2021, June 8). *U.S. job openings, quits hit record highs in April.* Reuters. Retrieved September 6, 2021, from https://www.reuters.com/business/us-trade-deficit-narrows-april-2021-06-08/

Schaufeli, W., Bakker, A., Hoogduin, K., Schaap, C., & Kladler, A. (2001). On the clinical validity of the Maslach burnout inventory and the burnout measure. *Psychol Health, 16*, 565–582.

Seppala, E., & King, M. (2017). Burnout at work isn't just about exhaustion. It's also about loneliness. *Harvard Business Review, 29*, 2–4.

Sharifi, M., Asadi-Pooya, A. A., & Mousavi-Roknabadi, R. S. (2021). Burnout among healthcare providers of COVID-19; a systematic review of epidemiology and recommendations. *Archives of Academic Emergency Medicine, 9*(1).

Thomas, N. K. (2004). Resident burnout. *JAMA, 292*, 2880–2889.

Torrès, O., Benzari, A., Fisch, C., Mukerjee, J., Swalhi, A., & Thurik, R. (2022). Risk of burnout in French entrepreneurs during the COVID-19 crisis. *Small Business Economics, 58*(2), 717–739.

U.S. Bureau of Labor Statistics. (2022, March 29). *Table 4. quits levels and rates by industry and region, seasonally adjusted – 2022 M02 results.* U.S. Bureau of Labor Statistics. Retrieved April 6, 2021, from https://www.bls.gov/news.release/jolts.t04.htm

West, C. P., Dyrbye, L. N., & Shanafelt, T. D. (2018). Physician burnout: contributors, consequences and solutions. *Journal of Internal Medicine, 283*(6), 516–529.

Yanchus, N. J., Beckstrand, J., & Osatuke, K. (2015). Examining burnout profiles in the Veterans Administration: All Employee Survey narrative comments. *Burnout Research, 2*(4), 97–107.

10 Working from home during a pandemic: A theoretical perspective on work–home spillover and risk of burnout

Igor Portoghese and Maura Galletta
Department of Medical Sciences and Public Health, University of Cagliari,
Monserrato, CA, Italy

Introduction

The Covid-19 pandemic has not only impacted the global economy and health system but also changed the way people work. Authorities worldwide implemented restrictions measures such as lockdown and social distancing in order to limit the infection spread. In the workplace context, work-from-home was one such measure. Notably, it brought into effect significant changes in both work and personal lives, as well as to the interaction between the two. Even though for some occupations such as healthcare, food, postal/delivery sectors, is necessary to be physically present in the workplace, for most others, transitioning from in-person to remote work was forced (Eurofound, 2020a).

According with Peters et al. (2022), among the different novel working practices adopted during the pandemic scenario, the most important was the transition to working remotely. However, many employees found this transition to be challenging because of the simultaneous coexistence of both work and family domains within the same physical space, without any distinct boundaries between the two (Cho, 2020; Trógolo et al., 2022). Although working from home is not a new working arrangement, the pandemic forced employers toward a massive adoption of teleworking to curb the infection diffusion. This compelled employers, academics, and policymakers to face several challenges in the workspaces (Wang et al., 2021). As the transition was major and came into effect rather overnight due to the unprecented pandemic, employees did not receive sufficient guidance regarding the same (Sinclair et al., 2020). Consequently, several major problems arose, which resulted in employees feeling that instead of working at home, they were living at work. This has highlighted the need to discuss the effects of remote work on the workplace, organisational practices, and labour market, as well as how it can impact the workers' wellbeing. Of all the problems arising due to this transition, the most significant one is the diminishing boundary between work and domestic life; for instance, work can spill over into domestic life, or work can take a backseat because of increased familial responsibilities.

DOI: 10.4324/9781003250531-11

Working remotely has potential benefits such as increased flexibility to organise the workday and opportunities to balance home and work demands (Felstead & Henseke, 2017). Nevertheless, working from home exposes workers to an increased risk of work spilling over to the home domain (Putnam et al., 2014) because private life and work end up being mixed. In addition, prolonged hours at home while in isolation increases home demands, such as childcare, which may negatively interlope with work demands, thus leading to a home–work conflict.

According to Peters and colleagues (2022), the Covid-19 pandemic increased stress among workers due to changes experienced in both work organisation and environment. Exposure to the infection, changes in working hours and patterns, work overload, job roles and responsibilities, negatively impacted work–life balance, decreased working social support, and lack of adequate paid leave policies are the main stressors for employees (Cotofan et al., 2021; Prasad et al., 2021; Wang et al., 2021). Moreover, some worker categories such as young individuals, employees with children, ethnic minority workers, and workers with prolonged Covid symptoms are found to be at high risk for work–life imbalance (Cotofan et al., 2021). Hwang et al. (2021) showed a high prevalence of anxiety, depression, stress, and burnout among university employees, as well as worsened well-being after four/five weeks of home working (Evanoff et al., 2020). Therefore, it is important to analyse the long-term effects of this change on employees' well-being to offer evidence-based suggestions for employers, organisations, and governments for them to develop effective interventions.

Definition of remote working

Remote working began in the 1970s. It was first referred to as telecommuting (Nilles, 1975) because employees working from home were dependent on technology to carry out work and communicate with their co-workers. Nilles et al. (1976) thus emphasised the need to increase knowledge regarding smart technology to make telework a successful practice. Despite the subtle differences, the term "remote work" is often interchangeably used with telecommuting, telework, home-based work, flexible work, distance work, multilocational work, and mobile work.

Both telework and remote work involve work being performed outside office premises, through the use of technology (Bailey & Kurland, 2002; Golden & Veiga, 2005). However, the literature highlights the difference between the two concepts owing to their differing approaches. Garrett and Danziger (2007) described teleworking as work performed at home or fieldwork or a combination of both. Similarly, according to Fonner and Roloff (2010) and Konradt et al. (2000), telework is work carried out either in parts or completely outside the company premises, with knowledge shared among the employees through telecommunication service. Therefore, in short, teleworking is performance of work by employees situated in different locations, through information and communication technologies (ICTs) (Nilles, 1997; Perez et al., 2003). Over the recent years, with the rapid adoption of teleworking, scholars and professional alike are paying increased attention in understanding the various aspects, advantages, and obstacles faced during teleworking and how to enhance work experience. Teleworking is advantageous for both employees and employers, as it helps recruit based on talent and not location, reduce infrastructure cost, and ensure work–family balance (Madsen, 2003). The ILO, in a recent report (2020), outlined four similar concepts related to teleworking: (1) remote work, (2) telework, (3) work at home, and (4) home-based work. Remote work encompasses situations in which all or part of the work is performed at locations other than the predefined work location.

The main difference between working from home and working at home should be emphasised. Working from home refers to home-based teleworking, whereas working at home refers to work that is "done at home using the home as a place of work and production without ICT" (Eurofound and the ILO, 2017, p. 5). The latter can be exemplified by workers who sew garments at home and sell their products to a firm, which is a system based on piecework pay. Teleworking as a concept is considered a subcategory of remote work. Finally, home-based work just refers to work carried out at home, even if their home is not the traditional workplace.

The term "e-work" refers to work performed virtually. Kirk and Belovics (2006) described e-workers as full-time telecommuters who work at home and communicate primarily via electronic means (e-mail, corporate intranet) and have few face-to-face interactions with co-workers. Remote working has grown in popularity over the last 40 years owing to the development of personal computers and the diffusion of the Internet. #DigitalNomad and #WorkFromAnywhere are common hashtags in social media and are a good representation of how telecommuting has evolved, becoming a kind of lifestyle.

Working from home before the pandemic

The Joint ILO–Eurofound report (2017) shows the rapid increase in remote working across Europe. For example, in France, from 2017 to 2012, the e-worker population strength increased from 7% to 12.4%; similarly, in Sweden, from 2003 to 2014, the said population increased from 36% to 51%.

The 2015 Labour Force Survey (UK) shows that, from 1997 to 2014, the frequency of working away from office, at least one day a week, increased from 13.3% to 17.1% (Eurofound & ILO, 2017). They also highlighted that high-skilled (14%) and middle-skilled workers (16%) are the most likely to work away a traditional from office, as opposed to factory-based workers (8%). In 2015, teleworkers comprised about 37% of the US population (Gallup, 2016). In the European Union (EU), it was 17% in 2015, 7% in Italy, and 37% in Denmark (Eurofound and the ILO, 2017).

Certain specific sectors are more likely to promote teleworking (Fana et al., 2020; Messenger & Gschwind, 2016; OECD, 2020; Sostero et al., 2020), for instance, wholesale and retail trade (10.7%), ICT (7.8%), scientific and professional activities (7.2%), and the public sector (7.2%) (Eurofound, 2017).

Remote working in the pandemic scenario

Since the beginning of the Covid-19 pandemic, the ILO (2020a) has considered work from home as the most effective measure to mitigate the spread of the infection and enable the continuation of productive activities that are critical to the functioning of national economies. According to the ILO (2021), the global number of workers working from home was estimated at 558 million, representing 17.4% of global workers (between 477 and 638 million workers). In 2020, 12.3% of employed people in the EU routinely worked from home, and of these, 13.2% were women. Considered at the level of individual nations, the percentage of workers from home was highest in Finland (25.1%), Luxembourg (23.1%), Ireland (21.5%), Austria (18.1%), and the Netherlands (17.8%). The countries with the lowest prevalence were Bulgaria (1.2%), Romania (2.5%), Croatia (3.1%), Hungary (3.6%), and Latvia (4.5%) (OECD, 2021).

Recently, the ILO (2021) reported that 7.9% of the global workforce, about 260 million workers, are home-based workers. This represents a figure almost triple that of the pre-pandemic context (3%) (ILO, 2020b).

Effects of working from home

Pre-pandemic research showed benefits of working remotely for different stakeholders (worker, organisation, and community/society (Fana et al., 2020; Messenger, 2019; Perez et al., 2003). According to a recent systematic review (Charalampous et al., 2019), remote working is linked to increased job satisfaction, increased job autonomy, increased organisational commitment, decreased emotional exhaustions, and better balance of work and life demands. Usually, organisations always supported working from home because it allowed workers to meet work–life balance needs. Further, this way teleworks can be more productive (Golden & Veiga, 2008; Martinez-Sanchez et al., 2008; Tremblay & Thomsin, 2012). For example, Hoeven and Zoonen (2015) suggested that when organisational flexibility increases effective communication, work-life balance, and job autonomy, thus resulting in enhanced well-being.

Despite these countless advantages and recognised benefits, existing empirical evidence on the association between working from home and employee well-being is inconclusive and rather controversial (Vartiainen, 2021). Thus, the reality is quite different, and it has been argued (Vartiainen, 2021) that benefits come at the cost of work intensification and an increased inability to unplug. For example, Bailey and Kurland (2002) found limited clear evidence of greater overall job satisfaction among telecommuters, while they highlighted satisfaction with the freedom and flexibility of working at home.

The European Working Conditions Surveys (EWCS) analysed teleworkers' working conditions in relationship to perceived job quality (Eurofound and ILO, 2017). Findings suggested that perceived health was linked to exposure to physical (e.g., static postures, prolonged sitting; EU-OSHA, 2021b) and psychosocial (e.g., quality of the relationships with supervisors and colleagues, job intensity) risk factors (EU-OSHA, 2021b; Eurofound, 2020b).

Concerning the pandemic scenario, in their systematic review, Lunde and colleagues (2022) analysed associations between home working and health outcomes, and they found different results. Indeed, in both cross-sectional and longitudinal studies, little evidence was found regarding the relationship between working from home and general health, well-being, stress, and burnout. Soga et al. (2022) in their recent review that analysed how pitfalls were associated with flexible work practices, were wondering about the concept of flexibility in remote work models. In effect, if on the one hand telecommuters may have uninterrupted time to perform their activities (e.g., read, plan, coordinate, research ...), on the other hand, they are exposed to frequent interruptions from home with the risk of longer work hours, thus negatively impacting on work–life balance (Bailey & Kurland, 2002). In addition, working from home may require working longer hours to solve work-related problems, and no one (co-workers or supervisors) notices the excessive demand, setting the stage for negative work-to-home spillover. For example, workers who live with other people face a greater set of challenges than those who live alone, because they also have to navigate others' spaces and collaborate in household activities, for example. In other words, the home has turned into a hub for carrying out both domestic and professional work (Soga et al., 2022; Soroui, 2021).

Mandatory work from home is a phenomenon different from the pre-pandemic conditions where employers and employees were aware of the opportunity to adopt arrangements of working remotely and its advantages. The pandemic changed the traditional concept of open office and shifted the focus to home as the main work context. Most studies on employee mental health during the pandemic highlighted the dangers associated with the synergic effect of Covid-19-related anxiety, social isolation due to lockdowns, job loss or fear of job loss, stress, and burnout (De Kock et al., 2021; Evanoff et al., 2020). However, the literature lacks information on the impact of the almost-overnight transition to remote work on individuals with little or no prior experience with it. In fact, many workers had to face various challenges such as difficulty in finding a space at home to work, lack of technological resources such as internet connection or personal computer, and poor support to perform home and work activities. Thus, working from home during the pandemic has changed the representation of physical and temporal boundaries that before the pandemic were an important prerequisite, thus raising concerns about a high degree of overlap between private and work life.

According to Ramarajan and Reid (2013), to maintain a clear boundary between work and personal life, workers must act deliberately. Until the 1970s,

194 Igor Portoghese and Maura Galletta

work and personal life were considered as two separate domains both physically and temporally (Parsons & Bales, 1955). Between the two domains that are assumed to be characterised by physical and temporal boundaries and assumes that emotions and behaviours of one domain spill over into the other. For people who are highly involved in work, the boundary between the two domains is likely to be highly permeable, thus allowing emotions felt at work to spill over into private life (Ashforth et al., 2000). Later, Katz and Kahn (1978) changed this perspective to an open-system approach based on the assumption that the two domains can potentially influence each other. The spillover theory (Staines, 1980), based on Katz and Kahn's approach, affirms the interdependence between the two domains that are assumed to be characterised by physical and temporal boundaries and assumes that emotions and behaviours of one domain spill over into the other. In this sense, there is an increased chance of work life affecting domestic life, especially in the case of workaholics (Ashforth et al., 2000). Moreover, the chances of work life spilling over to domestic life increase when a clear boundary between the two is missing, the roles lack distinction, and/or any sort of role conflict across the two domains is negligible (Greenhaus & Powell, 2006; Ilies et al., 2009). Conversely, negative spillover occurs if negative experiences in one sphere spill over into the other and there is a high level of overlap between the two spheres in terms of space, time, resources, and commitment (Sirgy, 2002). To avoid going into negative repercussions, workers often create psychological boundaries between the two spheres (Ashforth et al., 2000) by constructing mental and physical fences to organise the different work and family roles. For example, employees must set distinct boundaries between home and work domains (Judge et al., 2001; Sonnentag, 2012). Further, they must create a mental boundary that ensures that they leave work-related issues at work, instead of fussing over them at home; maintaining this distinction and balance enhances overall satisfaction with life (Sonnentag et al., 2008).

During this pandemic, these fences were dramatically destroyed overnight, and workers who had clear segmentation between work and personal lives were forced to redefine (sometimes without any negotiation) these boundaries.

Another important point that this pandemic made evident was that most of the work–home interaction theories/models were developed considering the dominant pre-pandemic labour market, where working remotely represented only a not very common working condition, usually conceived as a voluntary work arrangement. Although the large body of research focused on the remote working modality in the last 30 years, the unprecedented scale of the diffusion of this modality during the Covid-19 pandemic raises the question with respect to the validity of the accumulated knowledge on this topic, as it probably might lack contextual relevance, such as the consideration of the voluntary choice in adopting this modality (Wang et al., 2021). The lack of research and organisational theories regarding telework makes it difficult to pinpoint and understand the expectations and consequences of telework (Bailey & Kurland, 2002), especially when it becomes the only (mandatory) working modality. A few comparative research findings regarding the effects of telework and remote or digital online work are available globally (Eurofound, 2020b; International Labor Organisation, 2021), but there is no clear theoretical framework to be adopted. Now, everything has changed, and working remotely has the potential to become a more common strategy for many countries in the next few years. In this sense, the quality of the relationship between remote work and work–life balance depends on several factors. If working from home was a work arrangement adopted for reducing the likelihood of experiencing negative spillover from work to family because employees are left with more resources that can be used to actively participate in the family role(s), now it might not apply. In fact, now home and work environments do not have distinct boundaries and coexist at the same time and place, competing for resources. In this sense, the spillover effect has the potential to become constant—negative experiences of working from home can spill over to the home domain and vice versa. For example, issues with internet connection that delay the quality of work meetings may require other members of the house to limit internet connection, generating conflicts with family members. In turn, this would not be possible if kids are attending virtual lessons or if the partner is attending a meeting in another room.

Another critical point is that the impact of this massive remote work on employee burnout is still under-researched. The forced confinement of workers during the pandemic has further complicated this issue. Worsening mental health, psychological distress, burnout, and substance use accelerated substantially during the pandemic (Peters et al., 2022). These effects are associated with job uncertainty and loss of income (Wilson et al., 2020), as well as with substantive changes to working conditions.

Burnout is a chronic problem reflecting uneasy relationships between people and their work (Leiter 2005). It is a psychological syndrome involving three key dimensions: exhaustion–energy, cynicism–involvement, and inefficacy–efficacy (Maslach et al., 2001; Maslach & Leiter, 2008). In line with this definition, chronic exposure to psychosocial risks may represent an important condition for burnout development. However, the main characteristic of this pandemic is the acute exposure to different and sometimes risk factors underrated in the pre-pandemic literature. Among the dominant theoretical perspectives presented in the burnout literature, the Areas of Work Life Model (AWL; Leiter & Maslach, 2005) explains the processes of burnout and suggests ways in which organisations can address this prevalent problem. The AWL brings together both person and job context factors in a more integrated way. In other words, when identifying the source of burnout, instead of focusing on the relationship between the individual and the job environment, this model frames job stressors in terms of person–job imbalance or mismatches (Leiter & Maslach, 2004). The greater the perceived mismatch, the greater the likelihood of burnout.

This model identifies six key areas prone to imbalance: workload, control, reward, community, fairness, and values. The AWL model outlines six factors essential for a workplace to be called healthy: (a) a sustainable workload; (b) choice and control; (c) recognition and reward; (d) a supportive work community; (e) fairness, respect, and social justice; and (f) clear values and meaningful work. Further, Maslach and Banks (2017) believe that the quality of relationship between a person and their work is mostly decided by the degree of satisfaction of core psychological needs

Six areas of working life and teleworking in the Covid-19 scenario

An important question is whether working from home in the pandemic scenario opens the door to the consideration of alternative theoretical models. As previously stated, scholars have highlighted the strong limitation of the pre-pandemic literature in helping scholars, managers, and policymakers in understanding if remote working in pandemic scenarios requires a new definition of working environment or if previous studies are still valid.

Considering the actual worldwide context, there is a need for an evidence-based model that signs the line of possible interventions that could be implemented in fostering healthy remote-working environments.

Workload

As postulated in the model, workload has the strongest association with the exhaustion dimension of job burnout. In this sense, lack of resources to fulfil job demands increases perceived workload, thereby aggravating burnout. Employees feel their physical, cognitive, or emotional energy are depleted by lack the time, expertise, equipment, or support staff essential to deal with the requests of their job (Semmer et al., 2007).

The Covid-19 pandemic has well-being-related costs for employees, such as an increase in technology-related job demands and technostress (Donati et al., 2021; Molino, et al., 2020; Ghislieri, et al., 2022), as well as in terms of anxiety, depression, and sleep quality (Afonso et al., 2021). Further, the pandemic has accelerated digitalisation, globally. With the ICT, in this pandemic, the office literally moved to the home of employees, increasing workload (Wang, Liu, Qian, & Parker, 2021; Yang et al., 2022), and techno overload (Molino 2020). Techno overload results from the pressure to work faster and longer or alter work habits, thereby resulting in technostress (Ragu-Natha et al., 2008). In this sense, the pandemic dramatically changed working context exposing teleworkers to a significant increase in terms of number of emails, virtual meetings, and mobile phone apps, requiring keeping workers to remain permanently connected even when not formally on the job (Boswell & Olson-Buchanan, 2007; Soga et al., 2022). Techno overload refers to the technology-related demand to work longer and faster, whereas constant connectivity and, consequently, a diffusion of work into private life are defined as techno-invasion (Galanti et al., 2021). According with Derks and colleagues (Derks, & Bakker, 2014; Derks et al., 2015), being constantly connected and available anytime and anywhere, exposes workers to a higher risk of blurring the boundaries between work and personal life, further exacerbating stress and burnout. Being constantly connected is associated with permeable boundaries between work and home domains, which implies that it might contribute to the experience of work–home interference. Wang et al. (2021) showed that workers struggled with work–home interference while trying to balance roles. For example, being online all the time became an exhausting experience, reducing people's ability to meet home obligations. In this sense, the techno-invasion refers to "invasive effect of IT in situations where employees can be reached anytime and feel the need to be constantly connected, thus blurring work-related and personal contexts" (Ragu-Nathan et al., 2008, p. 427). Communication technology creates that environment in which employers, colleagues and\or customers can contact workers anywhere, activating that vicious cycle that leads to work on unresolved tasks even when it would be necessary to take a break from work (Eichberger et al., in press). Indeed, previous studies have associated being constantly connected with difficulties in managing work–home balance (Derks & Bakker, 2014). This condition represents the spillover of work to the family domain (Amstad et al., 2011) and fosters conflict between the two roles. In this sense, in the early phase of the adoption of remote working methods, technology and lockdowns acted as catalysts in requiring workers to move rapidly from one sphere to another, not only moving from rooms in the house but adapting "working corners" on the fly. The lack of separate physical space for work diminishes the mental boundaries between work and personal life (Kubo et al., 2021). A recent study (Nolan et al., 2020) showed that work-from-home during the pandemic was associated with low recovery and low wellbeing among those workers who spent more time in working than in personal life activities, suggesting significant difficulties in transitioning from work to home roles. Furthermore, virtual meetings from home at night and during weekends and long working days have led to breakdowns in the work–life balance and problems with family members. Johnson and Mabry (2022) suggested that this spread of virtual engagement was referred to in the social media as "Zoom fatigue." This techno-invasion facilitated the negative spillover of work on personal life, invading not only the time but the space.

Another important condition was that living alone, marital status, and family structure were important contextual factors in increasing the likelihood of negative spillover. Whereas living alone may expose workers to unclear boundaries between work and private life as a coping strategy for surviving loneliness, especially during lockdowns, it may have a different impact when all members of the family live, study, and work in the same home. This pandemic pushed everyone to stay at home, which resulted in multiple invasions into private life and multiple spillovers. The United Nation Global Communications chief Melissa Fleming posted a picture on social media where she ironised about her experience of working from home: she transformed the ironing board into a desk. In this way, she was able to "escape with it into a different room when the three of us living here need a separate quiet workspace". Furthermore, whether workers have small children or not was an important condition for a positive effect on the work–life balance (Eurofound, 2020b; Eurofound & ILO, 2017; Messenger, 2019). However, if in the pre-pandemic literature this condition was associated to the reduced need to commute, as well as work hour flexibility, with the ongoing pandemic, the same reasons do not apply.

As a matter of fact, these individuals are now faced with the challenge of fulfilling their roles successfully on both the work and home domains, as the demands from both roles have increased (Prottas & Hyland, 2011). As not all demands from both roles can be effectively met, that may require extra re-sources, such as time and energy, thereby aggravating the stress (Hobfoll, 2001; Eby et al., 2005; Bakker & Demerouti, 2007; Brummelhuis & Bakker, 2012) and burnout (Maslach et al., 2001; Brewer & Shapard, 2004). According to Wethal et al. (2022), employees who have children are the most likely to reduce their work hours or shift outside a 9-to-5 rhythm to accommodate caretaking demands, for instance, organising work schedule around the chil-dren's timetable. For instance, some families reported on planning childcare responsibilities based on which parent had scheduled virtual meetings at work, while others set temporal limits for homeschooling or scheduled some working duties when children were sleeping.

Another important point raised by the EU work-from-home data was that being women with small children was linked to more negative spillover than men (Eurofound, 2020b). Power (2020) found that during the early stages of the pandemic women were extremely impacted by work-family stress and burnout. Specifically, working mothers were found to be spending approxi-mately 20 extra hours a week on housework than men. Having and taking care of children has always been considered a driver of telework (Vyas & Butakhieo, 2021). As remote work became a compulsion during the pan-demic, attaining work-life balance became a task more complex than in the past. Since all members of the family had to remain isolated at home because of the pandemic, the work performance of employees, especially women, got severely affected, and various studies observed that the presence of children at home was associated with employees' decreased physical and psychological well-being (Xiao et al., 2021), enhanced perceived workload (Santos et al., 2021) and boundary management issues (Graham et al., 2021; Syrek, Kühnel, Vahle-Hinz, & de Bloom, 2018). For example, during the pandemic, many parents were not ready to become informal educators while balancing work responsibilities and providing childcare simultaneously (Lee et al., 2021). Therefore, parents were at risk of experiencing parental burnout due to the chronic stress they encountered (Brown et al., 2020) because the demands that they carried outweighed the resources available to them (Bornstein, 2020).

Control

According with the AWL model, when workers cannot make decisions re-garding resources or the authority to work efficiently, the risk to develop burnout increases. A control mismatch is also evident when workers have responsibilities that extend beyond their authority. The critical issue is whether individuals or groups have the authority and access to resources that are appropriate to their responsibilities. At the root of this concept, there is the notion that job control can buffer the relationship between job demands and strain. The control dimension entails that workers perceive to be able to influence decisions relating to their work, to exercise personal autonomy, and to gain access to resources (for example, social support and reward) in order to complete their work. That is, even when the demands become too challenging, such as in the Covid-19 scenario, having high control over one's own job reduces strain and can diminish the negative outcomes of high job demands (Karasek, 1979).

According to pre-pandemic studies, teleworking was associated to enhanced flexibility, autonomy, and control (Kossek et al., 2006). According to Becker et al. (2022), in the pandemic scenario, shifting to remote work may have increased job control over the work environment and schedule, enhancing workers' sense of autonomy in the early phase. In general, teleworking enables workers to organise their professional activities more flexibly, for example, beginning the day with the tasks that require greater concentration, as this is when they feel more alert, and/or making up for work interruptions (e.g., preparing lunch or going out to make a last-minute purchase), and extending their working hours at the end of the day or working during the weekend (Borpujari et al., 2020). Accordingly, this perceived high control has been noted as the autonomy paradox, as these arrangements contrarily lead to work intensification and self-exploitation (de Mazmanian et al., 2013).

Furthermore, the generally increased uncertainty during the pandemic in all life domains (social, family, community, work) reduced employee control over other aspects of their lives and may have strengthened the saliency of remote work's perceived high job control (e.g., one of the few things employees could control was the way they performed their jobs). In fact, some employees may have reacted more to the forced nature of the change itself, as well as to the lack of structure and physical separation between work and nonwork, leading to lower perceptions of job control. According to Becker et al. (2022), high perceived job control is generally considered to be beneficial, but the benefits are attenuated for employees with high separation between work and home boundaries. In this sense, in the pandemic context and for teleworkers, the definition of control should be extended by considering if individuals are able to control the border between home and work domains and, consequently, attain a good balance between work and family demands. In the pandemic context, Verteinen (2021) suggested that the main sources of well-being and job satisfaction at home are the opportunities to concentrate and exert control over one's own jobs and time. For example, Wethal et al. (2022) highlighted that parents were most likely to have fewer work hours or to shift outside a 9-to-5 rhythm to make room for additional caring demands. According to the boundary theory (Ashforth et al., 2000; Clark, 2000), integrating work and family in time and space, as in flextime and flexplace job designs, means that borders between the two domains are permeable. For workers to really have control over how and when they telework and manage family demands, they may need to have a boundary management strategy. Kossek et al. (1999) define boundary management strategy as "the principles one uses to organise and separate role demands and expectations into specific realms of home (e.g., dependent caregiving) and work (i.e., doing one's job)". When teleworking, they work in a home office with a door closed to shut out family interruptions. Others may prefer to integrate. They may take personal calls as work. When at home, they may work at the kitchen table and be accessible to their families at the same time. For example, in the Sixth European Working Conditions Survey (2017), time management was assessed in teleworking, and findings showed that 22.9% of workers were free to decide their working hours, while for 34.1% of workers, their working hours were decided by the company.

Reward

Lack of reward is closely related to the burnout dimension of inefficacy (Maslach et al., 2001). It is about the lack of appropriate compensation or recognition for the work that people do. The critical issues pertaining to reward vary with people and situations. A reward shortfall could be in terms of benefits, social appreciation, or intrinsic reward. In the pre-pandemic context, teleworking was considered a kind of reward/benefit that workers received from employers and supervisors (Gabriel & Aguinis, 2022). Proper rewards can help the employees to feel that their efforts are recognised, which drives their level of engagement and motivation to work better. Notably, it should be emphasised that, when focusing on efforts to reduce burnout, non-monetary rewards must be prioritised over monetary benefits, as the feeling of just treatment by the organisation reduces the psychological impact of stress. Now remote working poses the risk of not being recognised for their work and subsequently, not receiving any benefit. Recognition requires a clear system of benefits, and symbolic recognition is based on support, monitoring, and performance assessment systems. For example, social isolation or communication blocks may present an important issue for reward recognitions. According with Metallo, Agrifoglio, and Maria (2022), professional isolation associated to remote working would increase workers' fear to be not considered for promotions and other rewards. Johnson and Mabry (2022) found that video meetings can be a rewarding source of productivity and social connection. This, in turn, may spill over into home life, as teleworkers may invest more resources in working in a kind of compensation system, feeling home demands to be a kind of obstacle to their work activities.

Community

According to the AWL model, burnout exacerbates when employees lack positive connections with others in the workplace. Positive connection with others provides social resources (such as social support) and instrumental assistance, and it makes the person feel like a part of a group with shared values. In this sense, the social environment plays a critical role reducing burnout risk and fostering work engagement (Leiter & Stright, 2009). According to Mäkiniemi et al. (2021), social support, positive perception of team climate, and good interpersonal relationships at work have been shown to be positively associated with better employee well-being. Thus, family, friends, colleagues, and supervisor(s) at work can act as effective sources of social support (Halbesleben, 2006). Social support can be expressed through several ways, such as actively listening to a person's problems, making suitable suggestions to help them solve the problem, provide guidance of material assistance, or merely talking to them and expressing how much their efforts are valued and appreciated. On the contrary, social isolation leads to employees feeling disconnected from the working environment, leading to lower performance and reduced work motivation (Wojcak et al., 2016; Contreras et al., 2020). Long-term isolation has adverse effects on employees' performance and increases turnover intention, as well as family–work and work–family conflict (Golden et al., 2008).

Concernig the pandemic scenario, as reported by Wang and colleagues (2021), social isolation (mainly loneliness) was among the main challenges associated to working from home. In fact, as face-to-face interactions became a non-essential social activity, workers lost social opportunities such as conversations and drinking coffee with colleagues. Despite the endless benefits of information and communication technology, their negative effects cannot be ruled out. For instance, the reduced in-person communication with co-workers has hindered social interaction (Baruch, 2000; Cooper & Kurland, 2002; Nakrošienė et al., 2019). Furthermore, teleworkers reported that the increased physical distance often was as an important obstacle for sharing organisational values and goals (Madsen, 2003; Cooper & Kurland, 2002) and it might influence their career opportunities (Khalifa & Davison, 2000) and might be a critical concern in terms of uncertainty.

Supervisor support plays a crucial role in teleworking as the immediate supervisor is in charge of evaluating employees' job performance and communicating organisational goals and vision. Thus, high quality relationship with the supervisor is viewed as a signal of positive organisational voluntary actions and helps employees to build a positive perception of organisational support (Eisenberger et al., 2001). According to Richardson et al. (2008), teleworking-related support offered by the organisation also serves to enhance employees' perceived control over their environment, thereby regenerating their coping efficacy.

The way a supervisor manages telework arrangements could affect the individual perception of job demands, job control, justice, values, and rewards system. According to Sinclair and colleagues (2020), the role of supervisor support in teleworking modality become crucial, especially in pandemic scenario. Fear and consequent stress arising in such situations can significantly impact individuals' work performance; thus, supervisors must put in efforts to address this issue in order to ensure that their teams' performance remains consistent and that their employees experience job satisfaction. Furthermore, supervisor support for ensuring employees' healthy work–life balance has been shown to lead to improvements in employee health, well-being, and work outcomes (Hammer et al., 2011).

Fairness

Reflects employees' perception of organisational justice in workplace. Fairness concerns issues of equity in workload or pay or fairness of treatment in terms of evaluations and promotions. Fairness is about employees' evaluation of the results of organisational decisions, such as whether they are fair or unfair decisions. It is also about procedural fairness, that is, whether the decision-making process reflects qualities of openness and adherence to relevant criteria. Particularly important in assessing fairness is relational justice, such as the consideration and respect shown during the decision-making process. If employees experience unfair treatment, such as exclusion from the organisational community, they tend to reciprocate by distancing themselves from the organisation through a cynical approach to work.

Most of the pre-pandemic scientific literature focused on employees' perceived justice in facilitating telework arrangements and the supervisor's role in granting autonomy to perform work and offering support for work–life balance (Kim et al., 2021). According to Gálvez et al. (2020), since work arrangements are significantly transformed in teleworking and remote settings, there could be the need to clearly redesign and strength standards, guidelines, processes, rules, norms, and policies (Thatcher & Zhu, 2006; Gálvez et al., 2020). However, since this is often not the case, unpredictability and the blurring of boundaries (longer and lonelier hours or denser workloads which diminish aspirations for work-life balance) are frequently the unexpected results of teleworking (Glass & Noonan, 2016; Gálvez et al., 2020).

Value

The extent to which employees believe that their contribution to the organisation is furthering the employees' core values. A positive balance is more likely when the organisation and its employees share core values. Values could involve ethical or moral principles, aspirations, or practices (Maslach et al., 2001). Concerning working from home, the value system should be considered in a wider context, as life values now are an important part of work values and can generate conflicts (Greenhaus & Allen, 2011). Specifically, workers may face a dilemma if they pay more attention to their personal needs and simultaneously (but ineffectively) try to cope with work, which threatens to violate their work values. On the other hand, ignoring their foremost concern about their personal life and engaging in work tasks can violate their preferred life values. In a teleworking context, it encompasses the values, norms, and expectations for each of the domains, work and personal life, requiring negotiation and integration of values from both domains.

Future research and implications for applications in work psychology

According to Soga and colleagues (2022), this pandemic made evident the main pitfalls of remote working arrangements, emphasising the need to investigate its impact on changes to work-family relationship, the strong dependence on technology, and the adoption of a sharing culture. Worldwide, employers are beginning to encouraging workers to gradually return-to-office, planning return to the office three days a week or introducing hybrid solutions. For example, many organisations are requiring workers to returning back to the office full time and the debate about what kind of work arrangements should be considered is still ongoing.

According to ILO (2020) and OSHA (2021), ensuring a safe return to work is crucial for many occupational groups. The adoption of safety plans not necessarily is in contrast with the use of work-from-home arrangements. In fact, in 2021, 91% of people in the US who work from home said they would continue to work remotely in the future. In the Gallup study (2021), 54% of workers reported that they believe their company will continue to sustain remote work, while 33% expect it to be reduced. Despite the uncertainty of the longer-term impacts of this situation, some companies began discussing the possibility of making remote work a permanent fixture for some employees (Best, 2021). A recent publication by Microsoft's Work Trend Index (2021), based on findings from a global survey conducted on more than 30000 workers across 31 countries, showed that the pandemic experience of working from home is likely to have a permanent influence on the workplace. A recent report from the UK (2022) investigated the "lessons from lockdowns" and the impact of working from home arrangement. This report highlighted that "hybrid working is the new workforce expectation" (p.8). In anticipation of this scenario, more than two thirds of the workers with managerial responsibilities stated that they are already considering redesigning the physical spaces of the workplace to adapt it to hybrid work arrangements.

However, employers should take into consideration the possibility that not all workers are available to continue to work from home at the same conditions. Paradoxically, while many workers are not ready (or happy?) to return to the office, it may help some workers in rebuilding the boundaries between work and personal life. Furthermore, these new scenarios raise the possibility that multiple roles with high negative spillover may increase the risk of other forms of burnout, such as parental burnout (Nyanamba et al., 2022). In this sense, organisations should learn from the pandemic experience, considering to implement clear guidelines aimed at supporting both the transition to remote-working and vice versa from remote working to in-person workplace, fostering more flexible work-life schedules for those who prefer hybrid arrangements. Then, the next new normal workplace would considering the (new) transition from remote working to hybrid work plan arrangements and giving support is the key to a successful transition. It may require a new corpus of scientific researches as a new workplace definition is coming: remote colleagues and\or supervisors, forced virtual collaboration, new organisational cultures, and e-meetings are just some examples. In this sense, longitudinal studies are needed as there is no evidence that hybrid working or forced return to the office may imply new risks for mental health of workers. In fact, after almost two years where workers literally crafted and balanced their life to working from home, now this new change (and not necessarily is going back to the pre-pandemic condition as the world changed) may require new efforts in balancing work and home life.

References

Afonso, P., Fonseca, M., & Teodoro, T. (2021). Evaluation of anxiety, depression and sleep quality in full-time teleworkers. *Journal of Public Health (Oxford, England)*, fdab164. 10.1093/pubmed/fdab164. Epub ahead of print. PMID: 34036369; PMCID: PMC8202819.

Amstad, F. T., Meier, L. L., Fasel, U., Elfering, A., & Semmer, N. K. (2011). A meta-analysis of work–family conflict and various outcomes with a special emphasis on cross-domain versus matching-domain relations. *Journal of Occupational Health Psychology*, *16*(2), 151.

Ashforth, B. E., Kreiner, G. E., & Fugate, M. (2000). All in a day's work: Boundaries and micro role transitions. *Academy of Management review*, *25*(3), 472–491.

Bailey, D. E., & Kurland, N. B. (2002). A review of telework research: Findings, new directions, and lessons for the study of modern work. *Journal of Organizational Behavior: The International Journal of Industrial, Occupational and Organizational Psychology and Behavior*, *23*(4), 383–400.

Bakker, A. B., & Demerouti, E. (2007). The Job Demands-Resources model: State of the art. *Journal of Managerial Psychology*, *22*(3), 309–328.

Baruch, Y. (2000). Teleworking: benefits and pitfalls as perceived by professionals and managers. *New Technology, Work and Employment*, *15*(1), 34–49.

Becker, W. J., Belkin, L. Y., Tuskey, S. E., & Conroy, S. A. (2022). Surviving remotely: How job control and loneliness during a forced shift to remote work impacted employee work behaviors and well-being. *Human Resource Management*, *61*(4), 449–464. https://doi.org/10.1002/hrm.22102

Best, S. J. (2021). The future of work: Remote work in the emerging new normal. *The Business & Management Review*, *12*(1), 285–292.

Bornstein, M. H. (2020). "Parental burnout": The state of the science. *New Directions for Child and Adolescent Development*, *174*, 169–184.

Borpujari, R., Chan-Ahuja, S., & Sherman, E. L. (2020, July). Time fungibility: an inductive study of workers' time-use during COVID-19 stay-at-home orders. In *Poceedings of the 80th Virtual Meeting*, Briarcliff Manor, NY: Academy of Management.

Boswell, W. R., & Olson-Buchanan, J. B. (2007). The use of communication technologies after hours: The role of work attitudes and work-life conflict. *Journal of Management*, *33*(4), 592–610.

Brewer, E. W., & Shapard, L. (2004). Employee burnout: A meta-analysis of the relationship between age or years of experience. *Human Resource Development Review*, *3*(2), 102–123.

Brown, S. M., Doom, J. R., Lechuga-Peña, S., Watamura, S. E., & Koppels, T. (2020). Stress and parenting during the global COVID-19 pandemic. *Child Abuse & Neglect, 110*, 104699.

Charalampous, M., Grant, C. A., Tramontano, C., & Michailidis, E. (2019). Systematically reviewing remote e-workers' well-being at work: A multidimensional approach. *European Journal of Work and Organizational Psychology, 28*(1), 51–73.

Clark, S. C. (2000). Work/family border theory: A new theory of work/family balance. *Human Relations, 53*, 747–770.

Cho, E. (2020). Examining boundaries to understand the impact of COVID-19 on vocational behaviors. *Journal of Vocational Behavior, 119*, 103437.

Colvin, G. (2022, April 6). *Many CEOs want workers back full-time. Here's how Twitter, Netflix, and other major companies are handling return to work.* https://fortune.com/2022/04/06/ceos-want-workers-back-in-office-twitter-rei-gm-citi-netflix/.

Contreras, F., Baykal, E., & Abid, G. (2020). E-leadership and teleworking in times of COVID-19 and beyond: what we know and where do we go. *Frontiers in Psychology, 11*, 590271.

Cooper, C. D., & Kurland, N. B. (2002). Telecommuting, professional isolation, and employee development in public and private organizations. *Journal of Organizational Behavior: The International Journal of Industrial, Occupational and Organizational Psychology and Behavior, 23*(4), 511–532.

Cotofan, M., De Neve, J. E., Golin, M., Kaats, M., & Ward, G. (2021). Work and well-being during COVID-19: impact, inequalities, resilience, and the future of work. *World Happiness Report*, 153–190.

De Kock, J. H., Latham, H. A., Leslie, S. J., Grindle, M., Munoz, S. A., Ellis, L., … & O'Malley, C. M. (2021). A rapid review of the impact of COVID-19 on the mental health of healthcare workers: implications for supporting psychological well-being. *BMC public health, 21*(1), 1–18.

Derks, D., & Bakker, A. B. (2014). Smartphone use, work–home interference, and burnout: A diary study on the role of recovery. *Applied Psychology, 63*(3), 411–440.

Derks, D., van Duin, D., Tims, M., & Bakker, A. B. (2015). Smartphone use and work–home interference: The moderating role of social norms and employee work engagement. *Journal of Occupational and Organizational Psychology, 88*(1), 155–177.

Donati, S., Viola, G., Toscano, F., & Zappalà, S. (2021). Not All Remote Workers Are Similar: Technology Acceptance, Remote Work Beliefs, and Wellbeing of Remote Workers during the Second Wave of the COVID-19 Pandemic. *International Journal of Environmental Research and Public Health, 18*(22), 12095.

Eby, L. T., Casper, W. J., Lockwood, A., Bordeaux, C., & Brinley, A. (2005). Work and family research in IO/OB: Content analysis and review of the literature (1980–2002). *Journal of vocational behavior, 66*(1), 124–197.

Eichberger, C., Derks, D., & Zacher, H. (in press). A daily diary study on technology-assisted supplemental work, unfinished tasks, and sleep: The role of problem-solving pondering. *International Journal of Stress Management, 29*(1), 61–74. https://doi.org/10.1037/str0000237

Eisenberger, R., Armeli, S., Rexwinkel, B., Lynch, P. D., & Rhoades, L. (2001). Reciprocation of perceived organizational support. *Journal of applied psychology, 86*(1), 42.

EU-OSHA (2021b). *Home-based teleworking and preventive occupational safety and health measures in European workplaces: evidence from ESENER-3.* Luxembourg: Publications Office of the European Union.

Eurofound (2020a). *Regulations to address work–life balance in digital flexible working arrangements, New forms of employment series.* Luxembourg: Publications Office of the European Union. Retrieved from: https://www.eurofound.europa.eu/sites/default/files/ef_publication/field_ef_document/ef19046en.pdf

Eurofound (2020b). *COVID-19: Policy responses across Europe.* Luxembourg: Publications Office of the European Union. Retrieved from: https://www.eurofound.europa.eu/sites/default/files/ef_publication/field_ef_document/ef20064en.pdf.

Eurofound and the International Labour Office (2017). *Working anytime, anywhere: The effects on the world of work.* Publications Office of the European Union, Luxembourg, and the International Labour Office, Geneva.

Eurofound (2017). Sixth European Working Conditions Survey – Overview report (2017 update), Publications Office of the European Union, Luxembourg. https://www.eurofound.europa.eu/sites/default/fles/ef_survey/feld_ef_documents/6th_ewcs_-_technical_report.pdf (2017a) (accessed on 20 April 2022).

Evanoff, B. A., Strickland, J. R., Dale, A. M., Hayibor, L., Page, E., Duncan, J. G., ... & Gray, D. L. (2020). Work-related and personal factors associated with mental well-being during the COVID-19 response: survey of health care and other workers. *Journal of medical Internet research*, 22(8), e21366.

Fana, M., Milasi, S., Napierala, J., Fernandez-Macias, E., & Vázquez, I. G. (2020). *Telework, work organisation and job quality during the COVID-19 crisis: a qualitative study* (No. 2020/11). JRC Working Papers Series on Labour, Education and Technology.

Felstead, A., & Henseke, G. (2017). Assessing the growth of remote working and its consequences for effort, well-being and work-life balance. *New Technology, Work and Employment*, 32(3), 195–212.

Fonner, K. L., & Roloff, M. E. (2010). Why teleworkers are more satisfied with their jobs than are office-based workers: When less contact is beneficial. *Journal of Applied Communication Research*, 38(4), 336–361.

Gabriel, K. P., & Aguinis, H. (2022). How to prevent and combat employee burnout and create healthier workplaces during crises and beyond. *Business Horizons*, 65(2), 183–192.

Galanti, T., Guidetti, G., Mazzei, E., Zappalà, S., & Toscano, F. (2021). Work from home during the COVID-19 outbreak: The impact on employees' remote work productivity, engagement, and stress. *Journal of Occupational and Environmental Medicine*, 63(7), e426.

Gallup (2016). In US, telecommuting for work climbs to 37%. *Gallup.com*, (accessed on 20 April 2022).

Gálvez, A., Tirado, F., & Alcaraz, J. M. (2020). "Oh! Teleworking!" Regimes of engagement and the lived experience of female Spanish teleworkers. *Business Ethics: A European Review*, 29(1), 180–192.

Garrett, R. K., & Danziger, J. N. (2007). Which telework? Defining and testing a taxonomy of technology-mediated work at a distance. *Social Science Computer Review*, 25(1), 27–47.

Ghislieri, C., Dolce, V., Sanseverino, D., Wodociag, S., Vonthron, A. M., Vayre, É., ... & Molino, M. (2022). Might insecurity and use of ICT enhance internet addiction and exhaust people? A study in two European countries during emergency remote working. *Computers in Human Behavior*, 126, 107010.

Glass, J. L., & Noonan, M. C. (2016). Telecommuting and earnings trajectories among American women and men 1989–2008. *Social Forces*, 95(1), 217–250.

Golden, T. D., & Veiga, J. F. (2005). The impact of extent of telecommuting on job satisfaction: Resolving inconsistent findings. *Journal of Management*, 31(2), 301–318.

Golden, T. D., & Veiga, J. F. (2008). The impact of superior–subordinate relationships on the commitment, job satisfaction, and performance of virtual workers. *The Leadership Quarterly, 19*(1), 77–88.

Golden, T. D., Veiga, J. F., & Dino, R. N. (2008). The impact of professional isolation on teleworker job performance and turnover intentions: does time spent teleworking, interacting face-to-face, or having access to communication-enhancing technology matter?. *Journal of Applied Psychology, 93*(6), 1412.

Graham, M., Weale, V., Lambert, K. A., Kinsman, N., Stuckey, R., & Oakman, J. (2021). Working at home: The impacts of COVID 19 on health, family-work-life conflict, gender, and parental responsibilities. *Journal of Occupational and Environmental Medicine, 63*(11), 938.

Greenhaus, J. H., & Powell, G. N. (2006). When work and family are allies: A theory of work–family enrichment. *Academy of Management Review, 31*, 72–92.

Greenhaus, J. H., & Allen, T. D. (2011). Work-family balance: A review and extension of the literature. In Quick, J. C., & Tetrick, L. E. (Eds.), *Handbook of occupational health psychology* (pp. 165–183). American Psychological Association.

Halbesleben, J. R. (2006). Sources of social support and burnout: a meta-analytic test of the conservation of resources model. *Journal of Applied Psychology, 91*(5), 1134.

Hammer, L. B., Kossek, E. E., Anger, W. K., Bodner, T., & Zimmerman, K. L. (2011). Clarifying work–family intervention processes: The roles of work–family conflict and family-supportive supervisor behaviors. *Journal of Applied Psychology, 96*(1), 134.

Harpaz, I. (2002). Advantages and disadvantages of telecommuting for the individual, organization and society. *Work Study, 51*(2), 74–80.

Hobfoll, S. E. (2001). The influence of culture, community, and the nested-self in the stress process: Advancing conservation of resources theory. *Applied Psychology, 50*(3), 337–421.

Hwang, H., Hur, W. M., & Shin, Y. (2021). Emotional exhaustion among the South Korean workforce before and after COVID-19. *Psychology and Psychotherapy: Theory, Research and Practice, 94*(2), 371–381.

Ilies, R., Wilson, K. S., & Wagner, D. T. (2009). The spillover of daily job satisfaction onto employees' family lives: The facilitating role of work-family integration. *Academy of Management Journal, 52*(1), 87–102.

ILO (2020). A Safe and Healthy Return to Work during the COVID-19 Pandemic. Brief Note. https://www.ilo.org/global/topics/safety-and-health-at-work/resources-library/publications/WCMS_745549/lang- -en/index.htm

ILO (2020a). Working from Home: Estimating the worldwide potential. Available at https://www.ilo.org/global/topics/non-standard-employment/publications/WCMS_743447/lang--en/index.htm, (accessed on 20 April 2022).

ILO (2020b). *Working from Home: From invisibility to decent work.* Geneva: ILO.

ILO (2021). From potential to practice: Preliminary findings on the numbers of workers working from home during the COVID-19 pandemic. *ILO Brief,* Geneva.

International Labour Organization. (2020). Defining and measuring remote work, telework, work at home and home-based work (technical note). Available online: https://www.ilo.org/wcmsp5/groups/public/---dgreports/---stat/documents/publication/wcms_747075.pdf (accessed on 20 April 2022).

Johnson, B. J., & Mabry, J. B. (2022). Remote work video meetings: Workers' emotional exhaustion and practices for greater well-being. *German Journal of Human Resource Management, 36*(3), 380–408.

Judge, T. A., Thoresen, C. J., Bono, J. E., & Patton, G. K. (2001). The job satisfaction–job performance relationship: A qualitative and quantitative review. *Psychological bulletin*, *127*(3), 376.

Karasek Jr, R. A. (1979). Job demands, job decision latitude, and mental strain: Implications for job redesign. *Administrative Science Quarterly*, 285–308.

Katz, D., & Kahn, R. L. (1978). *The social psychology of organi- zations* (2nd ed.). New York: Wiley.

Khalifa, M., & Davison, R. (2000). Exploring the telecommuting paradox. *Communications of the ACM*, *43*(3), 29–31.

Kim, T., Mullins, L. B., & Yoon, T. (2021). Supervision of telework: a key to organizational performance. *The American Review of Public Administration*, *51*(4), 263–277.

Kirk, J., & Belovics, R. (2006). Making e-working work. *Journal of Employment Counseling*, *43*(1), 39–46.

Konradt, U., Schmook, R., Wilm, A., & Hertel, G. (2000). Health circles for teleworkers: selective results on stress, strain and coping styles. *Health education research*, *15*(3), 327–338.

Korunka, C. (2021). *Flexible working practices and approaches.* Psychological and Social Implications. Switzerland: Springer Cham, Springer Nature Switzerland: AG 2021.

Kossek, E. E., Lautsch, B. A., & Eaton, S. C. (2006). Telecommuting, control, and boundary management: Correlates of policy use and practice, job control, and work–family effectiveness. *Journal of Vocational Behavior*, *68*(2), 347–367.

Kossek, E. E., Noe, R. A., & DeMarr, B. J. (1999). Work-family role synthesis: Individualand organizational determinants. *International Journal of Conflict Management*, *10*(2), 102–129.

Kubo, T., Izawa, S., Ikeda, H., Tsuchiya, M., Miki, K., & Takahashi, M. (2021). Work e-mail after hours and off-job duration and their association with psychological detachment, actigraphic sleep, and saliva cortisol: A 1-month observational study for information technology employees. *Journal of Occupational Health*, *63*(1), e12300.

Lee, S. J., Ward, K. P., Chang, O. D., & Downing, K. M. (2021). Parenting activities and the transition to home-based education during the COVID-19 pandemic. *Children and Youth Services Review*, *122*, 105585.

Leiter, M. P., & Maslach, C. (2004). Areas of worklife: A structured approach to organizational predictors of job burnout. In P. L. Perrewé & D. C. Ganster (Eds.). *Emotional and physiological processes and positive intervention strategies* (pp. 91–134). Elsevier Science/ JAI Press.

Leiter, M. P., & Maslach, C. (2005). *Banishing burnout: Six strategies for improving your relationship with work.* John Wiley & Sons.

Leiter, M. P., & Stright, N. (2009). The social context of work life: Implications for burnout and work engagement. *International Handbook of Work and Health Psychology*, *3*, 25–47.

Lunde, L. K., Fløvik, L., Christensen, J. O., Johannessen, H. A., Finne, L. B., Jørgensen, I. L., ... & Vleeshouwers, J. (2022). The relationship between telework from home and employee health: a systematic review. *BMC Public Health*, *22*(1), 1–14.

Madsen, S. R. (2003). The effects of home-based teleworking on work-family conflict. *Human Resource Development Quarterly*, *14*(1), 35–58.

Mäkiniemi, J. P., Oksanen, A., & Mäkikangas, A. (2021). Loneliness and well-being during the COVID-19 pandemic: The moderating roles of personal, social and organizational resources on perceived stress and exhaustion among Finnish university employees. *International Journal of Environmental Research and Public Health*, *18*(13), 7146.

Martínez-Sánchez, A., Pérez-Pérez, M., Vela-Jiménez, M. J., & de-Luis-Carnicer, P. (2008). Telework adoption, change management, and firm performance. *Journal of Organizational Change Management, 21*(1), 7–31.

Maslach, C., & Banks, C. G. (2017). Psychological connections with work. In Cooper, C., & Leiter, M. P. (Eds.), *Routledge companion to wellbeing and work* (pp. 37–54). New York, NY: Routledge.

Maslach, C., & Leiter, M. P. (2008). Early predictors of job burnout and engagement. *Journal of Applied Psychology, 93*(3), 498.

Maslach, C., Schaufeli, W. B., & Leiter, M. P. (2001). Job burnout. *Annual Review of Psychology, 52*, 397–422.

Mazmanian, M., Orlikowski, W. J., & Yates, J. (2013). The autonomy paradox: The implications of mobile email devices for knowledge professionals. *Organization Science, 24*(5), 1337–1357.

Messenger, J. (2019). *Telework in the 21st century*. Cheltenham: Edward Elgar Publishing.

Messenger, J. C., & Gschwind, L. (2016). Three generations of Telework: New ICT s and the (R) evolution from Home Office to Virtual Office. *New Technology, Work and Employment, 31*(3), 195–208.

Metallo, C., Agrifoglio, R., & Maria, F. (2022). Effective management of a remote workforce for Covid-19: A proposed research model toward smart working adoption within organizations. In *HR Analytics and Digital HR Practices* (pp. 101–126). Singapore: Palgrave Macmillan.

Molino, M., Ingusci, E., Signore, F., Manuti, A., Giancaspro, M. L., Russo, V., … & Cortese, C. G. (2020). Wellbeing costs of technology use during Covid-19 remote working: An investigation using the Italian translation of the technostress creators scale. *Sustainability, 12*(15), 5911.

Nakrošienė, A., Bučiūnienė, I., & Goštautaitė, B. (2019). Working from home: characteristics and outcomes of telework. *International Journal of Manpower, 40*, 87–101.

Nilles, J. (1975). Telecommunications and organizational decentralization. *IEEE Transactions on Communications, 23*(10), 1142–1147.

Nilles, J. M. (1997). Telework: enabling distributed organizations: implications for IT managers. *Information Systems Management, 14*(4), 7–14.

Nilles, J. M., Carlson, F. R., Gray, P., & Hanneman, G. (1976). Telecommuting-an alternative to urban transportation congestion. *IEEE Transactions on Systems, Man, and Cybernetics*, (2), 77–84.

Nolan, S., Rumi, S. K., Anderson, C., David, K., & Salim, F. D. (2020). Exploring the impact of COVID-19 lockdown on social roles and emotions while working from home. *arXiv preprint arXiv:2007.12353*.

Nyanamba, J. M., Liew, J., & Li, D. (2022). Parental burnout and remote learning at home during the COVID-19 pandemic: Parents' motivations for involvement. *School Psychology, 37*(2), 160–172.

Occupational Safety and Health Administration (OSHA) (2021). Protecting Workers: Guidance on Mitigating and Preventing the Spread of COVID-19 in the Workplace. https://www.osha.gov/coronavirus/safework

OECD (2020). Productivity gains from teleworking in the post COVID-19 era: How can public policies make it happen? OECD Policy Responses to Coronavirus (COVID-19), Updated 7 September 2020, https://www.oecd.org/coronavirus/policy-responses/productivity-gains-from-teleworking-in-the-postcovid-19-era-a5d52e99/ (accessed on 20 April 2022).

OECD (2021). Teleworking in the COVID-19 pandemic: Trends and prospects. https://www.oecd.org/coronavirus/policy-responses/teleworking-in-the-covid-19-pandemic-trends-and-prospects-72a416b6/, (accessed on 20 April 2022).

Parent-Thirion, A., Biletta, I., Cabrita, J., Vargas Llave, O., Vermeylen, G., Wilczyńska, A., & Wilkens, M. (2016). Sixth European working conditions survey–overview report. *EUROFOUND.* https://policycommons.net/artifacts/1840857/sixth-european-working-conditions-survey/2583901/ (accessed on 20 April 2022).

Parry, J., Young, Z., Bevan, S., Veliziotis, M., Baruch, Y., Beigi, M., ... & Tochia, C. (2022). Work after lockdown: No going back: What we have learned working from home through the COVID-19 pandemic. https://eprints.soton.ac.uk/455918/ (accessed on 05 June 2022).

Parsons, T., & Bales, R.F. (1955). *Family, socialization, and interaction process.* Glencoe, IL: Free Press.

Pérez, M. P., Sanchez, A. M., & de Luis Carnicer, M. P. (2003). The organizational implications of human resources managers' perception of teleworking. *Personnel Review.*

Peters, S. E., Dennerlein, J. T., Wagner, G. R., & Sorensen, G. (2022). Work and worker health in the post-pandemic world: a public health perspective. *The Lancet Public Health,* 7(2), e188–e194.

Power, K. (2020). The COVID-19 pandemic has increased the care burden of women and families. *Sustainability: Science, Practice and Policy,* 16(1), 67–73.

Prasad, K., McLoughlin, C., Stillman, M., Poplau, S., Goelz, E., Taylor, S., ... & Sinsky, C. A. (2021). Prevalence and correlates of stress and burnout among US healthcare workers during the COVID-19 pandemic: A national cross-sectional survey study. *EClinicalMedicine,* 35, 100879.

Prottas, D. J., & Hyland, M. M. (2011). Is high involvement at work and home so bad? Contrasting scarcity and expansionist perspectives. *The Psychologist-Manager Journal,* 14(1), 29–51.

Putnam, L. L., Myers, K. K., & Gailliard, B. M. (2014). Examining the tensions in workplace flexibility and exploring options for new directions. *Human Relations,* 67(4), 413–440.

Ragu-Nathan, T. S., Tarafdar, M., Ragu-Nathan, B. S., & Tu, Q. (2008). The consequences of technostress for end users in organizations: Conceptual development and empirical validation. *Information Systems Research,* 19(4), 417–433.

Ramarajan, L., & Reid, E. (2013). Shattering the myth of separate worlds: Negotiating nonwork identities at work. *Academy of Management Review,* 38(4), 621–644.

Richardson, J., McBey, K., & McKenna, S. (2008). Integrating realistic job previews and realistic living conditions previews: Realistic recruitment for internationally mobile knowledge workers. *Personnel Review,* 37(5), 490–508.

Santos, M. H., Rosa, M., Correia, R. B., & Xavier, E. (2021). Gender roles and dynamics in COVID-19 times: Changes and continuities in sharing arrangements of housework and caregiving. *Psicologia,* 35(1), 147–156.

Semmer, N. K., Jacobshagen, N., Meier, L. L., & Elfering, A. (2007). Occupational stress research: The "Stress-As-Offense-to-Self" perspective. In J. Houdmont & S. McIntyre (Eds.), *Occupational health psychology: European perspectives on research, education and practice* (Vol. 2, pp. 43–60). Castelo da Maia: ISMAI.

Sinclair, R. R., Allen, T., Barber, L., Bergman, M., Britt, T., Butler, A., ... & Yuan, Z. (2020). Occupational health science in the time of COVID-19: Now more than ever. *Occupational Health Science,* 4(1), 1–22.

Sirgy, M. J. (2002). *The psychology of quality of life* (Vol. 12). Dordrecht: Kluwer Academic Publishers.

Soga, L. R., Bolade-Ogunfodun, Y., Mariani, M., Nasr, R., & Laker, B. (2022). Unmasking the other face of flexible working practices: A systematic literature review. *Journal of Business Research, 142*, 648–662.

Sonnentag, S. (2012). Psychological detachment from work during leisure time: The benefits of mentally disengaging from work. *Current Directions in Psychological Science, 21*(2), 114–118.

Sonnentag, S., Mojza, E. J., Binnewies, C., & Scholl, A. (2008). Being engaged at work and detached at home: A week-level study on work engagement, psychological detachment, and affect. *Work & Stress, 22*(3), 257–276.

Soroui, S. T. (2021). Understanding the drivers and implications of remote work from the local perspective: An exploratory study into the dis/reembedding dynamics. *Technology in Society, 64*, 101328.

Sostero, M., Milasi, S., Hurley, J., Fernandez-Macías, E., & Bisello, M. (2020). *Teleworkability and the COVID-19 crisis: a new digital divide?* (No. 2020/05). JRC working papers series on labour, education and technology.

Staines, G. L. (1980). Spillover versus compensation: A review of the literature on the relationship between work and nonwork. *Human Relations, 33*(2), 111–129.

Syrek, C., Kühnel, J., Vahle-Hinz, T., & de Bloom, J. (2022). Being an accountant, cook, entertainer and teacher—all at the same time: Changes in employees' work and work-related well-being during the coronavirus (COVID-19) pandemic. *International Journal of Psychology, 57*(1), 20–32.

Syrek, C. J., Kühnel, J., Vahle-Hinz, T., & De Bloom, J. (2018). Share, like, twitter, and connect: Ecological momentary assessment to examine the relationship between non-work social media use at work and work engagement. *Work & Stress, 32*(3), 209–227. https://doi.org/10.1080/02678373.2017.1367736

Ten Brummelhuis, L. L., & Bakker, A. B. (2012). A resource perspective on the work–home interface: The work–home resources model. *American psychologist, 67*(7), 545.

Ter Hoeven, C. L., & Van Zoonen, W. (2015). Flexible work designs and employee well-being: Examining the effects of resources and demands. *New Technology, Work and Employment, 30*(3), 237–255.

Thatcher, S. M., & Zhu, X. (2006). Changing identities in a changing workplace: Identification, identity enactment, self-verification, and telecommuting. *Academy of Management Review, 31*(4), 1076–1088.

Tremblay, D. G., & Thomsin, L. (2012). Telework and mobile working: Analysis of its benefits and drawbacks. *International Journal of Work Innovation, 1*(1), 100–113.

Trógolo, M. A., Moretti, L. S., & Medrano, L. A. (2022). A nationwide cross-sectional study of workers' mental health during the COVID-19 pandemic: Impact of changes in working conditions, financial hardships, psychological detachment from work and work-family interface. *BMC psychology, 10*(1), 1–11.

Vartiainen, M. (2021). Mobile multilocational work: benefits and drawbacks. In Korunka, C. (Ed.), *Flexible working practices and approaches* (pp. 117–147). Cham: Springer. https://doi.org/10.1007/978-3-030-74128-0_7

Vyas, L., & Butakhieo, N. (2021). The impact of working from home during COVID-19 on work and life domains: an exploratory study on Hong Kong. *Policy design and practice, 4*(1), 59–76.

Wang, B., Liu, Y., Qian, J., & Parker, S. K. (2021). Achieving effective remote working during the COVID-19 pandemic: A work design perspective. *Applied psychology*, *70*(1), 16–59.

Wethal, U., Ellsworth-Krebs, K., Hansen, A., Changede, S., & Spaargaren, G. (2022). Reworking boundaries in the home-as-office: boundary traffic during COVID-19 lockdown and the future of working from home. *Sustainability: Science, Practice and Policy*, *18*(1), 325–343.

Wilson, J. M., Lee, J., Fitzgerald, H. N., Oosterhoff, B., Sevi, B., & Shook, N. J. (2020). Job insecurity and financial concern during the COVID-19 pandemic are associated with worse mental health. *Journal of Occupational and Environmental Medicine*, *62*(9), 686–691.

Wojcak, E., Bajzikova, L., Sajgalikova, H., & Polakova, M. (2016). How to achieve sustainable efficiency with teleworkers: Leadership model in telework. *Procedia-Social and Behavioral Sciences*, *229*, 33–41.

Xiao, Y., Becerik-Gerber, B., Lucas, G., & Roll, S. C. (2021). Impacts of working from home during COVID-19 pandemic on physical and mental well-being of office workstation users. *Journal of Occupational and Environmental Medicine*, *63*(3), 181.

Yang, L., Holtz, D., Jaffe, S., Suri, S., Sinha, S., Weston, J., Joyce, C., Shah, N., Sherman, K., Hecht, B., & Teevan, J. (2021). The effects of remote work on collaboration among information workers. *Nature Human Behaviour*, *6*, 43–54. https://doi.org/10.1038/s41562-021-01196-4

11 Work/home spillover when working from home

Oi-ling Siu and Nuoxun Lin
Psychology Department Lingnan University, Hong Kong

Introduction

Employees are daily border-crossers between work and home (Clark, 2000). They perform different roles, fulfilling different responsibilities associated with different roles day and night, at home and at work. When ones' resources (time, energy, money, work skills, life skills, social support, etc.) are insufficient to cover all these roles and responsibilities simultaneously, s/he will be involved in the negative work-home spillover consequences, specifically work-home conflict. One's responsibilities at home and at work, and his/her relationships with others are dynamic throughout the different stages of his/her family life (Allen & Shockley, 2012). However, given the new requirement for many people to work from home, the prolonged COVID-19 pandemic has blurred the lines between work and home and impacted on the dynamics of responsibilities and relationships.

Work-home conflict for different age groups under the pandemic

When judging from a life course perspective, the analysis is concerned with the trajectories and transitions of ones' social roles and interpersonal relationships with others throughout a life span (Moen et al., 2008; Moen & Sweet, 2004). Work-home conflict may inevitably be perceived, though manifesting itself in different ways, depending on individual persons or families.

Referring to recent work arrangement in Hong Kong and mainland China, let us illustrate work-home conflict issues in two hypothetical scenarios. For instance, Sophia Can is a 30-year-old woman serving as the director in a marketing department. She has ten subordinates, and she is responsible to the senior marketing manager. Meanwhile, she has two competitive director colleagues and their competitive teams. During the pandemic, Sophia and her husband were working from home, and their 10-year-old boy was studying from home, too. They met and interacted with each other inside the confined space 24/7. One morning, when Sophia was in the bedroom having an important online meeting, she suddenly heard her husband shouting at their son

DOI: 10.4324/9781003250531-12

because he was playing computer games instead of attending his online course. Sophia apologise d to the online audiences immediately and continued the report, but she could not but feel angry at these two males at home. Waiting until the meeting had finished, Sophia quarrelled with her husband for not respecting her meeting time. The work from home policy forced Sophia to shift marketing strategies for the firm's products in order to maintain profits. Since this is demanding and challenging to her and her team, she had to devote more time and energy to work. After working at home in such way for a month, Sophia was burned out from this work–home conflict battle. She was eager to leave, she felt angry at why this virus existed, and the demanding profit target drained Sophia of energy all the time.

The work–home conflict situation might have a different picture when a family has elderly people. Mary Li is a clerk. It is her duty to deal with all kinds of daily chores. She is very busy. She lives with her parents, who have become concerned about her health during the pandemic. During the first several days when Mary worked from home, they witnessed how Mary had less time to take a break from work, and how tired she was at the weekends so that she spent the whole day in bed on Saturday then kept working on Sunday, and so on. The lack of organisa tional support (equipment, colleagues, etc.) and in-creased workload as a result drained Mary. Meanwhile, her parents kept asking her to take a break every hour, kept reminding her to slow down when eating, or kept sending fruits or other snacks into Mary's room when she was working. Mary understood the concern of her parents and felt their warmth, but she had no choice but to focus on addressing all the work demands. Mary could not balance her role as a clerk and her role as a daughter when working from home. Together the workload from work and the love from her parents burned her out.

The inescapable work–home conflict

Negative work–home spillover effect reflects the psychological carryover of strain between the work and home domains at the intra–individual level (Barnett, 1998; Krouse & Afifi, 2007). Significant research on the work–home interface has identified the high costs that negative work–home spillover has caused in personal, organisa tional, and societal domains (Allen et al., 2000). Theories of role stress and inter-role conflict are the foundation of negative work–home spillover research (Kahn et al., 1964). These theories point out that it is difficult to perform well in multiple roles (e.g., employee, parent, spouse) simultaneously due to the strain caused by role conflicts. This incompatibility creates conflicts and tension between work and home domains for a person (Greenhaus & Beutell, 1985). When the resources (e.g., time, energy, money, work skill, family skills) a person owns at the time are sufficient to fulfill different role demands, s/he could maintain the balance between these roles (Clark, 2000, p. 751). However, in most situations, the resources to support a person behaving in an ideal fashion in each role at any one time are limited. From the perspective of role stress theory, scholars adopted the term work-home conflict to describe this negative work-home interface (see e.g., Rothbard, 2001). Work-home conflict could be perceived in three ways. Time-based conflict refers to the time spent in one role constrains a person from having time to fulfill another role's responsibilities. Strain-based conflict refers to the fatigue experienced in one role hampering the performance in another role. Behaviour-based conflict refers to the behaviour incompatibility between roles (Greenhaus & Beutell, 1985). Meanwhile, conflict theory describes the constraints on a person's performance from one domain (e.g., work) carrying over into another (e.g., family) in a similar way. Compared to the time-, strain-, and behaviour-based conflicts, this highlights the deficiency of attitudes, beliefs, emotions, behaviour patterns, and skills involved when they are needed to fulfill different role demands (see Geurts & Demerouti, 2003).

It has been found that the work-home conflict is bidirectional (Frone 2003; see also Frone et al., 1992a, 1997b). The work-to-home conflicts reside in the home domain (e.g., marital dissatisfaction, poor parenting), whereas the home-to-work conflicts reside in the work domain (e.g., reduced work engagement, poor job performance, induced job burnout). Empirical evidence has added to our understanding that the bidirectional conflicts have effects on both the work and home outcomes simultaneously. As Wayne et al. (2004) identified, when there was a conflict, the originating role was associated with negative affective outcomes, while the receiving role was associated with behavioural outcomes. In the face of adversity, it is inevitable to experience some negative emotions, such as frustration, anxiety, depression, guilt, or rage. Previous studies discovered that negative emotions have destructive effects on social behaviours (Chen et al., 2012). Furthermore, improper behaviours influence whether employees can achieve their intra- and interpersonal meaningful goals or not (Gross, 2002). As a result, employees' mental health, physical health, job performance, safety behaviour, family satisfaction, etc. are damaged by these bidirectional work-home conflicts. Dual-earner couples are increasing in number world-wide due to the increased financial needs of families (Warren & Tyagi, 2004). Childrearing and family life calls for a father's return to support the tired mother and help more with the children's growth (Kaufman, 2013; Sayer, 2005). Consequently, men and women now juggle and suffer from the work-home conflict, especially the work-to-home conflict.

Job demands, role ambiguity, role overload, and work hours, etc., were found to be the antecedents of work-home conflict (Byron, 2005). The stressful events which employees encounter in their work environment are common conducive factors leading to the rise of work-home conflict (Bakker et al., 2005; Ernst Kossek & Ozeki, 1998; Ford et al., 2007; Ganster & Perrewé, 2011; Spector et al., 2004). When employees cannot mitigate these factors, work-home conflict can exhaust the employee physically and emotionally (Baeriswyl et al., 2016). The better these employees can be aware of their emotional and physical status, the better they will be able to develop adaptive coping strategies (Bernard, 2019).

The boundary theory offers a choice of active coping strategy tackling work-home conflict from the role integration–segmentation perspective. It is suggested that boundary permeability and boundary flexibility decide the extent to which a person would be impacted by work-home conflict (Ashforth et al., 2000). When employees insist on impermeable and segmenting boundaries, they are likely to prevent influence from one domain spreading to another; conversely, when employees choose to apply or have no choice but to apply permeable and integrating boundaries, they are less likely to avoid the spillover from one domain to another. Segmentation, therefore, was found to be an active coping strategy in the face of work-home conflict (Edwards & Rothbard 2000).

The COVID-19 pandemic has exacerbated work-home conflict as a stressor. The work from home (and study from home) anti-epidemic policy shifts our house into becoming a workplace (and classroom), which increases the likelihood of role conflicts for employees. Moreover, locationally and psychologically, segmenting boundaries between work and home has become harder than ever before (Fisher et al., 2020). In addition, when referring to those employees who still engage in work-at-workplace, such as nurses, the novel coronavirus exacerbated their work-home conflict in a different way (Zhan et al., 2020). For example, being worried about parents who might lose their single child, nurses who had single children at home felt more threatened about contracting the virus. The work-to-home spillover further increased nurses' anxiety and hampered their sleep (Mo et al., 2020).

Work-home conflict, job burnout, and safety behaviour

Work-home conflict analyses conducted after the outbreak of COVID-19 have established that job burnout became a prevalent outcome among employees across different occupation groups (e.g., Chi et al., 2021; Chong et al., 2020; Giurge & Bohns, 2020; Sahay & Wei, 2021; Shin et al., 2021).

Burnout is a psychological syndrome reflecting the accumulated difficult interaction between a person and his/her work (Maslach & Leiter, 2005). It includes three aspects: emotional exhaustion, the stress dimension of burnout; cynicism (or depersonalisa tion), the interpersonal correlation dimension of burnout; and ineffectiveness, the self-evaluation dimension of burnout (Maslach et al., 2001; Maslach & Leiter, 2008). The overwhelming exhaustion is the overextended feeling resulting from the depletion of physical and emotional resources. Cynicism is an excessively negative detachment from different aspects of the job. Finally, ineffectiveness portrays the feeling of unproductiveness, lack of competence and achievement at work (Maslach, 2003).

Maslach and Leiter (2008) categorise d six job characteristic antecedents of job burnout, namely workload, control, reward, community, fairness, and values. It is common sense that there is no perfect work setting and the extent to which different people could fit into the same work context varies. For instance, an outgoing employee might love a sales job since s/he enjoys going to different places and interacting with different people, whereas to keep talking and visiting day after day may be a burden and is painful for an introverted person. These six dimensions serve as a guidebook for employees to find out in which domain s/he is mismatched with the work setting, so as to further understand why s/he is trapped into job burnout.

Workload contributes most to exhaustion among these six areas. Employees perceive stress from workload when they lack sufficient resources (e.g., time, energy, expertise, colleague support, supervisor feedback) to address job requirements. Such under-resourced situations make what would otherwise be legitimate demands feel xcessive. Moreover, demands made beyond employees' psychological contracts with work would be treated as a burden (Semmer et al., 2007). When employees were required to display emotions that differ from their true feelings, their stress level increased (Brotheridge & Grandey, 2002). The consumption of cognitive, emotional, and physical resources in completing the job exhausted employees (Demerouti et al., 2001).

Control exacerbates burnout when employees lack effective authority at work and cannot access sufficient resources to fulfil job responsibilities. The degree of authority an employee commands at work and to what extent s/he could access proportionate resources decides whether job demands are stressful or not.

Reward aggravates burnout when the compensation or recognition for an employee is inappropriate. The lack of sufficient reward could be reflected in benefits, intrinsic reward, or social appreciation, etc, which are highly subject to individual differences. When employees perceive they are underappreciated by the surroundings, they might have a sense of inefficacy (Maslach et al., 2001).

Community exacerbates burnout when employees perceive insufficient emotional support from others in the workplace or lack a sense of belongingness in a group that share the similar values. Fairness accounts for burnout when employees feel they are treated inequitably at work. The unfairness could be reflected by injustice in workload, compensation, evaluation, and promotion depending on either the outcomes or the decision-making process.

Value contributes to burnout when employees cannot have shared core values with the organisa tion. If employees' contribution at work is a development of their own core values and accumulates through overlaps with the organisa tion's core values, it encourages employees to devote more and integrate more into the organisa tion, and vice versa (Maslach et al., 2001).

As Peeters and his colleagues (2005) argued convincingly, work-home conflicts mediate the relationship between different job stressors and job burnout. The effort-recovery (E-R) model gives an explanation to the mediation correlation (Geurts & Demerouti, 2003; Meijman & Mulder, 1998). The negative work-home spillover has demonstrated how different job stressors cause negative load effects on both the work and home domain that impair employees emotionally and physically. The E-R model highlights the importance of the quantitative and qualitative recovery an employee makes at home in response to the resources consumed at work. However, work-home conflicts aggravate any insufficient recovery and as a result accumulate negative influences on the employees' psychological health (including burnout).

Empirical research evidenced the stressors-work-home conflict-strain chain (e.g., Burke, 1988; Geurts et al., 1999; Geurts et al., 2003; Rudolph et al., 2020; Van Zoonen et al., 2021). Previous studies considered that moving quickly to remote working increases role stress and role overload when employees are trying to reconcile home and work demands (Bolger et al., 1989; Duxbury et al., 2018). Frequently that pushes employees into a stage that lacks organisa tional support (Stamper & Johlke, 2003). Regarding the COVID-19 epidemic context, employees were forced to face not only huge uncertainty about the development of the virus but also the rapid changes in the work-place, which increased their job insecurity (Cho, 2020). Employees who battled with the virus in the front line, such as nurses and doctors, faced graver life threats than before and experienced higher degrees of anxiety and fear (e.g., Zhan et al., 2020).

Multidimensional role overload stress spills over from work-to-home and home-to-work spheres (Bolger et al., 1989), aggravating the work-home conflicts (Fan et al., 2019; Lim & Kim, 2014). Unfortunately, these emotional, mental, and quantitative demands leading to work-home conflicts were sources of job burnout at the same time (Peeters et al., 2005). Even before the pandemic accentuated the situation women were found to suffer more than men from work-home conflicts and burnout. This is because females, com-pared to their male colleagues or husbands, are more vulnerable to pressure from role overload and suffer from a lack of family or organisa tional support (Duxbury et al., 2018; Fan et al., 2019; Peeters et al., 2005).

Safety behaviour is always vital no matter whether at home or at work. However, when an employee is drained by the emotional, mental, and quantitative demands in reconciling work home roles, s/he is less likely to have enough physical or mental energy to prevent him/herself from unsafe behaviour. For instance, burned out nurses were found to encounter more adverse events (Laschinger & Leiter, 2006). Siu et al. (2004) discussed a similar phenomenon that psychologically distressed construction workers were prone to injuries and accidents. In Siu et al.'s (2004) study, psychological distress was found to increase accident rates significantly. To protect workers from acci-dent and injuries, the authors suggested to heighten workers' safety attitudes. Survey data supported the proposition that better safety attitudes could sig-nificantly prevent accident rates and occupational injuries. This study pointed out the important role of the individual's attitude towards the adverse event in protecting them from accidents.

Recently, Siu and Ng (2021) reported the positive correlation between burnout and workplace injuries among employees in Chinese societies. In their study, a two-wave longitudinal survey data were obtained from 233 Chinese employees in two high-risk industries (nursing and railways) and analysed by structural equation modelling technique. In their theoretical model (see Figure 1, p. 2), they proposed that job demands (family-to-work conflict, FWC) bring forth a health impairment process that exhaust workers' physical and psychological resources and thus lead to burnout. On the other hand, Siu and Ng (2021) also proposed that job resource (family-to-work enrichment, FWE) allows workers to cope with demands and strains and hence reduce burnout. They also tested the mediating roles of burnout, safety violations, and work engagement. The results show that the association of FWE with workplace injuries was mediated by work engagement and then safety violations. Burnout was found to mediate the association of FWC with workplace injuries. Further, safety violations were also found to mediate the association of FWC with workplace injuries. In sum, the findings from Siu and Ng (2021) have provided information that the relation between FWC and workplace injuries was mediated by burnout and then safety violations.

A recent study undertaken in the context of COVID-19 has also confirmed this phenomenon. Du and Liu (2020) stated that burned-out employees were more likely to commit unsafe epidemic prevention behaviours. Demarcating psychological or spatial boundaries between work and home spheres properly protected employees from work-home conflicts before the outbreak of COVID-19. However, the remote work policy has confined families within the same space, making it less likely to set a delimitation between work and home. According to Folkman & Lazarus (1984), evaluation of whether a stress is a threat or a challenge accounts for different subsequent emotional, behavioural, and cognitive responses. When concerning functional coping strategies and alleviating the negative emotional impact, it is important to clarify when an adverse event was encountered and what kinds of personal factors drives an individual to evaluate it is stressful or not. In addition, whether the evaluation is rational and close to the reality of the adverse event, or it is covered by one's unrealistic subjective interpretation. Practice and research in the field of cognitive and behavioural psychology has argued that cognitive interpretation serves as the driver and source of emotional and behavioural consequences that, in turn, drive the subsequent cognition-affect-behaviour patterns. Regardless of the objective environments, an individual's intrapersonal interpretations and evaluations of the reality of him/herself and of the nature of the adverse events affect to what extent the events would affect this person, and whether the influence is constructive or destructive (e.g., Ellis, 1957; Kelly, 2020) on the efficiency of goal-attainment and individual health (e.g., Schnur et al., 2010).

Recognising our rational beliefs

One of such fruitful theory is the rational-emotive behaviour therapy theory (REBT) (David et al., 2018; Dryden et al., 2010; Ellis, 1957, 1984). This is a groundbreaking approach in empowering individuals to think rationally by using four structural self-knowledge beliefs which enable individuals to recover from their mental sufferings and reduce the damage caused by their improper social behaviour (Bernard & Dryden, 2019). Rational beliefs have been playing an important role in increasing employees' psychological well-being, personal flourishment, self-control, and desirable organisa tional outcomes for decades (Bernard, 2019). In addition, a recent two-wave survey conducted from the Greater Bay Area of China during the early outbreak of COVID-19 added to the REBT literature that rational beliefs could buffer the negative effect from work-home conflict to job performance via work engagement (Lin, 2021).

REBT divides individual's cognitive appraisals upon adverse events into two categories, the rational beliefs, and the irrational beliefs. Rational beliefs are defined as characteristics that are "flexible or non-extreme, consistent with reality, logical, largely functional in one's emotional, behavioural and cognitive consequences, and largely helpful to the individual in pursuing his basic goals and purposes" (Dryden & Branch, 2008, p. 8). These beliefs are powerful in equipping individuals to remain on track towards goal attainment when confronting adverse events (Bernard & Dryden, 2019; Ellis, 1957). The core assumption is that healthy emotions come from an individual's subjective rational, non-extreme, and pragmatic cognitive appraisal of the objective adverse events (Dryden, 2013; Ellis, 1957, 1962). Through this lens, rational beliefs overcome the damage from unhealthy affects and maladaptive social behaviour by leading individuals to think rationally from four types of thinking (Bernard, 2011; Bernard & Dryden, 2019; Ellis, 1957). Thus, rational beliefs draw people on a motivational adaptive cognition-affect-behaviour pattern for achieving personally meaningful goals (Bernard, 2011; Bernard & Dryden, 2019; Chrysidis et al., 2020; Ellis, 1957). Meanwhile, irrational beliefs drive individuals in a destructive, unhealthy, and maladaptive cognition-affect-behaviour downward spiral.

Rational beliefs refer to a comprehensive integration of four subtypes. The first one is non-dogmatic preference. It is defined as the flexible and accepting thinking of one's desire(s) (David, 2014). For example, in the first hypothetical scenario, Sophia expected a quiet working environment at home even though her husband and son might disrupt her occasionally. She could describe her non-dogmatic preference in this way: "I want to have a quiet environment at home when working to make myself concentrate, but a working place does not have to be in this way," instead of thinking in a rigid and extreme way that "I want to have a quiet environment at home when working to make myself concentrate, and that environment must be as quiet as I require." The latter places too many demands and rigid requirements on herself and the result (David, 2019, p. 269; Dryden, 2019, p. 27). The rationality in non-dogmatic preference is evident as follows: 1) Sophia is flexible in allowing for the possible result that she might not receive what she wants; 2) her desire for the quiet working environment in order to concentrate is consistent with the reality, and there being no general law to require that a working place is quiet is another reality; 3) how she describes her desire is logical, and her flexibility is closely related to her desire; 4) this flexibility helps Sophia to develop functional and healthy emotions, behaviours, and cognitions for goal-attainment, and motivates her to think about what she is doing and what to do next, instead of how well she is doing (Dryden & Branch, 2008, p. 9).

The second one is non-awfulising belief. Non-awfulising belief is defined as "a person believes, at the time, that something is bad, but not the end of the world." Thus, Sophia might think in this way: "I want the environment to be quiet when I am working, but it does not have to be so. It is bad if it is noisy, but not awful" (Dryden, 2019, p. 28). The rationality in non-awfulising belief is evident as follows: 1) Sophia is non-extreme in that she agrees that there would be other things in the world worse than not having a quiet work environment; 2) Sophia's admits that it is bad for her to work in a noisy place but that this result is not awful is consistent with reality; 3) how she admits to the badness is logical, and her non-awfulising allowing is closely related to her admission; 4) this non-awfulising admission helps Sophia to develop functional and healthy emotions, behaviours, and cognitions for goal-attainment, and motivates her to think about what she is doing and what to do next, instead of how well she is doing (Dryden, & Branch, 2008, p. 10).

The third one is high frustration tolerance belief. It is defined as "a person believes, at the time, that it is difficult tolerating the adversity that they are facing or about to face, but that they can tolerate it and that it is worth it for them to do so. In addition, they assert that they are willing to tolerate the adversity and commit themselves to doing so" (Dryden, 2019, p. 28). Thus, Sophia might think in this way: "If I do not have a quiet working environment, that will be difficult to bear, but I can stand it. It will not be intolerable, and it is worth it for me to tolerate it" (Dryden & Branch, 2008, p. 11). The rationality in high frustration tolerance belief is evident as follows: 1) Sophia is non-extreme in that she agrees that a noisy working environment is not an extreme result and it is tolerable; 2) based on the reality, Sophia admits that it is suffering to bear the adversity, but Sophia knows she could withstand this suffering, and she knows it is for her own sake to do so; 3) how she acknowledges the struggle during the tolerance period is logical, and her high level of tolerance of the frustration is closely related to her acknowledgment; 4) this high level of tolerance helps Sophia to develop functional and healthy emotions, behaviours, and cognitions for goal-attainment, and motivates her to think about what she is doing and what to do next that would prevent causing those "hard to tolerate" conditions at the same time, instead of focusing on how well she is doing, nor on the "unbearable" drawbacks when she is doing badly (Dryden & Branch, 2008, p. 12).

The last one is unconditional acceptance. Unconditional acceptance is defined as "a person acknowledges that they, others or life are far too complex to merit a global negative evaluation and that such an evaluation does not define self, others or life" (Dryden, 2019, p. 28). Thus, Sophia might think in this way: "I want to have a quiet working environment, but I do not have to do so. My husband and son are fallible humans whether they could remember what I told them in advance or not" (Dryden, 2019, p. 28). The rationality in unconditional acceptance belief is evident as follows: 1) Sophia is non-extreme in that she knows her husband and son could perform both well and badly; 2) this non-extreme belief is consistent with the reality that Sophia admits her husband and son are "fallible human beings" when they cannot keep quiet when she was working, but this failing will not lower their self-worth; 3) Sophia knows that her husband and son as a whole person cannot be defined by a single behaviour, so she does not overgeneralise them; 4) this unconditional acceptance helps Sophia to develop functional emotions, behaviours, and cognitions for goal-attainment. What is more, this unconditional acceptance enables her to learn from the past, especially the errors. The lessons learned from experience help her to better understand how to improve her performance when dealing with the same or similar issue next time, instead of being stuck similarly with her poor performance in the future (Dryden & Branch, 2008, p. 13).

These four rational beliefs together enhance a person's rationality 1) in being consistent with the reality of the adversity and their/others' self-worth, 2) in developing functional, healthy, and adaptive emotions, behaviours, and cognitions for goal-attainment, and 3) in learning from their errors to improve their performance instead of dwelling on their past poor performance or negative emotions. These evaluative appraisals could be applied in a broad array of contexts whenever the person faces a new or similar adversity. This sort of self-discovering requires an individual's ability to be aware of their subtle cognitive evaluations, as well as have a clear understanding of the framework of these four rational beliefs.

Lin (2021) conducted a two-wave survey during February and March 2020, which was right after the outbreak of COVID-19, trying to examine the relationships between irrational beliefs, the counterparts of rational beliefs, with work-home conflict and burnout. Employees ($N = 257$) from more than 10 industries from cities (e.g., Guangzhou, Shenzhen, Foshan) in the Greater Bay Area of China took part in the survey. Data confirmed the positive correlation between work-home conflict and burnout. Moreover, irrational beliefs exacerbate the negative relationship between work-home conflict and emotional exhaustion.

Lessons from the pandemic and beyond: How to nurture our rational beliefs

We are all tired of the COVID-19 and expecting a life without corona. However, the highly contagious Delta and Omicron variants of Covid-19 continue to spread around the world rapidly. Confirmed cases have raised to 414,525,183 globally by 16 February 2022. Given the potential that coronavirus might continue to exit in the foreseeable future, people in countries all around the world are experiencing high levels of anxiety and panic because of this notorious virus.

People may think they just experience the anxiety and depressed mood due to the COVID. However, the fact is people also suffer from emotional distress because of their negative thoughts and attitudes about what is going on. It is very important that people maintain awareness of the present moment of reality. If people take time to learn facts and evidence, that is the wonderful thing that can help them suffer less emotionally. REBT is one of the most used contemporary cognitive therapies (Matweychuk et al., 2019). Yet it is not only an effective psychological therapy, it is that, also, a way of life. These tools could work for people if people use them, their awareness.

Emotional and behavioural disorders occur more frequently for people holding irrational beliefs than holding rational beliefs (Ellis, 1994). The good news is people's emotional and behavioural disorders can be reduced or eliminated via replacing irrational beliefs with rational beliefs (Ellis, 1994). REBT-based intervention, coaching, and counselling has been playing an important role in reducing psychological strain such as occupational stress, depression, anxiety, rage, self-abasement, burnout, and etc. (e.g., David et al., 2018; Ogbuanya et al., 2017; Ogbuanya et al., 2018). Rational beliefs-oriented education and counselling have also been playing a role in parenting and family issues since their first appearance (Bernard, 2019).

What can organisa tions do to equip employees with a set of rational beliefs? First, rational beliefs could be one session in the training for newcomers to the organisation. By doing so, the organisation could nurture the employees with a set of structural coping strategies to tackle different subjective adverse events both at work and at home. Second, the organisation could try to nurture a climate of rational beliefs at group and organisation level. By doing so, HR staffs or managers could help individual employees to internalise the rational beliefs coping strategies in daily work and lives, thereby reducing their vulnerability to job burnout and stimulating a better job performance. Third, organisations could out-source or recruit a REBT-oriented therapist/coach to offer counselling and regular training. Employees are also recommended to read REBT-oriented self-help and self-development books so that they can have better understanding and application of these beliefs. Once employees could internalise rational beliefs and apply them at work and home, they would be more capable of protecting themselves from this stressful modern workplace.

Acknowledgement

Part of the research in this paper was supported by the General Research Fund from the Research Grants Council of Hong Kong (Project No. 341713); and Wofoo Joseph Lee Consulting and Counseling Psychology Research Centre.

References

Allen, T. D., Herst, D. E. L., Bruck, C. S., & Sutton, M. (2000). Consequences associated with work-to-family conflict: A review and agenda for future research. *Journal of Occupational Health Psychology*, 5, 278–308.
Allen, T. D., & Shockley, K. (2012). Older workers and work–family issues. In J. W. Hedge & W. C. Borman (Eds.). *The Oxford Handbook of Work and Aging* (pp. 520–537). New York, NY: Oxford University Press.

Ashforth, B. E., Kreiner, G. E., & Fugate, M. (2000). All in a day's work: Boundaries and micro role transitions. *Academy of Management Review, 25*, 472–491.

Baeriswyl, S., Krause, A., & Schwaninger, A. (2016). Emotional exhaustion and job satisfaction in airport security officers–work–family conflict as mediator in the job demands–resources model. *Frontiers in Psychology, 7*, 663.

Bakker, A. B., Demerouti, E., & Euwema, M. C. (2005). Job resources buffer the impact of job demands on burnout. *Journal of Occupational Health Psychology, 10*(2), 170.

Bernard, M. E. (2011). *Rationality and the pursuit of happiness. The legacy of Albert Ellis.* Chichester, UK: Wiley-Blackwell.

Bernard, M. E., & Dryden, W. (2019). *Advances in REBT.* Springer Nature Switzerland.

Bernard, M. E. (2019). REBT in the Workplace. In *Advances in REBT* (pp. 353–380). Cham: Springer.

Barnett, R. C. (1998). Toward a review and reconceptualization of the work/family literature. *Genetic Social and General Psychology Monographs, 124*(2), 125–184.

Bolger, N., DeLongis, A., Kessler, R. C., & Wethington, E. (1989). The contagion of stress across multiple roles. *Journal of Marriage and the Family, 51*(1), 175–183.

Brotheridge, C. A. & Grandey, A. A. (2002). Emotional labor and burnout: comparing two perspectives of 'people work'. *Journal of Vocational Behavior, 60*, 17–39.

Burke, R. J. (1988). Some antecedents of work–family conflict. *Journal of Social Behavior and Personality, 3*(4), 287.

Byron, K. (2005). A meta-analytic review of work–family conflict and its antecedents. *Journal of Vocational Behavior, 67*, 169–198.

Chen, P., Coccaro, E. F., & Jacobson, K. C. (2012). Hostile attributional bias, negative emotional responding, and aggression in adults: Moderating effects of gender and impulsivity. *Aggressive Behavior, 38*(1), 47–63.

Chi, O. H., Saldamli, A., & Gursoy, D. (2021). Impact of the COVID-19 pandemic on management-level hotel employees' work behaviors: Moderating effects of working-from-home. *International Journal of Hospitality Management, 98*, 103020.

Cho, E. (2020). Examining boundaries to understand the impact of COVID-19 on vocational behaviors. *Journal of Vocational Behavior, 119*, 103437.

Chong, S., Huang, Y., & Chang, C. H. D. (2020). Supporting interdependent telework employees: A moderated-mediation model linking daily COVID-19 task setbacks to next-day work withdrawal. *Journal of Applied Psychology, 105*(12), 1408.

Chrysidis, S., Turner, M. J., & Wood, A. G. (2020). The effects of REBT on irrational beliefs, self-determined motivation, and self-efficacy in American Football. *Journal of Sports Sciences, 38*(19), 2215–2224.

Clark, S. C. (2000). Work/family border theory: A new theory of work/family balance. *Human Relations, 53*(6), 747–770.

David, D. (2014). The empirical status of Rational Emotive Behavior Therapy (REBT) theory & practice. *Therapy, 3*, 175–221.

David, D., Cotet, C., Matu, S., Mogoase, C., & Stefan, S. (2018). 50 years of rational-emotive and cognitive-behavioral therapy: A systematic review and meta-analysis. *Journal of Clinical Psychology, 74*(3), 304–318.

David, O. (2019). REBT in Coaching. In *Advances in REBT* (pp. 267–287). Cham: Springer.

Demerouti, E., Bakker, A. B., Nachreiner, F., & Schaufeli, W. B. (2001). The job demands-resources model of burnout. *Journal of Applied psychology, 86*(3), 499.

Dryden, W. (2013). On rational beliefs in rational emotive behavior therapy: A theoretical perspective. *Journal of Rational-Emotive & Cognitive-Behavior Therapy, 31*(1), 39–48.

Dryden, W. (2019). The distinctive features of rational emotive behavior therapy. In *Advances in REBT* (pp. 23–46). Cham: Springer.

Dryden, W., & Branch, R. (2008). *Fundamentals of rational emotive behaviour therapy: A training handbook.* Chichester, UK:John Wiley & Sons.

Dryden, W., David, D., & Ellis, A. (2010). Rational emotive behavior therapy. In K. S. Dobson (Ed.), *Handbook of cognitive-behavioral therapies* (pp. 226–276). New York, NY: The Guilford Press.

Du, Y., & Liu, H. (2020). Analysis of the influence of psychological contract on employee safety behaviors against COVID-19. *International Journal of Environmental Research and Public Health, 17*(18), 6747.

Duxbury, L., Stevenson, M., & Higgins, C. (2018). Too much to do, too little time: Role overload and stress in a multi-role environment. *International Journal of Stress Management, 25*(3), 250.

Edwards, J. R., & Rothbard, N. P. (2000). Mechanisms linking work and family: Clarifying the relationship between work and family constructs. *Academy of Management Review, 25*, 178–199.

Ellis, A. (1957). Rational psychotherapy and individual psychology. *Journal of Individual Psychology, 13*(1), 38.

Ellis, A. (1984). The essence of RET. *Journal of Rational-Emotive Therapy, 2*(1), 19–25.

Ellis, A. (1994). *Reason and emotion in psychotherapy* (Rev. ed.). New York: Carol Publishing Group.

Ellis, A. (1962). *Reason and emotion in psychotherapy.* New York, NY: Polyglot Press.

Ernst Kossek, E., & Ozeki, C. (1998). Work–family conflict, policies, and the job–life satisfaction relationship: A review and directions for organizational behavior–human resources research. *Journal of applied psychology, 83*(2), 139.

Fan, W., Lam, J., & Moen, P. (2019). Stress Proliferation? Precarity and Work–Family Conflict at the Intersection of Gender and Household Income. *Journal of Family Issues, 40*(18), 2751–2773.

Fisher, J., Languilaire, J.-C., Lawthom, R., Nieuwenhuis, R., Petts, R. J., Runswick-Cole, K., & Yerkes, M. A. (2020). Community, work, and family in times of COVID-19. *Community Work & Family, 23*, 247–252.

Folkman, S., & Lazarus, R. S. (1984). *Stress, appraisal, and coping.* New York: Springer Publishing Company.

Ford, M. T., Heinen, B. A., & Langkamer, K. L. (2007). Work and family satisfaction and conflict: a meta-analysis of cross-domain relations. *Journal of applied psychology, 92*(1), 57.

Frone, M. R. (2003). Work-family balance. In J. C. Quick & E. Tertic (Eds.), *Handbook of occupational health psychology* (pp. 143–162). Washington DC: American Psychological Association.

Frone, M. R., Russell, M. & Cooper, M. L. (1992a). Antecedents and outcomes of work-family conflict: Testing a model of the work-family interface. *Journal of Applied Psychology, 77*, 65–78.

Frone, M. R., Yardley, J. K. & Markel, K. S. (1997b). Developing and testing an integrative model of the work-family interface. *Journal of Vocational Behavior, 50*, 145–167.

Ganster, D. C. & Perrewé, P. L. (2011). Theories of occupational stress. In J. C. Quick, and L. E. Tetrick (Eds.). *Handbook of Occupational Health Psychology* (pp. 37–53). Washington, DC: American Psychological Association.

Geurts, S. A. E. & Demerouti, E. (2003). Work/Non-work interface: a review of theories and findings. In M. J. Schabracq, J. A. M. Winnubst & C. L. Cooper (Eds.). *The handbook of work and health psychology* (pp. 279–312). Chichester: John Wiley & Sons.

Geurts, S. A. E., Kompier, M. A. J., Roxburgh, S., & Houtman, I. L. D. (2003). Does work-home interference mediate the relationship between workload and well-being? *Journal of Vocational Behavior, 63,* 532–559.

Geurts, S., Rutte, C., & Peeters, M. (1999). Antecedents and consequences of work-home interference among medical residents. *Social Science & Medicine, 48,* 1135–1148.

Giurge, L. M., & Bohns, V. K. (2020, April 3). 3 Tips to Avoid WFH Burnout. *Harvard Business Review.* https://hbr.org/2020/04/3-tips-to-avoid-wfh-burnout.

Greenhaus, J. H. & Beutell, N. J. (1985). Sources of conflict between work and family roles. *Academy of Management Review, 10,* 76–88.

Gross, J. J. (2002). Emotion regulation: Affective, cognitive, and social consequences. *Psychophysiology, 39*(3), 281–291.

Kahn, R. L., Wolfe, D. M., Quinn, R., Snoek, J. D., & Rosenthal, R. A. (1964). *Organizational stress.* New York, NY: Wiley.

Kaufman, G. (2013). *Superdads: How fathers balance work and family in the 21ˢᵗ century.* New York: New York University Press.

Kelly, G. (2020). *The psychology of personal constructs.* London: Routledge.

Krouse, S. S., & Afifi, T. D. (2007). Family-to-work spillover stress: Coping communicatively in the workplace. *Journal of Family Communication, 7*(2), 85–122.

Laschinger, H. S., & Leiter, M. (2006). The impact of nursing work environments on patient safety outcomes: The mediating role of burnout/engagement. *Journal of Nursing Administration, 36,* 259–267.

Lim, V., & Kim, T. (2014). The long arm of the job: Parents' work–family conflict and youths' work centrality. *Applied Psychology: An International Review, 63*(1), 151–167.

Lin Nuoxun. (2021). *The roles of growth mindset and rational beliefs as personal resources on employees' job performance and work engagement: applying the job demands-resources model in the Greater Bay Area* (PhD thesis). Lingnan University.

Maslach, C. (2003). Job burnout: new directions in research and innovation. *Current Directions in Psychological Science, 12,* 189–192.

Maslach, C. & Leiter, M. P. (2005). Reversing burnout: how to rekindle your passion for work. *Stanford Social Innovation Review,* Winter, 43–49.

Maslach, C. & Leiter, M. P. (2008). Early predictors of job burnout and engagement. *Journal of Applied Psychology, 93,* 498–512.

Maslach, C., Schaufeli, W., & Leiter, M. P. (2001). Job burnout. *Annual Review of Psychology, 52,* 397–422.

Matweychuk, W., DiGiuseppe, R., & Gulyayeva, O. (2019). A comparison of REBT with other cognitive behavior therapies. In *Advances in REBT* (pp. 47–77). Cham: Springer.

Meijman, T. F., & Mulder, G. (1998). Psychological aspects of workload. In P. J. D. Drenth, H. Thierry, & C. J. de Wolff (Eds.). *Handbook of work and organisational psychology* (2nd ed., pp. 5–33). Hove, England: Psychology Press/Erlbaum.

Mo, Y., Deng, L., Zhang, L., Lang, Q., Liao, C., Wang, N., Qin, M., & Huang, H. (2020). Work stress among Chinese nurses to support Wuhan in fighting against COVID-19 epidemic. *Journal of Nursing Management, 28*(5), 1002–1009.

Moen, P., Kelly, E., & Huang, Q. (2008). Work, family and life-course fit: Does control over work time matter? *Journal of Vocational Behavior, 73,* 414–425.

Moen, P., & Sweet, S. (2004). From 'work–family' to 'flexible careers': A life course re-framing. *Community, Work & Family, 7*, 209–226.

Ogbuanya, T. C., Eseadi, C., Orji, C. T., Ohanu, I. B., Bakare, J., & Ede, M. O. (2017). Effects of Rational Emotive Behavior Coaching on occupational stress and work ability among electronics workshop instructors in Nigeria. *Medicine, 96*(19), e6891.

Ogbuanya, T. C., Eseadi, C., Orji, C. T., Omeje, J. C., Anyanwu, J. I., Ugwok, S. C., & Edeh, N. C. (2018). Effect of rational-emotive behavior therapy program on the symptoms of burnout syndrome among undergraduate electronics work students in Nigeria. *Psychological Reports, 1*, 33294117748587.

Peeters, M. C., Montgomery, A. J., Bakker, A. B., & Schaufeli, W. B. (2005). Balancing work and home: How job and home demands are related to burnout. *International Journal of Stress Management, 12*(1), 43.

Rothbard, N. P. (2001). Enriching or depleting? The dynamics of engagement in work and family roles. *Administrative Science Quarterly, 46*, 655–684.

Rudolph, C. W., Allan, B., Clark, M., Hertel, G., Hirschi, A., Kunze, F., … Zacher, H. (2020). Pandemics: Implications for research and practice in industrial and organizational psychology. *Industrial and Organizational Psychology, 14*(1–2), 1–35.

Sahay, S., & Wei, W. (2021). Work-Family Balance and Managing Spillover Effects Communicatively during COVID-19: Nurses' Perspectives. *Health Communication*, 1–10.

Sayer, L. C. (2005). Gender, time, and inequality: Trends in women's and men's paid work, unpaid work, and free time. *Social Forces, 84*(1), 285–303.

Schnur, J. B., Montgomery, G. H., & David, D. (2010). Irrational and rational beliefs and physical health. *Rational and Irrational Beliefs: Research, Theory and Practice*, 253–264.

Semmer, N., Jacobshagen, N., Meier, L. & Elfering, A. (2007). Occupational stress research: the 'stress-as-offence-to-self' perspective. In J. Houdmont & S. McIntyre (Eds), *Occupational Health Psychology: European Perspectives on Research, Education and Practise, Vol. 2* (pp. 43–60). Maia, Portugal: ISMAI.

Shin, Y., Hur, W. M., & Park, K. (2021). The Power of Family Support: The Long-Term Effect of Pre-COVID-19 Family Support on Mid-COVID-19 Work Outcomes. *International Journal of Environmental Research and Public Health, 18*(19), 10524.

Siu, O. L., & Ng, T. K. (2021). Family-to-work interface and workplace injuries: The mediating roles of burnout, work engagement and safety violations. *International journal of environmental research and public health, 18*(22), 11760.

Siu, O. L., Phillips, D. R., & Leung, T. W. (2004). Safety climate and safety performance among construction workers in Hong Kong: The role of psychological strains as mediators. *Accident Analysis & Prevention, 36*, 359–366.

Spector, P. E., Cooper, C., Poelmans, S., Allen, T. D., O'Driscoll, M., Sanchez, J. I., … & Yu, S. (2004). A cross-national comparative study of work-family stressors, working hours, and well-being: China and Latin America versus the Anglo world. *Personnel Psychology, 57*(1), 119–142.

Stamper, C. L., & Johlke, M. C. (2003). The impact of perceived organizational support on the relationship between boundary spanner role stress and work outcomes. *Journal of Management, 29*(4), 569–588.

Van Zoonen, W., Sivunen, A., Blomqvist, K., Olsson, T., Ropponen, A., Henttonen, K., & Vartiainen, M. (2021). Understanding stressor–strain relationships during the COVID-19 pandemic: the role of social support, adjustment to remote work, and work–life conflict. *Journal of Management & Organization, 27*(6), 1038–1059.

Warren, E., & Tyagi, A. W. (2004). *The two-income trap: Why middle-class parents are going broke*. Basic Books.

Wayne, J. H., Musisca, N. & Fleeson, W. (2004). Considering the role of personality in the work-family experience: Relationships of the big five to work-family conflict and facilitation. *Journal of Vocational Behavior, 64*, 108–130.

Zhan, Y., Liu, Y., Liu, H., Li, M., Shen, Y., Gui, L., Zhang, J., Luo, Z., Tao, X., & Yu, J. (2020). Factors associated with insomnia among Chinese front-line nurses fighting against COVID-19 in Wuhan: A cross-sectional survey. *Journal of Nursing Management, 28*(7), 1525–1535.

12 Return to work and the workplace during the pandemic: Navigating new normal(s)

Jonathon R. B. Halbesleben
University of Texas at San Antonio

At this point, to state that the COVID-19 pandemic had a dramatic impact on the manner in which employees approach their work feels cliché. Nonetheless, we recognise that the pandemic has had widespread and lasting impact on employees' experiences of work and broader well-being. That said, the pandemic is certainly not the first significant event to have produced a major disruption to the manner in which employees approach work. Even the notion of shifts to remote work is not particularly new, as employees have experienced such shifts in the past due to natural disasters and other temporary impacts on their workplace. Some events have had transformative impacts on how specific jobs have been done. For example, the terrorist attacks of 11 September 2001 transformed many jobs within the airline industry changed across the world to address new security concerns.

The COVID-19 pandemic has been unique, however, due to the more widespread impact of changes to work across industries and occupations and the continual manner in which employers have had to adjust the requirements, procedures, and location of jobs as public health conditions have changed. In this chapter, I address issues associated with returning to work and the workplace during the COVID-19 pandemic.

This is by necessity a work-in-progress. Even as I write this chapter in spring of 2022, new variants of the coronavirus continue to emerge and require interventions such as restrictions on access to workplaces in some parts of the world. Nearly every day there are new reports in the popular press about challenges as organisations as their employees to return to work and their workplaces to attempt to return to work as it was performed pre-pandemic. Indeed, just as I was finishing my initial draft, a report from Future Forum (2022) based on a survey of knowledge workers in nearly 11,000 workers across six countries reported that "stress and anxiety has hit the highest levels since [their] surveying began in the summer of 2020" (p. 3) with particularly high levels of stress among those who had been impacted by the implementation of return-to-office policies. While the concerns about this topic continue to emerge, this is a good opportunity to begin exploring what we have learned from the experiences of employers and employees as they have gradually returned to their work and workplaces, how those lessons help us to

DOI: 10.4324/9781003250531-13

understand various psychological theories of well-being and burnout, and how we might utilise what we have learned to reduce burnout for employees as they continue to return to their work and workplaces.

In this chapter, I will refer both to return to work and return to workplaces, differentiating those processes where necessary. For many employees, the pandemic had little impact on their work, but only impacted where their work was done; in those cases, return to workplace is the more appropriate term. For others, the nature of their work was fundamentally altered by the pandemic. In still others, the shift in workplace necessitated a change in how they approached their work—a situation may academics have experienced as the need to provide instruction without use of a classroom meant not only teaching from a remote location, but considering the pedagogical adjustments necessary for successful distance learning. In all cases, "return" will be used merely as a term of convenience, with the understanding that many workers may never return to work as it was done previously or may experience permanent changes in where the work is located. This chapter will attempt to address all of those situations, attempting to highlight differences in those experiences where they are relevant.

To that end, I will begin by summarising the work on responses to changing stressors in the workplace using the lens of adaptation theories (e.g., Diener et al., 2006). I will integrate those theoretical concepts with our understanding of burnout via stress–reaction theories, specifically conservation of resources theory (Hobfoll, 1988), to understand how adaptation processes impact employees' resources and, thus, employees' well-being as manifest by burnout. I will review the emerging empirical literature concerning return to work after major life events, with the goal of informing practical solutions for easing the transition back to work and workplace and providing directions for future research that utilise the context of return to work and workplaces following the pandemic to advance our understanding of theories of adaptation and employee well-being.

Responses to stress: adaptation and stress–reaction theories

Over the years, a number of theories have been proposed to explain how people respond to stressors, change, and uncertainty over time. Broadly speaking, they can be separated into two categories: adaptation theories and stress–reaction theories.

Adaptation theories

Adaptation theories propose that negative events or stressors have an initial impact on well-being, but eventually well-being returns to a baseline level that is, for most people, somewhat more positive than neutral (Brickman & Campbell, 1971; Diener & Diener, 1996). For example, starting a new job generally introduces a new set of stressors, but over time individuals settle into their new position so that many of the stressors either are resolved (e.g., where the copier is) or don't have as strong a negative impact on well-being (e.g., the commute). These theories propose that each person has a specific level of happiness or well-being, often called a set point, that has a significant genetic component and, as such, is impervious to change (Lykken & Tellegen, 1996). Regardless of whether we experience positive or negative events, our level of well-being is proposed to return to our natural set point within a relatively short period of time.

Several studies have supported the notion of adaptation to stressors in the workplace (e.g., Bowling et al., 2005; Matthews et al., 2014; Nawijn, 2011). For example, Matthews and Ritter (2019) found evidence that employees adapt to incivility experienced at work, such that incidents of incivility have a lower impact on subsequent indicators of well-being, including burnout.

There are several important caveats to adaptation that are important, especially for understanding the impact of returning to work or the workplace during the pandemic. There are individual differences in employees' setpoints and their adaptation processes (Diener et al., 2006). That seems logical, as I suspect all of us have experienced co-workers who differ in their general levels of well-being as well as co-workers who differ in the extent to co-workers react to negative events. A number of researchers have suggested personality traits are a key individual difference in adaptation (e.g., Diener et al., 2006). Indeed, Liu et al. (2021) found that those who were higher in neuroticism and extraversion had greater increases in perceived stress through the early stages of the pandemic. Personality traits may translate in how people process negative events as well. Zacher and Rudolph (2021) collected data from nearly 1,000 Germans pre-pandemic and during the early stages of the pandemic (March 2020 and May 2020). While they found a number of markers of well-being decreased after March 2020, the amount of that decrease depended on factors such as the manner in which the participants appraised the source of the stress and strategies they utilised to cope with the stress of the pandemic.

In the context of the pandemic, we would expect that people would naturally adapt to the stressors associated with the pandemic, with some individual differences in how the adaptation process plays out. However, one challenge with regard to adaptation is the complexity of the stressors associated with the COVID-19 pandemic. In other words, while we may think about the COVID-19 pandemic as a singular event, understanding the impact of the myriad stressors associated with the pandemic requires some additional theorising.

Stress–reaction theories

Stress–reaction theories propose that stressors draw upon a reserve of resources that each of us maintains. For example, conservation of resources theory proposes that stress is a response to a loss of resources, threat to our resources, or poor investment of resources (Hobfoll, 1988, 1989). While the definition of resources remains a bit elusive, they are generally defined as something that is valued for its ability to help us achieve some goal (Halbesleben et al., 2014; Hobfoll et al., 2018). While there are mechanisms to replenish resources that are lost, conservation of resources proposes that each loss of resources increases the likelihood of subsequent loss of resources, a situation termed a resource loss spiral (Hobfoll, 2001). Recent studies have found support for the notion of resource loss spirals in a number of contexts, including inadequate sleep (Sayre et al., 2021), interpersonal conflict (Somaraju et al., 2022), and alienation (Guo et al., 2021). Chong et al. (2020) found that daily task setbacks caused by COVID-19 were associated with burnout at the end of the day, which was associated with withdrawal behaviours the next day, leading to a spiral of more task setbacks.

Resource losses are more likely among those who start with fewer resources. McElroy-Heltzel and colleagues (2022) found that resource losses during early parts of the pandemic were particularly pronounced for those below the poverty line and those with chronic disease. Similarly, Peck (2021) used a number of datasets to argue that women would be more negatively impacted by the COVID-19 pandemic in men because they were already at a disadvantage in terms of a number of important resources (see also Bazzoli et al., 2021).

The conclusion one can draw from conservation of resources theory and other stress–reaction theories is that stress has an accumulating negative impact, particularly for those individuals who do not have access to resources that might help them break from negative spirals. Loss spirals set off a series of reactions that make each successive loss experience worse; they seem especially likely to occur among people with fewer resources to start with. We will return to that issue a bit later, as it holds important implications for how we think about employees returning to work and workplaces during the pandemic.

Adaptation or accumulation?

These theories have commonly been positioned as competing theories because, on the surface, they sound like processes that would be mutually exclusive. However, while adaptation theory suggests that we become acclimated to stressors over time, that is not the same as suggesting we don't experience the stressors at all. Similarly, just as conservation of resources theory suggests that the accumulation of stressors puts us in a worse position to invest our resources and begets further losses, that is not the same as suggesting that each stressor accumulates in the same way. When considered together, it is indeed possible that stressors do accumulate, but the addition of each successive stressor to the "pool" of accumulated stressors may not be equal. Additionally, much of the work on adaptation has been about major life events and how the impact of those single events wanes over time. That's not quite the same as a loss spiral, which refers to situations where resources are lost successively. Indeed, the effects seen in adaptation to a single major event may simply be the recovery of lost resources following the negative event, which should manifest as stabilised or even increasing well-being (Matthews et al., 2014). On the other hand, Michel et al. (2021) suggested that when an employee is continually exposed to a stressor, and emphasised the pandemic specifically, those repeated exposures can have a negative, accumulated impact on well-being.

Along those lines, researchers are increasingly acknowledging that it may be possible for set points to change, especially if someone experiences a particularly traumatic experience (cf., Fujita & Diener, 2005; Headey, 2010). Unemployment and development of a disability have been suggested as stressors for which adaptation is unlikely and instead reset a person's set point (Lucas, 2007; Lucas et al., 2003, 2004); those also are outcomes that increased for employees during the pandemic, especially those that contracted COVID-19. This is consistent with the notion that stressors that draw significantly from one's pool of resources would be more likely to lead to a loss spiral. Put another way, a loss spiral might be seen as a resetting of one's set point after successive significant losses of resources.

On the flipside, a number of studies have found that the availability of resources keeps individuals from experiencing loss cycles, with the idea that while people may experience similar stressors, those who have access to other resources to draw from may not fall victim to a resource loss spiral (e.g., Breevaart & Tims, 2019). It may be that one way of thinking about adaptation is not so much that we "get used" to a stressor, but rather that we have other resources to draw from to reduce the continued negative impact of a repeated stressor.

Taken together, there is utility in both adaptation and stress–reaction theories of coping with stressors over time in the context of a major life event, particularly major events that are associated with a complex variety of stressors. For example, Michel et al. (2021) found that employees generally experienced fewer negative psychological health symptoms over the course of their study with the trajectory of change in symptoms levelling off toward the tail end of the study, which suggests support for adaptation theory, particularly since the study timeframe was a period of significant increases in COVID-19 cases in the USA. Their study found that on-site workers experienced increases in physical fatigue over the course of the study, which is perhaps not surprising given the timeframe of the study (data from April 2020 demonstrates one of the first "spikes" in hospitalisations in the USA during the pandemic), but would seem to support stress–reaction theories. Viewing the COVID-19 pandemic through this lens is helpful as we examine how employees experience the return to work and workplace.

Factors impacting employee responses to return to work during the pandemic

Applying the theories discussed above offers some guidance in understanding employees' responses to returning to work during or following the COVID-19 pandemic. From adaptation theories, we might expect that employees will naturally acclimate to some aspects of the pandemic in ways that reduce their burnout.

Uncertainty

One could argue that uncertainty has impacted nearly all aspects of life through the COVID-19 pandemic, but uncertainty would seem to be a particularly important factor in employee responses to returning to work (Wong et al., 2021). From work prior to the pandemic, we know that uncertainty plays a significant role in burnout (Meyerson, 1994), including uncertainty about how long negative conditions will persist in the workplace (e.g., abusive supervision, e.g., Wu et al., 2019).

Tolerance of uncertainty seems to play a factor in reducing the likelihood that stress translates to burnout. In an interesting exploration of health care workers in Italy during the COVID-19 pandemic, Di Trani et al. (2021) identified two clusters of workers: those high in burnout risk and those low in burnout risk. A key factor distinguishing the clusters was the level of (in) tolerance of uncertainty among those in the clusters.

Uncertainty has emerged in many forms in the context of returning to work and the workplace during and following the pandemic. Much of that uncertainty has been related to the novel and virulent nature of the coronavirus and its impact on people who are infected, from early uncertainty regarding how it was transmitted and how that impacted work to later uncertainty about whether vaccines would be effective against variants of the virus. These forms of uncertainty may be particularly challenging for organisations to confront, since they are largely outside of the organisation's control. For example, it appears that people have adapted somewhat to the idea that COVID-19 cases exist in their communities; however, the impact of changes in cases (i.e., spikes) appear to trigger larger changes in anxiety over time (Fu et al., 2021). Put another way, employees seem accustomed to the general idea that COVID-19 is sticking around, but are increasingly jittery when local cases of COVID-19 increase.

Remote work

One of the main challenges workers faced at the onset of the pandemic was a sudden shift in both how and where their work was done coupled with shifts in life outside the workplace (Mandeville et al., in press). For example, many employees had to take on family care responsibilities while also performing remote work. Arguably the biggest debate associated with returning to work during the pandemic has been the extent to which remote work should continue to be utilised. When considering the lingering health risks of contracting and transmitting the virus when working around other people (Sinclair et al., 2020), it is of little surprise that employees are increasingly expecting (and even demanding) the continuation of remote work arrangements that had been initiated early in the pandemic (Future Forum, 2022).

The impact remote work has on employee well-being and burnout is mixed (Bailey & Kurland, 2002). Several studies have found that employees experience less stress, greater engagement with work, and higher performance during teleworking days (Anderson et al., 2015; Delanoeije & Verbruggen, 2020; DuBrin, 1991). Other studies have found that remote work can be associated with higher levels of stress (Oakman et al., 2020; Song & Gao, 2020) and greater conflict between work and family on days when they telework due to more frequent interruptions to their work during the regular work day and more interruptions from work to their homelife after work hours (Delanoeije et al., 2019; Eddleston & Mulki, 2017). Still others have found telework associated with lower burnout and lower work engagement (Sardeshmukh et al., 2012). Golden (2012) found that the higher conflict between work and family associated with remote work can lead to higher levels of burnout. It is worth noting that the vast majority of studies prior to the pandemic were focused on intermittent remote work arrangements—cases where employees worked remotely perhaps a day or two per week—so we need to be careful in generalising those findings to exclusive remote work that has become more common during the pandemic.

To understand the impact of remote work on burnout, it is also important that we isolate characteristics of remote work that lead to both positive and negative impacts on employee well-being. Kubicek et al. (2022) separated out the cognitive demands associated with structuring one's own work while working remotely and coordinating with others when co-workers are distributed. They found that structuring one's own work is actually enriching, while coordinating work with others negatively impacted employee well-being. Kaduk et al. (2019) found that outcomes such as stress, burnout, and turnover intentions depended on whether the employee had chosen to engage in remote work, where remote work that is involuntary is associated with worse outcomes. Overall, this line of research highlights the need to delve deeper into the nuanced experiences of remote workers rather than treat remote work as a singular concept (Charalampous et al., 2019; Lecours et al., 2021).

As managers consider how best to manage increases in remote work, it is natural to wonder whether there is any evidence to support strategies to make remote work more effective. Following the findings of Kubicek et al. (2022), managers should consider strategies to make coordination of work with co-workers less demanding. That may involve common policies and procedures for coordination and the investment in technologies (and importantly, training in how to use those technologies; Bjursell et al., 2021; Shipman et al., 2021). Nordbäck et al. (2017) found evidence that setting general policies in support of remote work helped employees to more easily structure their workdays and adapt to the remote work strategies of their co-workers (as contrasted by organisations who treat remote work as an exception, which makes coordination with remote co-workers more of a perceived anomaly that must be

dealt with; see also Chong et al., 2020 for findings regarding perceived organisational telework support).

One consistent finding is that having a dedicated space at home for work
seems to help, including helping manage work–non-work balance (Allen
2021). Another strategy that seems to help remote workers manage well-being
is to intentionally disconnect from work during non-work hours (Allen et al.,
2021; Cho, 2020). This strategy is consistent with the extensive literature on
recovery experiences, suggesting that disconnecting from a situation that is
draining resources allows resources to be replenished (Sonnentag et al., 2022).
However, to the extent that telepressure (felt pressure to engage in work at all
times) makes detachment and other recovery experiences more difficult (cf.,
Barber & Santuzzi, 2015; Gillet et al., 2022), managers should consider clear
policies about availability and responsiveness—and importantly, follow their
own policies—to help ensure recovery actually happens.

A common assumption tied to remote work is that some employees will be
less productive without the supervision that comes with being on a job site.
For many organisations, the natural response is to increase monitoring of remote employee productivity (Groen et al., 2018), which unfortunately, is
associated with increased work-to-home interference (Wang et al., 2021). In a
qualitative study of telework in the context of COVID-19, employees stressed
the importance of trust and support from managers and leaders in order to be
productive and maintain well-being (Shipman et al., 2021).

In summary, the rapid shift to widespread remote work early in the pandemic presented challenges to organisations and employees and there remain
questions about whether remote work can be sustained as we emerge from the
pandemic. If there is a silver lining for organisations, qualitative work by
Franken et al. (2021) may provide it by tying the research findings back to our
theories regarding employee responses. A repeated theme in their work was
that remote work introduced all kinds of unforeseen challenges and stressors;
however, most employees were able to adapt to them over time.

Flexible work schedules

Remote work is often seen as a variant of flexible work scheduling. In response to
many of the initial financial uncertainties early in the pandemic and continued
challenges with the volatile labour, many organisations have shifted to flexible or
variable work scheduling. Some organisations have also seen this as a way to
accommodate employees with challenging family conditions but who must
complete their tasks on-site. Findings from prior to the pandemic suggested that
flexible work schedules (or flextime) were associated with less work interference
with family (Allen et al., 2013) and burnout (Grzywacz et al., 2008), though those
findings are dependent somewhat on whether employees actually feel as though
they can take advantage of flexible work opportunities (Mandeville et al., 2016).

However, Chung (2022) presents a compelling picture that should be
carefully considered. In a study of 1,678 locations of a quick-service restaurant

before and during the pandemic (October 2019-December 2020), she found that variable work schedules led to higher levels of turnover and, as a result, lower performance at the restaurant level. There are couple of important considerations here. First, there may be a key difference between variable and flexible, in that the variable work schedules in Chung's study may not have given the employees much choice (and as a result, not as much perceived flexibility). In that regard, Chung notes that the variability of the schedules may have provided some flexibility to the organisation, but added even more uncertainty to employees while they were already dealing with economic uncertainty (e.g., potential job loss) and health risks associated with the food-service industry.

So, what does this all mean for employees as they return to work and workplace? Based on the literature, it seems reasonable to conclude that flexible schedules might be a way to help reduce stressors that are associated with employee burnout (e.g., work interference with family). However, those effects will be dramatically reduced if the flexible scheduling is not within the employee's control. Further, while utilising flexible/variable work schedules controlled by the employer may seem like a viable strategy for organisations to mitigate risks, and may even be necessary in certain industries to have adequate staffing coverage, it is important for employers to understand where variable schedules fit with regard to uncertainty experienced by employees (Chung, 2022). One possible strategy is variability between the employees, but consistency for each employee (e.g., each employee consistently has the same schedule).

Carryover of coping strategies from earlier the pandemic

While the focus of this chapter is on returning to workplaces as the impact of the pandemic has receded, understanding the stress experiences of employees during the pandemic, and particularly the coping mechanisms they utilised to address those stressors, is informative. Research is emerging that shows that early experiences in the pandemic impacted employee experiences at work as the pandemic continued to unfold (Mandeville, Manegold, Matthews, & Whitman, in press).

Particularly concerning are coping mechanisms that may have provided short-term relief while isolated at home, but could be particularly problematic when returning to more consistent work in the workplace. For example, a number of studies have suggested that alcohol use increased as a mechanism to cope with the stress during the pandemic (Daly & Robinson, 2021; Rodriguez et al., 2020). To the extent to which employees relied more on such coping techniques during the pandemic, the impact of those coping techniques may carry over into their responses to returning to the workplace.

A source of optimism has been the increase utilisation of mental health services, including employee assistance plans (EAPs) during the pandemic (Attridge & Steenstra, 2021). That increased uptake could have a lasting impact as more employees see the value in utilising those benefits. Overall, the pandemic has sparked a more comprehensive evaluation of employee benefit programs meant to help employees navigate difficult situations, from increased mental health services, adjustments to paid and unpaid leave practices, child care, and even greater questioning of the employer-sponsored health insurance system in the USA (Klein, 2021; Lester et al., 2021).

Developing and enforcing policies

The dynamic nature of the COVID-19 pandemic, particularly when coupled with the politicisation of some public health remedies, put organisations in a position to have to develop and rapidly update policies for employees and customers related to masks, social distancing, occupancy capacity, and vaccines. This also put managers in the position of enforcing those policies for employees and, in some cases, employees in a position of enforcing those policies for customers (Berry et al., 2020). Enforcement of these new policies was particularly stress-inducing for front-line employees (Mayer et al., 2022; Northington et al., 2021), especially when customers were not cooperative (Sumner & Kinsella, 2021a; Voorhees et al., 2020) and in situations where government response was slow, requiring more front-line intervention (Sumner & Kinsella, 2021b).

In fact, Northington et al. (2021) found "customers not following rules" and "customers who are rude, mean, or disrespectful" were behind only "bringing COVID-19 back home to someone in family" and "contracting COVID-19" as the most concerning stressors for front-line employees, with nearly a third of their participants choosing the highest point on their scale ("causes me great concern") in response to those two questions. Unfortunately, the frequency with which front-line employees were exposed to policy violations was very high, with 29.6% of their participants indicating that policies were violated daily to multiple times per day and an additional 39.2% indicating violations occurred between once and several times per week.

A perception that policies are not uniformly enforced may be adding to the challenges. As of early 2022, Future Forum (2022) found that non-executive knowledge workers were more than twice as likely to be working in the office five days a week and were reporting levels of stress twice as high as executives. This perceived double-standard may have lasting impacts as it leads employees to perceive a lack of transparency in policies and how they are enforced—knowledge workers who perceived a lack of transparency in how organisations plan to manage the future of worker were more than three times more likely to say they will "definitely" be seeking new employment in the next year (Future Forum, 2022).

As the pandemic recedes, enforcement of rules will presumably become less of a concern. However, it is still something for managers to consider, as re-introduction of safety rules in response to new variants of the coronavirus may make enforcement even more challenging as employees and customers become accustomed to not engaging in strict protective actions. Perhaps more important, the COVID-19 pandemic has highlighted not just the importance of strong crisis management and communication plans, but plans that consider the experiences of all stakeholders involved (managers, employees, customers) and their interactions (Trachsler & Jong, 2020). Beyond that, Li et al. (2021) introduce a crisis management model that systematically accounts for issues that may have come as a surprise to some organisations, such as the intersection of the political environment with the public health information and expertise. Managers should utilise the lessons learned from the COVID-19 pandemic now to better prepare for future catastrophic events.

Directions for future research

In the spirit of better preparing for catastrophic events, there are a number of areas where additional research, or different approaches to research, may be necessary.

The convergence of stressors

Perhaps the most challenging issue associated with returning to work and workplace during the pandemic is that all of the issues above, as well as others not discussed, are converging to make an already-difficult situation even more difficult for many workers (Sinclair et al., 2021). The COVID-19 pandemic has set forward a string of unusual circumstances that enhance the risks workers face beyond just health risks. For example, employees may have first dealt with the economic uncertainties of high unemployment and wage cutbacks at the start of the pandemic. While they may now feel greater job security, the "great resignation" that has impacted so many sectors may now mean that secure job comes with greater demands as organisations scramble to keep up with turnover. Those issues, coupled with supply chain disruptions and other factors, have led to inflationary increases in the costs of many goods, presenting new economic challenges to workers.

Even at the more micro-level, employees have experienced the convergence of unique stressors in the pandemic. For example, uncooperative responses to safety rules by customers put employees in a position to deal with (1) risk of contracting COVID-19, (2) expectation by their employer that they enforce safety rules, and (3) potential aggression from the customer if the employee requested compliance.

What exactly is the "new normal?"

The COVID-19 pandemic provides an interesting context within which to continue to explore and extend adaptation and stress-reaction theories of stress. There is some literature concerning how employees psychologically navigate return to work after major events such as the death of a family member (e.g., Flux et al., 2019; Pitimson, 2021), natural disasters (Venn, 2012), and terrorist attacks (Kleinberg, 2005), including those who may have experienced symptoms of

226

 *J*Jonathon R. B. Halbesleben*

post-traumatic stress disorder as a result of their experiences (Precin, 2011). In most of the situations that have been studied previously, there may have been some fear that the major event could occur again, but generally returning to work was seen as indicative of some return to normalcy. Indeed, that insight might be one element to understanding differing responses to employees as they returned to work during the COVID-19 pandemic. To the extent that employees view their work, and particularly their workplace, as a core part of their work of their normal lifestyle, they may experience lower stress and burnout than employees who see their work as having dramatically changed or a place where the major event could be repeated (in this case, due to exposure to the virus).

However, the specific timing of return to one's set point has not been clearly explicated in theory and it's not entirely clear that even at the time of writing this piece (April, 2022) we can call the negative event of the pandemic "over." Presumably we will reach that point and have an opportunity to continue to explore the nature of adaptation. It remains to be seen whether a new normal will emerge and be associated with altered set points for well-being and burnout among employees.

Conclusion

The COVID-19 pandemic has served as a shock to everyone and has provided burnout researchers a rich context to understand how employees interact with their work and how that impacts their well-being. As researchers examine the notion of a new normal and adaptation, it will be important that they account for nuanced experiences across employees. While everyone experienced the pandemic, not everyone lost a loved one or lost a job. Some employees got their dream of an entirely remote work position; others are stretched thin due to massive shifts in the labour force. It seems likely that many people will settle back in to a level of well-being very close to where they were prior to the pandemic. What will be important and interesting for researchers, employers, and policy makers is a strong understanding of those who do not adapt.

References

Allen, T. D., Johnson, R. C., Kiburz, K. M., & Shockley, K. M. (2013). Work–family conflict and flexible work arrangements: Deconstructing flexibility. *Personnel Psychology*, 66(2), 345–376.
Allen, T. D., Merlo, K., Lawrence, R. C., Slutsky, J., & Gray, C. E. (2021). Boundary management and work-nonwork balance while working from home. *Applied Psychology: An International Review*, 70(1), 60–84. 10.1111/apps.12300
Anderson, A. J., Kaplan, S. A., & Vega, R. P. (2015). The impact of telework on emotional experience: When, and for whom, does telework improve daily affective well-being? *European Journal of Work and Organizational Psychology*, 24(6), 882–897. 10.1080/1359432X.2014.966086
Attridge, M., & Steenstra, I. (2021). Work outcomes and EAP use during the COVID-19 pandemic. *Journal of Employee Assistance*, 51(4), 30–31.

Bailey, D. E., & Kurland, N. B. (2002). A review of telework research: Findings, new directions, and lessons for the study of modern work. *Journal of Organizational Behavior: The International Journal of Industrial, Occupational and Organizational Psychology and Behavior, 23*(4), 383–400.

Barber, L. K., & Santuzzi, A. M. (2015). Please respond ASAP: Workplace telepressure and employee recovery. *Journal of Occupational Health Psychology, 20*(2), 172–189. 10.1037/a0038278

Bazzoli, A., Probst, T. M., & Lee, H. J. (2021). Economic stressors, COVID-19 attitudes, worry, and behaviors among US working adults: A mixture analysis. *International Journal of Environmental Research and Public Health, 18*(5), 2338. 10.3390/ijerph18052338

Berry, L. L., Danaher, T. S., Aksoy, L., & Keiningham, T. L. (2020). Service safety in the pandemic age. *Journal of Service Research, 23*(4), 391–395.

Bjursell, C., Bergmo-Prvulovic, I., & Hedegaard, J. (2021). Telework and lifelong learning. *Frontiers in Sociology, 6*, 642277. doi: 10.3389/fsoc.2021.642277

Bowling, N. A., Beehr, T. A., Wagner, S. H., & Libkuman, T. M. (2005). Adaptation-level theory, opponent process theory, and dispositions: an integrated approach to the stability of job satisfaction. *Journal of Applied Psychology, 90*(6), 1044–1053.

Breevaart, K., & Tims, M. (2019). Crafting social resources on days when you are emotionally exhausted: The role of job insecurity. *Journal of Occupational and Organizational Psychology, 92*(4), 806–824.

Brickman, P., & Campbell, D. T. (1971). Hedonic relativism and planning the good society. In M. H. Appley (ed). *Adaption-level theory: A symposium.* New York: Academic Press.

Charalampous, M., Grant, C. A., Tramontano, C., & Michailidis, E. (2019). Systematically reviewing remote e-workers' well-being at work: A multidimensional approach. *European Journal of Work and Organizational Psychology, 28*(1), 51–73. 10.1080/1359432X.2018.1541886

Cho, E. (2020). Examining boundaries to understand the impact of COVID-19 on vocational behaviors. *Journal of Vocational Behavior, 119*, 103437. 10.1016/j.jvb.2020.103437

Chong, S., Huang, Y., & Chang, C.-H. (D.). (2020). Supporting interdependent telework employees: A moderated-mediation model linking daily COVID-19 task setbacks to next-day work withdrawal. *Journal of Applied Psychology, 105*(12), 1408–1422. 10.1037/apl0000843

Chung, H. (2022). Variable work schedules, unit-level turnover, and performance before and during the COVID-19 pandemic. *Journal of Applied Psychology, 107*, 515–532. 10.1037/apl0001006

Daly, M., & Robinson, E. (2021). High-risk drinking in midlife before vs. during the COVID-19 crisis: Longitudinal evidence from the UK. *American Journal of Preventive Medicine, 60*, 294–297. 10.1016/j.amepre.2020.09.004

Delanoeije, J., & Verbruggen, M. (2020). Between-person and within-person effects of telework: A quasi-field experiment. *European Journal of Work and Organizational Psychology, 29*(6), 795–808. 10.1080/1359432X.2020.1774557

Delanoeije, J., Verbruggen, M., & Germeys, L. (2019). Boundary role transitions: A day-to-day approach to explain the effects of home-based telework on work-to-home conflict and home-to-work conflict. *Human Relations, 72*(12), 1843–1868. 10.1177/0018726718823071

Diener, E., & Diener, C. (1996). Most people are happy. *Psychological Science, 7*(3), 181–185. 10.1111/j.1467-9280.1996.tb00354.x

228   *Jonathon R. B. Halbesleben*

Diener, E., Lucas, R. E., & Scollon, C. N. (2006). Beyond the hedonic treadmill: Revising the adaptation theory of well-being. *American Psychologist*, *61*(4), 305–314. doi: 10.1037/0003-066X.61.4.305

Di Trani, M., Mariani, R., Ferri, R., De Berardinis, D., & Frigo, M. G. (2021). From resilience to burnout in healthcare workers during the COVID-19 emergency: the role of the ability to tolerate uncertainty. *Frontiers in Psychology*, *12*, 987.

DuBrin, A. J. (1991). Comparison of the job satisfaction and productivity of telecommuters versus in-house employees: A research note on work in progress. *Psychological Reports*, *68*(3_suppl), 1223–1234.

Eddleston, K. A., & Mulki, J. (2017). Toward understanding remote workers' management of work–family boundaries: The complexity of workplace embeddedness. *Group & Organization Management*, *42*(3), 346–387. 10.1177/1059601115619548

Flux, L., Hassett, A., & Callanan, M. (2019). How do employers respond to employees who return to the workplace after experiencing the death of a loved one? A review of the literature. *Policy and Practice in Health and Safety*, *17*(2), 98–111.

Franken, E., Bentley, T., Shafaei, A., Farr-Wharton, B., Onnis, L. A., & Omari, M. (2021). Forced flexibility and remote working: Opportunities and challenges in the new normal. *Journal of Management & Organization*, *27*, 1–19. 10.1017/jmo.2021.40

Fu, S. Q., Greco, L. M., Lennard, A. C., & Dimotakis, N. (2021). Anxiety responses to the unfolding COVID-19 crisis: Patterns of change in the experience of prolonged exposure to stressors. *Journal of Applied Psychology*, *106*(1), 48–61. 10.1037/apl0000855

Fujita, F., & Diener, E. (2005). Life satisfaction set point: Stability and change. *Journal of Personality and Social Psychology*, *88*(1), 158–164. 10.1037/0022-3514.88.1.158

Future Forum. (2022). Inflexible return-to-office policies are hammering employee experience scores. Accessed April 20, 2022 at https://futureforum.com/pulse-survey/

Gillet, N., Morin, A. J. S., Fernet, C., Austin, S., & Huyghebaert-Zouaghi, T. (2022). Telepressure and recovery experiences among remote and onsite workers. *Journal of Personnel Psychology*. Advance online publication. 10.1027/1866-5888/a000303

Golden, T. D. (2012). Altering the effects of work and family conflict on exhaustion: Telework during traditional and nontraditional work hours. *Journal of Business and Psychology*, *27*(3), 255–269.

Groen, B., van Triest, S., Coers, M., & Wtenweerde, N. (2018). Managing flexible work arrangements: Teleworking and output controls. *European Management Journal*, *36*(6), 727–735. 10.1016/j.emj.2018.01.007

Grzywacz, J. G., Carlson, D. S., & Shulkin, S. (2008). Schedule flexibility and stress: Linking formal flexible arrangements and perceived flexibility to employee health. *Community, Work and Family*, *11*(2), 199–214.

Guo, L., Cheng, K., Luo, J., & Zhao, H. (2021). Trapped in a loss spiral: how and when work alienation relates to knowledge hiding. *The International Journal of Human Resource Management*, 1–30. 10.1080/09585192.2021.1937672

Halbesleben, J. R., Neveu, J. P., Paustian-Underdahl, S. C., & Westman, M. (2014). Getting to the "COR" understanding the role of resources in conservation of resources theory. *Journal of Management*, *40*(5), 1334–1364. 10.1177/0149206314527130

Headey, B. (2010). The set point theory of well-being has serious flaws: on the eve of a scientific revolution? *Social Indicators Research*, *97*(1), 7–21.

Hobfoll, S. E. (1988). *The ecology of stress*. New York: Taylor & Francis.

Hobfoll, S. E. (1989). Conservation of resources: a new attempt at conceptualizing stress. *American Psychologist*, *44*(3), 513–524.

Hobfoll, S. E., Halbesleben, J., Neveu, J. P., & Westman, M. (2018). Conservation of resources in the organizational context: The reality of resources and their consequences. *Annual Review of Organizational Psychology and Organizational Behavior, 5*, 103–128. 10.1146/annurev-orgpsych-032117-104640

Hobfoll, S. E. (2001). The influence of culture, community, and the nested-self in the stress process: Advancing conservation of resources theory. *Applied Psychology, 50*(3), 337–421.

Kaduk, A., Genadek, K., Kelly, E. L., & Moen, P. (2019). Involuntary vs. voluntary flexible work: Insights for scholars and stakeholders. *Community, Work & Family, 22*(4), 412–442.

Klein, J. A. (2021). The impact of the coronavirus pandemic on employee benefits. *Benefits Quarterly, 37*(1), 8.

Kleinberg, J. (2005). On the job after 9/11: Looking at Worker's block through a group lens. *Group Analysis, 38*(2), 203–218.

Kubicek, B., Baumgartner, V., Prem, R., Sonnentag, S., & Korunka, C. (2022). Less detachment but more cognitive flexibility? A diary study on outcomes of cognitive demands of flexible work. *International Journal of Stress Management, 29*(1), 75–87. 10.1037/str0000239

Lecours, A., Gilbert, M. H., Lord, M. M., Labrecque, C., & Boucher, F. (2021). Telework in a pandemic context: protocol of a participatory study on the effects of teleworking conditions on the well-being and social participation of workers. *BMJ Open, 11*(8), e051099. 10.1136/bmjopen-2021-051099

Lester, G. V., Brock Baskin, M. E., & Clinton, M. S. (2021). Employer-sponsored benefits in the United States: The past, present, and future. *Compensation & Benefits Review, 53*(1), 24–42.

Li, B., Zhang, T., Hua, N., & Wang, Y. (2021). A dynamic model of crisis management from a stakeholder perspective: The case of COVID-19 in China. *Tourism Review, 76*, 764–787. Doi 10.1108/TR-09-2020-0413

Liu, S., Lithopoulos, A., Zhang, C. Q., Garcia-Barrera, M. A., & Rhodes, R. E. (2021). Personality and perceived stress during COVID-19 pandemic: Testing the mediating role of perceived threat and efficacy. *Personality and Individual Differences, 168*, 110351.

Lucas, R. E. (2007). Adaptation and the set-point model of subjective well-being: Does happiness change after major life events? *Current Directions in Psychological Science, 16*(2), 75–79.

Lucas, R. E., Clark, A. E., Georgellis, Y., & Diener, E. (2003). Reexamining adaptation and the set point model of happiness: reactions to changes in marital status. *Journal of Personality and Social Psychology, 84*(3), 527.

Lucas, R. E., Clark, A. E., Georgellis, Y., & Diener, E. (2004). Unemployment alters the set point for life satisfaction. *Psychological Science, 15*(1), 8–13.

Lykken, D., & Tellegen, A. (1996). Happiness is a stochastic phenomenon. *Psychological Science, 7*(3), 186–189.

Mandeville, A., Halbesleben, J., & Whitman, M. (2016). Misalignment and misperception in preferences to utilize family-friendly benefits: Implications for benefit utilization and work–family conflict. *Personnel Psychology, 69*(4), 895–929.

Mandeville, A., Manegold, J., Matthews, R., & Whitman, M. V. (in press). When all COVID breaks loose: Examining determinants of working parents' job performance during a crisis. *Applied Psychology.* 10.1111/apps.1237

Matthews, R. A., & Ritter, K. J. (2019). Applying adaptation theory to understand experienced incivility processes: Testing the repeated exposure hypothesis. *Journal of Occupational Health Psychology, 24*(2), 270–285. 10.1037/ocp0000123

Matthews, R. A., Wayne, J. H., & Ford, M. T. (2014). A work–family conflict/subjective well-being process model: A test of competing theories of longitudinal effects. *Journal of Applied Psychology, 99*(6), 1173–1187. 10.1037/a0036674

Matthews, R. A., Wayne, J. H., & McKersie, S. J. (2016). Theoretical approaches to the study of work and family: Avoiding stagnation via effective theory borrowing. In T. D. Allen and L. T. Eby (Eds.). *The Oxford handbook of work and family* (pp. 23–35). London: Oxford University Press.

Mayer, B., Helm, S., Barnett, M., & Arora, M. (2022). The impact of workplace safety and customer misbehavior on supermarket workers' stress and psychological distress during the COVID-19 pandemic. *International Journal of Workplace Health Management*, 15, 339–358. 10.1108/IJWHM-03-2021-0074

Meyerson, D. E. (1994). Interpretation of stress in institutions: The cultural production of ambiguity and burnout. *Administrative Science Quarterly*, *39*, 628–653. https://doi.org/10.2307/2393774

McElroy-Heltzel, S. E., Shannonhouse, L. R., Davis, E. B., Lemke, A. W., Mize, M. C., Aten, J., … & Miskis, C. (2022). Resource loss and mental health during COVID-19: Psychosocial protective factors among US older adults and those with chronic disease. *International Journal of Psychology*, *57*(1), 127–135.

Michel, J. S., Rotch, M. A., Carson, J. E., Bowling, N. A., & Shifrin, N. V. (2021). Flattening the Latent Growth Curve? Explaining Within-Person Changes in Employee Well-Being during the COVID-19 Pandemic. *Occupational Health Science, 5*(3), 247–275. 10.1007/s41542-021-00087-4

Nawijn, J. (2011). Happiness through vacationing: Just a temporary boost or long-term benefits? *Journal of Happiness Studies, 12*(4), 651–665.

Nordbäck, E. S., Myers, K. K., & McPhee, R. D. (2017). Workplace flexibility and communication flows: A structurational view. *Journal of Applied Communication Research, 45*(4), 397–412. 10.1080/00909882.2017.1355560

Northington, W. M., Gillison, S. T., Beatty, S. E., & Vivek, S. (2021). I don't want to be a rule enforcer during the COVID-19 pandemic: Frontline employees' plight. *Journal of Retailing and Consumer Services, 63*, 102723.

Oakman, J., Kinsman, N., Stuckey, R., Graham, M., & Weale, V. (2020). A rapid review of mental and physical health effects of working at home: how do we optimise health? *BMC Public Health, 20*(1), 1–13.

Peck, J. A. (2021). The disproportionate impact of COVID-19 on women relative to men: A conservation of resources perspective. *Gender, Work & Organization, 28*, 484–497.

Pitimson, N. (2021). Work after death: an examination of the relationship between Grief, emotional labour, and the lived experience of returning to work after a bereavement. *Sociological Research Online, 26*(3), 469–484.

Precin, P. (2011). Return to work after 9/11. *Work, 38*(1), 3–11.

Ritter, K. J., Matthews, R. A., Ford, M. T., & Henderson, A. A. (2016). Understanding role stressors and job satisfaction over time using adaptation theory. *Journal of Applied Psychology, 101*(12), 1655–1669. 10.1037/apl0000152

Rodriguez, L. M., Litt, D. M., & Stewart, S. H. (2020). Drinking to cope with the pandemic: The unique associations of COVID-19-related perceived threat and psychological distress to drinking behaviors in American men and women. *Addictive Behaviors, 110*, 106532.

Sardeshmukh, S. R., Sharma, D., & Golden, T. D. (2012). Impact of telework on exhaustion and job engagement: A job demands and job resources model. *New Technology, Work and Employment, 27*(3), 193–207.

Sayre, G. M., Grandey, A. A., & Almeida, D. M. (2021). Does sleep help or harm managers' perceived productivity? Trade-offs between affect and time as resources. *Journal of Occupational Health Psychology, 26*(2), 127–141. 10.1037/ocp0000192

Shipman, K., Burrell, D. N., & Mac Pherson, A. H. (2021). An organizational analysis of how managers must understand the mental health impact of teleworking during COVID-19 on employees. *International Journal of Organizational Analysis.* 10.1108/IJOA-03-2021-2685

Sinclair, R. R., Allen, T., Barber, L., Bergman, M., Britt, T., Butler, A., ... & Yuan, Z. (2020). Occupational health science in the time of COVID-19: Now more than ever. *Occupational Health Science, 4*(1), 1–22.

Sinclair, R. R., Probst, T. M., Watson, G. P., & Bazzoli, A. (2021). Caught between Scylla and Charybdis: How economic stressors and occupational risk factors influence workers' occupational health reactions to COVID-19. *Applied psychology, 70*(1), 85–119. 10.1111/apps.12301

Somaraju, A. V., Griffin, D. J., Olenick, J., Chang, C.-H. (D.), & Kozlowski, S. W. J. (2022). The dynamic nature of interpersonal conflict and psychological strain in extreme work settings. *Journal of Occupational Health Psychology, 27*(1), 53–73. 10.1037/ocp0000290

Song, Y., & Gao, J. (2020). Does telework stress employees out? A study on working at home and subjective well-being for wage/salary workers. *Journal of Happiness Studies, 21*(7), 2649–2668.

Sonnentag, S., Cheng, B. H., & Parker, S. L. (2022). Recovery from Work: Advancing the Field Toward the Future. *Annual Review of Organizational Psychology and Organizational Behavior, 9*, 33–60. 10.1146/annurev-orgpsych-012420-091355

Sumner, R. C., & Kinsella, E. L. (2021a). "It's Like a Kick in the Teeth": The Emergence of Novel Predictors of Burnout in Frontline Workers During Covid-19. *Frontiers in Psychology, 12*, 1875.

Sumner, R. C., & Kinsella, E. L. (2021b). Grace under pressure: Resilience, burnout, and wellbeing in frontline workers in the United Kingdom and Republic of Ireland during the SARS-CoV-2 pandemic. *Frontiers in Psychology*, 3757.

Trachsler, T., & Jong, W. (2020). Crisis management in times of COVID-19: game, set or match?. *Journal of contingencies and crisis management, 28*(4), 485–486.

Venn, D. (2012). "Helping Displaced Workers Back Into Jobs After a Natural Disaster: Recent Experiences in OECD Countries". *OECD Social, Employment and Migration Working Papers*, No. 142, OECD Publishing. 10.1787/5k8zk8pn2542-en

Voorhees, C. M., Fombelle, P. W., & Bone, S. A. (2020). Don't forget about the frontline employee during the COVID-19 pandemic: Preliminary insights and a research agenda on market shocks. *Journal of Service Research, 23*(4), 396–400.

Wang, B., Liu, Y., Qian, J., & Parker, S. K. (2021). Achieving effective remote working during the COVID-19 pandemic: A work design perspective. *Applied Psychology: An International Review, 70*(1), 16–59. 10.1111/apps.12290

Wong, A. K. F., Kim, S. S., Kim, J., & Han, H. (2021). How the COVID-19 pandemic affected hotel employee stress: Employee perceptions of occupational stressors and their consequences. *International Journal of Hospitality Management, 93*, 102798.

Wu, T. Y., Chung, P. F., Liao, H. Y., Hu, P. Y., & Yeh, Y. J. (2019). Role ambiguity and economic hardship as the moderators of the relation between abusive supervision and job burnout: An Application of uncertainty management theory. *The Journal of General Psychology, 146*(4), 365–390.

Zacher, H., & Rudolph, C. W. (2021). Individual differences and changes in subjective wellbeing during the early stages of the COVID-19 pandemic. *American Psychologist, 76*(1), 50–62. 10.1037/amp0000702

Index

Printed in the United States
by Baker & Taylor Publisher Services